John Bunyan's *Pilgrim's Progress*:
Themes and Issues

John Bunyan

John Bunyan's
Pilgrim's Progress

Themes and issues

Barry E. Horner

 **EVANGELICAL PRESS**

Solid Ground Christian Books

EVANGELICAL PRESS
Faverdale North Industrial Estate, Darlington, DL3 0PH, England

Evangelical Press USA
P. O. Box 925, Webster, NY 14580, USA

e-mail: sales@evangelical-press.org

web: http://www.evangelicalpress.org

SOLID GROUND CHRISTIAN BOOKS
P.O. Box 660132, Vestavia Hills, AL 35266, USA

e-mail: Solid-ground-books@juno.com

web: http://solid-ground-books.com

First published 2003
Second Impression 2007

British Library Cataloguing in Publication Data available

ISBN 0 85234 529 1

Unless otherwise indicated, Scripture quotations in this publication are from the New American Standard Bible. Copyright © The Lockman Foundation 1963. All rights reserved.

All Scripture quotations marked AV are taken from the Authorized / King James Version.

Printed and bound in the USA

Contents

Acknowledgements

As the years pass, my indebtedness has grown with regard to those who, out of love for the truth of God as Bunyan expressed it, have contributed in so many encouraging ways. In particular, I must mention my wife Ann, Jeff Kendal, John and Leona Heffelfinger, Galen Johnson, Henry and Naomi Ansell and John Coleman.

Preface

OVER the last few years, interest in seminars that I have conducted on *The Pilgrim's Progress* has greatly increased. It has been a privilege to speak at churches, family camps, colleges and seminaries, in England, Australia, New Zealand and many parts of America. During the course of these meetings, I have been encouraged in a large measure by the intense interest that has been shown in the substance of John Bunyan's allegory. On many occasions people have wanted to talk for hours on the numerous intricacies of Bunyan's weaving. So often I have been stimulated by various enquiries concerning details of the text and related doctrinal matters, and as a result have been forced to do further study. On the other hand, there have been certain questions which I have found people asking time and time again. A number of those who attended these talks have admitted their previous misunderstanding of Bunyan's real meaning, and have been really enthused and captivated as a result of perceiving for the first time the depth of Bible teaching that he intended.

Through all of this — and it is very much an ongoing journey — many matters have arisen which I felt needed clarification for the benefit of an evangelical world that sadly, to its shame, hardly knows Bunyan. This book is the product of such concern. While some chapters may include more scholarly substance than others, I believe that all the issues raised are of considerable importance. I do not apologize for being critical of the general aura of Bunyan studies over the past century which, although contributing much with regard to textual and historical matters, have been at best politely distant, and in some cases even positively disdainful, in their attitude towards the evangelical doctrine that was unquestionably of supreme concern for Bunyan himself.

For my own part, I hold the ministry of John Bunyan in high regard principally because of his unswerving commitment to the gospel of God's sovereign grace, and also for his winsome portrayal of that truth. Anyone who loses sight of this priority, for whatever reason, is guilty of emasculating the allegory of its most vital feature. The reality is that, at an academic level, many want to admire Bunyan with secular discrimination, while at the same time repudiating his doctrine as being at best passé and at worst 'fundamentalist'. In this situation, such assessments are usually filtered through the presuppositions of secular humanism, religious liberalism, or neo-orthodoxy. However, the biblical truth of *The Pilgrim's Progress* stands firm, whatever modern man may say. Therefore, the need of the hour is not detachment grounded upon the pretence of scholarly objectivity, but instead the recovery of that intelligent and heartfelt pursuit of the truth which does not stop short of personally embracing it. Rather, it acknowledges Bunyan as a whole, and gives the Bedford tinker that regard which esteems above all else the priority that he gave to evangelical truth.

Barry E. Horner

The writings of John Bunyan

FOR 150 years, the standard publication of *The Works Of John Bunyan* has been the three-volume set edited by George Offor. More recently the Banner of Truth Trust has reprinted this work, except that *A Map shewing the Order and Causes of Salvation and Damnation* has been omitted.

The original Offor edition contained fifty-nine separate compositions, though it appears that even this warmly appreciative editor had serious doubts about the inclusion of *An Exhortation to Peace and Unity*. In deference to the judgement of others he included it, yet expressed eight reasons why he questioned its authenticity, and even put forward the suggestion that it may have been written by Paul D'Anvers, a leader among London Baptists who opposed Bunyan's views on baptism.[1]

More recently, Oxford University Press has completed the publication of a totally new edition of Bunyan's writings, though, sadly, it is very expensive. This scholarly production commenced with the publication of the definitive text of *The Pilgrim's Progress* in 1960, edited by J. B. Wharey and later revised by Roger Sharrock. Subsequently *Grace Abounding to the Chief of Sinners* was published in 1962, then *The Holy War* in 1980 and *The Life and Death of Mr Badman* in 1988. Finally, in 1994, the thirteen-volume set of Bunyan's *Miscellaneous Works* was completed. In this overall Oxford University Press Edition enterprise, Roger Sharrock was the General Editor.

In the Oxford edition, it should be noted that the more recently discovered *Profitable Meditations*, first published in 1661, is included.[2] On the other hand, *An Exhortation to Peace and Unity*, *Reprobation Asserted* and *Scriptural Poems* have been omitted. With regard to *Reprobation Asserted*, John Brown, Bunyan's foremost biographer to date, rejected the work as spurious.[3] Richard Greaves has written an article in which he cautiously agrees with this opinion. He also declares: 'Henri Talon and G. B. Harrison rejected Brown's arguments and instead affirmed Bunyan's authorship, whereas Roger Sharrock, while rejecting Brown's arguments as inconclusive, decided after a more intensive analysis that the work was, in fact, not Bunyan's.'[4] In this regard, one thing remains certain, and it is that, quite apart from this disputed work, which represents high Calvinism (considered in more detail in chapter 9), Bunyan's convictions concerning the sovereignty of grace remain both pervasive and substantial.

With regard to *Scriptural Poems*, Offor writes, 'This very interesting little volume of poems, we believe, has not been reprinted since the year 1701, nor has it ever been inserted in any edition or catalogue of Bunyan's works... The style and substance of these scriptural poems are entirely Bunyan's.'[5] On the other hand, Graham Midgley, editor of volume VI of the recent Oxford edition, and no doubt with Sharrock's agreement, omits this work.[6] It has to be admitted that, on the basis of Midgley's evidence, together with the supporting opinion of John Brown, this rejection seems warranted.

1.
Why *The Pilgrim's Progress* is a book for our time

'This wonderful work is one of the very few books which may be read over repeatedly at different times, and each time with a new and a different pleasure' (Samuel Taylor Coleridge).

THE
Pilgrim's Progreſs
FROM
THIS WORLD,
TO
That which is to come:
Delivered under the Similitude of a
DREAM
Wherein is Diſcovered,
The manner of his ſetting out,
His Dangerous Journey, And ſafe
Arrival at the Deſired Countrey.

I have uſed Similitudes, Hoſ. 12:10.

By *John Bunyan.*

𝔏𝔦𝔠𝔢𝔫𝔰𝔢𝔡 𝔞𝔫𝔡 𝔈𝔫𝔱𝔯𝔢𝔡 𝔞𝔠𝔠𝔬𝔯𝔡𝔦𝔫𝔤 𝔱𝔬 𝔒𝔯𝔡𝔢𝔯.

LONDON
Printed for *Nath. Ponder* at the *Peacock*
in the *Poultrey* near *Cornhil*, 1678.

Title-page of the first edition of *The Pilgrim's Progress*

1.
Why *The Pilgrim's Progress* is a book for our time

THE first edition of *The Pilgrim's Progress* in 1678 was an immediate runaway best-seller, at least amongst the common populace within England, and then beyond its shores. As a result, publisher Nathaniel Ponder became increasingly troubled with numerous attempts to pirate the work and infringe upon his licence. Three editions were published within the first year, and by the time of Bunyan's death in 1688, thirteen editions overall had produced at least 100,000 copies. Even in 1686, eight years after the first edition, Bunyan could not refrain from expressing, in the introductory poem to Part II, his delight at such unparalleled and international success:

My Pilgrim's book has travell'd sea and land,
Yet I could never come to understand
That it was slighted, or turn'd out of door
By any kingdom, were they rich or poor.
In France and Flanders, where men kill each other,
My Pilgrim is esteem'd a friend, a brother.
In Holland too, 'tis said, as I am told,
My Pilgrim is with some worth more than gold.
Highlanders and wild Irish can agree

My Pilgrim should familiar with them be.
'Tis in New England under such advance,
Receives there so much loving countenance,
As to be trimm'd, new cloth'd, and deck'd with gems
That it may show its features and its limbs,
Yet more; so comely doth my Pilgrim walk,
That of him thousands daily sing and talk.[1]

During the 1690s several booksellers placed exceptionally large orders, including two of approximately 10,000 copies.[2] Thus *The Pilgrim's Progress* became 'by far the most popular work of seventeenth-century prose fiction'.[3]

Although the eighteenth-century Great Awakening under Whitefield and Wesley spawned an even more widespread enthusiasm, once again amongst multitudes of the lower classes, acceptance within 'cultured' and 'refined' circles was still reluctant. Even William Cowper could reflect this hesitancy when, in anonymously endorsing *The Pilgrim's Progress*, he writes:

I name thee not, lest so despised a name
Should move a sneer at thy deserved fame.
Yet, e'en in transitory life's late day
That mingles all my brown with silver grey,
Revere the man whose *Pilgrim* marks the road,
And guides the *Progress* of the soul to God.[4]

However, the early nineteenth century saw a sudden burst of learned enthusiasm, as Lord Macaulay acknowledges: '*The Pilgrim's Progress* is perhaps the only book about which, after the lapse of a hundred years, the educated minority has come over to the opinion of the common people.'[5] Thus, right up to the early part of the twentieth century, more often than not only the highest praise could be offered to Bunyan.

For example, the esteemed historian G. M. Trevelyan, writing in 1928, began by commenting on the allegory's opening paragraph: 'Of all the works of high imagination which have enthralled mankind, none opens with a passage that more instantly places the reader in the heart of all the action that is to follow; not Homer's, not Milton's invocation of the Muse; not one of Dante's three great openings; not the murmured challenge of the sentinels on the midnight platform at Elsinor — not one of these better performs the author's initial task. The attention is at once captured, the imagination aroused. In these first sentences, by the magic of words, we are transported into a world of spiritual values, and impressed at the very outset with the sense of great issues at stake — nothing less than the fate of a man's soul... He [Bunyan] shines, one of the brightest stars in the firmament of English literature. Yet he never had an ambition in anything he wrote save to turn poor sinners to repentance.'[6]

Nevertheless, as the twentieth century progressed, there gradually spread, like a cloud obscuring the light, a dullness in relation to the real heart of Bunyan that has left us, in the main, with an obsession on the part of secular academics with Bunyan's literary talent and with embroilment in the historic facts of related Puritan life, while, sadly, the substance of his overriding evangelical concern seems to have become more and more lost to view.

Is *The Pilgrim's Progress* valid for the present?

So why should *The Pilgrim's Progress* be enthusiastically recommended to modern man as he now finds himself facing all the uncertainties of the twenty-first century? Why indeed, when a survey of readers by Columbia University Press in 1950, designed to identify the most boring of all literary classics, revealed that *The Pilgrim's Progress* by John Bunyan ranked at number one in that category? (*Das Kapital* by Karl Marx ranked at number thirteen.)[7] In the 1980s a survey of seventeen-year-olds in the USA indicated that less than one in seven could identify the book.[8] Further, why ever should we, in this enlightened and secular age, consider a biblical allegory that is over three hundred years old, that is so militantly Protestant and of the very essence of English seventeenth-century Puritan thought? And again, why should we give so much as the time of day to a book written by an uneducated mender of pots and pans who lacked even a secondary education?

Why? Because all these responses are merely symptoms of the fact that biblical Christianity is currently in decline, of a lethargy of soul that shuns stimulation of the mind, of blinding modernity. They indicate a condition of pervasive spiritual dullness and indifference that requires, not a capitulation to further drifting, but rather that we take heed to Jeremiah's exhortation to backslidden Israel: 'Ask for the ancient paths, where the good way is, and walk in it; and you shall find rest for your souls' (Jer. 6:16).

It must be stressed that a rallying call of this type is not to past tradition and antiquarian loyalties. But I would strenuously maintain that there is a desperate need for Christian churches today to return to 'the faith which was once for all delivered to the saints' (Jude 3), and that Bunyan's classic allegory is ideally suited for stimulating such a recovery in its faithful undergirding of essential Bible truth. Yes, as we shall see in more detail in later chapters, *The Pilgrim's Progress* must be presented in a suitable manner to this modern secular generation, while at the same time keeping in view the media and image-consciousness of today, which are things that Bunyan never even remotely dreamed about. Nevertheless I would vigorously contend that *The Pilgrim's Progress* is an ideal and proven medium for reaching our present generation. Seminar experience has demonstrated this point over and over again. What is needed is passionate recommendation, communication and making known of this peerless allegory. And in so doing the Word of God, and the gospel in particular, will be set forth with a purity and power that will prove to be both uncommonly refreshing and effectual. During one seminar which I conducted, between sessions a man confessed that his wife had recently left him. Then he added: 'However, in spite of participation in counselling, this teaching of John Bunyan's has been far more helpful.'

Some necessary qualifications

Because literary awareness is at an all-time low within Christendom, it has become necessary to deal first with certain misunderstandings which a previous generation would not have entertained. For instance, I have on several occasions heard the opinion expressed that *The Pilgrim's Progress* was an account of the Pilgrim Fathers' journey from Europe to America! At other times people have confused John Bunyan with Paul Bunyan, the American folklore hero! And multitudes have, on eventually studying this great classic, freely confessed their former ignorance concerning what *The Pilgrim's Progress* really taught. Hence, four qualifications are given here for the purpose of clearing the air and allowing Bunyan's real intentions and content to stand out with biblical clarity.

1. *The Pilgrim's Progress* was not primarily written for children

The Christian book market is becoming increasingly flooded with simplified versions of *The Pilgrim's Progress* that are apparently designed to make the allegory appealing to children and young people. Not surprisingly, some have been led to believe that *The Pilgrim's Progress* was principally written for children, but nothing could be further from the truth, since it is definitely an adult book that deals with a multitude of very adult situations. Luther scholar Gordon Rupp confirms this estimate when he describes how 'Coleridge called it [*The Pilgrim's Progress*] a compendium of evangelical doctrine, and we shall be wise not to treat it as a long outmoded pious book for

children.'⁹ (For a more detailed consideration of this misunderstanding see chapter 19.)

2. *The Pilgrim's Progress* was not written for academic study

John Bunyan and his writings have proved to be a happy
hunting ground for twentieth-century academics who, while
repudiating his Calvinistic doctrine and his literalist understanding of the Bible, have bowed to his natural abilities and
analysed his person and works from a multitude of perspectives.
These include:

- Literary criticism, concerning style, sources, influences
and allegorical structure.
- Historical investigation, concerning a turbulent, revo-
lutionary seventeenth century.
- Psychological analysis, concerning Bunyan's Puritan
mores and supposedly sensitive psyche.
- Political theory, concerning secular partisan conflicts,
class struggles and influences.
- Theological appreciation, concerning a biblicist Puritan era that is usually assessed from a modern sceptical
perspective.

For a more detailed consideration of these areas of specialist
study refer to chapter 18. However, Bunyan's fundamental
purposes in writing *The Pilgrim's Progress* were spiritual and
pastoral, as his introductory and concluding poems so clearly
indicate. He desired to gain the attention of the uninterested
and indifferent, and even to attract them with his engaging style.
His concern was for the souls of men, both the lost in com-
mending Christ to them at the Wicket-gate, and authentic
Christians in encouraging them to persevere towards the
Celestial City.

3. *The Pilgrim's Progress* is not merely a simple gospel tract

While the gospel pervades the allegory as a whole, in Part One 10.5% of the text is concerned with the beginning of the allegory up to Christian's reception at the Wicket-gate and conversion, while 89.5% of the text takes us from the Wicket-gate up to the conclusion at the Celestial City. As the title plainly suggests, *The Pilgrim's Progress* is chiefly about the progress of a Christian pilgrim.

4. *The Pilgrim's Progress* is not a non-doctrinal moral novel

Truncated versions of *The Pilgrim's Progress* are inevitably pruned of the more doctrinal discourse sections. However, it comes as a surprise to the serious student of the allegory to discover that Bunyan deals with theological issues with considerable precision and detail. Dr J. Gresham Machen perceptively writes of 'that tenderest and most theological of books, the *Pilgrim's Progress* of John Bunyan ... that is pulsating with life in every word'.[10]

The essential purposes of *The Pilgrim's Progress*

From the outset, and in view of the preceding disclaimers, it would seem important to declare positively, in a summary fashion, what in substance John Bunyan intends to communicate in *The Pilgrim's Progress* that is buried beneath the surface of his allegorical style. In the concluding poem of Part One he challenges his readers as follows:

> Take heed also, that thou be not extreme,
> In playing with the outside of my dream:
> Nor let my figure or similitude
> Put thee into a laughter or a feud.

Leave this for boys and fools; but as for thee,
Do thou the substance of my matter see.[11]

Hence, the obvious question that has to be considered here is: what does Bunyan mean when he directs the reader to the 'substance' of his allegory? Clearly it involves the essence of his biblical emphases, and it is suggested that these concern four recurring themes:

- The gospel of the Lord Jesus Christ's saving, substitutionary righteousness as the ground of the advancing pilgrim's justification and sanctification.
- Progressive sanctification, from entrance at the Wicket-gate by means of transforming conversion to entrance into the Celestial City, with resultant glorification.
- Church fellowship under faithful pastoral leadership, as the only sure place of earthly refuge and support for pilgrims in transit.
- Anticipation of ultimate deliverance from the evil and trials of this world, along with future glory in the presence of Christ, when entrance is gained at the Celestial City.

The *Pilgrim's Progress* is thoroughly biblical

Even a casual acquaintance with *The Pilgrim's Progress* will reveal its biblical solidity. C. H. Spurgeon has vividly described this intrinsic quality as follows: 'Read anything of his [Bunyan's], and you will see that it is almost like reading the Bible itself. He had studied our Authorized Version … he had read it till his whole being was saturated with Scripture; and, though his writings are charmingly full of poetry, yet he cannot give us his *Pilgrim's Progress* — that sweetest of all prose poems — without continually making us feel and say, "Why, this man is a living Bible!" Prick him anywhere; and you will find that his blood is Bibline, the very essence of the Bible flows from him. He cannot speak without quoting a text, for his soul is full of the Word of God.'[12]

As a composite presentation of Bible truth

Aside from the basic marginal Scripture references which Bunyan supplies, there are countless other biblical passages that are almost seamlessly woven together. Often this interweaving is so smooth that the reader may be unaware that the Bible is in fact being quoted.

Consider just one instance, when Evangelist reappears to discover Christian paralysed with fear as he cowers under the threatening sheer slopes of the mountain — in reality Mount Sinai — that separates him from the village called Morality. Evangelist's first words of stern enquiry are: 'What doest thou here?'[13] Christian's only response is shameful silence, since he has departed from the narrow way. But does this not recall a similar scene in the Old Testament, that in which the word of the Lord addresses the prophet Elijah in a similarly shameful situation, after his flight from wicked Jezebel to a desert cave, with the question: 'What doest thou here, Elijah?' (1 Kings 19:9, AV). In this case, Bunyan gives no Scripture reference even though the specific biblical situation is clearly implicit. Hence, it is possible to study *The Pilgrim's Progress* without being fully aware of the biblical content that is being assimilated.

As a multi-level composition

It would also be true to say that Bunyan has incorporated levels of biblical understanding in *The Pilgrim's Progress* which account for its appeal to a wide range of age levels. There is the *basic* level of graphic spiritual adventure that is so captivating for young children and simply identified by character and situation names. There is the *biblical* level which transcends the allegorical framework so that the broad panorama of redemption is identified. There is the *doctrinal*, or substantial level, which deals with such categories as justification, imputation, Christ's person and work, the church, the world, sanctification, glorification, etc.

As a systematic presentation of Bible truth

Hence, it is perhaps most significant of all that Bunyan's use of Scripture is ultimately systematic rather than indiscriminate. He uncompromisingly presents a unified body of doctrine that clearly portrays the great truths of God, man, sin, Jesus Christ, grace, redemption, sanctification, the final judgement, glorification, etc. Nowhere is this emphasis clearer than in Bunyan's many-faceted, overall presentation of the gospel. In Christian we see mirrored Bunyan's own distinctive experience of saving faith in Christ, with its disjunction between the Wicket-gate and the Place of Deliverance, whereas in Hopeful's testimony we have the process of conversion described in its more normative expression (see chapter 6). Immediately following this, by way of contrast, we are shown Ignorance's faith in a false gospel; that is, his trust in an infused, or inner, righteousness that enables him, as he supposes, to produce works of righteousness by which he expects to be justified before God.

In all of this Bunyan is adamant that only the imputed substitutionary righteousness of Jesus Christ, received through faith alone, is able to reconcile any sinner to God. In full agreement with Luther, he insists that this gift of justifying righteousness is of the very essence of the gospel. And it is for this reason, this pervasive centrality of the gospel, that *The Pilgrim's Progress* is of such great importance for these days of clouded doctrine, for it is not only thoroughly biblical, but also truly evangelistic.

The Pilgrim's Progress has proven universal appeal

In the 1986 edition of *The Norton Anthology of English Literature*, a somewhat paradoxical comment is made to the effect that, while '*The Pilgrim's Progress* is no longer a household book' (as it formerly was), yet it remains 'the most popular allegory in our literature'.[14] We shall return later to the question of the book's fall in popularity in more recent times, but our concern at this point is to show that Bunyan's masterpiece deserves the recognition and circulation which, according to this assessment, it still enjoys in the field of allegory, not only in that limited sphere, but in a much wider one.

It is second only to the Bible

While both William Shakespeare and Bunyan's contemporary rival John Milton may have cause to challenge him in the field of general literary stature, even they cannot offer a single title that equals Bunyan's sustained universal popularity with regard to the circulation of his magnum opus. In other words, it is no exaggeration to claim that *The Pilgrim's Progress* remains the most popular and widest-circulating single piece of English literature, allegory or otherwise, outside of the Bible.[15] And this being the case, such a book continues to merit careful study.

Leading Bunyan scholar Roger Sharrock has written in this vein as follows: '*The Pilgrim's Progress* is a book which in three hundred years of its existence has crossed most of those barriers of race and culture that usually serve to limit the communicative power of a classic. It has penetrated into the non-Christian world; it has been read by cultivated Moslems during the rise of religious individualism within Islam, and at the same time in cheap missionary editions by American Indians and South Sea Islanders. Its uncompromising evangelical Protestantism has not prevented it from exercising an appeal in Catholic countries.

But to English readers it is bound to appear as the supreme classic of the English Puritan tradition.'[16]

It derives its very essence from the Bible

However, is this worldwide popularity simply due to an appealing simplicity of style contained within an arresting allegorical form? Surely the answer to this question must be in the negative if these two elements are all that we perceive Bunyan's method to contain. For as well as style and form, he has forged a biblical epic that derives its very essence from, and at all times sticks close to, the most popular book in all of human history — that is, the Bible. Here is the primary cause of the Bedford tinker's unrivalled success. In *The Cambridge History of English Literature* this conclusion is well supported: 'There are now [in 1949] versions of *The Pilgrim's Progress* in no fewer than one hundred and eight different languages and dialects, so that it is no mere poetical figure to say, as has been said, that it follows the Bible from land to land as the singing of birds follows the dawn.'[17] The number of languages has since risen to 200.

It merits optimistic recognition

What, then, is the point for us today concerning this sustained, though fading, universal recognition of Bunyan's allegory? It is simply that the present neglect of *The Pilgrim's Progress* ought to lead us to admit our own impoverishment in comparison with previous centuries, rather than to adopt a patronizing attitude towards what is often seen as a literary curiosity from the past containing only outmoded theology. But further, it is my belief that such repentance ought to be evidenced by a new sense of urgency in making Bunyan's classic more widely known and proclaiming its message. The favourable judgement of the last three centuries is not something that should be lightly tossed aside. Perhaps the fault really lies with a modern generation that is neglectful of history, intoxicated with the senses, mentally lazy, biblically illiterate and rebellious towards God. However, more particularly, even evangelical Christianity has drifted from its historic godly heritage towards the dangerous reefs of disabling humanism and modernity.

Nathaniel Hawthorne recognized this deterioration within Christendom as long ago as the middle of the nineteenth century, so that he was stimulated to write his short parody of Bunyan's allegory which he called *The Celestial Railroad*. In it he caricatures the prevailing interest of nominal Christians in desiring to travel towards heaven, no longer by means of a narrow way strewn with trials, but rather by a more comfortable rail journey, which promises the same destination by means of a less laborious form of transportation.[18] But something more than such insightful satire is required at this hour.

However true such an analysis may be concerning the subtle seduction of the church by the world, the assessment of *The Pilgrim's Progress* for the future by Cambridge scholar George Sampson ought to be seriously pondered and optimistically embraced: 'There is no need to say anything about the book by way of criticism; for its characters, its scenes and its phrases have become a common possession. Of course in *every* age there has been, and there always will be, the kind of superior person who disdains it. Such people are naught. *The Pilgrim's Progress* goes on for ever. Creeds may change and faith may be wrecked; but the life of man is still a pilgrimage, and in its painful course he must encounter the friends and the foes, the dangers and the despairs that Bunyan's inspired simplicity has drawn so faithfully that even children know them at once for truth.'[19]

The Pilgrim's Progress is winsome in character

In an allusion to Jesus Christ's command to the disciples Peter and Andrew, 'Follow me, and I will make you fishers of men' (Matt. 4:19), John Bunyan includes the following lines in his introductory poetic apology to *The Pilgrim's Progress*:

> You see the ways the fisherman doth take
> To catch the fish; what engines doth he make!
> Behold! How he engageth all his wits;
> Also his snares, lines, angles, hooks and nets.
> Yet fish there be, that neither hook nor line,
> Nor snare, nor net, nor engine can make thine:
> They must be grop'd for, and be tickled too,
> Or they will not be catch'd, whate'er you do.[20]

The evangelistic rationale here is clear, unambiguous and somewhat bold. Even though persuasion as a broad category may be open to abuse through extreme and gimmicky application, nevertheless gospel truth ought to be presented in a manner suitable to the sensitivities and peculiarities of the audience. In particular, for the indifferent masses there needs to be something more than just dangling a baited hook before them; rather a little gentle pressure may need to be applied; the truth must be packaged in such a way that it arouses attention, awakens curiosity, stimulates interest, goads reaction and promotes a response.[21]

In this same poem Bunyan continues:

> Art thou for something rare and profitable?
> Wouldest thou see a truth within a fable?
> Art thou forgetful? Wouldst thou remember
> From New-Year's-Day to the last of December?
> Then read my fancies, they will stick like burs,
> And may be to the helpless, comforters.

This book is writ in such a dialect,
As may the minds of listless men affect;
It seems a novelty, and yet contains
Nothing but sound and honest gospel strains.[22]

Here again the judgement of history is that this imprisoned pastor's goal was achieved beyond his most extravagant hopes. From the outset of its publication, *The Pilgrim's Progress* has captivated successive levels of society, except for the latter part of the twentieth century and onward. The nineteenth-century engraving by J. D. Watson depicted below well illustrates this former universal popularity.

It represents various characters coming out from under the Sign of the Peacock, the address of Bunyan's publisher, Nathaniel Ponder. They include a scholar, a finely dressed gentleman and his lady, schoolboys, a soldier and various men and women, all busily reading their copy of the best-selling allegory. Furthermore there is a rustic character with a whip in one hand and money in the other just going into the shop.

It is doctrinally winsome

From a slightly different perspective, namely that of Bunyan's doctrinal emphasis, poet Samuel Taylor Coleridge describes his appeal in this regard as follows: 'This wonderful work [*The Pilgrim's Progress*] is one of the very few books which may be read over repeatedly at different times, and each time with a new and a different pleasure. I read it once as a theologian — and let me assure you that there is great theological acumen in the work — once with devotional feelings — and once as a poet. I could not have believed beforehand that Calvinism could be painted in such exquisitely delightful colours.'[23]

It is biblically arresting

The question, then, that faces us today is whether this acknowledged appeal of the past is adequate for the present. While admitting the original attractiveness of Bunyan's style and content, is it nevertheless suitable for an age that has moved from typography to television, from discourse to sound-bites, from objectivity to subjectivity, from facts to feelings, from reality to sensuality, from tradition to modernity? In other words, can an old-fashioned literary garment, though popular in its time, continue to wear well and admirably in the present and therefore be communicated today in a manner that is up-to-date, faithful to Bible truth and equally captivating? My own undoubted conviction is, with the weight of history to support it, that *The Pilgrim's Progress* can be effectively communicated by teaching and proclamation that is both passionate and persuasive; indeed when a person, gifted of God, brings forth the Word of God that Bunyan has so marvellously enshrined in his allegorical style, he will find it quite easy to move into the mode of preaching and proclamation. One of the prime reasons for a lessening of interest has simply been misunderstanding about the essential message of the tinker preacher; when the truth has been pointed out in the setting of teaching or seminar, time and time again the enthusiastic response has been one of astonishment at what Bunyan is really saying, especially in terms of the gospel, sanctification, local church life and pastoral leadership.

The Pilgrim's Progress speaks to the spiritual needs of the hour

Unfortunately, as was mentioned earlier, *The Pilgrim's Progress* has more recently been perceived as a book that primarily addresses the thinking level of children. It has been regarded as designed for the presentation of simple Bible truth in an imaginative, adventurous, even fairy-tale manner. However, such an assessment is far from the truth. One has only to consider the variety of characters in the cast to realize that no child with only a few years' experience of life could fully comprehend the developed traits, both perverse and godly, that are embodied in the persons depicted, most of whom are adults. When we understand that Faithful is propositioned by a seductress, that Christian is at one point inclined to commit suicide and that Hopeful has a fleeting appetite for mammon, only then do we begin to grasp that *The Pilgrim's Progress* is about perennial adult problems that can only be dealt with by means of God's timeless gospel remedy.

If someone suggests that *The Pilgrim's Progress* is completely outdated and incapable of addressing the complex struggles of our technological and sophisticated generation, my usual response is a series of questions that goes something like this: 'Do you know of anyone today who could be designated as a Mr Worldly-Wiseman or a Mr Save-self? Amongst your neighbours or friends at work, do you recognize a Mr Money-love or a Mr Love-lust? In your experience in church life, have you ever encountered a minister like Mr Two-tongues, who says one thing and believes another? Do you know religious people who could be just as boldly hypocritical as Talkative? Have you from time to time met a real Christian who, like Hopeful, proved to be buoyant and encouraging in the midst of trying circumstances?' On so many occasions, people who hear this challenge grin as they acknowledge that times have not really changed, at least with regard to the basic characteristics of man.

Hence there are the best of reasons for maintaining that *The Pilgrim's Progress* is well able to address the spiritual torpor and ignorance of these modern times. In particular it confronts the growing corrosion of evangelical Christianity from a number of perspectives.

1. The need for clear proclamation of the gospel

While the apostle Paul was zealous in upholding the truth of the gospel with great exactness (Gal. 1:6-9; 2:4-5,14-16), present-day evangelism has degenerated into mere abstract, emotional and relational encounter with an ill-defined Christ. In particular, the modern gospel has blurred the centrality of the atonement and the fundamental moral conflict between God and man addressed by the doctrine of justification by faith alone.

However, *The Pilgrim's Progress* calls us back to the gospel precision of Paul's epistles. Bunyan was a great admirer of Martin Luther, and especially of the Reformer's commentary on Galatians.[24] It is no surprise, then, to discover that the Bedford pastor was rooted and grounded in that same gospel of free justification. The conversion testimony of Hopeful and the detailed dispute between Christian and Ignorance are model expositions of the nature of both true and false conversion, and the gospel as God's gift of imputed perfect righteousness received through faith alone.

2. The need for clear proclamation of sovereign grace

Avoid the emotive terms of 'Calvinism' and 'Arminianism' if we will, yet in the last hundred years or so the groundswell in Christian circles has been predominantly towards the powers of human autonomy at the expense of the sovereignty of God. Free-will doctrine has dominated the frontiers of evangelism, and thus it ought to be no surprise that the resulting harvest has produced a large number of doubtful conversions and spiritual stillbirths.

However, in this arena the Calvinist Bunyan has much to teach us. To quote from Coleridge again, 'Calvinism never put on a less rigid form, never smoothed its brow and softened its voice more winningly than in *The Pilgrim's Progress*.'[25] Yes, the portrayal of the man in the iron cage, with its emphasis on reprobation, is extremely sobering. Even so, the doctrines of human inability and sovereign grace, and the clear distinction between the particular elect of God and the reprobate, simply flow forth as part of a larger canvas; these truths are taught integrally rather than topically.

Nevertheless, in Bunyan's overall ministry, there is no logical constriction regarding the free offer of the gospel, but rather the most passionate, repeated, reasoned and entreating gospel invitations. It is not surprising that C. H. Spurgeon, who was such a lover of the doctrines of sovereign grace, not only had a great admiration for Bunyan, but likewise manifested that same unfettered evangelistic zeal.

3. The need for clear proclamation of sanctification

In the last hundred years or so, two movements within conservative evangelicalism have promoted views of sanctification in the Christian life that have resulted in widespread confusion and error among believers on this topic. On the one hand, there was the teaching of the classic English Keswick / Higher Life Movement that justification through faith is paralleled by sanctification through faith, or passive surrender to the Holy Spirit.[26] On the other hand, and even more influential in recent years, there is the Pentecostal / charismatic movement, which teaches that advanced sanctification should come by means of a sudden, cataclysmic, post-conversion experience described as the baptism in the Holy Spirit and evidenced by phenomena such as speaking in tongues.

As we shall see in chapter 7, the message of *The Pilgrim's Progress* provides a biblically based counterbalance to both of these false emphases. It graphically represents the Christian life as a journey in which spiritual growth and advancement towards the ultimate goal of being welcomed into heaven and the presence of Jesus Christ are achieved through a process of ongoing struggle and conflict. The advancement of pilgrims in this venture is aided by the use of the means provided for this purpose by the Lord whom they serve.

4. The need of clear proclamation that honours God

In his poetic introduction to *The Pilgrim's Progress*, Bunyan indicates just how sensitive he was to criticism of his allegorical method. He sought advice from pastoral colleagues. He did not rush into publication. He considered biblical standards of communication, eventually deciding to go to print and let history be the final arbiter. The verdict of general universal approval has of course been in for some time, and without question there has never been any ongoing criticism with regard to Bunyan's literary style in terms of its being irreverent or lacking in spiritual taste.

Yes, there are moments of very droll humour, though these are far outweighed by the more numerous scenes of transfixing solemnity. But there are no vain or flippant expressions to be found in his work, no coarseness or vulgarity, especially where the person and work of God are concerned.

It is true that numerous objectionable and worldly characters are described, and with such clarity that one becomes convinced that their names are simply pseudonyms for specific acquaintances of the author. However, these are also representative of personality traits that are equally common in today's society. There are just as many Obstinates and Pliables, Messrs Worldly-Wisemen and Talkatives abounding today. Our fashions and emphases may have modified over the past three hundred years, but, as Bunyan so convincingly demonstrates, the essential characteristics of man prove to be unchanging. And this is why *The Pilgrim's Progress* continues to be ongoing in its popularity, for it communicates with reverence and contemporaneity — at least it does, provided it is presented in a suitable way.

5. The need for clear proclamation that is competitive

Many of life's choicest experiences have come to us, not so much by means of self-discovery as through the recommendation and enthusiastic persuasion of a friend. For instance, consider the case of a particular foreign cuisine in which formerly you may have expressed no interest whatsoever — perhaps, say, Indian curry dishes. But then a friend presses you to join him at an Indian restaurant for a sample dinner, and so, without any great enthusiasm, you accept his gratuitous invitation. He is rapturous in his description of the menu. But still you remain unmoved — that is until you cautiously sample the distinctive fare for yourself and suddenly awaken to the delights of a whole new world of taste.

Now as a convert to this type of cuisine, and wanting to persuade others to share in its delights, is it enough to show your friends a book of Indian recipes, tell them where to buy the curry powder and spices, and then expect them to proceed to cook an Indian dinner for themselves? No, of course not! You need to excite the interest of your friends, in the same way as your own was aroused, through persuasive communication that awakens interest and introduces the hearer to a whole new world of delicious, enjoyable food. Of course, the ingredients must be intrinsically good and appetizing — that is, competitive in a world of food. And of prime importance is the necessity for various recipes to be well prepared, and promoted with fervent recommendation.

And so it is with *The Pilgrim's Progress* at this time. It is a neglect of responsibility today simply to believe that it is sufficient for Bunyan's allegory to be available on the shelves of bookstores. It would certainly be a neglect of responsibility to suggest that the Bible only needs to be made available in bookshops; otherwise preaching and personal evangelism would be regarded as superfluous. However, in the same way as the Bible needs proclamation, so does *The Pilgrim's Progress* to this present, spiritually dull generation. As a spiritual classic it is essentially good and appealing. History proves just how supremely competitive it really is. Yes, contemporary taste has degenerated. But that is only all the more reason why better food ought to be offered. *The Pilgrim's Progress* needs skilful and applicatory exposition that awakens those who are lethargic in their souls and introduces them to a new spiritual taste sensation!

The truth remains that modern man is on a pilgrimage, whether he recognizes it or not, though it is a sad journey to behold. Gordon Rupp (writing in 1957) describes it this way: 'Modern man, in the ruins of Hiroshima and Nagasaki, in the prisons of Europe, in the cities of Hungary, knows as poignantly as Christian the dilemma of human existence. But modern man, unlike Christian, has no book in his hand, he has no faith in Evangelist, and a heavenly city seems to him much more likely to be a mirage. The God-dimension is missing, and he does his thinking in a curious parody of Christian verities. He too moves along a road of human experience: meets mishap and disaster: knows what comforts comradeship and love, joy and laughter, may bring: knows the besetting impact of evil and temptation: moves inexorably towards the lonely experience of dying. But he cannot answer the question 'Whence?' or 'Whither?'[27]

However, it is the truth of the Bible, engagingly embedded throughout *The Pilgrim's Progress*, that can direct him to the answers.

John Bunyan commends his book to the reader

This book it chalketh out before thine eyes
The man that seeks the everlasting prize:
It shows you whence he comes, whither he goes;
What he leaves undone, also what he does;
It also shows you how he runs and runs,
Till he unto the gate of glory comes.
It shows, too, who set out for life amain,
As if the lasting crown they would obtain;
Here also you may see the reason why
They lose their labour, and like fools do die.
This book will make a traveller of thee,
If by its counsel thou wilt ruled be;
It will direct thee to the Holy Land,
If thou wilt its directions understand:
Yea, it will make the slothful active be;
The blind also delightful things to see.
Art thou for something rare and profitable;

Would'st thou see a truth within a fable?
Art thou forgetful? Wouldest thou remember
From New Year's day to the last of December?
Then read my fancies; they will stick like burs,
And may be, to the helpless, comforters.
This book is writ in such a dialect
As may the minds of listless men affect:
It seems a novelty, and yet contains
Nothing but sound and honest gospel strains.

John Bunyan
Introductory 'apology' to *The Pilgrim's Progress*

2.
Biblical reality through allegory

'Art thou for something
rare and profitable?
Wouldest thou see a
truth within a fable?...
Then read my fancies,
they will stick like burs,
And may be to the
helpless comforters'
(John Bunyan).

2.
Biblical reality through allegory

WHILE *The Concise Oxford Dictionary* defines an 'allegory' as 'a story in which the meaning or message is represented symbolically',[1] John Bunyan in *The Pilgrim's Progress* has a much broader understanding in view. Within the introductory and concluding poems of Part One are to be found eight terms in all which describe his style. They are 'allegory', 'similitude', 'metaphor', 'parable', 'figure', 'type', 'fable' and 'shadow'. In other words, to force his method into too technical a literary definition is inevitably to suggest a degree of inconsistency or contradiction which does not in fact exist.

Instead let us simply define *The Pilgrim's Progress* as a literary representation of life and truth that, although painted on a broad canvas, incorporates a blend of various stylistic elements; these include dialogue, muse, poetry, characterization, emblem, droll humour, fantasy, drama, saga, intrigue, polemic, spiritual romance and mystery. The weaving together of these various strands also incorporates continuity, contrast, progression in anticipation of a glorious, yet sober, climax, and so contributes to the fulfilment of the author's spiritual purposes.

Bunyan's justification of his allegorical style

Again, both the introductory and concluding poems of Part One give a comprehensive explanation of the author's rationale for what was, in Puritan circles, truly a literary novelty. The following list of arguments that Bunyan proposes in support of his allegorical method is to a large extent a response to early critical assessments of his work, particularly at a pastoral level.

The introductory poem

- Even though his style may appear dark, as some suggest, it may yet yield fruit.
- Hard souls will only be caught by means of a literary style that stimulates and arouses their interest.
- Difficult souls can only be snared by appropriate means.
- Treasure is often contained in a tawdry casket.
- 'Feigned' — that is, invented and contrived — words have been used by others to bring the truth to light.
- Metaphors, types and shadows have in the past been used by God to communicate solid truth.
- Impartial men will admit that truth, however it is wrapped up, is always better than lies, even though the latter may be set in silver.
- Paul does not forbid the use of parables in his warnings to Timothy of what he should avoid.
- This use of allegory is permitted provided it does not go to extremes and the truth is not in any way distorted.
- No one objects to the use of dialogue as a literary style. How much more appropriate, then, is it to use such a method to convey the truth of God!

- This style of teaching through illustrations is found in Scripture and, far from smothering truth, makes it shine more brightly.
- This style sets forth the realities of Christian pilgrimage and encourages the reader to become a pilgrim.
- This style helps the forgetful to retain truth and captures the interest of the listless.
- This style stimulates enquiry.

The concluding poem

- The style, though open to abuse, will do good provided it is rightly interpreted.
- Beneath the veil of literary form there is real substance.
- When one penetrates beyond the veil of the outward figures the substance which is revealed will prove helpful to the honest enquirer.
- The reader is free to reject any dross but should not discard the gold with it.
- When the ore in which it is wrapped is stripped away the inner gold of biblical truth will be revealed.

Bunyan's purposes with his allegorical style

While we might wish to discover some grand, ambitious design which compelled Bunyan to commence writing *The Pilgrim's Progress*, he tells us in his introductory poem to Part One that this was not in fact the case. He appears to have been well into the composition of *The Heavenly Footman*,[2] in the course of his imprisonment, when suddenly the first glimmer of an idea flashed into his fertile brain. At first it was more of a literary challenge to his sanctified spirit than anything else, but one idea sparked off another until the blaze gradually took hold and threatened to take over his writing completely. He tells us he used it as a means of shunning the evil thoughts and deeds which are the products of idleness. Did he, then, entertain in his thinking some noble missionary vision whereby he might confront an ungodly world that needed the truth using the means of literary titillation? This was not the case, since Bunyan tells us, quite honestly, that he wrote simply, 'mine own self to gratify'.[3] Nevertheless, using the imagery of a woman spinning flax, he describes how, '... as I pull'd it came; and so I penn'd it down',[4] till it rapidly grew in size.

However, we know something of the spiritual earnestness of Bunyan — a quality which he, in genuine humility, would have been most reluctant to boast about, or to put in writing in any self-congratulatory sense. Hence we must surely read between the lines at this point and attribute to him a more specific and edifying purpose, even if he would certainly be unwilling to admit to a deeper, altruistic intent. Clearly the introductory poem was written when Part One had been completed and publication was imminent. Nevertheless, its concluding lines contain a strong statement concerning several purposes that need to be appreciated by both the reader in general and the teacher of *The Pilgrim's Progress* in particular.

He intended to gain the attention of the indifferent

As a pastor, Bunyan was an astute observer of his fellow man and also of the world of nature. By means of this capacity for keen perception, he both learned many lessons and acquired a degree of flexibility in making applications to his hearers, or readers, while always keeping strictly within the bounds of holy propriety. Convinced Calvinist though he was, Bunyan did not hesitate to write in the following terms concerning the need to be winsome in evangelistic outreach, using principles which he had learned, not only from skilful fishing (see Matt. 4:19), as has been noted earlier, but also from 'fowling', or hunting birds. Such means he considered to be perfectly legitimate:

How does the fowler seek to catch his game?
By divers means! All which one cannot name:
His gun, his nets, his lime-twigs, light and bell:
He creeps, he goes, he stands; yea, who can tell
Of all his postures? Yet, there's none of these
Will make him master of what fowls he please.
Yea, he must pipe and whistle, to catch *this*,
Yet if he does so, *that* bird he will miss.[5]

Nevertheless, with regard to the present day, great discernment is certainly needed at this point concerning the critical question that immediately comes to mind about what is appropriate inducement. When are 'piping' and 'whistling' legitimate and when are they illegitimate? Bunyan, while incorporating in some of his writings a modest amount of material presented in an amusing style, would doubtless have abominated the gimmickry often to be found in ministry today, such as the concept of 'Christian comedy' and the entertainment syndrome so prevalent in contemporary local churches. The Bunyan Meeting would have been considered very strict and sober by today's standards.[6] Even so, the dry and witty humour of *The Pilgrim's Progress* does seem to indicate just how far he was prepared to go with his 'hunting', and no further. It is most likely that this indicates the limits of his spiritual 'stalking'.

However, it needs to be stated clearly that the number of passages in the allegory where a lighter note is sounded are far outweighed by the sobriety which pervades the work as a whole. This proportion is evident in the totality of Bunyan's ministry, including his other writings. The brief moments where he expresses himself in a very droll fashion are far eclipsed by the extended passages in which he is intensely serious. Certainly both the commencement and the conclusion of the allegory are marked by great solemnity. And, as has already been mentioned, there is not the slightest hint of coarseness or worldly banter.

He Intended to communicate biblical reality through allegory

In a world which frantically attempts to avoid reality by immersing itself in fantasy or diversionary escapades, whether through television, science fiction, music, drugs, or a hundred other sensual indulgences, Bunyan presents us with a contrasting scenario. He is passionately concerned that men and women should be confronted with the biblical reality concerning themselves that they so desperately seek to evade. This he does by engaging their attention with allegory that sets out to attract and then proceeds to turn our amusement and enjoyment into a sober reminder about truth and real life, about sin and God, about guilt and our ultimate destiny.

Of course, the reader of *The Pilgrim's Progress* can still purposely avoid Bunyan's warning and determine only to 'play with the outside of his dream', as he puts it, though he does so at his own peril and incurs Bunyan's condemnation of such foolishness. Lord Macaulay has significantly written that 'Bunyan is almost the only writer who ever gave to the abstract the interest of the concrete.'[7] Surely herein lie the wonder and intrigue and the captivating quality that continue to appeal even to the twenty-first century reader, provided he or she is prepared to spend sufficient time to give the gifted pastor of Bedford a fair hearing.

Modern man increasingly engrosses himself in flights of fancy, from many of which he has yet to wake up; his only prospect is the depressing jolt of a return to hard-core reality, and often before a yawning grave. On the other hand, Bunyan invites his audience to take a flight of fancy into reality and thus to avoid the necessity of experiencing the same wrench of adjustment to the waking state. Admittedly he reveals the reality about sin and guilt and ultimate judgement, not fantasy, and that can be profoundly disturbing. Yet the honest person senses that this revelation has integrity in spite of its allegorical form. But furthermore, Bunyan reveals, not the reality of a necessary resignation to the status quo, but rather the glory of the gospel alternative that transfers the awakened sinner to the kingdom of God's grace. When Bunyan concludes, 'So I awoke, and behold it was a dream,'[8] he does not leave us feeling deflated. He simply strips away the allegorical form and leaves us with the unchanging gospel truth of biblical revelation.

He intended to communicate truth through a novel form

On several occasions the Son of God indicates that at times his servants lacked that proper initiative and shrewdness which the children of the devil manifested only too frequently (Matt. 10:16; Luke 16:1-9; cf. Josh. 9:3-27). However, it is doubtful whether the Bedford tinker could be charged with being negligent in this regard. In the introductory poem of *The Pilgrim's Progress* we read the lines:

> Art thou for something rare and profitable?
> Wouldest thou see a truth within a fable? ...
> Then read my fancies, they will stick like burs,
> And may be to the helpless comforters.[9]

So the wily literary artist declares here both his spiritual priority and his strategy of appealing to the reader.

1. The priority of truth

Amidst the solicitous carnival atmosphere at Vanity Fair, and even the gaiety for which this scene has become proverbial, the intractable commitment of Christian and Faithful to the pilgrim way, without the slightest deviation, is certainly representative of Bunyan's own consecration to biblical Christianity. What is it that keeps the two travellers from sampling the wares, either to the left or to the right, on their transit through the city? The answer is to be found in the response of both pilgrims to the hucksters' solicitations: 'We buy the truth.'[10] Of course no such merchandise was on sale there, although the visitors were not slow to recommend this rare commodity in the face of much opposition.

So, for Bunyan, truth — that is, Bible truth about God, man, sin and grace; truth that could not possibly communicate error; objective and concrete truth — is his chief concern, even though in this instance it is packaged in such an engaging exterior.

2. The strategy of attractive literary form

To read only *The Pilgrim's Progress* might lead one to conclude that this style is representative of the author in general, but nothing could be further from the truth. The works of Bunyan as a whole convey a far more sober spirit, though one no less lacking in imaginative expression. Even *The Holy War* and, in particular, *The Life and Death of Mr Badman* are not impregnated to anything like the same degree with subtle and serious wit. Most often Bunyan is direct, intimate and solid, combining evangelistic fervour and pressing application with close doctrinal reasoning while at every point he is unflinching in his defence of the truth of Scripture. Like his mentor Martin Luther, he throbs with life and is never dull.

However, *The Pilgrim's Progress* is distinctive because it is aimed at a difficult and resistant market. Who specifically comprises this audience? According to the introductory poem of Part One, it is the slothful, blind, forgetful, listless, melancholy, etc. This being so, what inducement is offered? It consists of fancies, novelty, riddles and amusement, but not in an over-whelming measure so that the truth is all but lost sight of. No, there is enough bait to cause the fish to bite, but the hook of truth remains substantial just below the surface.

He intended to persuade the reader to become a traveller

It is true, as George Offor writes, that 'All mankind are pilgrims; all are pressing through this world.'[11] Nevertheless, the problem remains that all mankind are not headed in the same direction, and it is this matter of destiny that causes Bunyan, so anxious for the souls of men, to set them earnestly upon a very specific and unique course. So, again in the introductory poem of Part One, we find an invitation for the spiritually adventurous to become travellers:

> This book will make a traveller of thee,
> If by its counsel thou wilt ruled be;
> It will direct thee to the Holy Land,
> If thou wilt its directions understand.[12]

However, as our spiritual travel agent, Bunyan is not one to recommend the journey without having first had experience of the route heavenward himself. *Grace Abounding to the Chief of Sinners* is a faithful publicity testimonial and brochure, although, unlike advertising material in general, it does not describe the cost in small print, but rather spells it out with bold honesty. On the other hand, the resting places and the graphic descriptions of the scenery ahead, portrayed as it were in full colour, are enough to appeal to any serious pilgrim.

From another perspective, one of the recurring elements in this whole matter of allegorical journeying, of progress to a destination, is that of recapitulation. On numerous occasions the major pilgrims are to be found recollecting their former experiences, either to prove their authentic status, or to reassure themselves and fellow travellers: 'Thus far the Lord has helped us' (1 Sam. 7:12). All in all, Bunyan is intently involved in stimulating his readers to move and not be static. He is very sympathetic to the backsliding of a Christian or the slowness of a Little-faith insofar as they resume progress. But the inertia of a Simple, Sloth or Presumption is greatly distressing to him.

He intended to animate the reader to persevere to the end of the journey

For the apostle Paul it was not enough for sinners to be converted to Christ through his ministry. Rather he never ceased to be concerned about the safe arrival home of these saints into the very presence of the Lord Jesus Christ. So to the Thessalonians he writes, 'For who is our hope or joy or crown of exultation? Is it not even you, in the presence of our Lord Jesus at his coming?' (1 Thess. 2:19). With a similar interest Bunyan writes to his readers in *Grace Abounding to the Chief of Sinners*, 'I now once again ... do look yet after you all, greatly longing to see your safe arrival into the desired haven... The milk and honey is beyond this wilderness. God be merciful to you, and grant that you be not slothful to go in to possess the land.'[13]

So in *The Pilgrim's Progress*, this same long-term goal is even more graphically portrayed. It is not an allegory about 'successful' evangelistic crusades, but rather the faithful shepherding of souls who, having entered the Wicket-gate, are guided towards their safe reception in the Celestial City. The dominant perspective of the major pilgrims is not merely that of present sanctification, but anticipation of God's consummate 'eternal glory in Christ', something of which we have as yet had only a small taste (1 Cor. 2:9; 13:12; 1 Peter 5:10). Typical of this priority is Bunyan's rapturous final description of the Celestial City and his wistful comment as narrator recounting the entrance of Christian and Hopeful into that holy metropolis of heaven when he says that 'I wished myself among them.'[14]

Bunyan's critics and his allegorical style

The introductory poem to Part One of *The Pilgrim's Progress* makes it abundantly clear that the initial criticism of the innovative approach adopted by Bunyan was more a matter of moral propriety, and the suitability of allegory as a means of conveying Christian truth, than of literary correctness of style, or doctrinal orthodoxy. However, today a change of emphasis has taken place, to the point where the classic is regarded primarily as a literary specimen of an outdated species that is chiefly suitable for the endless mining of historic minutiae, exotic stylistic speculation and antiquarian conjecture. The one common factor that unites all this delving into Bunyan's allegory is a studied avoidance of any commitment to the truth of his message.

Roger Sharrock describes this development in a very honest and revealing fashion when he says, 'The greater part of the writing about *The Pilgrim's Progress* in the eighteenth, nineteenth, and into the twentieth century, was in the nature of pious commentary and moral exhortation, much of it by writers in the Free Church tradition. For a book that lay in the window-seat with the Bible there was no possibility of pure literary criticism; that was only to come, like the concept of "the Bible designed to be read as Literature", in the decadence of the English religious tradition.'[15]

What a confession this is! One could hope that this writer does indeed mean that the 'pure literary criticism' of today is in fact associated, detrimentally as many of us believe, with contemporary religious 'decadence'. But most disturbing of all is the inference that a 'pious' regard for *The Pilgrim's Progress* inevitably inhibits 'pure literary criticism'. Herein lies, from the pen of the quintessential twentieth-century Bunyan scholar, a frank, albeit misguided, admission that objective study is only possible when one retains a personal detachment from Bunyan's evangelical substance. Mind you, it does not matter if a scholar has a strong socialist / secularist / theologically liberal commitment, by which he is openly revisionist in his approach to the doctrine of Bunyan's writings; in that case, such 'scholarship' is regarded as acceptable, and even roundly applauded!

Seventeenth-century criticism

History appears to have delivered its verdict that Bunyan's own apology for his innovative allegorical style has been vindicated. The poetic defence of Part One is thorough and persuasive, especially insofar as it is a matter of convincing Christians who are sensitive about capitulation to worldliness. Furthermore, we need to remember that prior to 1678 when *The Pilgrim's Progress* was first published, the author had incurred strong opposition from some Baptist leaders concerning his *Differences in Judgement about Water Baptism No Bar to Communion*, which was published in 1673. However, it should once again be stressed that this difference of opinion concerning *The Pilgrim's Progress* was about the appropriateness of the genre rather than literary style.

At the time of Bunyan's increasing popularity, he also manifested a creative, though restrained, boldness that certainly challenged the more staid of his Puritan acquaintances. In 1664 he had published his *Map Shewing the Order and Causes of Salvation and Damnation*, an uncommon chart for his time.[16] The third edition of *The Pilgrim's Progress* to be published in 1679 included what came to be known as 'The Sleeping Portrait'. This was a drawing of himself dreaming his dream, and also depicted Christian progressing from the City of Destruction towards the Wicket-gate.[17] This was bold iconography. Yet with the work probably receiving the endorsement of John Owen[18] as well as that of multitudes of the common people, the debate soon gave way to an astonishing rate of distribution, acceptance and blessing. As John Brown writes, 'The fact that three editions were thus called for within a year shows that *The*

The sleeping portrait

Pilgrim's Progress leaped at a bound to that popularity which it has retained.'[19]

Eighteenth-century criticism

However, such initial renown fell chiefly within the ranks of the less cultured strata of society. Christopher Hill explains that '*The Pilgrim's Progress* was a best-seller from the start among the middling and poorer sort, though despised by the literary establishment.'[20] Although Dr Samuel Johnson attributed great merit to the work in 1773, the prevailing consensus amongst the sophisticated classes was the view expressed in 1757 by David Hume that such writing was in poor taste.[21] Even as late as 1784 William Cowper, though writing appreciatively, thought it best to refer to Bunyan's classic without actually naming it. In considering the elements of a good education he includes the allegory, yet, as mentioned earlier, makes the following explanation:

> I name thee not lest so despised a name
> Should move a sneer at thy deserved fame.[22]

Nevertheless, the amalgam of *The Pilgrim's Progress* with the dawning Evangelical Awakening was a fruitful marriage indeed. As a result, the 'reading of Bunyan contributed to the conversion or rededication of many who were, or would become, dissenting ministers. Leaders of the Evangelical Revival and of Methodism were inspired by him, returned to him often, and recommended him constantly.'[23]

George Whitefield, John Wesley, Howel Harris and John Newton, to name but a few, were all enthusiasts for Bunyan's pen. For instance, in 1768 Newton writes to some Christian ladies as follows: 'Soon after I returned [to Olney] from Yorkshire, I began to expound the *Pilgrim's Progress* in our meetings on Tuesday evenings; and, though we had been almost seven months travelling with the pilgrim, we have not yet left the House Beautiful; but I believe [we] shall set off for the Valley of Humiliation in about three weeks. I find this book so full of matter, that I can seldom go through more than a page, or half a page at a time. I hope the attempt has been greatly blessed among us; and for myself, it has perhaps given me a deeper insight into John Bunyan's knowledge, judgement, and experience in the Christian life, than I should ever have had without it.'[24]

However, it needs to be pointed out that up to this point, estimates of *The Pilgrim's Progress* were based primarily upon its biblical substance, even though there was fascination with the captivatingly new style and background.

Nineteenth-century criticism

While, to apply to Bunyan the words recorded concerning his Lord and Master, 'the common people heard him gladly' (Mark 12:37, AV), during the 1830s a remarkable number of opinions were voiced by notable literary critics and essayists, expressing a previously unknown appreciation of *The Pilgrim's Progress*. For instance, the classical scholar and educationist Thomas Arnold writes, 'I hold John Bunyan to have been a man of incomparably greater genius than any of them [i.e. of the Anglican divines and theologians], and to have given a far truer and more edifying picture of Christianity. His *Pilgrim's Progress* seems to be a complete reflection of Scripture, with none of the rubbish of the theologians mixed up with it.' In the same manner, Samuel Taylor Coleridge, Sir Walter Scott and Lord Macaulay also heaped praise on the author who by then had been dead for over 140 years. Similarly Robert Southey joined this parade of recognition, according to Keeble: 'That the poet laureate [Southey] should not feel it beneath his dignity to write a hundred page introduction to *The Pilgrim's Progress* implicitly testified to Bunyan's new-found status.'[25]

Yet at this apex of esteem, there also seems to have been injected a shift of emphasis, as noted earlier, from evangelical substance to style and background for their own sake. Also it ought not to escape our notice that as a rationalistic approach to the Bible began to infect Christendom in general, so this change of emphasis with regard to *The Pilgrim's Progress* seemed to run in parallel with the birth of a supposedly 'higher' critical enlightenment.

Thus in 1880 J. A. Froude, while declaring Bunyan to be distinguished as an 'English Man of Letters', nevertheless suggests a more accommodating approach to the universal concept of pilgrimage than the more specific Puritan model: 'His [Christian's] experience is so truly human experience, that Christians of every persuasion can identify themselves with him; and even those who regard Christianity itself as but a natural outgrowth of the conscience and intellect, and yet desire to live nobly and make the best of themselves, can recognize familiar footprints in every step of Christian's journey.'[26]

So by 1905 Robert Bridges can offer the patronizing comment: 'It is pleasanter to write about Bunyan without reference to his theology… Bunyan himself would have been horrified to find that the secret of his fame was literary excellence, yet without that he would have perished long ago. In this regard his book [*The Pilgrim's Progress*] is like Milton's epic [*Paradise Lost*], which was at first esteemed for its plot and theological aspect, and now is read in spite of them... Over-praise will do his [Bunyan's] reputation no service; and his theology needs so much allowance that anything which dislocates him from his time does him vast injury.'[27]

Sad to say, for the decades that have followed, with few exceptions, this new emphasis upon various aspects of style and background, rather than evangelical content, has remained of the essence of Bunyan scholarship.

Twentieth-century criticism

To assess the overall merits of a new motor vehicle today requires a complex of appreciative skills. Manufacturing excellence, aesthetics, performance and purpose are all inseparable elements necessary for a true judgement to be made. This is not to say that all of these factors necessarily may be of equal importance. For example, if the intended purpose of the vehicle is strictly utilitarian, then the opinion of the aesthetic analyst that its appearance is poor becomes a matter of only minor importance. And so long as the purpose for which it is designed is totally fulfilled, then it is hardly accurate to pronounce the vehicle poor on the grounds that one minor aspect of its standard of manufacture is merely mediocre. The same principle applies today with regard to the assessment of *The Pilgrim's Progress*. Many a secular scholar applies a distinctive area of analysis to the famous allegory while in fact his particular line of enquiry is of only minor importance when considered in the light of Bunyan's essential purposes.

1. The neglect of Bunyan's purposes

There are at least six closely related elements that confront the modern reader of the famous allegory in the realm of Bunyan studies. These are: literary style, history, psychology, sociology, theology and experience. Of these the last two are of pre-eminent importance according to Bunyan's stated purposes. However, the great danger is that a contemporary analytical approach may, for instance, very easily focus on the first two elements and give them unwarranted prominence in relation to the rest. Sad to say, so much modern criticism of Bunyan reveals its fatal weakness at this point. Often an expert in the field of literature will be found to be woefully ignorant of theology as a dynamic of the soul; or a specialist in history will, while having some appreciation of theology (usually from a liberal perspective), be quite ignorant with regard to Bunyan's biblical reasons for his Calvinism. Yet the literary and historical essays of this eclectic genre pour forth unabated and are frequently elevated to considerable heights in the forum of scholastic investigation, even though the topics to which they relate are of only secondary importance.

2. The neglect of Bunyan's evangelicalism

Thus, what has come to be most conspicuous by its absence in Bunyan studies today is a truly evangelical sympathy with the Bedford pastor's experience; indeed, as Sharrock has intimated, such an attitude would most probably be regarded as a dis-qualification for objective study. Mind you, antipathy towards Bunyan's literalist understanding of the Bible would be thought of as no hindrance whatsoever!

Furthermore, in this same vein, another failure today is the avoidance of the expressed purposes of Bunyan in writing *The Pilgrim's Progress,* especially in any practical sense. Indeed, it might not be at all ridiculous to suggest that any modern scholar who experientially identified with Bunyan's gospel might be in danger of academic ostracism!

Of course, the problem here is that to consider seriously such a realm is to enter immediately into the area of biblical author-ity, biblical theology and resultant personal application. If one agrees with Bunyan, according to his understanding of Scripture that the predicament of sin in the human soul is of supreme importance and that the evangelical gospel is man's only remedy, then such matters rise far above mere questions of literary style. As a consequence, academic burrowing of fanciful proportions becomes of far less importance. In this scenario, allegory is a bridge and not an end in itself; literary style is a vehicle that is far transcended in importance by the substance of the gospel freight that it bears and by the ultimate heavenly destination of redeemed sinners.

3. The developing critical spirit

However, the literary quibbling continues. Even during the nineteenth century Macaulay could write, '*The Pilgrim's Progress* undoubtedly is not a perfect allegory. The types are often inconsistent with each other; and sometimes the allegorical disguise is altogether thrown off. The river, for example, is emblematic of death; and we are told that every human being must pass through the river. But Faithful does not pass through it. He is martyred, not in shadow, but in reality, at Vanity Fair.'[28] Of course, the simple answer here is that the river represents the normal encounter with death. There are abnormal encounters, such as, for example, the translation to heaven of Enoch and Elijah, to which an angel on the riverbank refers, as well as martyrdom.

More recently, concerning Christian's sudden discovery of the key called Promise, Keeble seems to join with Sharrock in suggesting that such a turn of events is 'fictionally implausible'.[29] However, Bunyan has experience in mind here so that this representation is most appropriate. When a Christian is depressed, his Bible, though at hand, may nevertheless seem remote to him. This was Bunyan's own experience, as he relates in *Grace Abounding*: 'I have sometimes seen more in a line of the Bible than I could well tell how to stand under, and yet at another time the whole Bible hath been to me as dry as a stick; or rather, my heart hath been so dead and dry unto it, that I could not conceive the least drachm of refreshment, though I have looked it all over.'[30]

More harsh in tone is Brian Nellist in his analysis of the first scene at the House of the Interpreter: 'Interpreter ... presents his emblems as though they were simple pictures but uses them to disconcert the beholder as though they were hieroglyphs. For example, Christian sees first a man with lifted eyes, book in hand, the world behind him, pleading with men, while a golden crown hangs over his head. "Christian witness," we may think. The hero only confirms his naivety in our eyes by asking, "What means this?" Yet the interpretation provided is more perplexing than the emblem itself: "This is one of a thousand; he can beget children, travail in birth with children, and nurse them himself when they are born." This static figure, moreover, grotesquely distorted, eyes upwards, mouth on the level, back to the world ("Where is the audience, then?"), this is the authorized guide "in all the difficult places thou meetest with in the way". If the pictures were in themselves puzzling, their sequence increases our bemusement.'[31]

And on and on read the irritated comments. That such remarks could be considered scholarly is difficult to conceive, since they hardly merit notice. Doubtless Bunyan intends to make his readers think and dig. The fifth scene in the House of the Interpreter concerning the persevering valiant pilgrim concludes with such a prod.[32] Is Christian 'naïve'? Yes, since, having recently entered the Wicket-gate, he represents a new rather than a mature believer. Here is portrayed the ideal godly pastor. He is likened to a spiritual midwife, after the model of John Gifford, who is depicted in a stance now attributed to Bunyan himself by Boehm's statue of Bunyan at the corner of St. Peter's Green in Bedford, and one which can hardly be described as 'grotesque'. Surely it is obvious that 'the world behind him' refers to his own spiritual priority, since he is next described as if 'pleading with men' — that is, with the world.

In conclusion, Gordon Wakefield describes Ignorance as having 'been judged one of Bunyan's artistic failures. His fate is perplexingly severe. It almost dims the glories of the pilgrims' entry into the Celestial City.'[33] But what are the grounds of such judgement? With Wakefield it is not difficult to discover since he admits, not only to being at odds with Bunyan's doctrine — specifically with the gospel and with Bunyan's Calvinism, which he compares unfavourably with the Arminianism of John Wesley — but also to having an apparent sympathy with universalism.[34] On the other hand, no doubt Bunyan's sober conclusion has in mind the teaching of Jesus Christ as reflected in Matthew 7:21-23, according to which many will, with shockingly misplaced confidence, find themselves spurned by this same Judge Jesus at the Great Assize!

4. The preferable perspective on Bunyan

What, then, would be Bunyan's response to all of this? It is my opinion that he would be scathing in his denunciation of all such learned 'playing with the outside of my dream' while studiously avoiding, or even sneering at, 'the substance of my matter'.[35] It is one thing to love *The Pilgrim's Progress* for a multitude of reasons, whether sentimental or academic; it is quite another to love the truth of the allegory. Herein lies the distinguishing factor whereby the evangelical Christian alone has true fellowship with the author of *The Pilgrim's Progress*.

3.
The Bible and *The Pilgrim's Progress*

'The influence of the Bible upon *The Pilgrim's Progress* is so pervasive that one must be alert to it continuously even when Bunyan does not point to specific biblical passages with citations in the margin' (John R. Knott, Jr.).

3.
The Bible and *The Pilgrim's Progress*

IN spite of frequent depreciatory remarks at a contemporary scholarly level concerning John Bunyan's 'literalist' and 'Calvinist' regard for the Bible — and that at a period in history when the authority of Scripture has waned in influence — the truth is that his understanding of the Book of God was representative, not only of his time, but also of that stream of conservative evangelical Christianity that continues to the present day.

Concerning the seventeenth century, J. A. Froude writes, 'No doubts or questions had yet risen about the Bible's nature or origin. It was received as the authentic word of God Himself... No one questioned it, save a few speculative philosophers in their closets. The statesman in the House of Commons, the judge on the Bench, the peasant in a midland village, interpreted literally by this rule the phenomena which they experienced or saw.'[1]

But now, in this era of modern Bunyan studies, Roger Sharrock has adopted a snide tone not only in relation to Bunyan's 'reliance on the literal text of the Bible', but also when speaking of his 'intense, peculiar reading of Scripture [that] has guided the structure of his narrative [in *The Pilgrim's Progress*]'.[2] Elsewhere he comments: 'In Bunyan's spiritual sickness [a reference to his conversion struggles related in *Grace Abounding*] the extreme Protestant idea of the Bible as the Word of God was always present to him. Like the majority of Puritan Englishmen of his day, he believed that each verse of the Bible, taken out of its context, still held a message of truth.'[3] Bunyan's fear that he might have committed the unpardonable sin and have identified himself with Judas, draws forth a further comment from Sharrock: 'Here we see the remarkable way in which the tradition of bibliolatry harmonized with the psychological temperament of Bunyan, so abnormal in its subjection to verbal automatisms.'[4]

Then again, consider Richard Greaves' opinion which, in a pejorative style, implies a reluctance to admit what is patently clear — namely, conviction concerning the verbal inspiration of the original manuscripts as the prevailing belief of the Puritans, along with a normative literalist hermeneutic: 'In practice, most Nonconformists treated Scripture *as if* it were infallible, though without addressing this issue. For the most part they were content to think of the Bible as the perfect rule of faith and obedience, the authority of which was divine, at least to the extent that the Spirit suggested the words and aided the authors in expressing their thoughts... In contrast several Dissenters enunciated a view closer to that expressed in our own century by such neo-orthodox theologians as Karl Barth and Emil Brunner' (emphasis added).[5]

However, John Owen did address the issue of the divine nature of Scripture in great detail.[6] Further, the evidence supplied hardly proves a seventeenth-century neo-orthodox existentialist approach to fallible manuscripts, or to the Bible's being regarded as a scratchy record and a witness that directs man to Christ as revelation.[7] Such a view would have been anathema to Bunyan, Owen and their contemporaries who strenuously opposed Quaker subjectivism and upheld the Bible as a concrete and propositional revelation.[8]

Bunyan's high view of the Bible

The Bible is inerrant and truthful

In *A Relation of my Imprisonment*, Bunyan describes his encounter with Paul Cobb, Clerk of the Peace in Bedford, at the commencement of his imprisonment, in which he was exhorted to submit to the Church of England. The exchange concerning Bunyan's claim to have the gift of preaching continues as follows:

Cobb. But, said he, how shall we know that you have received a gift?

Bun. Said I, Let any man hear and search, and prove the doctrine by the Bible.

Cobb. But will you be willing, said he, that two indifferent persons shall determine the case, and will you stand by their judgement?

Bun. I said, Are they infallible?

Cobb. He said, No.

Bun. Then, said I, it is possible my judgement may be as good as theirs. But yet I will pass by either, and in this matter be judged by the Scriptures; I am sure that is infallible, and cannot err.[9]

In approaching the doctrine of the Trinity, Bunyan recommended the faultlessness and purity of Scripture to be of first priority: 'Suffer thyself, by the authority of the word, to be persuaded that the scripture indeed is the word of God; the scriptures of truth, the words of the holy one; and that they therefore must be every one true, pure, and for ever settled in heaven.'[10] Thus for Bunyan, the Bible is the product of verbal and plenary inspiration, with the result that it is thoroughly truthful and inerrant; his numerous references to John 10:35 give added support to this contention.[11]

The Bible is inerrant and truthful as a copy of the original

On one occasion, Bunyan was castigated by a Cambridge scholar since, unlike himself, the tinker did not have access to 'the original' — presumably the Greek and Hebrew texts. Bunyan enquired if the scholar had 'the very self-same original copies'. In response to his, 'No ... but we have the true copies of those originals,' Bunyan then asked, 'How do you know that?' The scholar answered, 'Why, we believe what we have is a true copy of the original.' In reply to this Bunyan concluded: 'Then, so do I believe our English Bible is a true copy of the original.'[12]

This understanding of biblical authority, insofar as it applies to translations in current use, is virtually identical with that enunciated in Article X of *The Chicago Statement on Biblical Inerrancy* produced in 1978: 'We affirm that inspiration, strictly speaking, applies only to the autographic text of Scripture, which in the providence of God can be ascertained from available manuscripts with great accuracy. We further affirm that copies and translations of Scripture are the Word of God to the extent that they faithfully represent the original.'[13] On the subject of translations, we know, of course, that Bunyan was familiar with both the Geneva Bible and the Authorized or King James Bible; also on one occasion he refers to Tyndale's version.[14]

The Bible is the only sure guide for salvation and life

Concerning Bunyan's personal life, *Grace Abounding to the Chief of Sinners* is saturated with instances of the Bible's being his one and only guide. In the midst of doubts, fears and struggles, even, as a young believer, concerning the mysteries of the Bible itself, Scripture is the undoubted final authority. Hill describes the Bible as 'Bunyan's sheet-anchor, his defence against despair and atheism'.[15] In his defence when on trial at the commencement of his imprisonment, this foundational resort to the Bible becomes vividly apparent, especially in his upholding of nonconformity.[16] However, *The Pilgrim's Progress* provides the most graphic representation of this principle. It is the book in Christian's hand — clearly the Bible, by virtue of its divine character — that alone is able to guide the pilgrim through many trials and testings to the Celestial City.

As Roger Sharrock comments, '*The Pilgrim's Progress* is soaked in the imagery of the Bible and deeply pervaded by the Puritan belief that the Bible provided the key to every problem of life and thought.'[17] So Bunyan himself tells the reader: 'Wouldst thou know what thou art, and what is in thine heart? Then search the Scriptures and see what is written in them (Rom. 1:29-31; 3:9-18; Jer. 17:9; Gen. 6:5; 8:21; Eph. 4:18), with many others. The Scriptures, I say, they are able to give a man perfect instruction into any of the things of God necessary to faith and godliness, if he hath but an honest heart seriously to weigh and ponder the several things contained in them.'[18]

Further, in his pocket volume entitled *Christian Behaviour,* published in 1674, Bunyan supplies copious biblical references to justify his instruction concerning the godly duties of family life, especially with regard to relationships among husband, wife, children and servants. Then follows a consideration of neighbours and the sins that inhibit a godly testimony before them, such as covetousness, pride and unclean behaviour. In conclusion, Bunyan addresses the believer whose zeal has cooled: 'I know thou wilt be afflicted with a thousand temptations to drive thee to despair, that thy faith may be faint, etc. But against all them set thou the word of God, the promise of grace, the blood of Christ, and the examples of great backsliders that are for thy encouragement recorded in the scriptures of truth.'[19]

The Bible in tension with Bunyan studies today

The foregoing obviously reveals a conflict that inevitably arises between Bunyan's regard for the Bible and modern liberal scholarship. As far back as 1928, G. B. Harrison could pompously declare: 'Puritanism is an unattractive creed, and its holiness is not beautiful... With the [modern] change of attitude towards the Old Testament the Puritan dogma has crumbled. If there was no first Adam, there was no actual compact between him and God; the sacrifice on Calvary ceases to be the bloody retribution for Adam's sin, and a new interpretation must be sought if the Bible is to be regarded as a record of God's dealings with man. It is difficult for an educated man in the twentieth century, accustomed to see the natural laws of God revealed through the microscope, to realize the full horror of literal belief in the Old Testament; but it is illustrated very clearly in the development of the mind of John Bunyan... Many of his books survive as little more than curious examples of an extinct theology. But four stand out — *Grace Abounding, The Pilgrim's Progress, Mr Badman*, and *The Holy War* — perennial monuments of a man who was greater than his creed.'[20]

But over seventy years later, the evangelical cause, with an authoritative Bible and a redeeming Christ, is very much alive while modernity is more jaded, especially in the moral sphere, and not nearly so attractive in its fading bloom under the pall of a nuclear world. Bunyan's analysis of human nature and his biblically-rooted gospel remain true when the heart of contemporary man is honestly plumbed.

Bunyan's interpretation of the Bible

The hermeneutic (or method of interpretation) of John Bunyan is classically Protestant, even if it is not perceived as such in terms of the looser principles of contemporary interpretation.

According to Bernard Ramm, Luther replaced 'the four-fold system [historical, allegorical, anagogical, tropological] of the scholastics' with 'the literal principle'. Likewise Calvin 'rejected allegorical interpretation ... [calling it] Satanic because it led men away from the truth of Scripture... "Scripture interprets Scripture" was a basic conviction... This meant many things. It meant *literalism* (as defined in this book) in exegesis with a rejection of the medieval system of the four-fold meaning of Scripture.'[21]

So in the seventeenth century, the Reformation hermeneutic was thoroughly embraced by the Puritans. J. I. Packer confirms this point when, in naming their governing principles, he sets out the first as follows: 'Interpret Scripture literally and grammatically. The Reformers had insisted, against the medieval depreciation of the "literal" sense of Scripture ... that the literal — i.e., the grammatical, natural, intended — sense was the only sense that Scripture has... The Puritans fully agreed.'[22]

Bunyan seems to have well understood this matter, as the following exchange with Mr Justice Foster, again taken from *A Relation of my Imprisonment*, indicates:

Fost.   He told me that I was the nearest the Papists of any, and that he would convince me of immediately.

Bun.   I asked him wherein?

Fost.   He said, in that we understood the Scripture literally.

Bun.   I told him that those that were to be understood literally, we understood them so; but for those that were to be understood otherwise, we endeavoured so to understand them.

Fost.   He said, which of the Scriptures do you understand literally?

Bun.   I said this, 'He that believeth shall be saved.' This was to be understood just as it is spoken; that

whosoever believeth in Christ shall, according to
the plain and simple words of the text, be saved.[23]

Bunyan's emphasis on the literal interpretation of Scripture
did not, of course, prevent him from writing *Solomon's Temple
Spiritualized*, but at the same time he explains: 'I have, as thou
by this little book mayest see, adventured, as this time, to do my
endeavour to show thee something of the gospel-glory of
Solomon's temple: that is, of what it, with its utensils, was a type
of … I may say that God did in a manner tie up the church of
the Jews to types, figures, and similitudes.'[24]

So John R. Knott, Jr., rightly concludes: 'Bunyan would
have seen no inconsistency between his strong commitment to
the literal truth of biblical narrative and his increasing interest in
the "spiritual" or "mystical" sense of Scripture. He operated
within the Protestant tradition that acknowledged only one,
literal sense and saw "spiritual" interpretations as, in the words
of Elizabethan Puritan William Whitaker, "not various senses,
but various collections from one sense, or various applications
and accommodation of that one meaning".'[25]

Bunyan's experience with the Bible

The period up to his conversion

Grace Abounding to the Chief of Sinners is a remarkably clear
window on the soul of John Bunyan, and one unclouded by
abnormal neuroses — contrary to the allegations of some, who
are not experientially acquainted with the Christian gospel. The
role of the Bible in this account is extremely pervasive, and the
author's initial interest in the Word of God, however casual it
may have been, takes us back to his earliest unrecorded days as
a child while growing up in a turbulent religious society. In this

regard, Bunyan's mention of some early schooling would presuppose Bible instruction of some sort.[26]

Up to the time of his marriage, after a period of military service, he recounts, 'The thoughts of religion were very grievous to me; I could neither endure it myself, nor that any should … I was now void of all good consideration, heaven and hell were both out of sight and mind.'[27] Then his new wife recommended some Christian books which gained a reading, and he followed this by regular church attendance. Subsequently he began to read the Bible, and did so with some pleasure, so that his curiosity was aroused and guilt stimulated. At first only historical passages appealed rather than doctrinal epistles.[28] But then, Bunyan explains, 'I began to look into the Bible with new eyes, and read as I never did before; and especially the epistles of the apostle Paul were sweet and pleasant to me; and, indeed, I was then never out of the Bible, either by reading or meditation; still crying out to God [like Christian], that I might know the truth, and the way to heaven and glory.'[29]

In his quest for peace with God, he tells us that in searching from Genesis to Revelation, he came upon many perplexing questions: 'Then darkness seized upon me … blasphemous thoughts were such as also stirred up questions in me, against the very being of God, and of his only beloved Son; as, whether there were, in truth, a God, or Christ, or no? And whether the holy Scriptures were not rather a fable, and cunning story, than the holy and pure Word of God?'[30] Yet, on numerous occasions we read, 'These words [of Scripture] broke in upon my mind …', or 'That Word came in upon me…', or, 'That scripture did also tear and rend my soul…'

Then follows his conversion: 'I remember that one day, as I was travelling in the country and musing on the wickedness and blasphemy of my heart, and considering of the enmity that was in me to God, that scripture came in my mind, He hath "made peace through the blood of his cross" (Col. 1:20). By which I was made to see, both again, and again, and again, that day, that God and my soul were friends by this blood; yea, I saw that the justice of God and my sinful soul could embrace and kiss each other through this blood. This was a good day to me; I hope I shall not forget it.'[31]

The period following his conversion

The subsequent period of struggle, lasting from two to three years, nevertheless must be understood as being watered by the influential, stimulating and solid biblical ministry of John Gifford, Bunyan's pastor and mentor, as well as that of Martin Luther in his *Commentary on Galatians*. Even in the midst of spiritual wrestling that oscillated between fervent hope and near despair, many great biblical issues arose in the soul of the Bedford tinker about which he sought biblical resolutions.

For instance, concerning his yielding to temptation, was he to be likened to the apostates Esau and Judas rather than to Peter? Had he committed the unpardonable sin? Throughout all of this, the Word of God continues to make its presence felt in Bunyan's soul. He is constantly studying the Bible and recollecting its truth, yet there are those more notable times when, as he puts it, 'Suddenly this sentence bolted in upon me...', or 'This word took hold of me...', or 'Scripture would come running after me...', or 'Then did that scripture seize upon my soul...', or 'This scripture would strike me down as dead...', or 'Now was the word of the gospel forced upon my soul...', or 'That scripture fastened on my heart...' In these instances, Bunyan happily understands their being impressed upon his mind as divine intervention.

He also writes, 'That piece of a sentence darted in upon me, "My grace is sufficient." At this methought I felt some stay, as if there might be hopes. But, oh how good a thing it is for God to send his Word! ... Therefore I still did pray to God, that he would come in with this Scripture more fully on my heart.'[32] This was followed by assurance and stability when '... that was brought to my remembrance, he [Christ] "of God is made unto us wisdom, and righteousness, and sanctification, and redemption" (1 Cor. 1:30).'[33]

This resultant peace and rest in Bunyan's soul, at his 'Place of Deliverance', led to formal membership in the Bedford nonconformist church, his 'Palace Beautiful', and in time to the commencement of itinerant preaching. Thus, in all of this, the Word of God retained the pre-eminent place in Bunyan's personal life and ministry.

However, this is not to suggest that he never experienced further instability, since he later confesses: 'I have sometimes seen more in a line of the Bible than I could tell how to stand under, and yet at another time the whole Bible hath been to me as dry as a stick; or rather, my heart hath been so dead and dry unto it, that I could not conceive the least drachm of refreshment, though I have looked it "all" over.'[34]

The Bible in *The Pilgrim's Progress*

One of the most remarkable features of *The Pilgrim's Progress* is the author's ability to blend Scripture into his narrative in such a way that the reader is often unconscious of his absorption of Bible truth. John R. Knott, Jr. puts it this way: 'The influence of the Bible upon *The Pilgrim's Progress* is so pervasive that one must be alert to it continuously even when Bunyan does not point to specific biblical passages with citations in the margin.'[35] Nevertheless, in addition to more direct references to the Bible, there are a variety of emblems that add colour and also speak of distinctive biblical functions. We shall now consider a number of these.

The book in the hand of Christian

In the opening scene of *The Pilgrim's Progress*, Christian simply appears with 'a book in his hand', which is clearly the instrumental cause of the 'great burden' that he carries 'upon his back'.[36] If we bear in mind that Christian is a distinct portrayal of Bunyan himself, the most likely parallel to this in *Grace Abounding to the Chief of Sinners* is the occasion already noted when, having begun to study the more historical parts of the Bible, Bunyan then advances to admiration of Paul's epistles. In refuting at that time the arguments of a licentious friend named Harry, as well as the claims of the antinomian Ranters, he declares: 'The Bible was precious to me in those days.'[37]

The Scriptures are then described, by means of Evangelist's direction, as 'a shining light' which is, according to 2 Peter 1:19, 'the prophetic word made more sure … a lamp shining in a dark place'.

Christian's book is subsequently mocked by Obstinate, toyed with by Pliable and repudiated by Mr Worldly-Wiseman.

The parchment-roll provided by Evangelist

This gift of an inscribed exhortation to 'Fly from the wrath to come' originates from the ministry of John the Baptist (Matt. 3:7). The Christocentric context of this passage (Matt. 3:3,11-12) suggests that the pilgrim is being urged to flee towards Christ at the Wicket-gate. The exhortation here is merely a faithful evangelist's exposition of the truth that Christian holds in his hand.

The inscription over the Wicket-gate

The invitation, 'Knock and it shall be opened unto you,' is in fact taken directly from the words of the Lord Jesus Christ, as recorded in Scripture (Matt. 7:7-8), here represented by Good-will.

The instruction at the House of Interpreter

The Interpreter is the Holy Spirit, who is inseparably associated with the Word of God. It is he who makes the Word 'living and powerful' (Heb. 4:12), who communicates and illuminates the truth (2 Tim. 3:16), and especially as it concerns the person and work of the Lord Jesus Christ (John 15:26). Thus Interpreter is, as Good-will declared, the one who 'would shew him excellent things'.[38]

The instruction at the Palace Beautiful

This representation of a faithful local church ministers the Word of God by means of exhortation, instruction, edification and the Lord's Table.

1. The exhortation of palace leadership

Prudence, Piety and Charity give wholesome instruction as a result of considering Christian's cases of conscience.[39]

2. The fellowship supper

This memorial banquet involves reminiscing about the person and work of the pilgrims' Lord.

3. The records in the study

Here focus is placed upon the great saving works of God by his warrior Son and through his faithful servants, as well as prophetic instruction.

4. The sword of the Spirit

This weapon is the Word of God, according to Ephesians 6:17, and is none other than a more militant version of Christian's book which is to be used both defensively and offensively.

The key called Promise in Christian's bosom

This key, revealed at Doubting Castle, is a representation of the light of truth, or the promises of the Word of God, which the Spirit of God brings to mind; as a result the darkness of despair is cast out (Ps. 119:130).

The exhortation of the shepherds at the Delectable Mountains

This pastoral scene represents another provision of spiritual nourishment by means of the ministry of the local church; it involves the truth of Scripture imparted by knowledgeable, experienced, watchful and sincere men of God.

The nourishment from the gardener in Beulah Land

Here appetizing food is provided; again this is the Word of God, which is mediated to them by means of the gardener, yet another representation of the pastoral office. This nourishment is particularly satisfying for senior pilgrims who are longing to gain entrance into the Celestial City.

The inscription over the gate of the Celestial City

This quotation from Revelation 22:14, 'Blessed are they that do his commandments, that they may enter in through the gates into the City,' is a warning that false claimants will not be admitted. Only those who have believed the Word and obeyed it will gain entrance.

The Bible in Bunyan's progress

Hence this magisterial dominion of Scripture in *The Pilgrim's Progress*, void of any focus through Aristotle and Plato such as might have been received at Oxford or Cambridge, is, however, subject to tutelage by Luther and Gifford, and probably also by Owen and Dell. It is representative of Bunyan's intention to embody the principle of *sola Scriptura* in all of his ministry: 'Wherefore "I will not take" of them [the learned] "from a thread even to a shoe-latchet — lest they should say, We have made Abram rich" (Gen. 14:23)… What you find suiting with the Scriptures take, though it should not suit with [the learned] authors; but that which you find against the Scriptures, slight, though it should be confirmed by multitudes of them [the learned]. Yea, further, where you find the Scriptures and your [learned] authors jump [agree], yet believe it for the sake of Scripture's authority. I honour the godly [learned] as Christians, but I prefer the Bible before them; and having this still with me, I count myself far better furnished than if I had without it all the libraries of the two universities [Oxford and Cambridge]. Besides, I am for drinking water out of my own cistern; what God makes mine by the evidence of his Word and Spirit, that I dare make bold with.'[40]

The Bible to be valued above the writings of men

Pray and read [the Word of God], and read and pray; for a little from God is better than a great deal from men. Also, what is from men is uncertain, and is often lost and tumbled over by men; but what is from God is fixed as a nail in a sure place... There is nothing that so abides with us as what we receive from God; and the reason why Christians at this day are at such a loss as to some things is, because they are content with what comes from men's mouths, without searching and kneeling before God, to know of him the truth of things.

John Bunyan
Christ a Complete Saviour,
Bunyan, *Works,* vol. I, p. 238.

4.
The concept of progress in pilgrimage

'Manner and matter too was all mine own,
Nor was it unto any mortal known,
'Till I had done it...
the whole, and every whit, is mine'
(John Bunyan).

4.
The concept of progress in pilgrimage

THE title of John Bunyan's classic allegory, *The Pilgrim's Progress*, is pregnant with meaning insofar as a comprehensive understanding of his essential purpose is concerned. It immediately identifies the composition as a connected whole that, fittingly without chapter divisions — as is the case with many of the author's writings — is designed to be understood in continuity, and not in a piecemeal fashion.

Furthermore, the reader is impressed straightaway with the guiding principle of movement that offers the prospect of journeying, of scenic change, of variation in pace, of challenging encounter, of blessed arrival. At the same time we are immediately confronted with a real-life pilgrimage of such vital importance that it calls for nothing less than the total commitment of a person's immortal soul.

Thus pilgrimage is to advance from the secular to the sacred, from this ugly world to that of holy beauty to come, with its commencement finding timeless expression in the opening line: 'As I walked through the wilderness of this world, I came upon a certain place.'[1] To begin with we are introduced, in a captivating fashion, to Bunyan's own journeying, and then to its representation by Christian. Hence the title guides us to the beginning of the journey which aptly portrays the world as one in which we all groan at the present time. Such a beginning is not so much chronological or metaphorical as theological; it is a description of the moral pit or quarry in which we all find ourselves by nature (Isa. 51:1).

The pilgrim who progresses

According to *The Concise Oxford Dictionary*, a 'pilgrim' is 'a person who journeys to a sacred place for religious reasons, a person regarded as journeying through life, a traveller',[2] as, for example, the Pilgrim Fathers who immigrated to New England. That the Puritans, and Bunyan in particular, happily identified with this title of 'pilgrim' is readily understandable if one recalls the biblical truth that Christians are, among other titles, called to be 'strangers and pilgrims' (1 Peter 2:11; Heb. 11:13, AV) and 'sojourners' (1 Chr. 29:15; Ps. 39:12) while on earth. So William Haller comments that '... the vocation of the elect [Puritans] was to go through this life as pilgrims'.[3]

The progress of the pilgrim

While the modern understanding of 'progress' as improvement and advancement may come quickly to mind at this point, nevertheless Philip Edwards challenges this idea with regard to Bunyan's original intent. He musters considerable authority when he explains: 'In fact, Bunyan's "progress", correctly quoted by the *Oxford English Dictionary* under sense 1, means, quite neutrally, travelling, a movement from one place to another, how Christian got from this world to the world which is to come.'[4]

However, if this perspective is correct at this juncture, then two problems arise that must be addressed. First, if 'progress' simply means travelling and movement, then it would seem that

Bunyan is guilty of a tautology, as if in fact the title of his work meant no more than 'The Pilgrim's Pilgrimage'. Second — and this seems to add more conclusive weight to the argument — the whole allegory is full of indications of advancement that includes the aspect of improvement, which is certainly a legitimate alternative meaning in seventeenth-century usage, according to *The Oxford English Dictionary.* Consider some examples of this internal evidence.

- To journey from the City of Destruction to the Celestial City is more than travel; rather it is advancement of the highest kind, from condemnation to justification, from sin to salvation, from earth to heaven.
- There is advancement on the part of the pilgrims in their understanding of many doctrinal issues, and especially with regard to an expanding revelation concerning the gospel and sanctification. Consider the more extensive, detailed and doctrinally profound later discourse that takes place as they traverse the Enchanted Ground.
- There is a geographic sense of moving on to higher and safer realms which offer increased blessing, as opposed to encounters with numerous trials and tribulations in the valleys. A point is reached by Christian and Hopeful in the land of Beulah where certain earlier evil influences, such as the Valley of the Shadow of Death, Giant Despair and Doubting Castle, are no longer a threat to the pilgrims in their present state of maturity.[5]
- The three leading pilgrims, especially Faithful and Hopeful, show clear evidence of spiritual growth. Christian, although like Peter in temperament, also becomes wiser, for example, with regard to his mature analysis of Little-faith while conflicts multiply.
- The number of pilgrims is reduced as the later stages are reached, in comparison with those who initially set out on the journey, although this order is reversed in Part Two. So the shepherds at the Delectable Mountains

declare: 'For but few of them that begin to come hither,
do show their face on these mountains.'[6]

The specific nature of the progress on pilgrimage

For many today, the name of *The Pilgrim's Progress* has come
to mean more than the title of a definitive, timeless Christian
classic. Rather it has now, in its historic popularity, taken on the
aura of a life-motif in general that need not be taken too
seriously in terms of its strictly biblical stance. The dominant
theme of life as a religious journey is cordially appreciated,
while a patronizing attitude is adopted towards the author's
literalist approach to the Bible and Calvinism, which is dis-
missed by these reviewers as outmoded theology. Such an
approach is by no means meant to suggest that Bunyan's
allegory is of little worth for today. On the contrary, as an
example of seventeenth-century literature, his teaching is
appreciated as a wonderful mine for modern extrapolation.[7] Yet
at the same time any study of his work must be filtered through
a grid of modern presuppositions with regard to the Bible that
are in reality diametrically opposed to Bunyan's essentially
evangelical convictions.

One recent biography of Bunyan is by Gordon Wakefield, a
modern English Methodist scholar who, in his decidedly interpretive account, quite plainly reveals his fundamental doctrinal
differences with the Bedford tinker. Concerning what he considers Bunyan's 'too narrow view' of the gospel, he writes, 'It
was one of the errors of Puritanism that everyone must undergo
conversion through conviction of sin and the agonized cry of
the Philippian gaoler [Acts 16:30]... [Bunyan believed that]
apart from Christ and the divine grace through him there is only
"a just God, a sin-revenging God, a God that will by no means
spare the guilty". In Christ there is infinite mercy and a love
which passes knowledge and grace to cover all sin. This seems
appallingly exclusive and discouraging to "virtuous and godly

living". Bunyan rules out so many whom the consensus of God-fearing humanity would regard as lights in their generation... Most will be left outside though they approach in hope and confidence. This would not worry Bunyan since Calvinism does not expect universal salvation.'[8]

Yet from a more general perspective, Wakefield is correct when he describes how the theme of a journey is innate in life itself: 'Behind us all is the journeying instinct of humanity... We are on a journey whether we like it or not from birth to death... The journey is the truest metaphor of life.'[9] Nevertheless, Bunyan would have seen these definitions as lacking in specific biblical application. His title, *The Pilgrim's Progress*, incorporates three connected key elements, namely, departure, transition and arrival, according to the historic interpretation of Scripture, stripped of all liberal and universalist presuppositions.

Certainly the life of Abraham is illustrative of this principle, for after his departure from Ur of the Chaldeans, the patriarch's life can be summed up as 'looking for the city which has foundations, whose architect and builder is God' (Heb. 11:9-10). In the same vein, the nation of Israel, having departed from Egypt, wandered in transition until the time appointed for its arrival in Canaan under the leadership of Joshua (Judg. 2:1).

However, Bunyan has something in mind that is even more significant than these literal historical events. Certainly he uses a narrative motif himself to convey his message. But his essential point is that it is the human soul, in all its militant alienation from God, that must depart, through the sovereignty of grace, from its enmity and bondage, make transition through an opposing wilderness world, and finally arrive acceptable in the presence of a holy and gracious heavenly Father. Here is the reality depicted by Bunyan's allegory, the substance of his shadows, the concrete embodiment of his imagination, the vital nerve of his title.

The origin of the pilgrimage motif

Because Bunyan makes no pretence of being a scholar and openly admits his lack of formal learning, many have attempted to discover, on the assumption that his concept must have been derived from elsewhere, exactly what sources he used to obtain his style. The literary excellence of his composition, which resides in its attractive simplicity of style, has led these same people to suspect that such a popular work could not possibly have originated from a poor, uneducated tinker. Bunyan himself faced charges that his allegory was not original. As a result, in 1682 at the publication of *The Holy War*, he penned the following apologetic poem:

> Some say the Pilgrim's Progress is not mine,
> Insinuating as if I would shine
> In name and fame by the worth of another,
> Like some made rich by robbing of their brother.
> Or that so fond I am of being sire,
> I'll father bastards; or, if need require,
> I'll tell a lie in print to get applause.
> I scorn it: John such dirt-heap never was,
> Since God converted him. Let this suffice
> To show why I my Pilgrim patronize.
> It came from mine own heart, so to my head,
> And thence into my fingers trickled;
> Then to my pen, from whence immediately
> On paper I did dribble it daintily.
> Manner and matter too was all mine own,
> Nor was it unto any mortal known,
> 'Till I had done it. Nor did any then
> By books, by wits, by tongues, or hand, or pen,
> Add five words to it, or write half a line
> Thereof: the whole, and every whit, is mine.[10]

Now while we recognize the integrity of Bunyan at this point, it will nevertheless be helpful to consider the relative validity of certain factors which may have had some influence on him, without detracting from the originality of his allegory.

The seventeenth-century literary antecedents

Just as investigation into Bunyan's doctrine, both in general and with regard to *The Pilgrim's Progress*, has been minimal, so the study of his possible literary antecedents has been prolific. George Offor, who was admittedly very sympathetic to the renowned author, made an extensive study of this matter during the first half of the nineteenth century. Amidst numerous suggested parallels, one is worth mentioning since it was, according to Bunyan himself, most influential in his early spiritual development. It concerns the dialogue structure of *The Plain Man's Pathway to Heaven* by Arthur Dent which, in *Grace Abounding*, he declares to have been a legacy that his first wife shared with him, and one which he found pleasing.[11]

Offor comments: 'It is singular that no one has charged him with taking any hints from this book, which is one of the very few which he is known to have read prior to his public profession of faith and holiness in baptism... This volume must have been exactly suited to the warm imagination of Bunyan. It had proved invaluable to him as a means of conversion; but, after a careful and delightful perusal, no trace can be found of any phrase or sentence having been introduced into *Pilgrim's Progress*.'[12]

Thus Offor concludes as a result of the whole of his investigation: 'Every attempt has been made to tarnish his [Bunyan's] fair fame; the great and learned, the elegant poet and the pious divine, have asserted, but without foundation in fact, or even in probability, that some of his ideas were derived from the works of previous writers... "It came from his own heart." The plot, the characters, the faithful dealing, are all his own. And what is more, there has not been found a single phrase, a sentence borrowed from any other book, except the quotations from the Bible, and the use of common proverbs. To arrive at this conclusion has occupied much time and labour, at intervals, during the last forty years.'[13]

Of course, this assessment has not stopped the literati of today from endeavouring to discover sources pillaged by Bunyan. However, Christopher Hill sums up the quest for the genesis of Bunyan's essential idea as follows: 'Much printer's ink has been spilt in the search for antecedents for *The Pilgrim's Progress*. I shall merely try to summarize what I take to be the present position. The concept of life as a pilgrimage goes back far into the Middle Ages, if not further. All attempts to tie Bunyan down to a single model have failed. The idea was common property in the fifteenth to seventeenth centuries.'[14]

The thorough absorption of biblical truth

In Richard Greaves' study of Bunyan's theology according to the major heads of Christian doctrine, there is one important area which he fails to consider and one which, strangely enough, has been little written about in recent times. This omission concerns the Bedford pastor's regard for the Bible.[15] Of course, the reason for this omission may be that Bunyan's attitude towards Scripture is so patently obvious and he accords it such dominance that this goes without saying.

His works convey an astonishing understanding of the content of the English Bible, and *The Pilgrim's Progress* in particular presents an almost seamless weaving of the sacred text into its very fabric which can be found in no other comparable work. But to move to the more doctrinal aspect of this matter, his understanding of the Bible was, to use modern parlance, 'literalist' and 'fundamentalist' — terms which his modern literary critics use pejoratively. On the other hand, the biblical liberalism and cultural relativism of today would have provoked just as severe a broadside of condemnation from Bunyan as did the Latitudinarians and Quakers of his time.

Hill is correct in his description of the importance of the Bible for the well-instructed tinker, although he also reflects the diminished sympathy that the modern spirit of literary scholarship has for Bunyan's fervent evangelical doctrine. To quote him again more fully: 'The Bible is Bunyan's sheet-anchor, his defence against despair and atheism. He would have been lost if he had abandoned it. This accounts for what seem today some of the less attractive features of Bunyan's thinking — his emphasis on hell-fire, or the inherent sinfulness of children, his racism and sexism.'[16]

Not that Bunyan was unaware of spurious ministry in his own day. Learned clergy led multitudes astray then, just as they do today. So he responded with fiery warnings: 'You who muzzle up your people in ignorance with Aristotle, Plato, and the rest of the heathenish philosophers, and preach little, if anything, of Christ rightly; I say unto you, that you will find you have sinned against God, and beguiled your hearers, when God shall, in the judgement-day, lay the cause of the damnation of many thousands of souls to your charge, and say, He will require their blood at your hands (Ezek. 33:6).'[17]

The subjective experience of a questing soul

The chief interior source of the substance of *The Pilgrim's Progress* is the author's self-exposure of his extremely sensitive soul. This Puritan inclination for heart-searching was based on Paul's exhortation to pilgrims to 'test yourselves to see if you are in the faith; examine yourselves!' (2 Cor. 13:5). In Bunyan's case he chronicled his intense analysis of himself in *Grace Abounding to the Chief of Sinners*, and it is this spiritual autobiography which becomes an indispensable tool for a right understanding of *The Pilgrim's Progress*.

Roger Sharrock explains that '*Grace Abounding* deals almost wholly with the development of his inner religious feelings; there are hardly any references to persons or places. Bunyan discards any attempt at literary adornment in order to achieve an absolutely naked rendering of his spiritual history... The movement into allegory serves to naturalize and familiarize Bunyan's religious perceptions to us... But *The Pilgrim's Progress* still retains the sense of personal urgency: it is his tremendous need to find a righteousness not his own [like Luther] by which to be saved that we encounter in the very first paragraph, and which is the force irresistibly driving Christian along the road to his final entry into the Celestial City.'[18]

Christopher Hill, while expressing his reliance upon Sharrock, adds: 'Perhaps the most significant prototype of *The Pilgrim's Progress* is *Grace Abounding*. The state of desperation in which the Pilgrim finds himself at the beginning of the story (GA, para. 9) mirrors that of Bunyan throughout *Grace Abounding*. The wicket-gate had been anticipated in Bunyan's dream of his exclusion from the company of the godly in Bedford (GA, paras. 53-5). The Slough of Despond recalls Bunyan finding himself "as on a miry bog that shook if I did but stir" (GA, para. 82). Christian's fear that Mt Sinai would fall on his head recalls Bunyan's fear that the church bells or steeple might fall on him whilst watching bell-ringing (GA, paras. 33-4). The blasphemies whispered to Christian by a devil in the Valley of the Shadow of Death echo those which Bunyan himself had been tempted to utter. Hopeful is as influenced as Bunyan had been by the text "My grace is sufficient for thee" (GA, paras. 204-6, 213). The "very brisk lad" called Ignorance, and Mr Brisk in Part II, remind us that Bunyan himself had been a brisk talker in matters of religion (GA, paras. 16, 29-32, 37).'[19]

The personal cultivation of natural ability

Had Bunyan been formally trained at either Oxford or Cambridge, his evident natural intellectual ability leaves little doubt that he would have achieved brilliant academic results. Providentially this was not to be, and the result was a life of distinctive freshness and originality that was not subjected to the structuring of classical studies, or Aristotelianism, or any other school of philosophy, except, of course, the school of Christ with its only textbook, the Bible.

Notwithstanding his lack of secular schooling, there is evidence of a very determined spirit that sought improvement through self-tutelage, though John Gifford, William Dell and John Owen seem to have been welcome guides. The poems in Part Two of *The Pilgrim's Progress* show a marked improvement in style over those contained in Part One. Add to this an inventive frame of mind and the result is a variety of forms of personal expression that produced such diverse results as a *Map Shewing the Order of Salvation and Damnation*, emblematic poems for children, a flute hewn in prison from a chair leg, a metal fiddle fashioned according to Bunyan's own metal-working skills, mental acuity in doctrinal reasoning and debate, close friendship with Sir John Shorter, the Lord Mayor of London, and an invitation to sit as a member of the Corporation of Bedford, an offer which he declined. These and other admirable, colourful and innovative characteristics portray a man who possessed exceptional abilities. John Bunyan had no need to borrow his creativity from other sources.

The biblical origin of the pilgrimage motif

Within the Bible there are many possibilities with regard to the concept of progress in pilgrimage that is so integral to *The Pilgrim's Progress*. To select a primary source here is not easy, and it seems probable that a combination of biblical texts and scenes best explains Bunyan's essential concept of a spiritual pilgrimage. For a man so saturated with Scripture, it is to be expected that a composite image drawn from a number of scriptural accounts of journeying would form the basis of his allegorical idea. Yet six strands of influence seem to emerge from the multitude of biblical examples that describe spiritual travelling in a wilderness world.

The journeying of the patriarch Abraham

In Hebrews 11:8-10,13-16 and 13:14 we certainly have a major statement concerning the journeying which characterized the life of Abraham, who, '... when he was called, obeyed by going out to a place which he was to receive for an inheritance; and he went out, not knowing where he was going ... for he was looking for the city which has foundations, whose architect and builder is God' (cf. Gen. 11:28 – 12:5).[20] This same spiritual adventure is described in Joshua 24:2-3, and again by Stephen in Acts 7:2-4. It is possible that Bunyan associated Ur of the Chaldeans with the City of Destruction; this may be one reason why Christian and Hopeful are told by the angels escorting them to the gates of the Celestial City, 'You are going now to Abraham, Isaac, and Jacob, and to the Prophets.'[21]

Lot's flight from Sodom

A parallel is drawn between The City of Destruction and Sodom when Christian warns his wife and children that '... our city will be burned with fire from heaven ... fire and brimstone', in the same way that Christian's escape can be compared to Lot's flight when he flees for his life (Gen. 19:23-28). Significantly, the Great Fire of London occurred in 1666, just prior to the period when Bunyan probably commenced his writing of *The Pilgrim's Progress*. So we read, '[Christian] looked not behind him, but fled towards the middle of the plain' (cf. Gen. 19:17). At the Palace Beautiful, Christian testifies to Charity that he warned his loved ones, '"but I seemed to them as one that mocked," and they believed me not' (cf. Gen. 19:14). Later, just beyond the silver mine at the hill Lucre, Christian and Hopeful encounter the monument to Lot's wife with its inscription, 'Remember Lot's wife' (Luke 17:32), on account of her 'looking behind her' (Gen. 19:26).[22]

The Exodus journeying of the nation of Israel

The pilgrimage of Israel from Egypt to Canaan, with the intervening sojourn in the wilderness, is frequently described in terms of 'the way' (Exod. 32:8; Josh. 24:1-17) or 'the straight [right, AV] way' (Ps. 107:4-7). So Evangelist enquires of Christian, after the latter has been led astray by the counsel of Mr Worldly-Wiseman, 'How is it, then, that thou art so quickly turned aside? For thou art now out of the way.'[23] At the Wicketgate Good-will warns Christian of many ways ahead, but tells him, 'Thou may'st distinguish the right from the wrong, the right only being straight and narrow.'[24] Faithful advises Christian that Pliable 'hath forsaken the way'.[25] Christian exhorts Hopeful, on account of Demas' seductive overtures, 'Let us not stir a step, but still keep on our way.'[26] At By-Path Meadow, 'The souls of the pilgrims were much discouraged because of the way' (Num. 21:4).[27] Then, having been led astray by Vain-confidence, the pilgrims are exhorted, 'Let thine heart be towards the highway, even the way that thou wentest, turn again' (cf. Jer. 31:21).[28] Christian enquires of the hospitable shepherds, 'Is there in this place any relief for pilgrims that are weary and faint in the way?' (Deut. 25:17-18).[29] Following release from the Flatterer's net by an angel, the pilgrims are asked, 'if they had not of those Shepherds a note of direction for the way'.[30] After discipline, they 'went softly along the right way'.[31]

The spiritual journeying of the psalmist

The definitive passage here is Psalm 23:3-4. In verse 3 David is a pilgrim who declares, 'He guides me in the paths of right-eousness for his name's sake.' Then he goes on to utter the words which Christian hears spoken by a voice ahead of him as he passes through the Valley of the Shadow of Death: 'Though I walk through the valley of the shadow of death, I will fear no evil; for thou art with me.'[32] The Psalms are full of references to life as a spiritual journey, whether the psalmist speaks of a 'way' (Ps. 1:1,6; 2:12; 5:8; 119:32,101; 142:3), or a 'path' (Ps. 16:11; 27:11; 119:35,105; 142:3), or of walking (Ps. 56:13; 101:2; 116:8-9; 138:7; 143:8).

The redemptive journeying of Jesus Christ

Undoubtedly Jesus Christ is the entrance to the way at the Wicket-gate (John 10:7), while at the same time he is the person of Good-will.[33] However, at Vanity Fair Bunyan weaves in the journey implicit in the incarnation of the Son of God with the explanation: 'The Prince of princes himself, when here, went through this town to his own country, and that upon a fair day too; yea, and as I think, it was Beelzebub, the chief lord of this fair, that invited him to buy of his vanities; yea, would have made him lord of the fair, would he but have done him reverence as he went through the town.'[34] This appears to portray Jesus Christ as travelling from the Celestial City, through Vanity Fair, towards the Place of Deliverance and the Wicket-gate. Overall, John 14:6 describes this redemptive journeying: 'I am the way, and the truth, and the life; no one comes to the Father, but through me' (cf. Isa. 40:3; John 16:28; Eph. 4:10).

The imagery of a journey as used by the apostle Paul

To the church at Corinth, Paul gives the following exhortation: 'Know ye not that they which run in a race run all, but one receiveth the prize? So run, that ye may obtain' (1 Cor. 9:24, AV). On the basis of this verse, Bunyan produced a further allegorical work entitled *The Heavenly Footman*, in which he exhorted his readers, 'Arise, man! be slothful no longer; set foot, and heart, and all into the way of God, and run; the crown is at the end of the race.'[35] Concerning this work Sharrock comments: 'Gradually, as if Bunyan cannot help himself, the metaphor turns from a cross-country race into a long journey.'[36] We should also take note of Paul's understanding of his earthly ministry as a 'course' to be obediently completed, according to the commission he had been given (Acts 20:24; 2 Tim. 4:7).

Thus all the learned energy expended for the purpose of discovering some subterranean source which led to Bunyan's composing of *The Pilgrim's Progress*, all the investigations that have attempted to unveil the underlying motions of his being, while proving fruitless in terms of discrediting the author's originality or diminishing his creative ability, have in fact only served all the more to uphold the obvious. In the words of Offor, '… the simple Christian will rejoice and triumph in the amazing superiority of a poor unlettered preaching mechanic, guided only by his Bible. Sanctified learning is exceedingly valuable; yet [the production of an unlettered man], wholly influenced by the Holy Oracles, shines resplendently over the laboured, murky productions of lettered men, who, forsaking the simplicity of the gospel, are trammelled with creeds, confessions, canons, articles, decretals, fathers, and, we may almost add, grandfathers.'[37]

How to run to the kingdom of Christ

Well then, sinner, what sayest thou? Where is thy heart? Wilt thou run? Art thou resolved to strip? Or art thou not? Think quickly, man, it is no dallying in this matter. Confer not with flesh and blood; look up to heaven, and see how thou likest it; also to hell! If thou dost not know the way, enquire at the Word of God. If thou wantest company, cry for God's Spirit. If thou wantest encouragement, entertain the promises. But be sure thou begin betimes; get into the way; run apace and hold out to the end; and the Lord give thee a prosperous journey. Farewell.

John Bunyan
The Heavenly Footman
Works, vol. III, p. 394

5.
The gospel in *The Pilgrim's Progress*

`... I gathered, that I must look for righteousness in his [Christ's] person, and for satisfaction for my sins by his blood...'

(Hopeful's testimony in *The Pilgrim's Progress*).

5.
The gospel in *The Pilgrim's Progress*

OF all the emphases concerning the truth of God incorporated in *The Pilgrim's Progress*, none is equal in importance
to Bunyan's multifaceted representation of the authentic
Christian gospel. In these days of spiritual declension, this
foundational evangelistic thrust in allegorical form is of crucial
importance for the following reason: the contemporary presentation of the gospel has become so diluted of truth, and as a
consequence so anaemic, that in most cases it has become
'another gospel' (Gal. 1:6). On the other hand, as we shall see
in chapter 7, the predominant concern of *The Pilgrim's Progress*
is with regard to sanctification rather than salvation. Thus at first
sight a contradiction seems to arise, in that the gospel is of
supreme importance, yet the major thrust of *The Pilgrim's
Progress* is sanctification. However, the supposed contradiction
is more apparent than real.

The explanation is this: while the gospel is foundational to
The Pilgrim's Progress as a whole, it is also of the essence of
initial salvation and is the ground of resultant sanctification. This
formal distinction between salvation and sanctification, on the
one hand, and the inseparable relationship between salvation
and sanctification, on the other, is one which not only the

sixteenth-century Reformers upheld, but also their seventeenth-century descendants. In this regard Bunyan was no exception. He explains this vital matter most clearly when, by means of Christian's animated response to the false gospel propounded by Ignorance, he expresses his own conviction concerning the gospel, as to both its root and fruit, and does so in very dogmatic terms: 'Ignorance is thy name, and as thy name is, so art thou... Ignorant thou art of what justifying righteousness is, and as ignorant how to secure thy soul, through the faith of it, from the heavy wrath of God. Yea, thou art also ignorant of the true effects of saving faith in this righteousness of Christ, which is, to bow and win over the heart to God in Christ, to love his name, his Word, ways, and people, and not as thou ignorantly imaginest.'[1]

Hence, throughout *The Pilgrim's Progress* the gospel is a pervasive saving and sanctifying reality that manifests itself according to three related and important perspectives.

The Pilgrim's Progress is Christ-centred

Comprehensive proof of this assertion will be provided in chapter 11. Furthermore, even a cursory review of the contents of Bunyan's *Works* will only serve to reinforce the pervasive aspect of this claim. One might say, that if, to borrow an expression from Spurgeon, the tinker's 'blood was bibline', then it circulated by means of a heart animated by Christ. The Christ whom Bunyan worshipped was revealed in, and faithfully represented by, both the Old and New Testaments, but especially within the Gospels and the epistles of Paul.

In *The Pilgrim's Progress* Christ is most frequently designated as the 'Lord of the Hill' — that is, as the sovereign Saviour and Lord of that hill Difficulty upon which his church, the Palace Beautiful, has been built for the refuge and comfort of weary pilgrims. [2]

To begin with, as in Bunyan's own experience recorded in his autobiography *Grace Abounding to the Chief of Sinners*, Christian's vision of Christ is ever so dim, and this is so even at the Wicket-gate, which he was formerly unable to see at all. Thus his initial perception of the gospel, although effectual, is only very basic. However, following the revelation of the grace of Christ, first at the House of Interpreter and then at the Place of Deliverance, the pilgrim's deep longing and desire is to 'see him alive that did hang dead on the cross'[3] — that is, to 'see him as he is' (1 John 3:2) — and he declares this glorious prospect to be his goal in response to the enquiries put to him by the inhabitants of the Palace Beautiful.

The Pilgrim's Progress is atonement-centred

The pre-eminence of Christ for Bunyan is not measured simply in terms of perfectly wedded deity and humanity; not his divine incarnate person only, but also his saving work and atoning sacrifice. Further, granted that Christ has come to deliver man from his overwhelming predicament, his hopeless bondage to sin and consequent judgement, more specifically the allegorist considered the question, how it can be possible for a holy God to maintain his integrity and at the same time save the sinner, to be a matter of vital importance. In simple terms, how could a just God pardon the ungodly? This was not so much a concern of the Latitudinarians and Quakers of Bunyan's day, who claimed that an inward and gradual work of renovation took place, in co-operation with grace provided by Christ's atonement, resulting in justifying works on the part of the individual. The Roman Catholic view of justification was virtually identical at this point.

However, for Bunyan the moral issue concerning God's holy character (Isa. 6:1-3) was of paramount importance since, to deal rightly with sin, satisfaction of his offended righteousness was absolutely necessary. Thus Richard Greaves comments:

'The necessity of an atonement was based by Bunyan upon the assumption that grace could only be extended to the sinner in a way which was not contradictory to divine justice, hence the rhetorical question was asked: "If the Promise, and God's grace without Christ's Blood would have saved us, wherefore then did Christ die?" For Bunyan there could be no thought of even the theoretical possibility that God could be gracious and merciful to sinners without an atonement for their sins.'[4] Hence in *The Pilgrim's Progress* this penal, satisfactory, substitutionary understanding of the atonement is of pervasive importance, just as it is in *Grace Abounding*.

Of course, as for Luther and the other Reformers, the doctrine of Paul in particular was of crucial significance here. Concerning his own experience, the Bedford pastor relates in his autobiography: 'One day, as I was passing in the field, and that too with some dashes on my conscience, fearing lest yet all was not right, suddenly this sentence fell upon my soul, Thy righteousness is in heaven; and methought withal, I saw, with the eyes of my soul, Jesus Christ at God's right hand there, I say, as my righteousness; so that wherever I was, or whatever I was a-doing, God could not say of me, He wants [lacks] my righteousness, for that was just before him. I also saw, moreover, that it was not my good frame of heart that made my righteousness better, nor yet my bad frame that made my righteousness worse; for my righteousness was Jesus Christ himself, the same yesterday, and today, and for ever (Heb. 13:8). Now did my chains fall off my legs indeed, I was loosed from my affliction and irons, my temptations also fled away.'[5]

Hopeful also tells of the advice he received from Faithful: 'He told me, that unless I could obtain the righteousness of a man that never had sinned, neither mine own, nor all the righteousness of the world, could save me... He bid me say to this effect, God be merciful to me a sinner, and make me to know and believe in Jesus Christ; for I see, that if his righteousness had not been, or I have not faith in that righteousness, I am utterly cast away.'[6]

Finally, revelation from Christ breaks through to Hopeful, as he confesses: 'From all which I gathered, that I must look for righteousness in his [Christ's] person, and for satisfaction for my sins by his blood... And now was my heart full of joy, mine eyes full of tears, and mine affections running over with love to the name, people, and ways of Jesus Christ.'[7]

The Pilgrim's Progress is justification-centred

When Christian's clothing of filthy rags (representing his own shabby righteousnesses — see Isa. 64:6), is taken away at the Place of Deliverance and replaced with a free coat, all as a result of his look of faith at the crucified Christ, Bunyan graphically portrays the essential truth of the Reformation doctrine of justification by faith alone. Christian further explains to Formalist and Hypocrisy: 'As for this coat that is on my back, it was given me by the Lord of the place whither I go; and that ... to cover my nakedness with. And I take it as a token of his kindness to me; for I had nothing but rags before.'[8]

The Latitudinarian[9] Edward Fowler, later to be a bishop, with whom Bunyan strenuously disputed over this matter in his *Defence of the Doctrine of Justification*, maintained that justification before God was a co-operative work whereby the sinner and internal grace produced justifying works. This synergistic gospel, being much like that of Roman Catholicism, meant that man was saved through gradual moral improvement. In stark contrast to this, Bunyan upheld an objective, rather than a subjective atonement, whereby the believing sinner, by looking to Christ's complete and satisfactory sacrifice, was justified and accredited with Christ's perfect righteousness.

Pieter de Vries is right when he comments: 'Bunyan was a staunch advocate of the forensic nature of justification. God clothes us with the righteousness that lies altogether outside ourselves and resides solely in the person of Christ... The grounds of salvation lie in the work of Christ *for* us and not in that of the Holy Spirit *in* us.'[10]

In contrast, Fowler maintained that co-operation with infused and subjective grace was the ground of human works which obtained progressive justification. For Bunyan, on the other hand, faith in objective grace, that is the atonement made at Calvary independently of the sinner, was also works-based, but the works concerned were exclusively those of Christ himself, in his life of obedience and his substitutionary death.

In the detailed dispute between Christian and Ignorance as they cross the Enchanted Ground, this objective/subjective conflict concerning the atonement is at the heart of their disagreement. Ignorance declares: 'I believe that Christ died for sinners; and that I shall be justified before God from the curse, through his gracious acceptance of my obedience to his law. Or thus, Christ makes my duties, that are religious, acceptable to his Father, by virtue of his merits; and so shall I be justified.'[11] To this Christian responds: 'Thou believest with a false faith; because it taketh justification from the personal righteousness of Christ, and applies it to thy own... This faith maketh not Christ a justifier of thy person, but of thy actions; and of thy person for thy action's sake, which is false ... true justifying faith puts the soul, as sensible of its lost condition by the law, upon flying for refuge unto Christ's righteousness, which righteousness of his is not an act of grace, by which he maketh, for justification, thy obedience accepted with God; but his personal obedience to the law, in doing and suffering for us what that required at our hands; this righteousness, I say, true faith accepteth, under the skirt of which, the soul being shrouded, and by it presented as spotless before God, it is accepted, and acquit from condemnation.'[12]

In response to this, Ignorance recoils with the objection: 'What! Would you have us trust to what Christ, in his own person, has done without [external to][13] us? This conceit would loosen the reigns of our lust, and tolerate us to live as we list [as we please]; for what matter how we live, if we may be justified by Christ's personal righteousness from all, when we believe it?'[14] Such a response is not unlike that of Paul's hypothetical opponent in Romans 6:15.

The scenes of the gospel

During the course of *The Pilgrim's Progress* there are numerous areas of focus where the content of the gospel is portrayed with distinctive emphasis. When this truth is considered as a whole, it can be concluded with the greatest certainty that the biblical gospel has abiding significance for the Christian; it is not merely initiatory, but perennially glorious.

Evangelist directs Christian to the Wicket-gate

While reading the Bible in the City of Destruction causes Christian to experience an increasing load of guilt, it is Evangelist who first points him in the direction of the gospel remedy. This is by way of his exhortation to flee towards the Wicket-gate, even though at that stage the distressed pilgrim's sight is too dim for him to identify this entrance into the narrow way. However, it is 'yon shining light', or 'a lamp shining in a dark place', that shows the way ahead to Jesus Christ, 'the morning star' (2 Peter 1:19). Upon his arrival at the Wicket-gate, the burdened pilgrim is confronted with a composite representation of the gospel in which Jesus Christ is depicted as the door (John 10:9), the way (John 14:6) and also by the person of Good-will (Luke 2:14). Thus Christian's course is set and a short way ahead, at the Place of Deliverance, the clarity of the gospel of free grace through an imputed righteousness results in assurance that his sin has been borne away (Ps. 103:12). As Christian travels onward, numerous incidents cause him to recall his hope in a crucified Christ. These include testifying about his coat to Formalist and Hypocrisy, the memorial supper at the

Palace Beautiful and his subsequent victory over Apollyon, when he is strengthened by eating bread and drinking from the bottle of wine given to him at the palace by Discretion, Prudence, Piety and Charity.

Evangelist rescues Christian from a false gospel

The seduction of Christian by Mr Worldly-Wiseman is countered by the genuine pastoral interest of Evangelist, who exposes this charlatan's fraudulent gospel. Such a deceitful evangel, supposedly offering relief from burdens by means of Legality at the village of Morality just beyond a 'high hill', is in fact encouragement to attempt what is humanly impossible — that is, the scaling of Mount Sinai so as to attain its demands of a perfect righteousness (Gal. 5:3). Thus Mr Worldly-Wiseman, while denouncing Christian's book, as well as free grace through the cross, is one who proclaims 'justification by the works of the law' (Rom. 3:20; Gal. 2:16). Further, this false gospel or 'administration of death' (2 Cor. 3:7-11) only results in condemnation. Nevertheless Evangelist redirects Christian towards Christ at the Wicket-Gate with words of encouragement: 'Yet will the man at the gate receive thee, for he has good-will for men.'[15]

Christian's encounter at the Wicket-gate

Although the apparent disjunction between the Wicket-gate and the Place of Deliverance is a reflection of Bunyan's particular experience, as explained in detail in chapter 6, it ought to be understood that, biblically speaking — and the author of *The Pilgrim's Progress* would have heartily agreed here — this entrance is the great gospel transition-point from darkness to light, from condemnation to justification, from the broad road leading to destruction to the narrow road leading to eternal life

(Matt. 7:13-14). Entrance requires a felt load of guilt before God and an earnest response to the gospel invitation (Matt. 7:7); this is simple though earnest faith in the Lord Jesus Christ as the only way of salvation and reconciliation with God (Matt. 11:28; John 14:6). The gospel, when seriously approached, is not complex, but it does demand the prerequisite of a 'broken and a contrite heart' (Ps. 51:17). Furthermore, even after this gate has been passed, this same gospel retains ongoing importance since entrance through the Wicket-gate has become the fundamental insignia of a bona fide pilgrim, and by this means the illegitimacy of Formalist and Hypocrisy, and of Ignorance, is identified.

If the specifics of the atonement seem to be missing at this juncture, Christian is certainly pulled through the Wicket-gate by the nail-pierced hands of Good-will, who is later identified in Part Two as Jesus Christ.[16]

The House of Interpreter

Of the seven scenes that instruct Christian here, two in particular have a gospel emphasis which, being communicated by the Holy Spirit, enlarges the understanding of the new pilgrim concerning the narrow way along which he now travels.

1. The distinction between the law and the gospel

This second scene, depicting the dusty room, illustrates the distinction between the law and the gospel which Bunyan, according to the particular influence of Luther, believed to be of great importance. In simple terms, the new Christian is to understand that, having been initially saved by the gospel, he will also be maintained and sanctified by the gospel, and not by the law. As he puts it, unlike the gospel, 'it [the law] doth not give power to subdue'.[17]

Elsewhere Bunyan writes, 'That thou mayest know the nature of the love of Christ ... be much in acquainting of thy soul with the nature of the law, and the nature of the gospel (Gal. 3:21)... The law is a servant, both first and last, to the gospel (Rom. 10:3-4): when therefore it is made a Lord, it destroyeth: and then to be sure it is made a Lord and Saviour of, when its dictates and commands are depended upon for life.'[18]

2. The grace of Christ conquers Satan's assault on the heart

This fourth scene, depicting the inextinguishable blaze, illustrates the surpassing greatness of the sustaining grace of Christ in the face of Satan's furious attempts to douse the fire in the soul that has been ignited in the first place by Christ (Rom. 5:20). As Bunyan explains, 'This is Christ, who continually, with the oil of his grace, maintains the work already begun in the heart.'[19] In other words, gospel grace began the work in the soul, and only gospel grace can uphold that work in the soul to the end.

The Palace Beautiful

This representation of a faithful nonconformist church indicates the pastoral centrality of the gospel in a number of ways. To begin with, there is careful investigation by the Palace Beautiful inhabitants in order to establish whether Christian has had an authentic encounter with the gospel via the Wicket-gate, and that his new affections reflect genuine conversion. In testifying that he has occasional spiritual victories, Christian points out that these are obtained through meditation on the cross and his coat of imputed righteousness.

However, it is at supper time, when the Lord's Table is so graphically portrayed, that the gospel is seen to be of such sustaining influence for the residents. Here the details of Christ's atonement are explained in graphic and applicatory detail as the household partakes of 'fat things ... with wine that was well refined'.[20] In conversation around the table, they discuss the fact that the Lord of the Hill had been a 'great warrior' and that this had involved 'the loss of much blood'.[21] Furthermore, 'He had stripped himself of his glory, that he might do this for the poor... They said moreover, that he had made many pilgrims princes, though by nature they were beggars born, and their original had been the dunghill.'[22] And when the pilgrim leaves the palace, having been strengthened as a result of his stay, he is given gospel tokens for the frequent and nourishing remembrance of Christ's saving work.

Faithful's conversion and witness

Convinced by Christian's witness in the City of Destruction that he should go on pilgrimage, Faithful is propositioned by the bewitching Wanton just outside the Wicket-gate. In resisting her, presumably he too is snatched in through the gate by Goodwill, as Christian was, and is thus brought into a saving relationship with Christ. He subsequently incurs the severe condemnation of Moses for being for a time inclined towards the seductive proposal of the old man Adam the First, yet he is delivered by the man with holes in his hands and side.

Up to this point Faithful's apprehension of Christ seems to be weaker than that of Christian, though it grows rapidly stronger as he disputes with Talkative and witnesses at Vanity Fair. Here he explains to Hopeful in the plainest possible terms that only the saving perfect righteousness of the Lord Jesus Christ, received for justification through faith alone, could save him. This gospel witness and Faithful's subsequent martyrdom make a considerable impression upon the town of Vanity, as is evident in Part Two when Christiana finds Christian fellowship there, and the populace is reported to have become less aggressive towards pilgrims.

Hopeful's conversion and witness

This testimony of conversion given to Christian on the Enchanted Ground is the model presentation of the gospel in *The Pilgrim's Progress*. In contrast with Christian's experience, there is no disjunction here between conversion and assurance. A summary of this testimony is as follows:

- At first Hopeful is fully immersed in worldliness without any consciousness of guilt.
- He begins to experience conviction of sin in various circumstances.
- He makes attempts at self-reformation by means of religious duties.
- Conviction grows stronger through the truth of Scripture.
- He consults Faithful, who tells him that:
    He needs a perfect righteousness.
    The Lord Jesus is the only righteous man.
    He must believe on the Lord Jesus for justification.
- He raises objections to Faithful's invitation:
    It is presumptuous to come to Christ.
    What is it to come to Christ?
- Christ is revealed to him from heaven inviting him to believe.
- He raises objections to Christ's invitation:
    He is a great sinner.
    What is it to believe?
- He exercises faith in Christ, looking to him alone for righteousness and salvation.
- He confesses Christ to Christian.

The false testimony of Ignorance

The stark contrast between the gospel attested to by Hopeful and the beliefs of Ignorance is of the highest importance to Bunyan. Described as 'a very brisk lad' at his first meeting with Christian and Hopeful, Ignorance is immediately identified as one whose profession of faith is false by the way he strenuously defends his entrance into the narrow way by means of 'a little crooked lane',[23] instead of through the Wicket-gate. He is firmly religious and intent on entering the Celestial City. When he and the two genuine pilgrims are reacquainted some distance ahead, during the crossing of the Enchanted Ground, the ensuing detailed dispute between Christian and Ignorance may be likened to Paul's animated concern for the purity of the gospel in Galatians 1:6-9; likewise for Bunyan, at this point essential truth is at stake (see Gal. 2:5).

As we saw earlier in this chapter, the controversy may be reduced to a question as to whether justification is by an objective and complete work of Christ crucified, carried out independently of, and externally to man, in which Christ's perfect righteousness is imputed to the sinner; or a subjective work taking place within the heart of man, on the basis of an infused righteousness and involving an element of co-operation with Christ on the part of the individual. Ignorance is constantly stressing his trust in what is going on within his heart, his own good thoughts, etc., so that he objects to the suggestion that he is thoroughly sinful. Thus he believes that a collaborative work with grace is taking place in his life whereby good works are produced that will result in his eventual justification before God. Christian is emphatic that faith alone must lay hold of what Christ has completed as an atonement on Mt Calvary, a work completed outside, and independently of, the sinful heart. However, Ignorance is unwavering to the end in his belief in a mystical gospel, and it is significant that when he finally arrives at the entrance to the Celestial City, he cites as his qualification for entrance, not Christ's righteousness but the fact that 'I have eat and drank in the presence of the King, and he has taught in our streets' (see Luke 13:26).'[24]

The doctrine of the gospel

At this point, those who have merely a sentimental and broadly evangelical regard for *The Pilgrim's Progress* will find themselves on the horns of a dilemma when they correctly understand what Bunyan's gospel doctrine is all about. Either they will have to walk away from their literary hero, since their contemporary grasp of the gospel is admitted to be radically different from that portrayed in the famous allegory, or else they will have to change their understanding of the gospel so dramatically that the change could be likened to a theological Copernican revolution. For instance, the contemporary terminology that describes Christian conversion as 'inviting Jesus Christ into your heart' will not mesh with Bunyan's representation of the gospel. It is more akin to the Roman Catholic gospel, in which justification is by infused grace.

First and foremost, Bunyan was a thoroughgoing biblicist who very conscientiously sought the truth in Holy Scripture for himself without relying upon numerous secondary sources. Of course, he had no knowledge of the original languages, and made no pretence of doing so; however, in no way did he disparage those more scholarly Puritans who were of like precious faith with him. Nevertheless his devotion to the English Bible was primary since he openly declared his preference for not drawing from the wells of other men.

Even so, other influences did impinge upon him, all claiming biblical roots. These shaped his theology in a secondary sense, particularly with regard to the gospel, while at the same time it must be acknowledged that Bunyan was very much his own man and not one to fall in line with a system of doctrine for the sake of loyalty and acceptance in some church association. We shall now consider the primary influences upon Bunyan's doctrine of the gospel.

His presuppositions concerning sin

Bunyan's understanding of sin, its historic commencement in the Garden of Eden and its universal consequences, is classically biblical and orthodox. He believed in an original, historical Adam who fathered the sinful human race: 'He [Adam] ... made them [his children] sinners — "By one man's disobedience many were made sinners" (Rom. 5:19)... [Adam] was the conduit pipe through which the devil did convey off his poisoned spawn and venom nature into the hearts of Adam's sons and daughters, by which they are at this day so strongly and so violently carried away, that they fly as fast to hell, and the devil, by reason of sin, as chaff before a mighty wind.'[25]

Elsewhere he writes of a person being at the present time 'under the wrath of God because of original sin (Rom. 5:12).'[26] Thus he believed in the doctrine of original, or congenital, sin whereby, even from birth and the cradle, sin is inherently present.

Furthermore, '[Sin] is that which hath stupefied and besotted the powers of men's souls, and made them even next to a beast or brute in all matters supernatural and heavenly (2 Peter 2:12). For as the beast minds nothing but his lusts and his belly, by nature, so man minds nothing but things earthly, sensual, and devilish, by reason of iniquity.'[27] This pollution is not only universal, but total and has resulted in man's being infected in all of his faculties, intellect, will and affections, so that every individual can only move with the freedom of this corrupt nature. '[Sin] has alienated the will, the mind, and affections, from the choice of the things that should save it, and wrought them over to a hearty delight in those things that naturally tend to drown it in perdition and destruction (Col. 1:21).'[28] Consequently, man retains no inherent ability to take pleasure in, or obey, the righteousness of God, such as through 'free will'.[29] Any holy response on man's part, even saving faith, can only be generated by particular grace sovereignly imparted (Eph. 2:8).[30]

Martin Luther

It is not difficult to understand Bunyan's feelings of spiritual kinship with the great Reformer, Martin Luther, at this point. As a tinker, newly married, he became increasingly aware of his own inner ungodliness; the misery was excruciating. It was at this juncture that he read a book which described this experience and at the same time prescribed the remedy with great animation and jealous regard for the supremacy of free and sovereign grace. Hence, it is not surprising that Bunyan wrote in *Grace Abounding* concerning Luther's *Commentary on Galatians* that 'I found my condition, in his experience, so largely and profoundly handled, as if his book had been written out of my heart... I do prefer this book of Martin Luther upon the Galatians, excepting the Holy Bible, before all the books that ever I have seen, as most fit for a wounded conscience.'[31]

As an Augustinian monk, Luther had faced the same struggle concerning his inward corruption and the great question as to how reconciliation might be made with a righteous God. So it seems that Bunyan considered himself forever indebted to Luther for his ministration of gospel truth, especially its description, in terms borrowed from the apostle Paul, of the free, objective, substitutionary 'righteousness of God' (Rom. 1:17) — that is, 'the gift of righteousness' (Rom. 5:15), or 'the righteousness which is by faith' (Rom. 9:30).

To illustrate this dependence on Bunyan's part, consider the conclusion of that turbulent period of over two years following his conversion and the way in which he finally came to a point of enlightenment and stability. In *Grace Abounding* he writes, '... suddenly this sentence fell upon my soul, *Thy righteousness is in heaven*; and methought withall, I saw, with the eyes of my soul, Jesus Christ at God's right hand; there, I say, as my righteousness... Now did my chains fall off my legs indeed, I was loosed from my affliction and irons, my temptations also fled away... So when I came home, I looked to see if I could find that sentence, *Thy righteousness is in heaven*; but could not find such a saying, wherefore my heart began to sink again, only that was brought to my remembrance, he *of God is made unto us wisdom, righteousness, sanctification, and redemption*; by this word I saw the other Sentence true (1 Cor. 1:30).'[32]

Now compare Luther's *Lectures on Galatians* where he comments on the words, 'For we through the Spirit, by faith, are waiting for the hope of righteousness' (Gal. 5:5): 'I conclude that perfect righteousness has been prepared for me in heaven ... in this hope I am strengthened against sin and look for the consummation of perfect righteousness in heaven... [Devout Christians] know that they have eternal righteousness, for which they look in hope as an utterly certain possession, laid up in heaven, when they are most aware of the terrors of sin and death; and that they are the lords of everything when they seem to be the poorest of all.'[33]

Thus it is the Reformer from Wittenberg, rather than Calvin from Geneva, who made such an indelible impression on Bunyan, and there is general agreement that this influence persisted throughout the length of the tinker's ministry. Although Bunyan was a strong believer in the doctrine of predestination, there was another doctrinal motif that guided him and which was far more influential in his thinking — namely, the reign of grace.

Richard Greaves describes this ascendancy of gospel grace in his teaching as follows: 'The influence of Luther on Bunyan's concept of the nature of God can be seen especially in Bunyan's view of God fundamentally in terms of the wrath–grace dichotomy rather than in terms of the Calvinist emphasis on the sovereign will of God. The controlling motif in Bunyan's theology was not the more philosophical principle of the divine will exercising supreme control in the universe, but the more personal and experiential conflict which raged in both the convicted sinner and the converted pilgrim who sensed on the one hand the dread of God whose wrath could not be mitigated because of the wrong done to his holiness and justice, and on the other hand the all-sufficient grace of a God whose love and mercy had triumphed in the salvation of his elect.'[34]

How then does this perspective find its outworking in *The Pilgrim's Progress*? It is evidenced in a consideration of the far greater degree to which sin and grace find emphasis in comparison with references to the sovereignty of the divine will. Of course, this is not an either/or situation but rather a matter of primacy, and in this respect, beyond doubt, *The Pilgrim's Progress* does manifestly give greater place to that sovereignty of grace which is greater than all our sin (Rom. 5:20). It is the grace of *sola scriptura, sola Christos, sola fide* (grace that is by Scripture alone, by Christ alone, by faith alone) of free justification, of imputed righteousness.

Law and gospel

This emphasis clearly confirms the dominant influence of the German Reformer over the Bedford pastor along with, as Hill points out, the impact of John Foxe, John Owen and William Dell.[35] For Luther, law and gospel were antithetical, reactive, though both in necessary tension. Law, as the declaration of God's perfect righteousness, thunders against incapacitated sinful man. More than that, it magnifies and arouses sin, in whatever crevice it hides. It offers no extenuating circumstances, no middle ground, no relativity, no truce, only relentless and accusatory demand.

On the other hand, grace rightly quenches and satisfies and has dominion over all that the law requires. It justly pardons sinners and thereby silences the condemnatory voice of the law. Whatever the law is able to arouse and terrify through guilt, grace is able to cleanse, quench and bring peace through pardon. The law, as represented by Moses, is a ministry of condemnation and death, while grace, as embodied in Jesus Christ, is a ministry of free righteousness and life and peace (John 1:17; Rom. 5:1,17-21; 2 Cor. 3:7-18).

So in *The Pilgrim's Progress* there are several indications of the major importance of this truth for Bunyan. Mr Worldly-Wiseman counsels Christian to lose his burden at the village of Morality just beyond 'yonder high hill'.[36] However, this hill, which represents Mount Sinai, only thunders at the pilgrim's attempt to scale the impossible heights of the law. Then at the House of Interpreter, the second scene presents a precise portrayal of the opposite roles of law and grace. The dusty room depicts man's heart, thoroughly polluted by sin — a situation which the sweeper (the law) only makes worse by stirring up the dust. But then the young woman sprinkles the water which represents the settling and cleansing influences of the gospel upon the life of the believer.

Further on in the narrative, Faithful is for a time inclined to pay heed to the old man Adam the First. For this reason Moses mercilessly and repeatedly knocks him down until Christ comes to the rescue and drives away the accuser.

Surprisingly, although Bunyan deals with this whole doctrinal matter in great detail in his *The Doctrine of the Law and Grace Unfolded,* published in 1659,[37] and in doing so uses modified covenantal terminology when he refers to 'the covenant of works' and 'the covenant of grace', he refrains from using this covenantal language in *The Pilgrim's Progress*, even though this was published later (Part 1 in 1678 and Part Two in 1684). This may well have been for the purpose of not confusing his readers with technical theological terms.

Calvinism

In consideration of more exact doctrinal definitions, while it is unquestionably true that Bunyan was a strict Calvinist, in the normal usage of the term, to be more precise he was really a predestinarian, like Luther, and was probably more familiar with the latter's *Bondage of the Will* than with Calvin's *Institutes of the Christian Religion*. Bunyan's *Works* nowhere express any regard for Calvin that is comparable to his acknowledged reliance upon Luther.

In this vein Greaves explains: 'On this Lutheran foundation Bunyan built an essentially Calvinistic superstructure with the ideas which he assimilated from the writings of Bayly and Dent,[38] the teaching of Gifford and Burton, his ministerial association with men such as Owen [and Dell], and his contact in general with the recurrent and often controversial discussion of basic Christian principles which absorbed the minds of so many in the seventeenth century... In the Westminster Confession and the writings of Owen, to use two obvious examples, predestination was a doctrine derived from the prior principles of the absolute sovereignty of the divine will and the concomitant decrees pronounced by that will, whereas in the writings of Bunyan the doctrine of predestination originated primarily in a soteriological concern, with men being predestined more on the basis of foreknowledge [fore-love, not prescience?] and gracious love than as the result of abstract philosophical principles. In order that predestination be accomplished there had to be the effectual and irresistible calling of those predestined to glory, and in stating this doctrine Bunyan continued to draw upon his Calvinist mentors and associates. The remainder of his soteriology manifested consistent if not especially noteworthy Calvinist influence.'[39]

From a twenty-first-century perspective, Bunyan would undoubtedly be regarded as a thoroughgoing, five-point Calvinist of Baptist convictions, rather than as a Lutheran, especially with regard to church structure and the ordinances. His belief in unconditional particular election, and rejection of free will as popularly understood, would mark him out as very different from the broad stream of evangelical Christendom.[40] Greaves also indicates that Bunyan seems to have professed belief in a limited or definite atonement, while not writing at length on this issue as did his friend John Owen.[41] (See chapter 9 for a more detailed consideration of this matter of sovereignty, election and free will.)

However, when we come to *The Pilgrim's Progress*, the author, while dealing in many instances with issues related to the sovereignty of God, yet adopts in most cases a mellower and more winsome tone than the direct and dogmatic approach we find in his other writings. This bares out the comment of Coleridge that 'Calvinism never put on a less rigid form, never smoothed its brow and softened its voice more winningly than in *The Pilgrim's Progress*.'[42]

What, then, are these gentler representations of a gospel that exults in the truth that salvation is wholly of the sovereign grace of God? In the first place, there is the simple expression, 'But as God would have it,' which explains the ability of Christian to regain his lost sword, just at the point when he seemed almost vanquished, and give Apollyon a deadly thrust.[43]

Likewise, following the martyrdom of Faithful, Bunyan relates, 'But he that overrules all things, having the power of their rage in his own hand, so wrought it about, that Christian for that time escaped them, and went his way.'[44]

Then there is the despairing reprobate in the iron cage (see chapter 10), who explains that 'God has denied me repentance. His Word gives me no encouragement to believe; yea, himself hath shut me up in this iron cage; nor can all the men in the world let me out. O eternity! eternity! how shall I grapple with the misery that I must meet with in eternity!'[45]

The shepherds declare to Christian and Hopeful, concerning the status of the way ahead, that it 'is safe for those for whom it is to be safe; but transgressors shall fall therein (Hosea 14:9).'[46]

However, with more specific regard to the gospel, Bunyan makes it quite clear that a saving understanding of this message is only possible by means of sovereign revelation from heaven. In Hopeful's account of his experiences to Christian as they cross the Enchanted Ground, he recounts how, when he sought counsel from Faithful, he was told to go to Christ. At this point in his narrative Christian asks of his companion, 'And did the Father reveal his Son to you?' Hopeful responds: 'Not at the first, nor second, nor third, nor fourth, nor fifth; no not at the sixth time neither.' Then when Hopeful has related how he eventually came to believe in Christ, Christian's comment is: 'This was a revelation of Christ to your soul indeed.'[47]

Towards the end of the succeeding incident, in which Christian disputes with Ignorance, Hopeful intervenes with the question whether 'he [Ignorance] ever had Christ revealed to him from heaven'. Ignorance is offended at the doctrinal implications of the question. Hopeful then tells him, 'Why, man! Christ is so hid in God from natural apprehensions of the flesh, that he cannot by any man be savingly known, unless God the Father reveals him to them.'[48] To Bunyan, then, the grace of God and his uncompromised sovereignty are inseparable elements (Rom. 11:5-6). He portrays the gospel in *The Pilgrim's Progress* as something which is strongly urged upon all men, yet the authentic embrace of this saving message will ultimately, and only, be the response of those 'as God would have it'.

Conclusion

There is no doubt that John Bunyan's preaching, teaching and writing had a vibrant quality about them, not unlike the animation and intensity one senses when reading the writings of Luther. Such a style was both infectious and captivating insofar as his hearers were concerned. And it is important to ask, 'Why?'

For instance, consider Bunyan's concluding exhortation in his *A Few Sighs from Hell*, based upon an exposition of Luke 16:19-31 concerning the destiny of the rich man and Lazarus: 'Reader, here might I spend many sheets of paper, yea, I might upon this subject write a very great book, but I shall now forbear, desiring thee to be very conversant in the Scriptures, "for they are they which testify of Jesus Christ" (John 5:39). The Bereans were counted noble upon this account: "These were more noble than those in Thessalonica, in that they received the Word with all readiness of mind, and searched the scriptures daily" (Acts 17:11). But here let me give thee one caution, that is, have a care that thou do not satisfy thyself with a bare search of them, without a real application of him whom they testify of to thy soul, lest instead of faring the better for thy doing this work, thou dost fare a great deal the worse, and thy condemnation be very much heightened, in that though thou didst read so often the sad state of those that die in sin, and the glorious estate of them that close in with Christ, yet thou thyself shouldst be such a fool as to lose Jesus Christ, notwithstanding thy hearing, and reading so plentifully of him.'[49]

Such earnestness, in the spirit of the apostle Paul, demonstrates a vital, heartfelt compassion that is to be found in all of Bunyan's writings, and yet sadly is so rare today. Greaves provides some help in our search for the reason for this fervency. It provokes careful thought concerning what ought to be at the heart of our gospel proclamation at this needy hour: 'Because grace was [Bunyan's] dominating motif, his thought retained a personal element which was often lacking in the writings of many Calvinists, notably those of Owen and the *Westminster Confession*. This sense of personal contact and vibrancy was, however, perhaps due more to the style of his writing than to his concern with grace; yet the concept of grace must be considered an important contributing factor to this personal element which pervaded his writings, since grace per se lent itself to a more personal treatment than did, for example, the more abstract concepts of sovereignty and will which were the basic principles of contemporary Calvinist theology. It was precisely this personal and living quality which made his sermons and writings so popular, for through the spoken and the printed word he made the workings of divine grace come alive.'[50]

The initiative of God in saving sinful men

It is expected among men that he which giveth the offence should be the first in seeking peace; but, sinner, betwixt God and man it is not so; not that we loved God, not that we chose God; but 'God was in Christ, reconciling the world unto himself, not imputing their trespasses unto them.' God is the first that seeketh peace.

What sayest thou now, sinner? Is not this God rich in mercy? Hath not this God great love for sinners? Nay, further, that thou mayest not have any ground to doubt that all this is but complementing, thou hast also here declared that God hath made his Christ 'to be sin for us, who knew no sin, that we might be made the righteousness of God in him' (2 Cor. 5:21). If God would have struck at anything, he would have struck at the death of his Son; but he 'delivered him up for us freely; how shall he not with him also freely give us all things?' (Rom. 8:32).

But this is not all. God doth not only beseech thee to be reconciled to him, but further, for thy encouragement, he hath pronounced, in thy hearing, exceeding great and precious promises; 'and hath confirmed it by an oath, that by two immutable things, in which it was impossible for God to lie, we might have a strong consolation, who have fled for refuge to lay hold upon the hope set before us' (Heb. 6:18-19; Isa. 1:18; 55: 6-7; Jer. 51:5).

John Bunyan
Saved by Grace,
(*Works*, vol. I, p. 350).

6.

The conversion of Christian

'How delightfully but solemnly is [the truth that Christ is the door] illustrated in ... the Wicket-gate at the head of the way, at which the poor burdened sinner must knock and obtain an entrance by Christ the door '
     (George Offor).

6.

The conversion of Christian

IN today's conservative evangelical environment, readers of *The Pilgrim's Progress* could easily be forgiven for assuming that the conversion of Christian occurred at the Place of Deliverance where, when he gazed at the uplifted cross, his burden was loosed from off his back. Yet it may come as a surprise to these same readers, even as it did to me several years ago, to discover that, beyond doubt, John Bunyan understood the conversion of Christian to have taken place earlier, at the Wicket-gate. Hence, first let us consider the proof of this assertion, and then attempt to understand Bunyan's conception of conversion with regard both to his own life and to the order of these particular narrative events.

Evidence in favour of the Wicket-gate

The assurance given to Christian by Good-will

To begin with, the exhortation of Evangelist is that Christian should flee to the distant Wicket-gate, not to the Place of Deliverance. Upon Christian's arrival at and sudden passage through this Wicket-gate, this entrance into the narrow way (Matt. 7:13-14), he is assured by Good-will, 'An open door is set before thee, and no man can shut it.'[1] Surely this reference to Revelation 3:7-8 is indicative of the new pilgrim's security, obtained at conversion, that will reassure him on his journey.

Christian's experience at the House of Interpreter

In accord with John 15:26, Good-will at the Wicket-gate, who represents Jesus Christ, directs Christian to proceed towards the House of Interpreter, which is representative of the ministry of the Holy Spirit. The substantial instruction which Christian then receives is very much reflective of the teaching and illuminating ministry of this same Holy Spirit (John 7:37-39; 14:26; 15:26; 16:13-15), in conjunction with the Bible that Christian has in his hand. However, such teaching in Scripture clearly has reference to the Holy Spirit's instructive ministry that commences in the life of the new believer. Hence the sequence of these events, and particularly the fact that this revelation immediately precedes Christian's arrival at the Place of Deliverance, is Bunyan's portrayal of that teaching as being most suitable for a new believer.

In the fourth scene at the Interpreter's house, Christian observes, not only Satan attempting to quench the fire of grace *already burning* in a true pilgrim's heart, but also the greater and more effectual outpouring of Christ's oil of grace which triumphantly maintains the blaze. In this regard Christian is told, 'This is Christ, who continually, with the oil of his grace, maintains the work *already begun in the heart*' (emphasis added).[2] This explanation would only make sense if Christian had already been converted.

The Illegitimacy of certain pilgrims

When Formalist and Hypocrisy tumble over the wall called Salvation, Christian questions their legitimacy since they have not made their entrance through the Wicket-gate. They are rebuked with a quotation from John 10:1, not because they ignored the Place of Deliverance, but rather because they avoided the legitimate gospel door, or Wicket-gate, at the head of the way, which is obviously Jesus Christ.[3] In the same manner, Ignorance is recognized as an illegitimate pilgrim by Christian, not because he ignored the Place of Deliverance, but because he too did not commence his journey through the Wicket-gate.[4]

Of course, it could be objected that the authentic pilgrim Hopeful, originating from the town of Vanity, apparently did not make an entrance through the Wicket-gate, either. However, this is no more of a problem than the fact that Faithful appears not to have been equipped with the necessary armour available at the Palace Beautiful. In the case of Hopeful, Bunyan takes liberty with his allegorical form so that this pilgrim is converted through the gospel preaching and witness of Faithful at Vanity prior to his martyrdom.

Good-will's testimony to Christiana

In Part Two of *The Pilgrim's Progress*, Christiana, with her four sons and Mercy, eventually arrives at the Wicket-gate as they follow in the steps of Christian. There, having sought pardon for their sins, they are told by the Keeper of the Gate, or Good-will, 'I [Christ — see next paragraph] grant pardon ... by word and deed; by word in the promise of forgiveness, by deed in the way I [Christ] obtained it.' Then we are told that this Keeper 'had them up to the top of the gate and showed them [at a distance] by what deed they were saved, and told them withal that that sight they would have again as they went along in the way, to their comfort'.[5]

Great-heart's testimony about Good-will

In Part Two, when Christiana and her company arrive at the Place of Deliverance, their escort Great-heart gives explanation of the atoning deed that was described immediately following their entrance through the Wicket-gate: 'The pardon that you and Mercy, and these boys *have attained*, was obtained by another, to wit, by him that let you in at the gate; and he hath obtained it in this double way. He has performed righteousness to cover you, and spilt blood to wash you in' (emphasis added).[6]

Grace Abounding

In Bunyan's spiritual autobiography, *Grace Abounding to the Chief of Sinners*, he describes dreaming of his miserable and cold isolation, obviously as an unbeliever, on the dark side of a mountain that faces a sunny mountain on the opposite side of the valley. The only means of access to the sunshine and warmth is through a narrow gap in a dividing wall that extends along the length of the valley separating the two mountains. After much struggle and repeated effort, Bunyan passes through. He then gives the following interpretation: 'The [sunny] mountain signified the church of the living God' (cf. 1 Tim. 3:15).'[7] Sharrock incorrectly identifies this as the tinker's admission to the local nonconformist Bedford congregation, an event which is far more certainly portrayed by his reception at the Palace Beautiful.[8] On this occasion, Bunyan's prime quest was for the light of the saving grace of God, not membership of a local church.

Bunyan continues: 'The sun that shone thereon, [was] the comfortable shining of his merciful face on them that were therein; the wall, I thought, was the Word, that did make separation between the Christians and the world; and the gap which was in this wall, I thought, was Jesus Christ, who is the way to God the Father (John 14:6; Matt. 7:14). But forasmuch as the passage was wonderful narrow, even so narrow, that I could not, but with great difficulty, enter in thereat, it showed me that none could enter into life, but those that were in downright earnest.'[9]

The context in *Grace Abounding*, and especially the quotation from Matthew 7:14, shows that Bunyan obviously regarded this incident as a preview of his conversion, which is also graphically depicted at the Wicket-gate.

The Strait Gate

In *The Strait Gate*, a treatise based upon Luke 13:24 published two years before *The Pilgrim's Progress*, Bunyan comments: 'There is the door of faith, the door which the grace of God hath opened to the Gentiles. This door is Jesus Christ, as also himself doth testify, saying, "I am the door," etc. (John 10:9; Acts 14:27). By this door men enter into God's favour and mercy, and find forgiveness through faith in his blood, and live in hope of eternal life.'[10]

At this point George Offor adds the editorial comment: 'How delightfully but solemnly is this illustrated in *The Pilgrim's Progress*, [that is, in] the Wicket-gate at the head of the way, at which the poor burdened sinner must knock and obtain an entrance by Christ the door.'[11]

Spurgeon's *Around the Wicket Gate*

In C. H. Spurgeon's tract, *Around the Wicket Gate*, which is wholly based upon *The Pilgrim's Progress*, he identifies with halting pilgrims who draw near to the way of salvation and yet, for various reasons, do not immediately pass through the entrance gate, that is the Wicket-gate: 'Millions of men are in the outlying regions, far off from God and peace; for these we pray, and to these we give warning. But just now we have to do with a similar company, who are not far from the kingdom, but have come right up to the Wicket-gate which stands at the head of the way of life... He who does not take the step of faith, and so enter upon the road to heaven, will perish. It will be an awful thing to die just outside the gate of life. Almost saved, but altogether lost!'[12] Clearly Spurgeon understood the Wicket-gate scene to be the place of conversion for Christian.

Can Christian's conversion be clearly located?

In support of the assertion that Christian's conversion took place at the Wicket-gate, we should note that this has certainly been the prevailing opinion amongst the more notable commentators on *The Pilgrim's Progress*, including George Offor, W. Mason, George Cheever, John Kelman, etc. However, more recently Richard Greaves has located this experience at the Place of deliverance.[13] Then another contemporary scholar has, to a certain degree, challenged any such attempt to locate exactly Christian's conversion with the following comment: 'From the fact that Bunyan, in *The Pilgrim's Progress*, Part Two, had the sealing of the Spirit occur, allegorically, before Christiana's entry through the Wicket-gate, we may learn that we had better be on our guard against attaching too much significance to the order in which Bunyan arranged his scenes.'[14]

In response, it appears quite clear from the text that Christiana's entrance through the Wicket-gate is the occasion of her conversion, as was the case with her husband. However, prior to this, Christiana receives a visitor in the City of Destruction, while still in her unconverted state, who passes on to her a letter from the King of the Celestial City inviting her to go on pilgrimage. Who, then, is this messenger who identifies himself as Secret? Probably he represents 'the Angel of the LORD' who responds to Manoah's enquiry concerning his name with the further question: 'Why askest thou thus after my name, seeing it is secret?' (Judg. 13:18, AV). There is probably also a reference to the statement that 'The secret of the LORD is with them that fear him; and he will show them his covenant' (Ps. 25:14, AV), as de Vries suggests.[15] Thus Christiana is to hold this letter close to her bosom, read it frequently, sing it as a song and present it, as validation of her original call, at the gate of the Celestial City.[16]

Now there is an obvious similarity between this item and the roll which Christian receives at the Place of Deliverance, 'the assurance of his life and acceptance at the desired haven'.[17] Further, according to a marginal reference to Ephesians 1:13, Bunyan, to some degree, associates this roll given to Christian with the sealing of the Holy Spirit. However, it should be understood that Christian's *perception*, new-found stability and heightened assurance at the Place of Deliverance reflect what had already been established, concerning the work of the Holy Spirit, at the Wicket-gate. In fact Bunyan gives no clear, definitive exposition regarding the sealing of the Holy Spirit in terms of an event occurring at a specific moment in time, in the way that many Calvinists understand this expression.

Hence de Vries is correct when he concludes: 'Surveying the whole we can say that Bunyan related being sealed with the Spirit to the whole field of personal, spiritual experience. Spiritual life, whatever measure of it there was, was to be seen as a fruit of the sealing work of the Spirit.'[18]

Therefore, when we consider the letter of invitation given by Secret to Christiana before her conversion at the Wicket-gate, there is no need to associate it with the sealing of the Spirit that is usually related with conversion. Rather it represents that prevenient work of the Spirit which offers hope, encouragement and promise of what will be formally inaugurated at the Wicket-gate (1 Peter 1:1-2).

Support for this understanding of Bunyan at this point is found in a segment of his poetic discourse entitled *A Discourse of the Building ... of the House of God*. Here runaways are addressed, those who qualify for the judgement of God and thus are distressed:

> But bring with thee a certificate,
> To show thou seest thyself most desolate;
> Writ by the master, with repentance seal'd,
> To show also that here thou would'st be heal'd,
> By those fair leaves of that most blessed tree,
> By which alone poor sinners healed be;
> And that thou dost abhor thee for thy ways.
> And wouldst in holiness spend all thy days;
> And here be entertained; or thou wilt find
> To entertain thee here are none inclin'd. [19]

Thus the desolate are invited to come to the church for salvation, and to bring with them a certificate of invitation issued by Jesus Christ. This is clearly a preceding work of the Spirit since it is productive of repentance that *leads* to spiritual healing, conversion.

The conversion of Christian according to John Bunyan

In *The Holy War*, published in 1682, military metaphor, familiar to the author, is used to describe the recapture by King Shaddai of the City of Mansoul, which has been subject to the tyrannical reign of giant Diabolus. The actual campaign represents Christian conversion, and George Offor more specifically relates several incidents here to Bunyan's own conversion as portrayed in *Grace Abounding*.[20] This being so, it ought not to surprise us if Bunyan similarly incorporates his own experiences into the conversion experience of Christian.

Why does Christian retain his burden?

While the author of *The Pilgrim's Progress* definitely portrays Christian as being converted at the Wicket-gate, release from this pilgrim's burden does not occur until, having been instructed at the House of Interpreter, he gazes at the uplifted cross at the Place of Deliverance. To twenty-first-century Christians, this may seem a conflicting order of events. What, then, is Bunyan's intention here? What does this deliberate hiatus represent? What is this post-conversion experience at the Place of Deliverance?

The opinion of C. H. Spurgeon

Consider once again the opinion of C. H. Spurgeon at this point who, as a devoted student and admirer of *The Pilgrim's Progress*, was second to none in his esteem for Bunyan. Yet this did not mean that he was in agreement with every detail concerning the tinker's allegory.[21] In fact he disagreed with two features that relate to the gospel, namely the initial directing of Christian to the shining light, and the apparent placing of the cross beyond the Wicket-gate.

1. The sermon illustration

In a sermon based upon 1 Corinthians 2:2, Spurgeon comments:

> By the way, let me tell you a little story about Bunyan's *Pilgrim's Progress*. I am a great lover of John Bunyan, but I do not believe him infallible; and the other day I met with a story about him which I think is a very good one. There was a wise young man; so he thought, 'If I am to be a missionary, there is no need for me to transport myself far away from home; I may as well be a missionary in Edinburgh.' ... Well, this young man started, and

determined to speak to the first person he met. He met one of those old fishwives; those of us who have seen them can never forget them, they are extraordinary women indeed. So, stepping up to her, he said, 'Here you are, coming along with your burden on your back; let me ask you if you have got another burden, a spiritual burden.' 'What!' she asked; 'do you mean that burden in John Bunyan's *Pilgrim's Progress*? Because, if you do, young man, I got rid of that many years ago, probably before you were born. But I went a better way to work than the pilgrim did. The evangelist that John Bunyan talks about was one of your parsons that do not preach the gospel; for he said, "Keep that light in thine eye, and run to the wicket gate." Why, man alive! That was not the place for him to run to. He should have said, "Do you see that cross? Run there at once!" But instead of that, he sent the poor pilgrim to the Wicket-gate first; and such good he got by going there! He got tumbling into the slough, and was like to have been killed by it.'

'But did not you,' the young man asked, 'go through any Slough of Despond?' 'Yes, I did; but I found it a great deal easier going through with my burden off from the commencement of the pilgrimage.'

If he [Bunyan] meant to show what usually happens, he was right; but if he meant to show what ought to have happened, he was wrong. We must not say to the sinner, 'Now, sinner, if thou wilt be saved, go to the baptismal pool; go to the Wicket-gate; go to the church; do this or that.' No, the cross should be right in front of the Wicket-gate; and we should say to the sinner, 'Throw thyself down there, and thou art safe; but thou art not safe till thou canst cast off thy burden, and lie at the foot of the cross, and find peace in Jesus.'[22]

2. The sermon illustration and the Wicket-gate

Now while we can to some extent sympathize with Spurgeon's criticism, it ought to be pointed out that, assuming that Bunyan understood the Wicket-gate to be a representation of Christ as the 'door' (John 10:7,9), or 'way' (John 14:6), then the exhortation of Evangelist was not altogether wrong. However, for a man as opposed to Quakerism as Bunyan was, the initial directive to follow the shining light is perhaps surprising. Though concerning this point, it is certain that by the light he had in mind passages such as, 'Thy word is a lamp to my feet, and a light to my path' (Ps. 119:105) and 'the prophetic word made more sure, to which you do well to pay attention as to a lamp shining in a dark place, until the day dawns and the morning star arises in your hearts' (2 Peter 1:19), as his marginal references indicate. In other words, the shining light was the illuminated Word of God which would lead to the dawning of Christ in the heart of the prospective Christian. Even so, the lack of clarification concerning the Wicket-gate and the subsequent Place of Deliverance is somewhat mystifying, though this could possibly be the reason why greater explanation is given in the account of Part Two concerning the conversion of Christiana, her four sons and Mercy.

John Bunyan's conversion as a model for Christian

However, it is important to understand that the conversion of Christian in *The Pilgrim's Progress* is undoubtedly a reflection of Bunyan's own experience, and herein lies the essential reason for the distinctive order of events that we are studying. Bunyan's tortuous and complicated conversion, unlike that of Spurgeon, involved an approximate period of up to four years, commencing with his first marriage in 1649 and continuing to 1653 when he was received into membership by the nonconformist church at Bedford. The definitive description of this period is Bunyan's own intense unveiling of his tender soul in *Grace Abounding to the Chief of Sinners*, and especially paragraphs 15-235.[23] To some more recent critics, this testimony appears extreme and indicative of a warped psyche born of strict Calvinism and a too literal understanding of the Bible.[24] However, in rejecting any merely secular psychological explanation of this classic confession, or the patronizing attitude of those who say that Bunyan was too hard on himself, I would propose that modern-day reticence in the realm of honest soul-searching, in the presence of a holy God, provides a better explanation of the scepticism of these times towards this account.

Let us consider, then, three significant aspects of Bunyan's own conversion experience, as revealed in *Grace Abounding*, which provide a basis for understanding the conversion of Christian in *The Pilgrim's Progress*.

1. An element of progression[25]

Having read his wife's Christian books with interest (para. 15), he then reads the Bible, first the narrative sections (para. 29) and then, with growing appreciation, the epistles of Paul (paras. 45-6). His early reformation of manners (paras. 28-31) is followed by a desire for light, as opposed to his present darkness (paras. 53-6), but assaults of the devil cause him to despair (paras. 101-2). He is also troubled in prayer with goading from the devil and wandering thoughts (paras. 107-8). Although encouraged by the gospel, he is also discouraged by Satan (paras. 109-10). Then comes a definite and assured trust in Christ (paras. 113, 115-16). Sitting under John Gifford's ministry subsequently strengthens his soul (paras. 117-18). Still wounded in conscience, he receives understanding and comfort from Luther's commentary on Galatians (paras. 19-30). Nevertheless, he is tempted to sell Christ, yet, in his weakness, is given grace that brings victory (paras. 132-4). He struggles with the possibility of falling from grace and the sins of those who make a false profession of faith (paras. 194-208). He is still troubled by the state of Esau, yet comes to understand, in some measure, that he himself is not of the same reprobate spirit (paras. 212-28). Finally, light floods his soul, resulting in stability based upon a surer trust in Christ's perfect imputed righteousness (paras. 229-35).

2. Bunyan strove with many questions

Would he leave his sins and go to heaven, or have his sins and go to hell? (para. 22). Were the Ranters' claims to licentious freedom and perfection true? (paras. 44-5). Would it be possible to accomplish a miracle by faith? (para. 51). Was he one of God's elect, or a reprobate? (paras. 58-61). Were the Moslem and the pagan lost? (para. 97). Was Paul a deceiver? (para. 98). Might he have committed the unpardonable sin against the Holy Spirit? (paras. 103, 153, 174, 180-81, 189). Was Jesus Christ both God and man? (para. 122). Did his sin resemble that of Judas? (paras. 158-60). Did he have the mark of Cain? (para. 165). Could the blood of Christ be sufficient to save his soul? (para. 203). What is the meaning of certain warning passages in Hebrews? (paras. 196, 208, 223-8).

3. A struggle with ambivalence

The latter part of this unsettled period in Bunyan's early Christian life involved extremes of oscillation. He describes how, 'I should be sometimes up and down twenty times in an hour, yet God did bear me up' (para. 191, cf. paras. 194-8, 203-5, 208). But then comes release, bringing stability to his still-burdened and wavering soul, as he suddenly grasps a clear understanding of the perfect substitutionary righteousness of Jesus Christ: 'Now did my chains fall off my legs indeed, I was loosed from my affliction and irons, temptations also fled away… Oh, I saw my gold was in my trunk at home [heaven]! In Christ, my Lord and Saviour! Now Christ was all; all my wisdom, all my righteousness, all my sanctification, and all my redemption [1 Cor. 1:30]' (paras. 228-32).

Christian's conversion represents that of John Bunyan

When we consider, then, the sequence of events in *The Pilgrim's Progress* in which Christian comes to the Wicket-gate, the House of Interpreter and the Place of Deliverance, we discover a close parallel with the conversion of Bunyan himself.

1. Christian at the Wicket-gate

Here Christian, like the wavering Bunyan, is pulled through, in spite of his hesitation, and thus enters into the narrow way with the gift of eternal life — that is, through Jesus Christ (Good-will) who is, according to the allegory, a composite representation of the 'door', the 'doorkeeper' and the 'good shepherd' (John 10:3,7,11,14). At this point the pilgrim has no deep understanding of the atonement, and uncertainty remains, yet his face is set heavenwards.

Early in *Grace Abounding*, Bunyan describes his conversion as follows: 'I remember that one day, as I was travelling into the country and musing on the wickedness and blasphemy of my heart, and considering of the enmity that was in me to God, that scripture came in my mind, He hath "made peace through the blood of his cross" (Col. 1:20). By which I was made to see, both again, and again, and again, that day, that God and my sinful soul could embrace and kiss each other through this blood. This was a good day to me; I hope I shall not forget it.'[26]

In George Offor's edition of Bunyan's *Works*, this early experience of *c.* 1650 is related in *Grace Abounding* under the editorial sub-heading, 'His [Bunyan's] conversion and painful exercises of mind, previous to his joining the church at Bedford.'[27] Certainly, according to Bunyan's perception of himself, a burden remained at this point, as it did for Christian, causing instability and leading to spasmodic assurance, although the comment of Kelman is helpful here: 'It will be observed that Christian does not take with him the love of sin, but only the weight of sin... The practical lesson of it is, in Dr Whyte's words, "get into the right way and leave your burden to God." It is thus that the labouring and heavy-laden find rest unto their souls.'[28]

2. Christian at the House of Interpreter

Having been directed by Good-will (Jesus Christ), burdened Christian arrives at the House of Interpreter (the Holy Spirit) for edification, in parallel with John 15:26. Here this new believer portrays Bunyan who, though still burdened, was likewise edified for his journey through the profitable instruction of Pastor John Gifford. So in *Grace Abounding* we are told, 'At this time, also, I sat under the ministry of holy Mr. Gifford, whose doctrine, by God's grace, was much for my stability.'[29] It is significant that the first room in Interpreter's house displays a portrait of the godly pastor, as epitomized by Gifford, thus following very closely, as we have just considered, the sequence of events described in *Grace Abounding*. For Christian, the burden remains while the balm of instruction is applied; and so he continues to struggle with temptation, troubling questions and fluctuations between hope and fear; and so it was the case with Bunyan until the cross came into clear view.[30]

Cheever comments concerning this condition: 'Young Christians are very apt to expect entire relief from all their burdens and a complete deliverance from sin the moment they are got within the Wicket-gate, the moment they have come to Christ. But very often this expectation is not realized, and then they faint and become disheartened or filled with gloomy doubts.'[31]

However, it ought to be noticed that Bunyan does critically address this period of spiritual turbulence that plagued him for up to four years, and he offers two principal reasons for its presence in the initial years of his Christian life.

First, his prayer in the face of trouble only focused upon the present. Rather, he adds, 'I also should have prayed that the great God would keep me from the evil that was to come... I do beseech thee, reader, that thou learn to beware of my negligence, by the affliction that for this thing I did for days, and months, and years, with sorrow undergo.'[32]

Second, he put God to the test, as if he were making a bargain, or looking for a sign, like Gideon (Judg. 6-7). Once, when he was troubled as his wife was prematurely experiencing the pangs of childbirth, he prayed that her suffering would be relieved as a proof that the Lord could discern his most secret thoughts. But later he realized that 'I should have believed his word, and not have put an *if* upon the all-seeingness of God.'[33]

3. Christian at the Place of Deliverance

Here Christian, like Bunyan as a believer who has at last come into a state of enlightenment, stability and assurance, gains a much clearer understanding of the atonement, with all its attendant benefits, and especially that of the saving substitutionary righteousness of Jesus Christ. Thus the burden of doubt falls away: 'Then was Christian glad and lightsome, and said with a merry heart, "He hath given me rest by his sorrow, and life by his death." '[34] So after approximately four years of restlessness, Bunyan tells us how he himself was similarly delivered (around the year 1653) 'from the guilt that, by these things, was laid upon my conscience ... from the very filth thereof; for the temptation was removed, and I was put into my right mind again, as other Christians were' (note the use of the word 'other', implying that he too was a Christian).[35]

Does Bunyan then endorse his own post-conversion experience as the norm? Not at all, for he seems, rather, to perceive it as none too common and as an unnecessary sequence of events. It represents a failing, rather than a biblical norm. We saw earlier how Spurgeon would agree with this assessment.

Hence it would appear that Bunyan incorporates his own testimony into the narrative of *The Pilgrim's Progress* as a help to those who, like himself, have needlessly floundered. Certainly he knows nothing of what Pentecostals and charismatics today would refer to as a post-conversion 'baptism of the Holy Spirit' — even though Bunyan was undoubtedly delivered through the sanctifying agency of the Comforter. Such a concept is foreign to the totality of his writings. Furthermore, his experience and that of Christian are atonement-centred rather than emphasizing the work of the Spirit.

However, Bunyan does gladly acknowledge several benefits that accrued to him as a result of his rescue from his prolonged trial:

- His appreciation of the being, glory, compassion and holiness of God and Christ was greatly enlarged, and he was deeply humbled, especially in the light of his having been formerly much perplexed with evil thoughts of unbelief, tending to atheism.
- The Scriptures appeared all the more wonderful and awesome. He was particularly impressed by the finality with which they promise blessing, on the one hand, and pronounce condemnation to eternal woe on the other. In this respect he saw them as the very keys of the kingdom of heaven.
- He paid much more attention to every detail of the promises of God as a result of trembling under the mighty hand of God and being torn apart with fearful thoughts of his holiness and justice.
- Whereas formerly he had hesitated to appropriate the promises of God, now he would seize eagerly on every promise and ventured to take Christ at his word when he promised not to cast out the one who came to him (John 6:37).
- Because great sins draw out great grace, so, at the point where he was most conscious of his own sinfulness

and guilt, the grace, love and mercy of God appeared all the greater and more exalted. Indeed, at times his sense of them was so overwhelming as to be greater than the capacity of his heart to comprehend. [36]

4. Assurance

The experience of Christian in the sequence of the three events, as he passes from the Wicket-gate, first to the Interpreter's house and then on to the Place of Deliverance, clearly reflects Bunyan's own early struggles as a believer. It is not intended to be seen as the biblical norm, as his confession cited above readily proves. However, it is evident that upon his entrance into authentic Christian life, Bunyan initially lacked sufficient assurance to produce steadiness in his soul. Only after prolonged struggle and exposure to faithful instruction did he reach a point of stability and confidence in Christ's substitutionary atonement. In contrast with this less usual and highly distinctive experience, Hopeful's testimony, given while crossing the Enchanted Ground, depicts something more akin to the norm.

Pieter de Vries is of a similar opinion when he concludes: 'In *The Pilgrim's Progress* [in this sequence of events] ... Bunyan symbolically intimated that in his opinion a longer or shorter period of time will elapse between coming to Christ and possessing the comfort and assurance that one's sins are forgiven. We find the same in *The Holy War*. After Mansoul had been invaded by Emmanuel's troops, there was not immediately joy in the hearts of Mansoul's citizens.'[37]

While Richard Greaves may be making too much of what he sees as a conflict as a result of Bunyan's failing to give sufficient weight to the gospel embraced at the Wicket-gate, yet he arrives at the right conclusion when he comments: 'Theologically the delay between entering the gate and the activities at the cross is intolerable, but it is experientially verifiable for Bunyan and various fellow Calvinists. The early stages of the pilgrimage do not bring unrelieved assurance'[38] — at least, we might add, in every case such as this. In addition, Greaves helpfully draws attention to a portion of *Law and Grace* in which Bunyan describes this particular early period of struggle following conversion.[39]

Christian's conversion and contemporary evangelism

In terms of the climate of evangelism today, and the penchant that Christians often have for calling upon unbelievers to 'make a decision for Jesus Christ' at a precise moment in time, it may be difficult for many of us to understand the concept of conversion in *The Pilgrim's Progress*. As stated earlier, Spurgeon's criticism of Bunyan is essentially correct, although it could have been expressed with a little more caution, in the same way as the fishwife's disagreement with Bunyan's imagery was not fully warranted. The Bible does urgently call upon sinners to repent and believe in Jesus Christ at a specific point of time, without delay (Mark 1:14-15; Acts 3:19; 17:30-31; 26:20). This crucified Saviour is to be the exclusive focus of the seeking sinner.

Yet are we not sometimes unduly eager to determine precisely when that true faith in Christ was expressed? Certainly Spurgeon identifies a very specific time in relation to his own conversion,[40] and it appears that even Bunyan was conscious of a particular period when he came to a saving knowledge of Jesus Christ, as he recounts in *Grace Abounding*.[41] However, his ensuing four-year struggle with lack of assurance has tended to blur the more normal and biblical experience of conversion for which Spurgeon argued, and which is indeed reflected in the testimony of Hopeful.[42]

A parallel can be drawn here with the problems sometimes associated with the birth process in the natural world, in which we find a variety of pre-natal irregularities and neo-natal conditions that contrast with the normal delivery process. Some babies — indeed a significant proportion — come forth from the womb with textbook precision. However, others are born with varying degrees of difficulty and with initial health problems that are later corrected. The suggestion that we ought to view the differences between Bunyan and Spurgeon in such a light is in no way intended to detract from the importance of radical and manifest conversion, or to obscure the evident spiritual life and fruit that distinguish the saved from the unsaved. In this respect, Bunyan himself is the clearest possible example of conversion leading to radical change in his interests and lifestyle. However, perhaps at the present time we are in need of discerning spiritual midwives in the life of local churches.

Even so, whether we side more with Spurgeon or Bunyan in this matter — and this will probably be according to our own experience — are not the essential indications of new birth and authentic conversion to be found in manifest godliness and true affections, rather than in a precisely defined regimen for spiritual delivery?

The narrow gate

I read in the scriptures of two gates or doors, through which they that go to heaven must enter... There is the door of faith, the door which the grace of God hath opened to the Gentiles; this door is Jesus Christ, as also himself doth testify, saying, "I am the door," etc. (Acts 14:27; John 10:9). By this door men enter into God's favour and mercy, and find forgiveness through faith in his blood, and live in hope of eternal life; and therefore himself also said, "I am the door, by me if any man enter in, he shall be saved," that is, received to mercy, and inherit eternal life. But ... there is another door or gate ... and that is the passage into the very heaven itself the entrance into the celestial mansion-house...

John Bunyan
The Strait Gate,
(Bunyan, *Works,* vol. I, p.365)

7.
Sanctification in
The Pilgrim's Progress

'If Christian in *Pilgrim's Progress* simply yielded himself to God, and never fought, or struggled, or wrestled, I have read the famous allegory in vain' (J. C. Ryle).

7.

Sanctification in
The Pilgrim's Progress

FROM the late nineteenth century onwards, two widespread movements within conservative evangelicalism have been responsible for promoting deviant views of practical Christian sanctification that have resulted in varying degrees of confusion, conflict and carnality. The influence of the English Keswick movement, though now considerably modified and less distinctive than formerly, was for many years pervasive at numerous convention centres throughout the world. It erroneously taught that justification by faith is paralleled by sanctification by faith, or passive surrender to the dominion of the Holy Spirit.[1] The impact of the more recent Pentecostal / charismatic movement has probably been even greater and certainly more intrusive in many denominational associations and fellowship groups. It teaches that sanctification comes by means of a sudden and cataclysmic post-conversion experience, a baptism in the Spirit that is often identified by phenomena such as expressed ecstasy and the evidence of speaking in tongues.

To both of these emphases, *The Pilgrim's Progress* speaks with clarifying freshness and honesty. The allegory's basic format, that of a journey requiring advancement towards a heavenly city, is a most graphic representation of the biblical pattern of encountering 'conflicts without' and 'fears within'

(2 Cor. 7:5), of '[pressing] on toward the goal for the prize of the upward call' (Phil. 3:14), of '[growing] in the grace and knowledge of our Lord and Saviour Jesus Christ' (2 Peter 3:18). Bunyan's title is most apt. It is not *Pilgrimage on the High Road* or *The Phenomenal Pilgrim*, but *The Pilgrim's Progress*, describing as it does participation in an endurance race that involves both disturbing 'sinful encumbrances' and the goal of being welcomed into the presence of Jesus Christ at the 'crossing of the line' (Phil. 3:12-14; Heb. 12:1-2). To deny that such ongoing struggle and conflict is a normal feature of this present Christian life — interspersed of course with periods of joyful confidence — is not only to delude oneself, but is spiritually counter-productive.

Sanctification in *The Pilgrim's Progress*

In the Wharey and Sharrock edition of *The Pilgrim's Progress* published by Oxford University Press (under the Clarendon Press imprint), the text of Part One is comprised of 5,607 lines. Of these, 10.5% cover the initial period from the commencement of the journey at the City of Destruction to the point where Christian reaches the Wicket-gate and knocks. The remaining 89.5% cover the second stage, starting with Christian's passage through the Wicket-gate and ending with Ignorance being consigned to hell from outside the very gates of the Celestial City. The obvious significance of these facts is that, while over 10% of the text deals with the time leading up to Christian's conversion, nearly 90% is concerned with the progressive sanctification of Christian through periods both of buffetings in the wilderness and of blessings experienced through Christian fellowship.

In other words, *The Pilgrim's Progress* is not primarily an evangelistic presentation, even though it most definitely has a pervasive evangelistic thrust. Rather, it is an allegorical tract that focuses mainly upon the authentic life-journey of a bona fide Christian, and especially upon his distancing of himself from the City of Destruction and all the agents of the devil seeking to drag him back there, and his advancement towards the Celestial City using the means provided by its King for the strengthening of pilgrims, especially godly companionship. Both the negative and positive elements here are of the very essence of biblical sanctification.

The response to the 'Higher Life' movement

The term 'Higher Life' movement is a broader title that includes not only the English Keswick movement, with its emphasis on the impact of Romans 5-8 upon Christian lives, but also the European and American antecedents of this ministry. The Boardmans, the Pearsall-Smiths and Bishop H. G. Moule are just a few representatives of an emphasis on practical sanctification which had a sweeping influence upon evangelical Christendom towards the end of the nineteenth century and in the early part of the twentieth.[2]

At that same time, another Anglican bishop, J. C. Ryle, Bishop of Liverpool, whom Spurgeon rated as the most stalwart evangelical minister of the Church of England of his time, wrote a classic book entitled *Holiness* which vigorously, though graciously, challenges the biblical basis of the traditional Keswick-type ministry. In his introduction to that volume he succinctly asks seven questions to all of which a right understanding of Scripture would imply negative responses.[3] These can be summarized as follows:

1. Is faith the one thing needful for sanctification?
2. Is practical exhortation to holiness in daily life to be neglected?

3. Is it wise to use language that implies that perfection in holiness can be attained in this life, when there is no scriptural warrant for this?

4. Is it true that Romans 7 does not describe the mature saint?

5. Is the doctrine of 'Christ in us' exalted to a position above that which it is given in Scripture?

6. Is it wise to make such a clear distinction between conversion and consecration?

7. Is it a biblical emphasis to encourage believers to 'yield themselves' passively to God, instead of urging them to fight and struggle against sin?

In answering the last of these questions Ryle comments: 'A holy violence, a conflict, a warfare, a fight, a soldier's life, a wrestling, are spoken of [in Scripture] as characteristic of the true Christian. The account of "the armour of God" in the sixth chapter of Ephesians, one might think, settles the question. Again, it would be easy to show that the doctrine of sanctification without personal exertion, by simply "yielding ourselves to God" ... is utterly subversive of the whole teaching of such tried and approved books as *Pilgrim's Progress*, and that if we receive it we cannot do better than put Bunyan's old book in the fire! If Christian in *Pilgrim's Progress* simply yielded himself to God, and never fought, or struggled, or wrestled, I have read the famous allegory in vain.'[4]

Indeed it would be true to say that *The Pilgrim's Progress* deals most naturally with all the questions raised by Ryle and does so in a manner which fully supports his teaching on both justification and progressive sanctification. In regard to this latter point the bishop goes to the real doctrinal heart of the problem when he adds: 'But the plain truth is, that men will persist in confounding two things that differ — that is, justification and sanctification. In justification the word to be addressed to man is "believe" — only believe; in sanctification the word must be "watch, pray, and fight". What God has divided let us not mingle and confuse.'[5] This vital matter will be dealt with in greater detail later in the chapter.

The response to the Pentecostal/charismatic movement

This more recent development has emphasized a post-conversion 'baptism with the Holy Spirit' that is often said to be evidenced by 'signs following', such as speaking in tongues and healing, etc. Other additional related aberrations have been similarly phenomenological and usually designed to appeal to the senses, such as 'slaying with the Holy Spirit', 'healing of the memories', 'exorcism', 'word of faith prosperity', 'word of knowledge prognostication', 'extra-biblical revelation', 'holy laughter', etc. It is true that this movement has required belief in the gospel as being mandatory for Christian conversion, but this has been so in only a very rudimentary, and even mechanical, sense. The transcending experience, insofar as being empowered for Christian living is concerned, has commonly been the supernatural 'baptism with the Holy Spirit'. Unfortunately the pursuit here of manifestations of the Spirit has been more of a quest for the animation and power of the Holy Spirit than an earnest desire to attain the righteousness of God through Christ.

To this whole scenario *The Pilgrim's Progress* speaks in much-needed theocentric, moral and remedial terms. It magnifies the gospel of grace through free justification as God's supreme saving work, rather than as some perfunctory transaction. It relates power for sanctification to regeneration and justification, rather than to some phenomenal experience that is subsequent to conversion. It exults in the wonder of moral transformation that reaches to the very depths of a sinner's being rather than mere physical stimulation. It emphasizes man's becoming conformed to God's holy image, especially as embodied in the Lord Jesus Christ.

It is certainly true that for the first four years of Bunyan's Christian life he struggled with doubts, fears and frequent spiritual ambivalence. Yet his deliverance from this instability was not due to some Spirit-baptism but, as he records in *Grace Abounding*, on account of an awakening to the certain knowledge, generated by the Spirit, that Christ's imputed righteousness had been credited to his heavenly account.[6] Further, Bunyan admits that this period of early instability was abnormal and was the result of spiritual negligence on his part.[7] (For greater detail on this matter see chapter 6.)

The response of biblical sanctification

By 'sanctification' is meant that work resulting from regeneration and justification whereby the 'new creation [or new species] in Christ' (2 Cor. 5:17) manifests increasing holy likeness to its divine Progenitor. This sanctification, being progressive, is to be distinguished from that definitive, or declarative, sanctification which is complete at the time of the sinner's conversion (1 Peter 2:9).[8]

Ryle gives his definition as follows: 'Sanctification is that inward spiritual work which the Lord Jesus Christ works in a man by the Holy Ghost, when he calls him to be a true believer. He not only washes him from his sins in his own blood, but he also separates him from his natural love of sin and the world, puts a new principle in his heart, and makes him practically godly in life.'[9]

Ryle goes on to list twelve points to qualify his definition of sanctification. These are set out below, along with parallels taken from *The Pilgrim's Progress*.[10]

1. Sanctification is the invariable result of that vital union with Christ which true faith gives to a Christian

Having passed through the Wicket-gate and concluded his period of instruction at the House of Interpreter, in which he learns much of substance concerning Christ, Christian declares:

> Here I have seen things rare and profitable;
> Things pleasant, dreadful, things to make me stable.[11]

On leaving the Place of Deliverance, 'Christian gave three leaps for joy, and went on singing.'[12] Subsequent growth towards spiritual maturity in Christ is stimulated by frequent reflection upon his new coat (representing the imputed righteousness of Christ) and scroll (his assurance).

2. Sanctification is the outcome and inseparable consequence of regeneration

The authentic pilgrim, having been saved by Good-will (Christ), is in immediate need of the ministry of Interpreter (the Holy Spirit) and so is sent to the latter's house.

Later, in rejecting Apollyon's former dominion over him, Christian states: 'I like his [Christ's] service, his wages, his servants, his government, his company, and country, better than thine.'[13]

3. Sanctification is the only certain evidence of the indwelling of the Holy Spirit

When Christian recovers his lost roll and thrusts it into his bosom 'with joy and tears [then] how nimbly ... did he go up the rest of the hill [Difficulty]!'[14] In other words, authentic assurance through the indwelling Spirit has victorious consequences (John 15:1-5,8,12-14,26-27).

4. Sanctification is the only sure mark of God's election

When Christian arrives at the gate of the Palace Beautiful, the initial investigation (for church membership) by the porter Watchful, along with Discretion, Prudence, Piety and Charity, is intended to discover whether Christian has the marks of a true pilgrim, and specifically from 'whence he was, and whither he was going … how he got in the way … what he had seen and met with in the way … his name'.[15]

5. Sanctification is a thing that will always be seen

Discussing Talkative's lack of sanctification the pilgrims say, 'His house is as empty of religion, as the white of an egg is of savour. There is there, neither prayer, neither sign of repentance for sin.' 'He cheweth the cud, he seeketh knowledge, he cheweth upon the Word; but he divideth not the hoof, he parteth not with the way of sinners…'[16] Contrast the saintly demeanour of Christian and Faithful at Vanity Fair in the face of persecution.

6. Sanctification is a thing for which every believer is responsible

Because Talkative fails to produce evidence of personal holiness, Faithful declares: 'The proverb is true of you which is said of a whore, to wit, that she is a shame to all women; so are you a shame to all professors.'[17]

Even Christian and Hopeful are accountable for their negligence and so are disciplined when they yield to the deceit of the Flatterer.

7. Sanctification admits of growth and degrees

In the early stages of the journey Faithful appears relatively weak, yet at Vanity Fair his testimony seems stronger than that of Christian.

When Christian and Hopeful arrive at Beulah Land, we learn that '… this was beyond the Valley of the Shadow of Death, and also out of the reach of Giant Despair, neither could they from this place so much as see Doubting Castle'.[18]

8. Sanctification depends greatly on a diligent use of scriptural means

Christian is strengthened in various ways: first by the Bible in his hand, then through fellowship by means of Faithful and Hopeful, and also at the Palace Beautiful, just before his encounter with Apollyon. In particular, while there he was taken to the armoury, where '… they harnessed him from head to foot with what was proof [resistant to penetration], lest, perhaps, he should meet with assaults in the way'.[19]

9. Sanctification does not prevent a man having a great deal of inward spiritual conflict

Faithful is at one stage inclined towards the overtures of the old man Adam the First, a sin of which he eventually repents and which he bemoans, saying, 'O wretched man [that I am]!'[20]

We also recall Hopeful's initial interest in the silver mine at the Hill Lucre. He then repents of this with the declaration: 'I am sorry that I was so foolish, and am made to wonder that I am not now as Lot's wife.'[21]

10. Sanctification cannot justify, yet it pleases God

Having crossed the River of Death, Christian and Hopeful are given a royal welcome as pilgrims who have persevered, yet their entrance into the Celestial City is by certificate only.

Over the gate is the inscription: 'Blessed are they that do his commandments, that they may have right to the tree of life, and may enter in through the gates into the city' (Rev. 22:14).[22]

11. Sanctification will be absolutely necessary as a witness to our character on the Day of Judgement

The man who dreamed of the Day of Judgement at the House of Interpreter admitted with shame: 'My sins also came into my mind; and my conscience did accuse me on every side… I was not ready for it.'[23] On the other hand, as Christian and Hopeful draw near to the Celestial City, they are described as 'the men that have loved our Lord when they were in the world, and have left all for his holy name'.[24]

12. Sanctification is absolutely necessary to train and prepare us for heaven

Pastoral edification both at the Palace Beautiful and at the Delectable Mountains has contributed to the holy preparation of the pilgrims. By the time that Christian and Hopeful have reached Beulah Land and enjoyed rich fellowship there, they are overcome with a desire for heaven so intense that they cry out with longing, 'If ye find my Beloved, tell him that I am sick of love' (S. of S. 5:8).[25]

Sanctification and justification

Unlike much contemporary evangelical practice, sanctification for Bunyan is not a soft option but rather a necessary result of justification, the possibility of backsliding notwithstanding. In other words, while he was second to none in upholding the doctrine of justification by faith alone, he was equally adamant that justification did not stand alone, but rather was productive of a spiritually fruitful life. So he writes, 'Now, he that shall not only see, but receive, not only know, but embrace the Son of God, to be justified by him, cannot but bring forth good works, because Christ who is now received and embraced by faith, leavens and seasons the spirit of this sinner … so then the soul being seasoned, it seasoneth the body; and the body and soul, the life and conversation... For the true beholding of Jesus to justification and life, changes from glory to glory (2 Cor. 3:18).'[26]

In other words, justification and its exaltation of free grace are the ground, substance and root from which sanctification blossoms and bears fruit. Now the root is not the fruit, and the fruit does not establish the root, though the root must give rise to fruit; therefore the root that does not produce fruit is dead (James 2:26), while fruit that does not come from the root is counterfeit. This truth permeates the whole of *The Pilgrim's Progress*. Consider four examples:

- In explaining to Talkative what are the indications of a true work of grace in the heart, Faithful comments: 'Now according to the strength or weakness of his [the true believer's] faith in his Saviour, so is his joy and peace, so is his love to holiness, so are his desires to know him more, and also to serve him in this world.'[27]
- When Formalist and Hypocrisy jeer at Christian's strange coat, he makes his defence as follows: '[It is] as you say, to cover my nakedness with. And I take it as a token of his kindness to me; for I had nothing but rags before. And, besides, thus I comfort myself as I go.'[28]
- In Hopeful's testimony of his conversion, shared with Christian, he tells how he finally came to understand that 'I must look for righteousness in his [Christ's] person, and for satisfaction for my sins in his blood.' The result was that 'It made me love a holy life, and long to do something for the honour and glory of the name of the Lord Jesus; yea, I thought that had I now a thousand gallons of blood in my body, I could spill it all for the sake of the Lord Jesus.'[29]
- When Ignorance disputes the very nature of the gospel itself, Christian solemnly tells him, 'Ignorant thou art of what justifying righteousness is, and as ignorant how to secure thy soul, through the faith of it, from the heavy

wrath of God. Yea, thou also art ignorant of the true effects of saving faith in this righteousness of Christ, which is, to bow and win over the heart to God in Christ, to love his name, his Word, ways, and people, and not as thou ignorantly imaginest.'[30]

Sanctification and the means of grace

For those of God's elect who have been regenerated and judicially reconciled to God through faith in Christ's imputed righteousness, there are made available means of grace whereby the new pilgrim is enabled to traverse this earthly wilderness safely (1 Cor. 5:9-10). Indeed it is the journeying saint's responsibility to use these means, though some do more so than others. Little-faith neglects his provisions and progresses very slowly as a spiritual hypochondriac. On the other hand, Great-grace uses well and valiantly the equipment at his disposal, notwithstanding his scars. So Ryle exhorts: 'Our God is a God who works by means, and he will never bless the soul of that man who pretends to be so high and spiritual that he can get on without them.'[31]

Perspective

By its very nature, pilgrimage is governed by departure, transition and arrival. At any point on this continuum the degree of progress may be assessed by both a retrospective and prospective review of the journey; to do so is to gain a sense of encouragement, direction and hope. So when Christian is challenged by Timorous and Mistrust to return to the City of Destruction on account of imminent danger, he reviews what is both behind him and ahead, and comes to the following conclusion: 'To go back is nothing but death; to go forward is fear of death, and life everlasting beyond it. I will yet go forward.'[32]

1. Retrospective views of the journey

On several occasions the major pilgrims review their progress thus far, just as Israel did (Ps. 106:6-46; 1 Sam. 7:12), for the purposes of mutual edification and being strengthened by the remembrance of God's keeping grace.

- At the Palace Beautiful Christian is required to review his travels thus far as a means of indicating his status as a as a legitimate pilgrim.
- When Christian catches up with Faithful they both reminisce concerning their individual experiences. These are to some extent related to the strengths and weaknesses of each.
- While crossing the Enchanted Ground, the pilgrims successfully combat drowsiness when Hopeful shares his testimony with Christian. This in fact amounts to a comprehensive review of the gospel, and this survey of the life of another pilgrim becomes instructive, by way of contrast with the experience of Christian, and at the same time encouraging.

2. Prospective assessments of the journey

Conversation and glimpses of future glory are major incentives for perseverance. Arrival will undoubtedly be better than anticipation, for we shall then 'know fully just as [we] have been fully known' (1 Cor. 13:12), and 'We shall see him just as he is' (1 John 3:2).

- Even before Christian is converted, he is able to share his enthusiasm with Pliable concerning 'an endless kingdom to be inhabited and eternal life to be given us; there are crowns of glory to be given us, and garments that will make us shine like the sun in the firmament of heaven.'[33]

• At the Palace Beautiful, Christian is taken to the roof-top, from where he gains a view of Immanuel's Land. He is told that, with the help of the shepherds resident there, he will be able to gain a distant sighting of the gate of the Celestial City. Then we read that, inspired by this future prospect, 'Now,' with renewed enthusiasm, 'he bethought himself of setting forward.'[34]

• At the conclusion of their time spent with the shep-herds, Christian and Hopeful are taken to the top of the hill called Clear and there, through a telescope, even though the view is blurred because their hands are trem-bling, they are able to make out the gate and something of the glory of the Celestial City. Encouraged by the sight, they immediately set forth once again, singing and with hope in their hearts.

• In the land of Beulah pilgrims obtain a more perfect view of the Celestial City and its radiant glory which makes them weak and faint with longing to arrive there. The increasing brilliance becomes 'so extremely glorious' that they cannot bear to look at it except through a dark-ened glass, or a veil (2 Cor. 3:18).[35] They seem oblivious of the River of Death which lies between and which they must soon cross.

The truth of God

This is imparted by a variety of means, all of which communi-cate the truth of Scripture. Again, the pilgrim is responsible for making use of the array of help available to him.

- Christian is first described as a man with 'a book in his hand'[36] — that is, the Bible or the Word of God. Its initial message — which is an essential preparation for the subsequent revelation of God's grace in the gospel — is one of conviction of sin and the warning of imminent judgement.
- When Christian asks Evangelist to tell him the way of escape, he is given a parchment roll on which is written: 'Fly from the wrath to come (Matt. 3:7).'[37]
- On meeting Formalist and Hypocrisy, Christian distinguishes between his own walking according to 'the rule of my Master' and their following after 'laws and ordinances' (Eph. 2:15; Col. 2:14).[38] Under the New Covenant, Christian is 'under the law of Christ' (1 Cor. 9:21) and not subject to the law of Moses (Rom. 7:1-4).
- At the House of Interpreter, Christian receives much illumination concerning vital doctrine. The instruction here is mediated by the Holy Spirit since his particular ministry is that of guiding pilgrims 'into all the truth' (John 16:13).
- In the armoury at the Palace Beautiful, Christian is equipped with the 'whole armour of God' and 'the sword of the Spirit, which is the word of God'.[39] In other words, the Palace Beautiful, or faithful local church, is to teach Christian how to use that book in his hand skilfully (Eph. 6:17) lest he meet with attacks from Apollyon!
- By the time Christian is incarcerated in Doubting Castle he has hidden much of the Word of God in his heart (Ps. 119:11). However, personal interest causes him to be forgetful — that is, until fellowship on the Lord's Day morning brings the promises of God to his consciousness with such freshness and vigour that he is set free from captivity to despair.

Church fellowship

For Bunyan personally, the fellowship of the local nonconformist church in Bedford had been of immense spiritual help and
stimulation. Pastor John Gifford had given him much individual
attention. Many of his portrayals of this encouragement in *The
Pilgrim's Progress* overlap so that they collectively represent the
church as an embassy of heaven upon earth:

- Evangelist represents just one facet of the pastoral office. He points people to Christ, delivers them from religious charlatans such as Mr Worldly-Wiseman and helps
new converts along by means of encouragement and
warning.
- Help, who rescues Christian at the Slough of Despond, is a further portrayal of that pastoral nurture which
Bunyan received from Pastor Gifford when, as he studied
the Scriptures, he increasingly wrestled with his own corrupt and sinful nature.
- The Palace Beautiful is, or ought to be, one of the
principal vehicles of grace for weary pilgrims who are under attack. It provides strengthening fellowship in the truth
about Christ, communion around the table of Christ, rest
in the grace of Christ, weaponry to fight for Christ and a
vision of the consummated kingdom of Christ.
- At the Delectable Mountains we have yet another representation of the faithful nonconformist church, except
that even greater emphasis is placed on the importance of
consecrated shepherding by means of the eldership ministry of Knowledge, Experience, Watchful and Sincere.
- Fellowship is of special importance when believers
meet together on the Lord's Day. This is emphasized by
Christian and Hopeful's release from Doubting Castle on
Sunday morning, the day of resurrection and church life,
the day of feasting on the promises of God, the day when

the light of truth casts out the darkness of doubt and despair accumulated during the preceding week.

Miscellaneous means

These all go to prove just how much provision of grace there is for pilgrims. These means are more than sufficient to deliver them from the snares and hellish devices of Satan. Furthermore, they are scattered throughout the journey to meet varying needs according to individual strengths and weaknesses.

• Help is also an agent of prevenient grace — that is, grace meted out to sinners who struggle towards Christ before conversion. However, Faithful was not similarly troubled at this juncture, for he perceived the provision of stepping stones, or 'wholesome instructions', that enabled him to cross this mire.

• Angels, or messengers, make frequent appearances, whether assisting Christian, as, for example, at the Place of Deliverance, or administering discipline, as when Christian and Hopeful foolishly allow themselves to be snared by the Flatterer. Further they encourage true pilgrims at the River of Death and escort them to the very gates of heaven.

• The spring at the foot of the hill Difficulty is most strategically placed, though not all ascending pilgrims are wise enough to drink there. As a result of Faithful's failure to do so, he becomes inclined to heed the carnal proposal of the old man Adam the First, halfway up the hill, and reaps much pain through his neglect.

• The arbour halfway up the hill Difficulty is a legitimate place for the refreshment of weary climbers, though it does at the same time test the flesh concerning indulgence. Hence, due to carnality, at this very place Faithful is mercilessly beaten by the accusatory Moses until rescued by Christ.

• The tokens of 'a loaf of bread, a bottle of wine, and a cluster of raisins'[40] supplied by the Palace Beautiful are obviously reflective of imagery connected with the Lord's Supper; they are to be carried by pilgrims since they represent that grace which is supplied during their ongoing travels, as they recall Christ's atoning merits.

• As Christian gingerly wends his way through the Valley of the Shadow of Death, he finds that his usual weapons of warfare are ineffective. Hence, when he finds himself tormented by the devil, he resorts to the instrument of 'All-prayer' (cf. Eph. 6:18).

• Memorials serve as warnings designed to deliver pilgrims from situations where they might easily be led astray. One such example is the monument to Lot's wife, which served as a deterrent from covetousness at the Silver Mine at the hill Lucre. Christian and Hopeful set up a similar pillar of warning at the stile leading to By-path Meadow.

Sanctification and the experience of grace

In common with other Puritans, Bunyan believed that authentic Christian experience was generated by the knowledge of Christian truth. J. I. Packer comments: 'The starting point was their certainty that the mind must be instructed and enlightened before faith and obedience become possible. All the Puritans regarded religious feeling and pious emotion without knowledge as worse than useless. Only when the truth was being felt was emotion in any way desirable.'[41] Therefore, when we come to *The Pilgrim's Progress*, it is obvious that 'truth within a fable', as Bunyan describes it, is very prominent as the ground of Christian's hope at all stages along the way. As a consequence this revelation is productive of profound experiences that are especially rooted in the grace of God.

Consider just one of many instances in *Grace Abounding* where the truth of the grace of God in Christ causes the author to burst into praise: 'Now I saw Christ Jesus was looked on of God, and should also be looked on by us as that common or publick person, in whom all the whole body of his elect are always to be considered and reckoned; that we fulfilled the law by him, died by him, rose from the dead by him, got the victory over sin, death, the devil, and hell, by him. Ah, these blessed considerations and scriptures, with many others of like nature, were in those days made to spangle in [sparkle before] mine eyes, so that I have cause to say, "Praise ye the Lord. Praise God in his sanctuary: praise him in the firmament of his power. Praise him for his mighty acts: praise him according to his excellent greatness" (Ps. 150:1-2).'[42] Here Bunyan vibrantly personifies sanctification through the contemplation and experience of grace.

Experience in emotion

Of all the emotions expressed in *The Pilgrim's Progress* it is that which is stimulated by the grace of God in the gospel that is the most passionate and pervasive. This truth is not to be comprehended merely in cerebral and matter-of-fact terms, but rather is presented as that which melts hardened souls and persuades them to be forever debtors to grace. While sin is shown to be exceedingly sinful, grace and mercy are heralded as being more abundant and powerful (Rom. 5:20-21). When this realization dawns upon Bunyan he is thrilled and enraptured. He portrays this ardent emotion in several scenes of his allegory:

- At the Place of Deliverance, with tears streaming down his face on account of a sudden surge of assurance,

Christian ponders with astonishment: 'Must here be the beginning of my bliss?'[43]

• Hopeful is similarly moved when the gospel is at last revealed to him: 'Now was my heart full of joy, mine eyes full of tears, and mine affections running over with love to the name, people, and ways of Jesus Christ.'[44]

Here is emotion in its rightful place. Here is evident sanctification.

Experience in singing

The first occasion when we find Christian singing is at the Place of Deliverance. Up to the time of his entry at the Wicket-gate he had little to sing about. But now we read:

Then Christian gave three leaps for joy, and went on singing —

'... Blest cross! blest sepulchre! blest rather be
The man that there was put to shame for me!'[45]

Following the martyrdom of Faithful, Christian can still rejoice as he intones:

Sing, Faithful, sing, and let thy name survive;
For, though they kill'd thee, thou art yet alive.[46]

Later, while being refreshed at the River of the Water of Life, both Christian and Hopeful sing in chorus:

The meadows green, besides their fragrant smell,
Yield dainties for them: and he that can tell
What pleasant fruit, yea, leaves, these trees do yield,
Will soon sell all, that he may buy this field.[47]

A further instance of this tendency on the part of genuine pilgrims to break into song can be found in the shepherd boy in Part Two who, although very poor in material terms, knows more of Heart's-ease than many who are richly clad and happily sings:

He that is down, needs fear no fall,
He that is low, no pride:
He that is humble, ever shall
Have God to be his guide.[48]

So for Bunyan, the child of God has a new song to sing (Ps. 40:1-3), and such spontaneous worship is just one more evidence of sanctification.

Experience in instruction

For Bunyan, the idea of any pilgrim shunning teaching in a local church was characteristic, not of a weak believer, but rather of one who was related to Ignorance. A genuine pilgrim would delight in the food of God's sanctifying truth (Matt. 4:4; 1 Peter 2:1-2).

So at the House of Interpreter we observe Christian earnestly seeking to understand and absorb the truth which the Holy Spirit imparts. He is deeply interested in asking questions and he responds with eager and thoughtful comment. When he sees the valiant man who thrusts his way into the stately palace, he seems readily to identify himself with this person as he smiles and asserts: 'I think verily I know the meaning of this.'[49] The despairing man in the iron cage causes Christian to exclaim: 'This is fearful! God help me to watch and be sober, and to pray that I may shun the cause of this man's misery!'[50] Thus he concludes that all seven scenes have put him in 'hope and fear':

Here I have seen things rare and profitable;
Things pleasant, dreadful, things to make me stable
In what I have begun to take in hand;
Then let me think on them, and understand.[51]

At the Palace Beautiful Christian is delighted to receive substantial further instruction and by this means he is encouraged to press forward. When Evangelist reappears, Christian seeks yet more teaching from him. Likewise the shepherds impart further truth which Christian and Hopeful gladly recommend to others:

Come to the Shepherds, then, if you would see
Things deep, things hid, and that mysterious be.[52]

Experience in discipline

When the narrow way becomes rough to the feet of Christian and Hopeful — obviously by the design of the Lord of the way — this testing causes them to murmur and grumble, as was the case with Israel in the wilderness (Num. 21:4-5). Thus it is not surprising that the stile leading to By-Path Meadow and Doubting Castle should appear at this point. The pilgrims' resultant imprisonment in the castle is discipline built into their act of rebellion. As they are to learn from the shepherds at the Delectable Mountains, it is only grace that delivers them from their folly. However, this whole incident is full of painful experiences reflective of Bunyan's own travail of soul. Yet the pilgrims become wiser for their trouble and thoughtfully take the initiative in warning others of lurking danger.

In a similar vein, Christian and Hopeful are subject to more direct discipline when they fall an easy prey to the Flatterer, and that in the face of warning from the shepherds. As a result, they lie 'bewailing themselves'[53] until rescued by an angel with a disciplinary whip in his hand. So the pilgrims submit to painful chastisement, after which, we read, they 'thanked him [the angel] for all his kindness, and went softly along the right way, singing'.[54] This too was a profitable incident for their progressive sanctification.

Experience in conflict

Immediately after moving on from the Place of Deliverance, the as yet naïve Christian is confronted with the indifference of Simple, Sloth and Presumption, and then with the illegitimacy of Formalist and Hypocrisy. Thus he proceeds 'sighingly and sometimes comfortable; also he would be often reading in the roll that one of the Shining Ones gave him, by which he was refreshed'.[55] Christian is now no longer naïve; he has advanced in his understanding of the counterfeit religious world about him and consequently has increased in sanctification.

However, when he encounters Apollyon, he learns about a different type of conflict. Residence at the Palace Beautiful has set him apart in a preparatory sense, but actual experience in spiritual warfare will substantially increase his sanctification, or growth in holiness. Following the initial verbal encounter, the battle becomes more bloody and exhausting; Christian's own strength gradually fails until he seems all but defeated; but sovereign grace enables him to retrieve his lost sword. When Apollyon retreats, he leaves Christian standing his ground and more sanctified as a result of this harrowing experience.

When Christian subsequently enters the Valley of the Shadow of Death, we read that he 'went on his way, but still with his sword drawn in his hand [and not in its scabbard as before]; for fear lest he should be assaulted'.[56] Here the conflict changes in character yet again. In this gloomy place the assaults are more subtle and difficult to distinguish from one's own thought-processes. The redeemed spirit is tormented by the devil; so Christian resorts to the more appropriate weapon of 'All-prayer' (Eph. 6:18). Eventually relief is anticipated when the resolute voice of Faithful is heard to be just ahead. So Christian's exit from this valley finds him to be a far more mature, though still very imperfect, pilgrim, and one who has been sanctified through the instrumentality of conflict.

Sanctification through the moral law

Be well acquainted with the Word, and with the general rules of holiness; to wit, with the moral law; the want of this is a cause of much unholiness of conversation. Let then the law be with thee to love it, and do it in the spirit of the gospel, that thou be not unfruitful in thy life. Let the law, I say, be with thee, not as it comes from Moses, but from Christ; for though thou art set free from the law as a covenant of life, yet thou still art under the law to Christ.

John Bunyan
A Holy Life the Beauty of Christianity,
Works, vol. II, p. 539

8.
Law and grace in
The Pilgrim's Progress

'Great sins do draw out
great grace; and where
guilt is most terrible and
fierce there the mercy
of God in Christ, when
showed to the soul,
appears most high and
mighty...'

(John Bunyan).

8.

Law and grace in
The Pilgrim's Progress

IT is common today, as, indeed, it has always been the case, for great saints to be claimed as supporters of a particular doctrinal cause. This is especially so amongst conservative evangelical Christians with regard to mustering the agreement of, say, Martin Luther, John Calvin, or more recently C. H. Spurgeon. It is sometimes claimed that while these men have not expressly stated their commitment to such-and-such a position, yet it is obviously implied in related matters. Spurgeon is a case in point since he has been claimed as a premillennialist, postmillennialist and amillennialist — and that in spite of the fact that he specifically aligned himself with historic premillennialism in general.[1]

A similar case is the question of John Bunyan and his commitment to the relationship between law and grace, and especially as it concerns certain Calvinistic emphases. Everyone wants John Bunyan on their side, and it may not be so pleasant to discover that he does not in fact hold to one's own preferred position. And in any case, as Richard Greaves confirms, he is not the sort of person who fits neatly into certain defined categories.[2] For instance some claim, in agreement with Greaves, and they are by far in the majority, that Bunyan steered very close to antinomianism, while others do not.[3] Certainly, like Paul, no one has ever charged him with being a legalist! Of course in this realm, as we shall see, it often becomes a matter of definitions.

Bunyan's views on law and grace

Influences concerning Bunyan's thought

At the outset, it needs to be reiterated once again that Bunyan's dominant emphasis owes more to Martin Luther than to John Calvin and the Westminster divines, whose writings were so influential in England during Bunyan's lifetime. He was a friend of both John Owen[4] of the Westminster fraternal and William Dell,[5] who was decidedly not aligned with all those who met at Westminster. Michael Mullett is correct when he writes, 'Though the church he joined was suffused with Calvinist thinking, Bunyan had also been strongly influenced by Luther, for whom justifying faith was more important than election and for whom predestination was not as explicitly salient as it became for the Calvinist school, especially in England.'[6]

Development in Bunyan's thought

In the lives of many notable men of God, it is noticeable that, over the course of a ministry of considerable length, a progress and maturity of thought develops, sometimes even leading to a change of opinion; otherwise we are forced to conclude that views have been expressed that contradict one another. Now where such a change is perceived to have taken place, this claim must be based upon solid evidence; otherwise the charge could well be levelled that an author's opinions are being twisted to suit a preconceived notion. Yet in the case of Bunyan, particularly with regard to the subject at hand, there does appear to be conclusive evidence of a change of opinion over the thirty-two-year period from the time of his first published writing in 1656, *Some Gospel Truths Opened, According to the Scriptures*, until his death in 1688. A clear case in point can be seen in the following paragraphs.

1. Teaching in *The Doctrine of the Law and Grace Unfolded*, published in 1659

Here Bunyan gives the most explicit exposition of his teaching with relation to the covenant. He emphasizes what he claims are the two essential covenants, the covenant of works and the covenant of grace, using these terms frequently, although nowhere else does he do so in such a relentless way. Concerning the covenant of works, he writes, 'The covenant of works or the law, here spoken of, is the law delivered upon Mount Sinai to Moses, in two tables of stone.'[7]

However, this point of origination is then qualified: 'But though this law was delivered to Moses from the hands of angels in two tables of stone, on Mount Sinai, yet this was not the first appearing of this law to man; but even this in substance, though possibly not so openly, was given to the first man, Adam, in the garden of Eden, in these words, "And the Lord God commanded the man saying, 'Of every tree in the garden thou mayest freely eat: but of the tree of the knowledge of good and evil, thou shalt not eat of it; for in the day that thou eatest thereof thou shalt surely die'" (Gen. 2:16-17). Which commandment then given to Adam did contain in it a forbidding to do any of those things that was and is accounted evil, although at that time it did not appear so plainly, in so many particular heads, as it did when it was again delivered on Mount Sinai; but yet the very same.'[8]

Then follows proof of this assertion, as he lists instances where each of the Ten Commandments were upheld or broken, from creation up to the giving of the law at Mount Sinai, involving, for example, Pharaoh, Jacob, Abimelech, Ham, Cain, the Sodomites, etc. In support of the teaching that the sabbath, or the Fourth Commandment, was given prior to the giving of the law at Mount Sinai, Bunyan writes, 'And we find the Lord rebuking his people for the breach of the fourth commandment (Exod. 16:27-29)'[9] — that is, just prior to their arrival at Mount Sinai.

2. Teaching in *Questions about the Nature and Perpetuity of the Seventh-Day Sabbath*, published in 1685

To begin with, it is interesting that while the terms 'law' and 'grace' are frequently used in this polemic directed against Seventh-Day Baptists, especially the former, there is no mention of the covenant of works, and the covenant of grace is only referred to once. The frequently used terms are 'the ministration of death/Sinai/condemnation' and 'the ministration of the Spirit/gospel/righteousness,' obviously drawing upon 2 Corinthians 3:7-11.

However, there appears to be a definite change with regard to the question of the Mosaic law having any antecedents back to Adam. It must be said that in the most absolute and repeated terms, the Fourth Commandment is described as being strictly ordained for Israel, the time of that endowment being the commencement of the wilderness wanderings. There is not one sentence that allows any latitude here.

Consider the following: 'Now as to the imposing of a seventh day sabbath upon men from Adam to Moses, of that we find nothing in holy writ either from precept or example... But of this [sabbath] you see we read nothing, either by positive law, or countenanced example, or any other way, but rather the flat contrary; to whit, that Moses had the knowledge of it first from heaven, not by tradition... The seventh day sabbath therefore was not from paradise, nor from nature, nor from the fathers, but from the wilderness, and from Sinai... What can be more plain ... that the seventh day sabbath, as such, was given to Israel, to Israel *only* [Bunyan's emphasis]; and that the Gentiles, as such, were not concerned therein!'[10]

It is readily acknowledged that Bunyan's vigorous defence of Sunday as the Christian's Lord's Day, or the Christian holy day, as he calls it, which has no continuity with the abolished Jewish Sabbath, takes on a rigid form which others, of a similar mind, would not fully endorse. For instance, he writes that 'Were I in Turkey with a church of Jesus Christ, I would keep the first day of the week to God, and for the edification of his people: and would also preach the word to the infidels on their sabbath day, which is our Friday.'[11]

What, then, is the explanation of this evident change of opinion? Most likely it is the length of time (twenty-six years) separating the composition of these writings — that is, between 1659 and 1685. Bunyan's understanding of the period from Adam to Moses has obviously modified. Certainly he seems to have come to the conclusion that the Fourth Commandment was not a creation ordinance. And this being the case, the publication date of 1678 for *The Pilgrim's Progress* should be kept in mind as we now consider the role of law and grace in its teaching.

The role of the law in *The Pilgrim's Progress*

When we recall the significance of Luther's influence upon Bunyan, it is not difficult to appreciate the Bedford preacher's indebtedness to the German Reformer concerning the distinction between law and gospel. It is here that Bunyan obtains his essential understanding of two covenants that are virtually identical with the Mosaic and new covenants.

It is well to remember that, as Greaves points out, 'Luther was in no sense even remotely a covenant theologian. Furthermore, Luther's pronouncements on law and grace in his commentary on *Galatians* were made predominantly in the context of the doctrine of justification rather than on the place of the law in the life of a justified believer. Yet it seems more than coincidence that Bunyan's first treatise of theological importance, published as early as 1659, should be entitled *The Doctrine of the Law and Grace Unfolded*, echoing as it did the theme of Luther's commentary.'[12] In other words, the substance of Bunyan's teaching on law and grace was derived more from Luther, even though it was clothed with a certain limited covenantal dress that was fashionable in Puritan conversation in the seventeenth century.

The role of the law illustrated in *The Pilgrim's Progress*

The role of the law, or the Ten Commandments, here to a large extent reflects Bunyan's overall views, which seem to have developed in a direction away from the distinctively Puritan emphasis in England, and one that at times led to his being charged with antinomianism by Richard Baxter, as we have already noticed. That is not to say that Bunyan totally discarded the law as being unnecessary for the child of God, but it is to indicate that in his opinion any such use, governed by Christian liberty, paled before the sanctifying revelation of the incarnate righteousness of God through his blessed Son.

1. The stimulus of Christian's growing burden

At the commencement of *The Pilgrim's Progress,* we discover that Christian already has a book in his hand and an increasingly heavy burden on his back — in other words, the Bible in his hand is stimulating his guilt to the point where it is crushing him. But what part of the Bible is he reading? Surely it is not only the Ten Commandments, but rather that more comprehensive revelation of the demands of God's perfect righteousness and his pronouncement of judgement on sinners, discovered in the totality of both the Old and New Testaments (cf. Rom. 3:19-20 where, in context, 'law' refers to the whole of the Old Testament).

In Christian's lament, 'What shall I do to be saved?' there is the inference that he finds himself in similar circumstances to those portrayed in Acts 2:36-37 and 16:30-32. That is, Bunyan has in mind the means by which the Jews at Pentecost and the Philippian jailer were convicted: for instance, Peter's use of the Old Testament to bring about such conviction (Acts 2:17-21,25-28,30,34-35). In *The Doctrine of the Law and Grace Unfolded*, Bunyan refers to these two incidents to explain the need of sinners to be convicted, or made dead to their own righteousness, by means of the old covenant, the covenant of condemning law.[13]

We know that later, when Faithful eventually heeds Christian's warning to escape from the City of Destruction, Moses (representing the law's ministry of condemnation) threatens to burn down his house if he does not flee.[14] So the pilgrims experience the awakening and accusatory ministry of the law of God in its broadest sense.

2. The threatenings of Mount Sinai

When Mr Worldly-Wiseman counsels Christian to lose his burden at the village of Morality, just beyond the 'high hill', he is in fact, as a Latitudinarian minister of a false gospel of works, exhorting the seeking pilgrim to obtain the release of his burden by means of the fulfilment of the law given at Mount Sinai. The recommendation of Mr Worldly-Wiseman seems so plausible, so attainable, while in fact it is utterly impossible. For Christian to scale the 'high hill' successfully would require that perfect, total and everlasting obedience to the law which the infinitely holy God requires. So the hill thunders, 'As many as are of the works of the Law, are under the curse; for it is written, Cursed is every one that continueth not in all things which are written in the Book of the Law to do them (Gal. 3:10).'[15]

This scene also conveys Bunyan's belief that the proclamation of the gospel presupposes a necessary revelation of God's
righteous judgement of sin before the saving character of his
righteousness is made known. So he writes, 'If thou wouldst
know the authority and power of the gospel, labour first to know
the power and authority of the law... That man that doth not
know the law doth not know in deed and truth that he is a
sinner; and that man that doth not know he is a sinner, doth not
know savingly that there is a Saviour... If thou wouldst, then,
wash thy face clean, first take a glass [mirror] and see where it is
dirty.'[16]

3. Law and grace at the House of Interpreter

In the connected sequence of events in *The Pilgrim's Progress*,
the scene of the dusty room that is swept clean occurs shortly
after Christian has entered through the Wicket-gate and thus
has become an authentic child of God. Hence, in the instruction
that he receives through the ministry of Interpreter (that is, the
Holy Spirit), the second room that he is shown is the one which
represents 'the heart of a man that was never sanctified by the
sweet grace of the gospel',[17] and thus not the heart of a child of
God. Here the contrasting roles of the law and the gospel, as
represented by Moses and Christ, are to be expounded. For
Bunyan, like Luther, this is a vital distinction that needs to be
firmly grasped for the purpose of new pilgrims making satisfactory, sanctified progress. Why is this so? Not because the law is
a means of sanctifying grace for the new believer, but rather
because its recommendation by misguided zealots, such as Mr
Worldly-Wiseman, may delude the new child of God into
believing that the law will assist him in his journeying and
growth in grace.

Thus Bunyan concludes that 'The law, instead of cleansing
the heart (by its working) from sin, doth revive, put strength
into, and increase it in the soul, even as it doth discover and
forbid it, for it doth not give power to subdue (Rom. 5:20; 7:6;

1 Cor. 15:56).'[18] Here the work of the law is described in terms of its ordained purpose, that is the conviction of an unconverted heart. This is a pre-conversion ministry of arousal and conviction, not a post-conversion ministry of assistance in Christian growth.

Then, following the man who sweeps the dusty room, but only succeeds in stirring up the dirt even more, there comes the gospel messenger, represented by the young woman who sprinkles water and thus subdues the inward corruption and facilitates cleansing. The point for Bunyan here is *not* that the already burdened pilgrim needs the sin-arousing influence of the law. Rather, as the allegorist well knows, the presence of remaining sin in the life of a new believer can be both a shocking and despairing discovery, especially through the indwelling ministry of the Holy Spirit, in conjunction with the Word of God, who both convicts and cleanses. Hence, the question arises as to *how* sin in the pilgrim is to be dealt with. For Bunyan, it is gospel grace alone that subdues and keeps sinful passions under control.

This truth is further illustrated when, in the fourth scene at the House of Interpreter, the pilgrim's heart is kept ablaze through Christ's continual supply of the oil of grace.[19]

George Offor appreciates this emphasis upon gospel sanctification when he quotes George Cheever as follows: 'Christian well knew this in his own deep experience; for the burden of sin was on him still, and sorely did he feel it while the Interpreter was making this explanation; and had it not been for his remembrance of the warning of the Man at the gate he would certainly have besought the Interpreter to take off his burden. The Law could not take it off; he had tried that; and grace had not yet removed it, so he was forced to be quiet and to wait patiently. But when the damsel came and sprinkled the floor and laid the dust, and then the parlour was swept so easily, there were the sweet influences of the Gospel imaged; there was divine grace distilling as the dew, there was the gentle voice of Christ hushing the storm; there were the corruptions of the heart, which the Law had but roused into action, yielding unto the power of Christ; and there was the soul made clean and fit for the King of glory to inhabit. Indeed this was a most instructive emblem. Oh that my heart might be thus cleansed, thought Christian, and then I verily believe I could bear my burden with great ease to the end of my pilgrimage, but I have had enough of that fierce sweeper, the Law. The Lord deliver me from his besom [broom]!'[20]

4. Moses' attack upon Faithful

When Christian joins in fellowship with Faithful, this new companion recalls his own distinctive experiences. Following the carnal propositioning of Madam Wanton, another challenge to his flesh came in his encounter, at the foot of the hill Difficulty, with old Adam the First. His offer of fleshly comfort and security, including marriage to his three daughters, Lust of the Flesh, Lust of the Eyes and the Pride of Life, was sufficiently tempting for Faithful to confess, 'Why, at first, I found myself somewhat inclinable to go with the man, for I thought he spake very fair.' Now even though he eventually repudiates these overtures (2 Tim. 2:22), as a result of his refusal old Adam the First is aroused to enmity that leads him not only to pinch Faithful until it hurts, but also to threaten 'that he would send such a one after me, that should make my way bitter to my soul'.

So soon afterwards Faithful is attacked by Moses, who as the embodiment of the law, repeatedly strikes the guilty pilgrim. To Faithful's cries for mercy, he responds pitilessly: 'I know not how to show mercy.' It is only when the man with the nail-prints in his hands comes along, the pilgrim's Lord, that Moses is beaten off.[21]

In a manner reminiscent of the previous scene at the House of Interpreter, Moses once again acts like a hound ferreting out unrighteousness, responding at the merest whiff of sin. And once he catches the guilty sinner, like a dog having caught its prey, he endeavours to shake the captive to death. Is Faithful guilty? Yes, since for a time he entertained a hankering after old Adam the First's proposal. That was all it needed for Moses to pursue his quarry. But Christ, in confronting Moses' 'ministry of death ... [his] ministry of condemnation,' beats him off by means of his 'ministry of the Spirit ... [his] ministry of [saving] righteousness' (2 Cor. 3:7-9).

Thus Bunyan warns in *The Heavenly Footman*, 'I will assure you, the devil is nimble, he can run apace, he is light of foot, he hath overtaken many, he hath turned up their heels, and hath given them an everlasting fall. Also the law, that can shoot a great way, have a care thou keep out of the reach of those great guns, the ten commandments.'[22]

The role of the law indicated in other works

I. *The Doctrine of the Law and Grace Unfolded*

Reference has already been made to this early work. But one quotation from it will help to illustrate Bunyan's understanding of the role of the law in relation to the unbeliever: 'The new covenant [grace] promiseth thee a new heart ... but the old covenant [law] promiseth none ... [the new covenant promiseth] a new spirit, but the old covenant promiseth none (Ezek. 36:26). The new covenant conveyeth faith, but the old one conveyeth none (Gal. 3). Through the new covenant the love of God is conveyed into the heart; but through the old covenant there is conveyed none of it savingly through Jesus Christ (Rom. 5). The new covenant doth not only give a promise of life, but also with that the assurance of life, but the old one giveth none; the old covenant wrought wrath in us and to us, but the new one worketh love (Rom. 4:15; Gal. 5:6).'[23]

2. Of the Law and a Christian

This late work, published posthumously in 1692, was discovered in a broadsheet format which Offor suggests was probably designed, as was then the popular mode, to be 'posted against a wall, or framed and hung up in a room',[24] for ready consumption. Though brief, occupying just over one page in Offor's edition, it presents us with the most mature expression of Bunyan's understanding of the role of the law in the life of a Christian.

Bunyan sees a contrast between the first giving of the law, in Exodus 19:16-20, where God revealed himself with terror and severity, and the second giving of the law, in Exodus 34:1-8 where God revealed himself as 'merciful, gracious, longsuffering, and abundant in goodness and truth, keeping mercy for thousands, forgiving iniquity, transgressions and sins'. Thus he expounds: 'My meaning is, when this law with its thundering threatenings doth attempt to lay hold on my conscience, shut it out with a promise of grace; cry, the inn is took up already, the Lord Jesus is here entertained, and here is no room for the law. Indeed if it will be content with being my informer, and so lovingly leave off to judge me [like the second giving of the law]; I will be content, it shall be in my sight, I will also delight therein; but otherwise, I being now made upright without it, and that too with that righteousness, which this law speaks well of and approveth; I may not, will not, cannot, dare not make it my saviour and judge, nor suffer it to set up its government in my conscience; for by so doing I fall from grace, and Christ Jesus doth profit me nothing (Gal. 5:1-5)... [The] Christian hath now nothing to do with the law, as it thundereth and burneth on Sinai, or as it bindeth the conscience to wrath and the displeasure of God for sin; for from its thus appearing, it is freed by faith in Christ. Yet it is to have regard thereto, and is to count it holy, just and good (Rom. 7:12); which that it may do, it is always whenever it seeth or regards it, to remember that he who giveth it to us is "merciful, and gracious, longsuffering, and abundant in goodness and truth," etc. (Exod. 34:6).'[25]

To sum up, Bunyan does not discard the law in a total sense. But he rejects the law as a necessary judge of the conscience, as a kind of additional system required by the Christian (Rom. 7:1-4). However, insofar as the ministry of the law essentially reveals the good character of God, like the second revelation of the law to Moses, then it is profitable.

The reign of grace in *The Pilgrim's Progress*

In *The Pilgrim's Progress*, as in Bunyan's works in general, the subject of 'saving grace' and its resultant effects upon the life of a progressing pilgrim is a topic of exquisite and supreme delight to his soul. And the Bedford preacher should be given his due here in acknowledging his faithfulness in according to grace a position of similar dominance to that which it occupies in the writings of Luther and the apostle Paul.

For example, he exults in *Saved By Grace*: 'O, when a God of grace is upon a throne of grace, and a poor sinner stands by and begs for grace, and that in the name of a gracious Christ, in and by the help of the Spirit of grace, can it be otherwise but such a sinner must obtain mercy and grace to help in time of need?'[26]

Grace illustrated in *The Pilgrim's Progress*

Whereas so many of Bunyan's works explicitly extol the saving and reigning grace of God, *The Pilgrim's Progress*, although in no way diminishing this emphasis, cloaks it with the allegorical style. Thus it has somewhat to be unveiled, by means of a more analytical and encompassing investigation.

1. The grace of God in the gospel

Christian's original name as a citizen in the City of Destruction was 'Graceless'. In such a condition he is directed by Evangelist towards Good-will at the Wicket-gate; this person, by his very name, is the incarnate fount of 'divine grace, Christ's mercy to sinners, revealed in the words used by the angels at the nativity (Luke 2:14; cf. Eph. 2:4,7; 2 Thess. 2:16; 1 John 4:9).'[27] So, during their brief companionship, Christian tells Pliable of the relief and riches of grace (Eph. 1:18; 2:7) that lie ahead for those who persevere. When Pliable asks, 'How shall we get to be sharers thereof?' Christian replies, 'The Lord, the governor of the country, hath recorded, that in this book, the substance of which is, if we be truly willing to have it, he will bestow it upon us freely [gratis, by grace alone].'[28]

Mr Worldly-Wiseman, on the other hand, with his dependence on the law, cannot offer the pilgrim the slightest particle of grace, notwithstanding his apparently congenial attitude — only relief from his burden on condition of successfully scaling Mount Sinai.

At the Wicket-gate, Good-will (who, as we have seen, represents Christ),[29] responds to Christian's request for entrance as follows: 'I am willing with all my heart,' so that as a consequence, '... with that he opened the gate'.[30] Here grace welcomes the new pilgrim into its embrace, by literally snatching him through the gate, from which point on he will 'grow in the grace and knowledge of our Lord and Saviour Jesus Christ' (2 Peter 3:18).

At the Place of Deliverance Christian is given a greater revelation of grace — something that, up to this point, he had only dimly perceived. He now comes into the enjoyment of a whole collection of benefits that all originate from the look of faith at the atoning Christ.

Even Talkative can speak of 'grace', when he expresses a desire for stimulating conversation with Christian and Faithful concerning 'the need of Christ's righteousness ... the necessity of a work of grace in their soul, in order to eternal life … a man can receive nothing except it has been given to him from heaven; all is of grace, not of works.'[31] However this charlatan's understanding of 'grace' is based only upon the problem of sin in others and he fails to understand his own need of it.

Some time later, when Hopeful recounts his conversion while traversing the Enchanted Ground, he explains to Christian that when he was tempted to quit praying and seeking for saving grace, he came to the conclusion that he could 'but die at the throne of grace'. As he still continued to wrestle with the enormity of his sin, the Lord Jesus encouraged him with the words: 'My grace is sufficient for thee.'[32] Finally, the Lord Jesus was revealed to him from heaven, by the gracious activity of God, and not as the result of his own seeking.

In contrast, the conversation with Ignorance which follows immediately afterwards reveals a man who trusts, not in Christ sovereignly revealed and objectively believed — a belief which he dismisses as the doctrine of 'distracted brains'[33] — but in justifying works of his own produced through his co-operation with grace. Christian roundly rejects this false gospel; it 'is not an act of [co-operation with] grace, by which he [Christ] maketh, for justification, thy obedience accepted with God; but his [Christ's] personal obedience to the law, in doing and suffering for us that required at our hands'.[34]

2. The grace of God as the pilgrim's dynamic

The perseverance of Christian, in the midst of many trials, is based upon the stimulus of various means, tokens and supplies of grace. The authenticating roll, the mark on his forehead and the embroidered coat are all indications of God's gracious and sovereign oversight which mean that he will not forsake the believer.

Then, at the House of Interpreter, there is not only the young woman who sprinkles 'the sweet grace of the gospel' upon the polluted heart, but also the man who keeps alight the blaze that the devil attempts to extinguish — in other words, 'Christ, who continually, with the oil of his grace, maintains the work already begun in the heart'.[35]

Further along on the journey, at both the Palace Beautiful and the Delectable Mountains, the pastoral fellowship and edification are vital stimuli that continuously remind the pilgrim of redeeming grace. We recall the supper with Discretion, Prudence, Piety and Charity, as well as the emblems of bread, wine and raisins for the traveller's sustenance. These all project the ongoing significance and stimulation of the grace of Christ. Consider also Great-grace, the King's champion, a valiant warrior for the Lord. But note that it is the greatness of the grace that he has received that makes him the defender of the faith that he is. In contrast, Little-faith, although an authentic pilgrim, neglects means of grace — for example, by travelling solo. By way of comparison observe how the companionship enjoyed by Christian, Faithful and, later, Hopeful is a source of mutual encouragement in the grace of God.

From all this it will be seen that, for Bunyan, Moses and the law are not to tag along behind the converted pilgrim, like some necessary perennial stimulus, or a code for daily life. The language of Luther in his commentary on Galatians, in which the law can still apply to the carnal believer,[36] is far more Bunyan's style than the emphasis of *The Westminster Confession of Faith*, where the law is, along with Christ, a rule for Christian living.[37] This is foreign to the spirit of *The Pilgrim's Progress*. Rather, it is grace in Christ that speeds the pilgrim along; it is grace in Christ that constrains him to keep looking heavenwards; it is grace in Christ that is productive of spiritual fruit in his life (Rom. 7:4).

Grace in Bunyan's other works

The following excerpts span Bunyan's early to his later ministry. It is very obvious that the doctrine of grace dominated his thinking in such a way as to overwhelm any legal emphasis that other Puritans more popularly manifested.

1. The Doctrine of Law and Grace Unfolded

While some attention has already been given to Bunyan's emphasis with regard to law in this early writing published in 1659, the aspect of grace should not be neglected, especially since Bunyan devotes a disproportionate two-thirds of the manuscript text to an enthusiastic discussion of this topic. The distinctive covenantal terminology in this work frequently speaks of a 'covenant of grace', which he refers to principally as 'the new covenant', but also identifies by such terms as' 'the second covenant', 'the better testament', 'the Son's covenant', 'the blessed covenant' and 'the gospel covenant'. In this regard, it is important to note that this 'second covenant' is to be distinguished from 'the first covenant' in a consecutive and superior sense, but not in the way proposed by systematic covenantalism — as, for example, in *The Westminster Confession of Faith* — that is, not in the sense of there being one comprehensive covenant of grace under which a law or works covenant is subsumed, or indeed all other covenants.[38] Thus a man is either under a 'covenant of works' or a 'covenant of grace' in the same way that he is under either the law or the gospel.

For example, in language reminiscent of Luther, Bunyan writes, '[If] these two be not held forth — to wit, the covenant of works and the covenant of grace, together with the nature of the one and the nature of the other — souls will never be able either to know what they are by nature or what they lie under. Also, neither can they understand what grace is, nor how to come from under the law to meet God in and through the other most glorious covenant, through which and only through which, God can communicate of himself grace, glory, yea, even all the good things of another world... [The] apostle [Paul] speaketh but of two covenants — to wit, grace and works — under which two covenants all are; some under one, and some under the other.'[39]

By way of definition Bunyan declares: 'The word "grace", therefore, in this scripture (Rom. 6:14), is to be understood of the free love of God in Christ to sinners, by virtue of the new covenant, in delivering them from the power of sin, from the curse and condemning power of the old covenant.'[40] This covenant of grace is between the Father and 'the seed of Abraham; not the seeds, but the seed, which is the Lord Jesus Christ [Gal. 3:16]'.[41] Thus Christ is the surety and mediator of the grace of this unchangeable covenant. 'Whatsoever any man hath of the grace of God, he hath it as a free gift of God through Christ Jesus the mediator of this covenant, even when they are in a state of enmity to him, whether it be Christ as the foundation-stone, or faith to lay hold of him, mark that (Rom. 5:8-9; Col. 1:21-22).'[42]

How, then, is a man brought into this covenant of grace? He is, according to Bunyan's terminology, 'killed' in relation to any attachment to the covenant of works. 'O, when the sinner is killed, and indeed struck dead to everything below a naked Jesus, how suitably then doth the soul and Christ suit one with another. Then here is a naked sinner for a righteous Jesus, a poor sinner to a rich Jesus, a weak sinner to a strong Jesus, a blind sinner to a seeing Jesus, an ignorant, careless sinner to a wise and careful Jesus.'[43]

Thus grace comprehends salvation as all of God through Christ while man is thoroughly guilty under the covenant of works, and at the same time totally impotent insofar as self-deliverance is concerned.

2. Grace Abounding to the Chief of Sinners

The triumph of grace in Bunyan's spiritual autobiography, published in 1666, is so evident even to a casual reader that it hardly needs further comment. The preface reads: 'It is profitable for Christians to be often calling to mind the very beginnings of grace with their souls… In this discourse of mine you may see much; much, I say, of the grace of God towards me. I thank

God I can count it much, for it was above my sins and Satan's temptations too… Oh, the remembrance of my great sins, of my great temptations, and of my great fears of perishing for ever! They bring afresh into my mind the remembrance of my great help, my great support from heaven, and the great grace that God extended to such a wretch as I.'[44]

Following his conversion and introduction to the helpful biblical instruction of Pastor John Gifford, especially his mentor's exhortation to seek divine confirmation of its truthfulness, Bunyan confesses: 'Wherefore I found my soul, through grace, very apt to drink in this doctrine, and to incline to pray to God that, in nothing that pertained to God's glory and my own eternal happiness, he would suffer me to be without the confirmation thereof from heaven.'[45]

However, the initial turbulent years brought an ambivalence of experience that could lead him to confess: 'Wherefore, still my life hung in doubt before me, not knowing which way I should tip; only this I found my soul desire, even to cast itself at the foot of grace, by prayer and supplication.'[46]

At another time he recounts: 'Wherefore, one day as I was in a meeting of God's people, full of sadness and terror, for my fears again were strong upon me; and as I was now thinking my soul was never the better, but my case most sad and fearful, these words did, with great power, suddenly break in upon me, "My grace is sufficient for thee, my grace is sufficient for thee, my grace is sufficient for thee," three times together; and, oh! methought that every word was a mighty word unto me.'[47]

Eventually this period of instability came to an end, and in retrospect Bunyan was able to see causes for thanksgiving even in this trial: 'I never saw these heights and depths in grace and love, and mercy, as I saw after this temptation. Great sins do draw out great grace; and where guilt is most terrible and fierce there the mercy of God in Christ, when showed to the soul, appears most high and mighty… I had two or three times, at or about my deliverance from this temptation, such strange apprehensions of the grace of God, that I could hardly bear up under it, it was so out of measure amazing, when I thought it could reach me, that I do think, if that sense of it had abode long upon me, it would have made me incapable for business.'[48]

3. *Saved by Grace*

First published in 1675, this exposition of Ephesians 2:5, while continuing the emphasis of Luther upon the vital distinction between law and gospel (grace),[49] very rarely mentions this antithesis in covenantal terms. But when he does employ this terminology his usage of it exactly parallels that in *The Doctrine of Law and Grace Unfolded.*

For example, concerning the terms of salvation, he writes, '[God] hath made all these things over to us in a covenant of grace. We call it a covenant of grace, because it is set in opposition to the covenant of works, and because it is established to us in the doings of Christ, founded in his blood, established upon the best promises made to him, and to us by him.'[50] Overall, his approach is typically one of extolling the grace of God, including its elective and prevenient aspects.[51]

Bunyan's passionate concern for this gospel truth can be seen in the following extract: 'Thou Son of the Blessed, what grace was manifest in thy condescension! Grace brought thee down from heaven, grace stripped thee of thy glory, grace made thee poor and despicable, grace made thee bear such burdens of sin, such burdens of sorrow, such burdens of God's curse as are unspeakable. O Son of God! Grace was in all thy tears, grace came bubbling out of thy side with thy blood, grace came forth with every word of thy sweet mouth. Grace came out where the whip smote thee, where the thorns pricked thee, where the nails and spear pierced thee. O blessed Son of God! Here is grace indeed! Unsearchable riches of grace! Unthought-of riches of grace! Grace to make angels wonder, grace to make sinners happy, grace to astonish devils. And what will become of them that trample under foot this Son of God?'[52] John Brown rightly comments: 'We seem to see the tears welling up to his eyes and to hear his voice, tremulous with emotion, as we read this characteristic passage about the grace of Christ to men.'[53]

Of particular significance at this point is Brown's recognition in this work of two instances which seem to foreshadow the forthcoming *The Pilgrim's Progress*.[54]

The first is an expression of the future riches of grace that the believer can anticipate in a manner that is very reminiscent of Christian's description of these ravishing delights to Pliable.[55]

Second, there is a variation of the scene at the House of Interpreter where Christ pours on the 'oil of grace' so that the fire in the heart of the child of God might continue to blaze in spite of Satan's extinguishing efforts: 'O what an enemy is man to his own salvation! I am persuaded that God hath visited some of you often with his Word, even twice and thrice, and you have thrown water as fast as he hath by the Word cast fire upon your conscience.'[56]

4. *The Saint's Privilege and Profit*

In this posthumous work published in 1692, Bunyan explains: '[The] word grace shows that God, by all that he doth towards us in saving and forgiving, acts freely as the highest Lord, and of his own good-will and pleasure, but also for that he now saith, that his grace has become a king, a throne of grace. A throne is not only a seat for rest, but a place of dignity and authority. This is known to all. Wherefore by this word, a throne, or the throne of grace, is intimated, that God ruleth and governeth by his grace. And this he can justly do: 'Grace reigns through right-eousness, unto eternal life, through Jesus Christ our Lord' (Rom. 5:21). So then, in that here is mention made of a throne of grace, it showeth that sin, and Satan, and death, and hell, must needs be subdued. For these last mentioned are but weakness and destruction; but grace is life, and the absolute sovereign over all these to the ruling of them utterly down. A throne of grace!'[57]

Covenant law and grace in *The Pilgrim's Progress*

It is interesting to note that there are no explicit covenantal references in *The Pilgrim's Progress*, and it is questionable whether any are even implied. Richard Greaves attempts to describe Christian as being under the covenant of works until he arrives at the Wicket-gate, but then admits to a difficulty: 'Christian is saved from damnation only because he is brought by Good-will (divine grace) into the new covenant, the covenant of grace. But the manner of entrance in *The Pilgrim's Progress* is more in keeping with Bunyan's experience as recorded in *Grace Abounding* than it is with Bunyan's [covenant] theology as it is set forth in *Law and Grace*.'[58]

This is precisely so because Bunyan's experience in *Grace Abounding* is unquestionably paralleled with Luther's experience rather than with the covenant theology of the Westminster divines. Consider the Bedford tinker's excitement of soul on reading the Wittenberg Reformer's commentary on Galatians: 'I found my condition, in his experience, so largely and profoundly handled, as if his book had been written out of my heart.'[59] The Luther scholar Gordon Rupp explains: 'As Bunyan found his own heart written out in Luther's Galatians, so there is much of Luther in "Grace Abounding" and in the "Pilgrim's Progress". Here is Luther, thinking of the Christian man as a St George against the dragon — and coming very close indeed to the immortal conference between Christian and Apollyon.'[60]

This is not to avoid the fact that in *The Doctrine of the Law and Grace Unfolded* there is a major emphasis on the terms 'covenant of works' and 'covenant of grace', though Bunyan's exact meaning here has to be carefully distinguished. Concerning Bunyan's covenantal beliefs, this early work, first published in 1659, is his most important writing, and that for an obvious reason. In this work, as in none of his other compositions, the terms 'covenant of works' and 'covenant of grace' are prolifically used, at least 115 times. Further, such synonymous terms as 'old / new covenant' and 'first / second covenant' etc. are used over 140 times.

However, as already mentioned, we need to make a careful distinction between Bunyan's repeated use of these expressions and the classic systematic definition, whereby there is only one comprehensive covenant of grace under which a variety of covenantal dispensations are subsumed.[61] This meaning is not stated even once in *Law and Grace*. How are we to account for this omission? By the simple fact that the distinction made by Luther between law and gospel is the undergirding principle which Bunyan here clothes in covenantal language, not the covenantalism of the *Westminster Confession*.

The covenant of law

In *Law and Grace* Bunyan proposes: 'The covenant of works or the law, here spoken, is the law delivered upon Mount Sinai to Moses, in two tables of stone, in ten particular branches or heads…Yet this was not the first appearing of this law to man; but even this in substance, though possibly not so openly, was given to the first man, Adam, in the garden of Eden.'[62] Nevertheless, as we noted earlier, Bunyan's opinion at this point appears to have changed so that later, in *Questions about the Nature and Perpetuity of the Seventh-day Sabbath,* the Decalogue is seen as having originated strictly by means of revelation to Moses.[63] Often this 'covenant of works' is described as the 'covenant of law', the 'old covenant' and the 'first covenant'. As such this covenant was established by God with man.

The covenant of grace

In *Law and Grace* the 'covenant of grace' is variously described as the 'covenant of the gospel', the 'new covenant' and the 'second covenant'. It is a free, unchangeable, covenant, or bargain, established exclusively between the Father and the Son in eternity past: 'This covenant was not made with God and the creature; not with another poor Adam, that only stood upon the strength of natural abilities; but this covenant was made with the second Person, with the eternal Word of God; with him that was everyways as holy, as pure, as infinite, as powerful, and as everlasting as God... This covenant or bargain was made in deed and in truth before man was in being.'[64]

Man was excluded, contrary to systematic covenantalism, according to which God and his elect are both parties to the covenant, and this again indicates, as Greaves rightly surmises,[65] Bunyan's identification with Luther in regard to preserving the gospel through the requirement of faith alone.

Bunyan, law and grace in summary

In spite of having such a variety of friends, John Bunyan was an individualist. His convictions concerning water baptism in relation to church membership provide ample proof of this. In 1672 he writes in *A Confession of my Faith, and a Reason of my Practice*, 'Touching my practice as to communion [church membership] with visible saints, although not baptized with water; I say it is my present judgement to do so, and am willing to render a farther reason thereof, shall I see the leading hand of God thereto.'[66] (The next year, in 1673, he published, *Differences in Judgement about Water Baptism No Bar to Communion*.)

Yet in this *Confession* just quoted, while he gives a very representative summary of his gospel convictions, even as they also relate to the believer, there is not so much as one mention of the tension that relates to the matter of law and grace. Rather he focuses on the main heads of the gospel. The reason, it would seem, is that while he was extremely sensitive to the plague and deceitfulness of sin, even as the Decalogue, or law of Moses, could expose it, yet the glories of grace so abundantly available in Christ, that ministry of righteousness so in excess of the ministry of condemnation (2 Cor. 3:9), caused him to focus chiefly on the incomparable superiority of the new covenant.

It is for this reason that Christopher Hill rightly declares, 'Bunyan often skirted near antinomianism.'[67] Indeed, it would seem that in terms of some of his opinions, he certainly was a 'mild antinomian'. As indicated earlier, his views expressed in *Questions about the Nature and Perpetuity of the Seventh-day Sabbath*, where the idea of the sabbath as a creation ordinance is expressly denied, indicate a rejection of the abiding significance of the fourth article of the Decalogue,[68] and especially as it is associated with Moses and Israel. However, in this instance, I would suggest that this charge of 'mild antinomianism' is in fact a compliment that any faithful gospel preacher ought to covet. If there was one charge which was repeatedly levelled against the apostle Paul by his Jewish opponents, it was that he was exhorting the Jews 'to forsake Moses ... [and] the Law' (Acts 21:21,28), or, in other words, to embrace antinomianism. There is no instance of Paul being labelled even a 'mild' legalist. And the same could likewise be said of John Bunyan.

Martyn Lloyd-Jones, commenting on Romans 6:1, makes a very searching application concerning the charge of antinomianism raised against the apostle Paul, Martin Luther and, we may add, John Bunyan: 'The true preaching of the gospel of salvation by grace alone always leads to the possibility of this charge being brought against it. There is no better test as to whether a man is really preaching the New Testament gospel of salvation than this, that some people might misunderstand it and misinterpret it to mean that it really amounts to this, that because you are saved by grace alone it does not matter at all what you do; you can go on sinning as much as you like because it will redound all the more to the glory of grace. That is a very good test of gospel preaching. If my preaching and presentation of the gospel of salvation does not expose it to that misunderstanding, then it is not the gospel. Let me show you what I mean. If a man preaches justification by works no one would ever raise this question… Nobody has ever brought this charge [of antinomianism] against the Church of Rome, but it was brought frequently against Martin Luther… It was also brought against George Whitefield two hundred years ago. It is the charge that formal dead Christianity — if there is such a thing — has always brought against this startling, staggering message, that God "justifies the ungodly", and that we are saved, not by anything that we do, but in spite of it, entirely and only by the grace of God through our Lord and Saviour Jesus Christ.'[69]

Yet many gospel preachers today have never known such a charge of even 'mild' antinomianism, and this being so, they ought to ask themselves, 'Why is this so?' John Bunyan has certainly suffered this accusation, and he is to be admired for it.

A new heart

Essential is, a new heart, and a new spirit or mind; and this also comes not by your principle, that being but the old covenant that gendereth to bondage, and that holds its Ishmaels under the curse for ever: there comes no new heart by the law, nor new spirit. It is by the new covenant, even the gospel, that all things are made new (Jer. 31:33; Ezek. 36; Heb. 8:8; 2 Cor. 5:17-19)… Now when the heart is turned to Christ, then the veil of Moses is taken off; wherefore then the soul 'with open face beholding as in a glass the glory of the Lord, is changed – from glory to glory, even as by the Spirit of the Lord' (2 Cor. 3:14-15).

John Bunyan
A Defence of the Doctrine of Justification,
Bunyan, *Works,* vol. II, p. 290

9.
Sovereignty, election and free will

'A man must first go to the little Grammar-school of Repentance and Faith, before he enters the great University of Election and Predestination'

(J. C. Ryle).

9.
Sovereignty, election and free will

EVEN a cursory study of *The Pilgrim's Progress* would lead one to conclude that John Bunyan makes few explicit references to the doctrine of the sovereignty of God and related matters. On the other hand, many of Bunyan's other writings do plainly and forcefully refer to what are designated as the doctrines of sovereign grace, or Calvinism. So what is the reason for this variation? To what extent is there implicit teaching on the sovereignty of God in *The Pilgrim's Progress*, and how does it find more direct expression in the Bedford pastor's other writings?

When one considers the stated purposes of Bunyan in the opening and concluding poems of the famous allegory, it becomes obvious that in consideration of his method of capturing the reader's attention, he purposely avoided a direct and full-blooded presentation of explicit Calvinism in much the same way as a fisherman must use appropriate bait to gain a catch, and even, as Bunyan puts it, resort to some 'groping' and 'tickling'.[1] To some this approach may appear as capitulation, a yielding to non-offensive evangelism that obscures and dishonours God's sovereignty in salvation; but Bunyan would have probably responded to such criticism along the lines of J. C. Ryle, who wrote, 'A man must first go to the little Grammar-school of Repentance and Faith, before he enters the great University of Election and Predestination.'[2]

However, we must also consider in this regard the comment of Coleridge who, having read *The Pilgrim's Progress*, readily admitted that 'I could not have believed beforehand that Calvinism could be painted in such exquisitely delightful colours.'[3] Here, then, is a clue that leads us to the conclusion that Bunyan's Calvinism is not really restrained as was initially suggested. Rather, according to his intention in adopting the allegorical style, he portrays the doctrines of sovereign grace in *The Pilgrim's Progress* integrally, rather than in a systematic manner, intrinsically rather than by formal definitions.

The sovereignty of God in *The Pilgrim's Progress*

The sovereignty of Good-will at the Wicket-gate

'So when Christian was stepping in, the other [Good-will, having opened the gate] gave him a pull. Then said Christian, What means that? The other told him. A little distance from this gate, there is erected a strong castle, of which Beelzebub is the captain; from thence, both he and them that are with him shoot arrows at those that come up to this gate, if haply they may die before they can enter in.'[4]

This exertion on the part of Good-will[5] is an indication of the sovereignty of the Son of God over not only Captain Beelzebub and his attacking hosts, but also over Christian himself. The true entrant into the kingdom of the Lord Jesus is indeed 'a brand plucked from the fire' (Zech. 3:2) by that same Christ. So James Inglis comments:

The pull given by Good-will ... shows that while we are saved by grace through faith, the faith is not of ourselves, but it also is the gift of God (Eph. 2: 8).

Why was I made to hear thy voice
And enter while there's room;
When thousands make a wretched choice,
And rather starve than come ?
'Twas the same love that spread the feast,
That sweetly forced us in,
Else we had still refused to taste,
And perished in our sin.[6]

God's sovereignty over the man in the iron cage

This sixth scene at the House of Interpreter is one of the most sobering in *The Pilgrim's Progress*, and the reason for this is not difficult to discover. While the topic as a whole is dealt with in detail in chapter 10, it is sufficient to note here that this despairing reprobate declares, 'God hath denied me repentance. His Word gives me no encouragement to believe; yea, himself hath shut me up in this iron cage; nor can all the men in the world let me out. O eternity! eternity! How shall I grapple with the misery that I must meet with in eternity!'[7] The essential problem is that God has sovereignly abandoned this wretch; human autonomy and free will cannot save him; his case is hopeless. Thus Christian's fearful response is acceptance of the warning that such a situation presents.

'But as God would have it...'

This expression, and others of a similar kind, are mentioned on three occasions. In every instance it reflects a trust that God, in his sovereignty, is able to overrule and thus preserve his children in the most disheartening of circumstances, including satanic assault, weakness of faith and overall frailty on the part of the pilgrims.

1. Christian is delivered from Apollyon

The fierce encounter between Christian and Apollyon reaches a dramatic climax when the doughty pilgrim nevertheless grows weary in combat and finds himself knocked to the ground. As a result his sword, representative of his only offensive weapon, the Word of God (Eph. 6:17), flies from his hand. Drawing close for the *coup de grâce*, Apollyon boasts, 'I am sure of thee now,' with the result that Christian 'despaired of Life'. Then we read, 'But as God would have it…', the pilgrim was enabled to regain possession of his sword and give Apollyon a 'deadly thrust, which made him give back, as one that had received his mortal wound'.[8] Clearly Christian's ultimate hope is the sovereignty of God, 'for the Lord is able to make him stand' (Rom. 14:4).

2. Christian is delivered from Vanity Fair

Following the martyrdom of Faithful, Christian is remanded back to prison. Then we are told that '… there [he] remained for a space; but he that overrules all things, having the power of their rage in his own hand, so wrought it about, that Christian for that time escaped them [the councillors of the town of Vanity], and went his way.'[9] So again Christian experiences the power of God's deliverance, for: 'The LORD has established his throne in the heavens, and his sovereignty rules over all' (Ps. 103:19).

However, we need to understand that the sovereignty of God evidenced in the preservation of Christian was no less manifest in the sufferings and martyrdom of Faithful.

3. Christian is delivered from Faint-heart, Mistrust and Guilt

Following a brief encounter with Turn-away, Christian is stimulated to introduce a discussion with Hopeful about Little-faith, who was so brutally beaten by the three rogues, Faint-heart, Mistrust and Guilt. After detailed interaction concerning Little-faith, a weak but authentic pilgrim, Christian relates that he too had experienced the fury of these three assailants. He confesses: 'I found it a terrible thing. These three villains set upon me, and I beginning, like a Christian, to resist, they gave but a call, and in came their master. I would, as the saying is, have given my life for a penny; but that, as God would have it, I was clothed with armour of proof [i.e. tried and tested armour].'[10] So once more Christian is delivered solely by God's sovereign provision, like the psalmist, who declares:

> They [the wicked] band themselves together against the
>   life of the righteous
> And condemn the innocent to death.
> But the LORD has been my stronghold,
> And my God the rock of my refuge
>
> (Ps. 94:21-22).

Sovereign grace along the narrow way

When the pilgrims Christian and Hopeful meet the four shepherds at the Delectable Mountains — namely, Knowledge, Experience, Watchful and Sincere — Christian enquires: 'How far is it thither [to the Celestial City]?' One shepherd responds: 'Too far for any but those that shall get thither indeed.' Christian then asks, 'Is the way safe or dangerous?' Another shepherd replies, '[It is] safe for those for whom it is to be safe; "but transgressors shall fall therein" (Hosea 14:9).'[11] Clearly this pastoral advice is governed by a perspective of Christian pilgrimage that views the genuine traveller as being overruled and directed by sovereign providence. Certainly the true pilgrim is responsible for walking carefully, 'not as unwise men but wise' (Eph. 5:15). On the other hand, there is a higher appointment and principle concerning 'those who are the called, beloved in God the Father, and kept for Jesus Christ', and 'him who is able to keep you from stumbling, and to make you stand in the presence of his glory blameless with great joy' (Jude 1,24).

An anonymous verse describes this sovereign preservation as follows:

Thou didst reach forth thy hand and mine enfold;
I walked and sank not on the storm-vexed sea;
'Twas not so much that I on thee took hold
As thou, dear Lord, on me.

The sovereign revelation of Jesus Christ

1. The testimony of Hopeful

To ward off drowsiness when traversing the Enchanted Ground, Hopeful testifies to Christian about his conversion. He explains how Faithful, in the town of Vanity, encouraged him to seek the righteousness of Christ through faith alone. As he describes his struggles in coming to saving faith with Christ, Christian enquires: 'And did the Father reveal his Son to you?' Hopeful explains that such understanding eluded him for some time, even to the point of desperation. So Christian asks again, 'And how was he [Christ] revealed unto you?' Hopeful tells how the light of gospel truth eventually dawned upon his soul, with the result that '... now was my heart full of joy, mine eyes full of tears, and mine affections running over with love to the name, people, and ways of Jesus Christ'. To this Christian responds: 'This was a revelation of Christ to your soul indeed.'[12]

Here Bunyan teaches that the true knowledge of the Lord Jesus Christ is not ultimately a matter of personal discovery, but rather particular divine revelation, just as the Son of God himself taught: 'All things have been handed over to me by my Father, and no one knows who the Son is except the Father, and who the Father is except the Son, and anyone to whom the Son wills to reveal him' (Luke 10:22; cf. Matt. 16:16-17).

2. The false hope of Ignorance

Here we discover a stark contrast with Hopeful's testimony. Again during their passage through the Enchanted Ground, Christian and Hopeful are reacquainted with Ignorance and a long discussion ensues concerning the precise nature of the gospel. Ignorance scornfully repudiates the doctrine of justification by faith alone and defends a gospel of infused righteousness whereby co-operation with grace produces works that gradually result in justification. Christian, with no uncertainty, roundly condemns this 'other gospel' (Gal. 1:8-9).

At this point Hopeful intervenes with the suggestion: 'Ask him [Ignorance] if ever he had Christ revealed to him from heaven.' To this Ignorance responds: 'What! you are a man of revelations! I believe that what both you, and all the rest of you, say about that matter, is but the fruit of distracted brains.' Hopeful replies, 'Why, man! Christ is so hid in God from the natural apprehensions of the flesh, that he cannot by any man be savingly known, unless God the Father reveals him to them.'

Finally Christian asserts: 'You [Ignorance] ought not so slightly to speak of this matter; for this I will boldly affirm, even as my good companion hath done, that no man can know Jesus Christ but by the revelation of the Father (Matt. 11:27); yea, and faith too, by which the soul layeth hold upon Christ, if it be right, must be wrought by the exceeding greatness of his mighty power; the working of which faith, I perceive, poor Ignorance, thou art ignorant of (1 Cor. 12:3; Eph. 1:18-19).'[13]

Here the illegitimate pilgrim indicates his aversion for the sovereignty of God in salvation; he does not merely express ignorance, but also a distaste for the truth that God 'will have mercy on whom he will have mercy' (Rom. 9:15-16).

The sovereignty of God in Bunyan's other writings

The fact that John Bunyan had a particular sense of divine calling is indicated by a revealing comment in *The Doctrine of the Law and Grace Unfolded*, published in 1659. He recounts how, when he at last came to a condition of stability as he rested in the saving grace of God, following the early turbulent period in his Christian life, '... methought I heard such a word in my heart as this — I have set thee down on purpose, for I have something more than ordinary for thee to do; which made me the more marvel, saying, What, my Lord, such a poor wretch as I. Yet still this continued, I have set thee down on purpose, and so forth, with more fresh incomes of the Lord Jesus and the power of the blood of his cross upon my soul... Reader, I speak in the presence of God, and he knows I lie not; much of this, and such like dealings of his could I tell thee of; but my business at this time is not so to do, but only to tell what operation the blood of Christ hath had over and upon my conscience, and that at several times, and also when I have been in several frames of spirit.'[14]

Sovereignty in *Grace Abounding to the Chief of Sinners*

1. Experiences of deliverance

This personal testimony is saturated with the unquestioned belief that God is ordering the whole process of Bunyan's life.

To begin with, consider four juxtaposed incidents described at the commencement of *Grace Abounding*:

> But God did not utterly leave me, but followed me still, not now with convictions, but judgements; yet such as were mixed with mercy. For once I fell into a creek of the sea, and hardly escaped drowning. Another time I fell out of a boat into Bedford river, but mercy yet preserved me alive. Besides, another time, being in the field with one of my companions, it chanced that an adder passed over the highway; so I, having a stick in my hand, struck her over the back; and having stunned her, I forced open her mouth with my stick, and plucked her sting out with my fingers; by which act, had not God been merciful to me, I might, by my desperateness, have brought myself to mine end.
>
> This also have I taken notice of with thanksgiving; when I was a soldier, I, with others, were drawn out to go to such a place to besiege it; but when I was just ready to go, one of the company desired to go in my room; to which, when I had consented, he took my place; and coming to the siege, as he stood sentinel, he was shot into the head with a musket bullet, and died.[15]

2. Concern about personal election

Prior to his conversion, Bunyan was disturbed as to whether he was one of God's elect: 'Though I was in a flame to find the way to heaven and glory, and though nothing could beat me off from this, yet this question did so offend and discourage me, that I was, especially at some times, as if the very strength of my body also had been taken away by the force and power thereof. This scripture did also seem to me to trample upon all my desires, "It is not of him that willeth, nor of him that runneth, but of God that showeth mercy" (Rom. 9:16)... Therefore, this would still stick with me, How can you tell that you are elected?

And what if you should not? How then? ... Why, then, said Satan, you had as good leave off, and strive no further; for if, indeed, you should not be elected and chosen of God, there is no talk of your being saved... By these things I was driven to my wits' end, not knowing what to say, or how to answer these temptations. Indeed, I little thought that Satan had thus assaulted me, but that rather it was my own prudence, thus to start the question.'[16] However, it is significant that following his conversion, Bunyan seemed no longer troubled by this doctrine, but rather fully endorsed it.

3. Revelation through Scripture

Throughout *Grace Abounding* there are over thirty references to the truth of Scripture bursting upon Bunyan's soul. Often he declares, 'That scripture did also tear and rend my soul...', or 'These words broke in upon my mind...', or 'Suddenly this sentence bolted in upon me...', or 'This word took hold upon me...', or 'This scripture would strike me down as dead...', or 'That scripture fastened on my heart...' or 'These words did, with great power, suddenly break in upon me...' etc.[17] The point here is that because of the divine initiative necessary for the soul to embrace the truth of the Bible, Bunyan recognized that the light of truth breaking in upon him was a sovereign revelation, and not simply due to self-discovery.

Sovereignty and particular election

In *A Confession of my Faith*, published in 1672, Bunyan provides a definitive statement concerning his belief in the doctrine of election under seven headings,[18] which proves to be very much in agreement with the particular, or Calvinistic, Baptists of his day. A parallel statement is found in *The Work of Christ as an Advocate*, published in 1688, which also is covered under seven headings.[19] The following summary comparison indicates that the later delineation of his beliefs, written in 1688, the year of Bunyan's death, is a fresh presentation rather than a revision of the earlier one. However, both lists emphasize the certainty of God's decree, particular election in Christ, the rejection of foreseen work and grace as sufficient to guarantee glory.

Confession of Faith 1672	*Christ as an Advocate* 1688
1. Election is free, being founded in grace, and the unchangeable will of God (Rom. 11:5-6; Eph. 1:11; 2 Tim. 2:19).	1. Election is eternal as God himself, and so without variableness or shadow or change, and hence it is called 'an eternal purpose', and a 'purpose of God' that must stand (Eph. 3:11; Rom. 9:11).
2. This decree, choice or election, was before the foundation of the world; and so before the elect themselves, had being in themselves (Rom. 4:17; Eph. 1:4; 2 Tim. 1:9).	2. Election is absolute, not conditional; and, therefore, cannot be overthrown by the sin of the man that is wrapt up therein. No works foreseen to be in us [were] the cause of God's choosing us; no sin in us shall frustrate or make election void (Rom. 8:33; 9:11).
3. The decree of election is so far off from making works in us foreseen, the ground or cause of the choice: that it containeth in the bowels of it, not only the persons, but the graces that accompany their salvation (Rom. 8:29; Eph. 1:4; 2:10; 3:8-11; 2 Tim. 1:9).	3. By the act of election the children are involved, wrapped up, and covered in Christ; he hath chosen us in him; not in ourselves, not in our virtues, no, not for or because of anything, but of his own will (Eph. 1:4-11).
4. Jesus Christ is he in whom the elect are always considered, and that without him there is neither election, grace, nor salvation (Acts 4:12; Eph. 1:5-7,10).	4. Election includes in it a permanent resolution of God to glorify his mercy on the vessels of mercy, thus foreordained unto glory (Rom. 9:15,18,23).
5. There is not an impediment attending the election of God that can hinder their conversion, and eternal	5. By the act of electing love, it is concluded that all things whatsoever shall work together for the good of

salvation (Jer. 51:5; Acts 9:12-15; Rom. 8:30-35; 9:7).	them whose call to God is the fruit of this purpose, this eternal purpose of God (Rom. 8:28-30).
6. No man can know his election, but by his calling. The vessels of mercy, which God afore prepared unto glory, do thus claim a share therein (Rom. 9:23-25).	6. The eternal inheritance is by a covenant of free and unchangeable grace made over to those thus chosen; and to secure them from the fruits of sin, and from the malice of Satan, it is sealed by this our Advocate's blood, as he is Mediator of this covenant, who also is become surety to God for them (John 10:28-29; Rom. 9:23; Heb. 7:22; 9:15,17-24; 13:20).
7. Election does not forestall or prevent the means which are of God appointed to bring us to Christ, to grace and glory; but rather putteth a necessity upon the use and effect thereof; because they are chosen to be brought to heaven that way: that is by the faith of Jesus Christ, which is the end of effectual calling (2 Thess. 2:13; 1 Peter 1:2; 2 Peter 1:10).	7. By this choice, purpose, and decree, the elect, the concerned therein, have allotted them by God, and laid up for them in Christ, a sufficiency of grace to bring them through all difficulties to glory (Acts 14:22; Eph. 1:4-5,13-14; 2 Tim. 1:9).

Sovereignty and free will

John Bunyan's understanding of particular election inevitably involved a denial of 'free will' as commonly understood by those holding to an Arminian concept of human autonomy. In other words, the appropriation of the gospel by God's elect was ultimately the consequence of sovereignly and particularly endowed faith rather than a universal, inherent human ability to believe or not believe.

Moreover, it was the gospel of salvation by pure grace which required that no human co-operation with the saving message — not even faith on the basis of free will — could be construed as a necessary and independent human contribution. So

Bunyan writes, 'Faith, as the gift of God, is not the Saviour, as our act doth merit nothing; faith was not the cause that God gave Christ at the first, neither is it the cause why God converts men to Christ; but faith is a gift bestowed upon us by the gracious God, the nature of which is to lay hold on Christ.'[20]

Such a perspective did not negate faith or the necessity for it, as Bunyan's evangelistic urging indicates; rather it made faith subservient to the power of God to save according to the ultimate truth of his good will and decree.

Thus Bunyan frankly declares in the last sermon he preached in 1688, 'I am not a freewiller; I do abhor it.'[21] He advises, 'Keep company with the soundest Christians, that have most experience of Christ; and be sure thou have a care of Quakers, Ranters, Freewillers.'[22] He is even sensitive to anything which 'savours too much of a tang of free will'.[23]

In response to the Latitudinarian Edward Fowler's *The Design of Christianity*, Bunyan writes in 1672: 'That there is no such thing in man by nature, a liberty of will, or a principle of freedom, in the saving things of the kingdom of Christ, is apparent by several scriptures. Indeed there is in men, as men, a willingness to be saved their own way, even by following, as you, their own natural principles, as is seen by the Quakers, as well as yourself; but that there is a freedom of will in men, as men, to be saved by the way which God hath prescribed, is neither asserted in the scriptures of God, neither standeth with the nature of the principles of the gospel.'[24]

We should not forget that, as with other aspects of Bunyan's doctrine of salvation by grace alone, his understanding at this point is more akin to the teaching of Luther than to that of the *Westminster Confession,* and it is not unreasonable to surmise that he may well have imbibed much of the German Reformer's polemic *On the Bondage of the Will.* Richard Greaves comments along this line of thinking as follows: 'In rejecting any notion of free will which would detract from the graciousness and sovereignty of God in salvation, Bunyan spoke more from a soteriological concern in a soteriological context (as did

Luther) than from the scholastic principles of a philosophical-theological system (as did Owen).'[25]

The authenticity of *Reprobation Asserted*

Up to this point, no reference has been made to *Reprobation Asserted* and its disputed authenticity, in order that the clear evidence offered for Bunyan's understanding of sovereignty, election and free will might stand beyond challenge.

While George Offor believes that *Reprobation Asserted* was written by Bunyan, he explains that the first publication of this work was undated, although Charles Doe suggested the date to have been about 1674.[26]

Richard Greaves informs us that 'The first independent claim of Bunyan's authorship appeared in a catalogue of his works printed by Nathaniel Ponder in the third edition of *One Thing is Needful: or, Serious Meditations upon the Four Last Things* in 1688. Ponder's criterion for attribution was whether or not a title-page printed Bunyan's name in full. *Reprobation Asserted* therefore qualified, in Ponder's judgement, as a genuine work of Bunyan. Although Ponder's reasoning is not compelling, it is a point in favour of Bunyan's authorship of *Reprobation Asserted* that the publisher of at least eight of his works regarded it as his. Ponder's testimony is additionally important in view of the fact that he published *The Pilgrim's Progress* (1678 and 1684) and was therefore acquainted with Bunyan's concern about pseudonymous imitations.'[27]

Conjecture as to whether Bunyan really was the author of this work commenced with the rejection of its authenticity in 1885 by his principal biographer to date, John Brown. Subsequent study of this matter led Roger Sharrock, general editor of the Oxford University Press (Clarendon) edition of Bunyan's *Miscellaneous Works* completed in 1994, to exclude it from this collection on the grounds that it was spurious.[28]

Challenges to the authenticity of *Reprobation Asserted*

1. John Brown

George Offor's belief that *Reprobation Asserted* was first published in 1674 is based upon a catalogue of Bunyan's works compiled by Charles Doe, a friend of Bunyan's. However, Brown comments that 'I venture to think that he [Doe] was mistaken, as he might very well be in reference to a book published several years before his personal acquaintance with Bunyan began.'[29]

Brown goes on to challenge what he claims are spurious publication details, and then comments regarding the style of composition: 'It [*Reprobation Asserted*] neither begins nor ends in Bunyan's characteristic fashion, nor is there in it a single touch to remind us of his own peculiar vein. Let him write on what subject he may, he writes not long before he either melts with tenderness or glows with fire. This writer never deviates into anything of the kind. He is hard and cold in style, thin in scheme and substance.'[30]

2. Roger Sharrock

Richard Greaves, drawing upon personal correspondence with Sharrock, relates that the latter, while 'rejecting Brown's arguments as inconclusive, decided after a more intensive analysis that the work was, in fact, not Bunyan's'.[31] The exact details upon which Sharrock based his conclusion do not appear to have been published, though it may be that Greaves relates all that is relevant.

3. Richard Greaves

This editor of four volumes of the Oxford edition of Bunyan's *Miscellaneous Works* cautiously rejects the authenticity of

Reprobation Asserted. While offering grounds for rejecting Brown's charge concerning spurious publication details, on the matter of stylistic differences he concludes: 'Its logical and well-ordered structure, involving eleven chapters in forty-four pages, is essentially without parallel in Bunyan's other writings… Only when Bunyan was directly embroiled in a theological controversy did he tend to omit popular phraseology, a direct appeal to the audience, and use of colourful metaphors.'[32]

Concerning some doctrinal inconsistency, Greaves writes, 'The most important difference is the affirmation of a general atonement in *Reprobation Asserted*, which conflicts with Bunyan's concept of a limited atonement. According to the author of the disputed treatise, "Christ died for all [2 Cor. 5:15], tasted death for every man [Heb. 2:9]; is the Saviour of the World [1 John 2:2]". The writer employs these verses to support a doctrine of general atonement. Elsewhere, Bunyan quoted Hebrews 2:9 and 1 John 2:2 when referring to the extent of the atonement, but qualified the latter verse by stating that Christ "as a Propitiation" is "not ours only, but also for the Sins of the whole World; to be sure, for the Elect throughout the World". Furthermore, the author of *Reprobation Asserted* clearly stated that, "the death of Christ did extend itself unto them [that is, the reprobate]: for the offer of the Gospel cannot, with God's allowance, be offered any further than the death of Jesus Christ doth go; because if that be taken away, there is indeed no Gospel, nor grace to be extended" (*Works*, II, 348). According to Bunyan, however, Christ "died for all his elect" (*Miscellaneous Works*, xi, p.216)… Bunyan may, of course, have changed his mind on this issue; most of the statements expressing his belief in a limited atonement come from a period subsequent to that when *Reprobation Asserted* was written. Yet he made at least two comments reflecting the concept of a limited atonement in 1672 and 1674, so that such a possibility is remote (*Miscellaneous Works*, iv, p. 64 (but cf. a statement on the same page: 'So he dyed for all'); viii, p. 61).'[33]

So Greaves concludes: 'When all the facts are analysed it is possible to argue plausibly either for or against Bunyan's authorship of *Reprobation Asserted*. Yet the discrepancies in style and theology, coupled with the uncertain external evidence and the distinct possibility that the treatise was written shortly after the publication of *Peaceable Principles and True* [1674] by an open-membership, open-communion Particular Baptist who admired Bunyan's role in that debate, point to the likelihood that *Reprobation Asserted* is a spurious, pseudonymous work.'[34]

Support for the authenticity of *Reprobation Asserted*

1. Henri Talon

The French author of *John Bunyan: The Man and his Works,* first published in 1948, simply rejects John Brown's arguments on the basis of Charles Doe's attestation and G. B. Harrison's brief arguments.[35]

2. G. B. Harrison

Harrison, whose book *John Bunyan: A Study of Personality,* was published in 1928, rejects John Brown's arguments, especially with regard to style: 'But the same hard, logical style [of *Reprobation Asserted*] is to be found in *Questions About the Nature and Perpetuity of the Seventh-day Sabbath,* wherein Bunyan was again arguing a point of doctrine. The arguments for reprobation and election arise quite naturally from Bunyan's doctrine of grace. Others of his disciples have felt no difficulty about the book; Doe included it in the list of Bunyan's works, though not in his folio, and Offor, who was the first to reprint it, calls down the Divine Blessing on his "attempt to spread this important, although to many, unpalatable doctrine".'[36]

3. Paul Helm

In a far more substantial assessment of the problem than that of either Talon or Harrison, Paul Helm has offered a detailed response to Greaves which, while giving plausible explanations for several matters, inevitably focuses on the chief problem, which is the charge that the writer of *Reprobation Asserted*, particularly in chapter IX, gives evidence of believing in a general atonement.[37] Helm declares that: 'This is the only place in the work in which a general atonement is asserted, if indeed it is asserted here.'[38]

This being the case, he further heightens the tension of the problem with the challenge: 'In the work objections to the doctrine of reprobation are constantly and candidly faced [and refuted]. But apparently the doctrine of general atonement, which is (to say the least) in extreme tension with the Calvinistic view of the decrees of God, is slipped in without a word of apology... Where else in this period, and from this theological quarter, is there another such work, a work that argues *both* that from all eternity God has decreed to elect some of the fallen race to salvation through Christ, and to pass over others who will be eternally condemned on account of their sin *and* that Christ's atonement was not for the elect but was general or indefinite in intent?'[39]

Helm's modus operandi is first to discover if a limited atonement is taught elsewhere in *Reprobation Asserted*. In the absence of explicit examples, he quotes two instances in chapters 1 and 5 where he suggests that this doctrine is *implicit*.

Second, he attempts to avoid a contradiction by suggesting that the language of chapter 9 describes a 'tender', or general *offer*, of the gospel to all men without distinction, in accordance with the practice of most Calvinists who believe in a limited atonement. It is pointed out that the main thrust of this chapter is concerned with the offer of the gospel to elect and non-elect alike. Thus Bunyan writes that 'The gospel is to be proffered to both, without considering elect or reprobate, even as they are sinners... The gospel is to be tendered to all in general ... to the reprobate as [well as] to the elect, *to sinners as sinners.*'[40]

But is this merely an offer of theoretical intention? Or is it a sincere offer? Helm responds: 'Christ's death extends itself to the reprobate in the sense that if they *were* to believe then Christ's death would suffice for their salvation' (emphasis added).[41] To this Greaves replies, 'Helm rightly acknowledges that nowhere in this tract does the writer explicitly indicate that Christ died for the elect alone ... if Christ died for the elect alone, any offer of the benefits of his death to the reprobate would be fraudulent.'[42] This point aside since it is not really germane to the main argument here,[43] Helm convincingly quotes a parallel passage from the bona fide *The Jerusalem Sinner Saved* to prove Bunyan's practical concern, as here in *Reprobation Asserted*, that the call and invitation must go out to all without distinction before the matter of election is considered.[44]

Probable Bunyan authorship

The claim that Bunyan is not the author of *Reprobation Asserted* for the principal reason that chapter 9 appears to profess belief in a general atonement is one which I find unconvincing. In particular it virtually ignores the unmistakable Calvinism of the work as a whole. More important than the question as to whether there is explicit, or even implicit, reference to a limited atonement in *Reprobation Asserted* overall is the vital question concerning whether this work clearly asserts particular election, involving the denial of universal ability or autonomy, in which case the offer of a general atonement would still appear anomalous and an issue to be dealt with. Particular election presupposes universal inability apart from the grace of genuine faith given to the elect. Hence the problem would still remain concerning the allegedly 'fraudulent' offer of the gospel to the impotent non-elect.

However as an emphatic believer in particular election I feel bound to consider the very charge of a 'fraudulent' offer that Greaves proposes. In the first place, consider the heading of chapter 9: 'Whether God would indeed and in truth, that the gospel, with the grace thereof, should be tendered to those that yet he hath bound up under Eternal Reprobation?'[45] Surely this is not the concern of a believer in a general atonement. The heading of chapter 10 reads: 'Seeing then that the grace of God in the gospel, is by that to be proffered to sinners, as sinners; as well ... to the reprobate as to the elect; Is it possible for those who are indeed not elect, to receive it, and be saved?' Then follows the heading of chapter 11: 'Seeing [that] it is not possible that the reprobate should receive this grace and live, and also seeing [that] this is infallibly foreseen of God; and again, seeing God hath fore-determined to suffer it so to be; Why doth he yet will and command that the gospel, and so grace in the general tenders thereof, should be proffered unto them?'[46]

Bunyan answers in closing: 'God willeth and commandeth the gospel should be offered to all, that thereby distinguishing love, as to an inward and spiritual work, might the more appear to be indeed the fruit of special and peculiar love. For in that the gospel is tendered to all in general, when yet but some do receive it; yea, and seeing these some are unable, unwilling, and by nature, as much averse thereto, as those that refuse it, and perish; it is evident that something more of heaven and the operation of the Spirit of God doth accompany the word thus tendered for their life and salvation that enjoy it (1 Thess. 1:4-7).'[47]

Thus further explanation is given that in some respects the elect and reprobate receive differing grace: 'There is present grace and present mercy [for the reprobate], eternal grace and eternal mercy [for the elect]... The non-elect perish by reason of sin, notwithstanding present mercy, because of eternal justice; and ... the elect are preserved from the death, though they sin and are obnoxious to the strokes of present justice, by reason of eternal mercy. What shall we say then? Is there unrighteousness with God? God forbid: "He hath mercy on whom he will have mercy, and compassion on whom he will have compassion" (Rom. 9:15).'[48]

Again, this is the reasoning of a thoroughgoing Calvinist who is confronting the antinomy of particular redemption and the explicit command of Scripture to invite elect and non-elect sinners universally to the gospel feast (Matt. 22:9).[49] It must be admitted that Bunyan's pastoral ministry epitomized this emphasis — namely, undoubted Calvinism by persuasion along with proclamation of Jesus Christ that included passionate, unrestricted invitations to sinners of every kind.

Conclusion

It seems evident that, while *The Pilgrim's Progress* does not contain explicit teaching on Calvinistic aspects of the sovereignty of God, Bunyan's overall commitment to the essential doctrines of sovereign grace was uncompromising, to say the least. In presenting the gospel to the unbeliever, he was fervent in his unqualified offer of grace to earnest sinners and at the same time vigorous in his solicitation of faith from indifferent sinners. Often he would reason about difficulties and objections from the unbeliever in much the same way as Spurgeon does in *Around the Wicket Gate.* Yet, in his evangelistic endeavours, he did not see the necessity of forcefully injecting details concerning election, reprobation, free will and foreknowledge, especially in *The Pilgrim's Progress.*

It could well be that, as Greaves has pointed out, the primacy of free grace was more important to Bunyan in his gospel witness than the proclamation of reasoned matters concerning God's decree. However, once a child of God began to mature, truth concerning the sovereignty of grace was plainly expounded as being necessary for stability and assurance.

What it means to be saved by grace

The words ['By grace ye are saved'] ... admit us these few conclusions —

1. That God, in saving of the sinner, hath no respect to the sinner's goodness; hence it is said he is frankly forgiven, and freely justified (Luke 7:42; Rom. 3:24).

2. That God doth this to whom and when he pleases, because it is an act of his own good pleasure (Gal. 1:15,16).

3. This is the cause why great sinners are saved, for God pardoneth 'according to the riches of his grace' (Eph. 1:7).

4. This is the true cause that some sinners are so amazed and confounded at the apprehension of their own salvation; his grace is unsearchable; and by unsearchable grace God oft puzzles and confounds our reason (Ezek. 16:62,63; Acts 9:6).

5. This is the cause that sinners are so often recovered from their backslidings, healed of their wounds that they get by their falls, and helped again to rejoice in God's mercy. Why, he will be gracious to whom he will be gracious, and he will have compassion on on whom he will have compassion (Rom. 9:15).

John Bunyan
Saved by Grace,
Bunyan, *Works*, vol. I, p.343

10.
The despairing reprobate in the iron cage

'And how if thou shouldst come but one quarter of an hour too late? I tell thee, it will cost thee an eternity to bewail thy misery in. Francis Spira can tell thee what it is to stay till the gate of mercy be quite shut...'

(John Bunyan).

10.

The despairing reprobate in the iron cage

OF all the scenes in *The Pilgrim's Progress*, this one presents the most solemn mystery. John Kelman declares it to be 'the darkest of all Bunyan's pictures'.[1] And it was obviously Bunyan's intention to produce a sober response, as we see from Christian's conclusion: 'Well ... this is fearful! God help me to watch and be sober, and to pray that I may shun the cause of this man's misery!'[2] Of course this stimulation to 'fear' was part of Bunyan's pastoral intention and was counterbalanced by the encouragements to 'hope' found in the preceding scenes.[3] In this regard, it is noteworthy that Christiana, the four children and Mercy were also exposed to this dreadful sight.[4] However, the response of readers through the centuries to this particularly grave episode has not always been as submissive as that of the pilgrims.

The essence of the problem

In its classical religious sense, 'despair' is the result when heinous sinners comprehend the fact of their irrecoverable abandonment by God. While they have previously been offered grace, they are now for ever without hope. God refrains from making any further particular saving moves towards such reprobates, so that their condition has become irremediable. There is also a lesser form of despair whereby a man *believes* that he is beyond the hope of God's grace, even though grace is in fact still offered. Such despair is born of stubborn unbelief rather than the result of God's turning from a sinner.

In the case of the man in the iron cage, although he formerly professed hope in grace, he now believes he is beyond the reach of saving mercy, and so declares that 'God hath denied me repentance. His Word gives me no encouragement to believe; yea, himself hath shut me up in this iron cage; nor can all the men in the world let me out. O eternity! eternity! How shall I grapple with the misery that I must meet with in eternity?'[5] While it could be maintained that the whole of this comment still remains within the realm of the man's *opinion* of his condition and God's attitude, other writings leave no doubt that Bunyan did believe that in certain instances, a man could be, to use his term, 'beyond grace',[6] or permanently abandoned, according to God's irrevocable determination.

Responses to the problem

Several commentators have expressed their dislike for Bunyan's teaching at this point. Out of respect for the tinker as a whole, such opinions are often stated in terms of what Bunyan is not supposed to have meant, even though his writings plainly state that a man may be abandoned by God while still living on earth.

George Cheever declares that 'Bunyan intended not to represent this man as actually beyond the reach of mercy, but to show the dreadful consequences of departing from God, and of being abandoned of him to the misery of unbelief and despair.'[7] Robert Maguire defensively comments: 'Surely God's mercy is universal, extending through time, through life, even to the end. There is no case that we would pronounce hopeless; no sin beyond the reach of pardon.'[8] Kelman similarly responds: 'It is certain that Bunyan did not believe that such a state of mind as this, represented the truth of the case as a necessary and final doom.'[9]

Here personal doctrinal preference seems to intrude so as to obscure the plain teaching that the author of *The Pilgrim's Progress* propositionally states: 'The day of grace ends with some men before God taketh them out of the world. I shall give you some instances of this... First. I shall instance Cain... Second. I shall instance Ishmael... Third I shall instance Esau.'[10]

The historical identification of the man in the iron cage

Since *The Pilgrim's Progress* closely parallels the real-life experiences of John Bunyan described in his spiritual autobiography *Grace Abounding to the Chief of Sinners*, it is probable that the 'despairing reprobate in the iron cage' is representative of a real character of his time, even a personal acquaintance. Bunyan was a penetrating observer of human nature. In *The Life and Death of Mr Badman*, he gives details of several unsavoury individuals whom he had come across in everyday life. But whom, in particular, does this despairing captive in the iron cage represent? There are two recognized possibilities.

The case for John Child

The support of George Offor

George Offor, editor of the standard three-volume set, *The Works of John Bunyan*, first published in 1854, supposes that the man in the iron cage is an allusion to an apostate named

John Child: 'He had been a Baptist minister, and was born at Bedford in 1638 ... he appears to have been an intimate friend of Bunyan's, so that when his *A Vindication of Gospel Truths* was published, John Child united in a recommendatory preface — this was in 1657. From a dread of persecution he conformed to the Church of England... This poor wretch afterwards became terrified with awful compunctions of conscience. He was visited by Mr Keach, Mr Collins, and a Mr B. (probably Bunyan). When pressed to return to the fold of Christ, he said, "If ever I am taken at a meeting, they will have no mercy on me, and triumph, *This is the man that made his recantation*; and then ruin me to all intents and purposes, and I cannot bear the thought of a cross nor a prison." ... His cries were awful. "*I shall go to hell; I am broken in judgement: when I think to pray, either I have a flushing in my face, as if it were in a flame, or I am dumb and cannot speak.*" In a fit of desperation he destroyed himself on the 15th October 1684.'[11]

The repudiation by John Stachniewski

While John Brown confirms this apostasy from the records of the Bedford church,[12] there is no reference to this sad episode in any of Bunyan's writings and, in particular, there is no hint of it in *Grace Abounding to the Chief of Sinners*. Although others hold this viewpoint, such as N. H. Keeble, who suggests that Roger Sharrock was of the same opinion,[13] John Stachniewski has more recently offered conclusive evidence that John Child could not have been the despairing reprobate in the iron cage, in the form of documentation indicating that *The Pilgrim's Progress* was written too early for a parallel with his case to have been incorporated.[14] Rather, a far more specific and more plausible identification has been proposed.

The case for Francis Spira

Spira identified in Bunyan's writings

In 1548, a lawyer in Italy of great repute named Francis Spira professed conversion to biblical and Protestant gospel truth. However, he later relapsed into Roman Catholicism and as a consequence became a victim of extreme despair. An account of his apostasy, with the title *A Relation of the Fearful Estate of Francis Spira*, tells of his subsequent remorse that found no hope in God's mercy. George Offor notes that his copy of this book 'has added to it a narrative of the wretched end of John Child, a Bedford man, one of Bunyan's friends'.[15] It is highly significant that, in his published works as a whole, Bunyan refers to Francis Spira on five occasions, over a period spanning from 1666 to 1682, and each time with regard to his irrecoverable condition. Let us consider each of these references separately.

1. In *Grace Abounding to the Chief of Sinners* (published 1666)

As we noted in chapter 6, the conversion of Bunyan, or his entrance through the Wicket-Gate, took place in approximately 1650, shortly before he came under the helpful influence of John Gifford's ministry (paras. 113-17). However, it was not until 1653 that Bunyan experienced lasting assurance that God had lifted away his burden of guilt; only subsequent to this did he become a member of the Bedford church (paras. 229-35, 253). In this intervening period of approximately four years, he experienced times of near despair, since he believed that he had 'sold Christ' (paras. 132-39) and committed the unpardonable sin (paras. 147-54).

At that time Bunyan also believed that he had sinned in the same manner as Judas and, in particular, Esau (Heb. 12:16-17). He lamented: 'It is too late, I am lost, God hath let me fall; not to my correction, but condemnation; my sin is unpardonable; and I know, concerning Esau, how that, after he had sold his birthright, he would have received the blessing, but was rejected. About this time, I did light on that dreadful story of that miserable mortal, Francis Spira; a book that was to my troubled spirit as salt, when rubbed into a fresh wound'(para. 163).[16]

2. Again in *Grace Abounding*

Here an oblique reference is made to Spira as Bunyan continues through his early period of ambivalence following conversion. In describing how he thought of asking for prayer by the fellowship of nonconformist believers in Bedford on account of the unsettled state of his soul, he tells of the anxiety he experienced: 'I feared that God would give them no heart to do it; yea, I trembled in my soul to think that some or other of them would shortly tell me, that God had said those words to them that he once did say to the prophet concerning the children of Israel, "Pray not thou for this people," for I have rejected them (Jer. 11:14). So, pray not for him, for I have rejected him. Yea, I thought that he had whispered this to some of them already, only they durst not tell me so, neither durst I ask them of it, for fear, if it should be so, it would make me quite besides myself. Man knows the beginning of sin, said Spira, but who bounds the issues thereof?'[17]

3. In *The Heavenly Footman* (published 1671)

Here Bunyan considers what it means when Christ is described as the one 'who shuts and no one opens' (Rev. 3:7). He concludes that the Son of God excludes with finality. 'And how if thou shouldst come but one quarter of an hour too late? I tell thee, it will cost thee an eternity to bewail thy misery in. Francis Spira can tell thee what it is to stay till the gate of mercy be quite shut; or to run so lazily, that they be shut before thou get within them.'[18]

4. In *The Barren Fig-Tree* (published 1673)

In this work, subtitled 'The Doom and Downfall of the Fruitless Professor', Bunyan demonstrates that a person may be excluded from saving grace long before his earthly life is ended. Of some who grievously sin against a profession of the gospel, he says, '... they are denied the power of repentance, their heart is bound, they cannot repent; it is impossible that they should ever repent, should they live a thousand years. It is impossible for those fall-aways to be renewed again unto repentance, "seeing they crucify to themselves the Son of God afresh, and put him to an open shame" (Heb. 6:4-6). Now, to have the heart so hardened, so judicially hardened, this is as a bar put in by the Lord God against the salvation of the sinner. This was the burden of Spira's complaint, "I cannot do it! Oh! now I cannot do it!"'[19] Here, then, are words that closely resemble the confession of the 'miserable reprobate in the iron cage' to Christian: 'I cannot get out; O, now I cannot... I have crucified him [the Son of God] to myself afresh.'[20]

5. In *The Greatness of the Soul* (published 1682)

Here Bunyan considers the sensitivity of the soul in the nether regions: 'Miseries as well as mercies sharpen and make quick the apprehensions of the soul. Behold Spira in his book, Cain in his guilt, and Saul with the witch of Endor, and you shall see men ripened, men enlarged and greatened in their fancies, imaginations, and apprehensions, though not about God, and heaven, and glory, yet about their loss, their misery, and their woe, and their hells.'[21]

Spira identified as the man in the iron cage

Hence it seems most likely that Bunyan's forlorn captive was, in fact, a representation of the spiritual derelict, Francis Spira. Certainly there may also be some secondary application to

John Child. However, it is obvious that the author of *The Pilgrim's Progress* has been indelibly impressed by the truth concerning a hopeless and abandoned soul such as Spira.

Furthermore, Bunyan was undoubtedly chilled by reading the following poem, which introduces the account of this religious man who, being spiritually and physically dead, still speaks:

> Here see a soul that's all despair; a man
> All hell; a spirit all wounds; who can
>   A wounded spirit bear?
> Reader, would'st see, what may you never feel
> Despair, racks, torments, whips of burning steel!
> Behold, the man's the furnace, in whose heart
> Sin hath created hell; O in each part
>   What flames appear:
> His thoughts all stings; words, swords;
>   Brimstone his breath;
> His eyes flames; wishes curses, life a death;
> A thousand deaths live in him, he not dead;
> A breathing corpse in living, scalding lead.[22]

The doctrinal identification of the man in the iron cage

For Bunyan, this man is in a cage very different from that in which Christian and Hopeful find themselves for a brief period at Doubting Castle.[23] It represents everlasting, rather than temporary hopelessness, and herein lies its horror. It cannot be doubted that Bunyan is teaching here, as he does in detail in *The Barren Fig-Tree*, that there are caged reprobates in this present earthly life who are beyond the rescue of divine mercy — and this notwithstanding the opinions of Cheever, Maguire and Kelman quoted earlier. Again, he expressly states that 'The day of grace ends with some men before God takes them out of this world.'[24] His support of this statement from Scripture includes Exodus 9:14; Deuteronomy 29:18-19; 1 Samuel 28:4-6; Isaiah 66:4; Romans 1:28-31; 2:3-5; Ephesians 4:18-19; 2 Thessalonians 2:10-12; 1 Timothy 4:2; Hebrews 6:4-6 and Jude 5-6,13.[25]

The influence of the unpardonable sin

Bunyan's personal experience

After his conversion, Bunyan's ambivalence in terms of his assurance led to the consideration that he might well have committed the unpardonable sin of Mark 3:29.[26] The reason appears to have been that, in his struggle against the temptation 'to sell and part with Christ', although he resisted for a period, he felt that he eventually yielded and consented to Satan's overtures. Thus he comments, 'Now was the battle won, and down fell I, as a bird that is shot from the top of a tree, into great guilt and fearful despair.'[27] The ongoing turmoil led him to compare himself with Judas, and with Esau in particular, who 'found no place for repentance, though he sought it with tears' (Heb. 12:17). When he was finally delivered from his fears and doubts through experiencing the assurance that trust in Christ's perfect righteousness brings, Bunyan seems to have been set free from any further personal concern in this matter.

Bunyan's early teaching

In 1659, just prior to his long imprisonment, Bunyan's *The Doctrine of the Law and Grace Unfolded* was published. This work contains a definitive statement which reveals his understanding of the unpardonable sin. It clearly parallels his belief that certain reprobates are past grace in this life, as detailed in *The Barren Fig-Tree*. He declares: 'But that [unpardonable] sin is a sin that is of another nature [from the sin of David and Peter], which is this — For a man after he hath made some profession of salvation to come alone by the blood of Jesus, together with some light and power of the same upon his spirit; I say, for him after this knowingly, wilfully, and despitefully to trample upon the blood of Christ shed on the cross, and to count it an unholy thing [as the man in the iron cage confesses], or no better than the blood of another man, and rather to venture his soul any other way than to be saved by this precious blood. And this must be done, I say, after some light (Heb. 6:4-5), despitefully (Heb. 10:29), knowingly (2 Peter 2:21), and wilfully (Heb. 10:26 compared with v. 29), and that not in a hurry and sudden fit, as Peter's was, but with some time beforehand to pause upon it first, with Judas; and also with a continued resolution never to turn or be converted again; "for *it is* impossible to renew such again to repentance," they are so resolved and so desperate (Heb. 6).'[28]

Certainly this description parallels the case of the reprobate in the iron cage, who was 'once a fair and flourishing professor,' and yet resolutely 'sinned against the light of the Word, and the goodness of God', so that he now says, 'I have provoked God to anger, and he has left me ... I have despised his [Christ's] person (Luke 19:14); I have despised his righteousness; I have "counted his blood an unholy thing"; I have "done despite to the Spirit of grace" (Heb. 10:28-29).'[29]

Bunyan's later teaching

In 1688, the year of his death, Bunyan's *The Jerusalem Sinner Saved* was published. In it he wrote, 'He that has sinned the sin against the Holy Ghost cannot come, has no heart to come, can by no means be made willing to come to Jesus Christ for life;

for that he has received such an opinion of him [Christ], and of his things, as deters and holds him back... He counteth this blessed person, this Son of God, a magician, a conjuror, a witch, or one that did, when he was in the world, what he did, by the power and spirit of the devil... His blood, which is the meritorious cause of man's redemption, even the blood of the everlasting covenant, he counteth "an unholy thing," ... of no more worth to him, in his account, than was the blood of a dog, an ass, or a swine.'[30]

The indications of being past grace

What evidence, then, are we to expect concerning a person who is, to use Bunyan's expression, 'past grace'? In *The Barren Fig-Tree — The Doom and Downfall of the Fruitless Professor*, which is based on Luke 13:6-9 and was published in 1682, he describes five signs, which are summarized as follows.[31]

• A person may be past grace when he has withstood and abused and worn out God's patience. Having come to the fig tree for fruit, and found none, God repeatedly shakes and warns it, yet still without result, so that he eventually calls for his axe!
• A person may be past grace when God lets him alone and allows him to do anything without the restraint of difficulties, or concern with regard to holiness. The fig tree is no longer tended, but left to grow wild.
• A person may be past grace when his heart becomes so hard and stony that it is discarded by God as impenetrable. This is the hardness of a Lot's wife or a Pharaoh. It is a hardness which God judicially hardens to a point of hopelessness.
• A person may be past grace when he determines to garrison his heart against the Word of God. This person

purposely shuts out the light so as to enjoy darkness. This fig tree has a root that bears gall and wormwood.

• A person may be past grace when he scoffs against the Lord and despises his messengers while being determined to pursue his own course. Thus God sets himself against such as these by causing them to perish rather than believe and be saved.

The qualifications relating to abandonment

1. Abandonment always follows persistent rebellion

In every instance proposed of a hopeless reprobate, such as Cain, Ishmael, or Esau,[32] or even Saul and Judas, Bunyan clarifies that God's abandonment follows after man's most heinous, barefaced and persistent rebellion. This is also evident in Romans 1:24, 26, 28, where God 'gives over', or abandons, certain men and women who persist in flagrant and extreme depravity.

2. Despair must be distinguished from a distraught condition

A distinction must be made between a despairing and a distraught soul. The one who is in the former case is abandoned by God and claimed by Satan, whereas in the latter case the person is kept by God but attacked by Satan. In *The Life and Death of Mr Badman*, Bunyan comments: 'And here I would put in a caution. Every one that dieth under consternation of spirit; that is under amazement and great fear, do not therefore die in despair. For a good man may have this for his bands in his death, and yet go to heaven and glory (Ps. 73:4). For, as I said before, he that is a good man, a man that hath faith and holiness, a lover and worshipper of God by Christ, according to his Word, may die in consternation of spirit; for Satan will not be wanting to assault good men upon their deathbed, but they are secured by the Word and power of God; yea, and are also helped, though with much agony of spirit, to exercise themselves in faith and prayer, the which he that dieth in despair can by no means do.'[33]

The fearful state of the hardened sinner

To some men that have grievously sinned under a profession of the gospel, God giveth this token of his displeasure: they are denied the power of repentance, their heart is bound, they cannot repent; it is impossible that they should ever repent should they live a thousand years. It is impossible for those fall-aways to be renewed again unto repentance, seeing they crucify to themselves the Son of God afresh, and put him to open shame...

This man sees what he hath done, what should help him, and what will become of him, yet he cannot repent; he pulled away his shoulder before, he shut up his eyes before, and in that very posture God left him, and so he stands to this very day. I have had a fancy that Lot's wife, when she was turned into a pillar of salt, stood yet looking over her shoulder, or else with her face towards Sodom; as the judgement caught her, so it bound her, and left her a monument of God's anger to after generations.

John Bunyan
The Barren Fig-Tree,
Bunyan, *Works*, vol. III, pp.582-3

11.
Images of Jesus Christ in
The Pilgrim's Progress

'In all things we are brought to Christ, and thrown upon him; and this is the sweet voice of the Pilgrim's Progress, as of the Gospel' (George Cheever).

II.
Images of Jesus Christ in
The Pilgrim's Progress

IT appears nothing short of astonishing that at least one modern author should deny the pervasive presence of Jesus Christ in John Bunyan's most famous allegory. Brian Nellist comments: 'So interiorized does he [Bunyan] make his model of the religious life it often seems close to those very Quakers and Ranters whom he so controverted so strenuously in his youthful days... One result of this interiorizing is remarkable — the comparative absence of Christ from the immediate experience of the Pilgrim. In *Grace Abounding* He is everywhere acknowledged, but in *The Pilgrim's Progress* He is only occasionally in Christian's mind. If we ask what takes His place in the work, then the answer is, I would suggest, the Road itself.'[1] Hence, it is hoped that the following summary of Bunyan's Christology in allegory will, once and for all, refute all such myopic assessments of *The Pilgrim's Progress*.

The images of Jesus Christ in *The Pilgrim's Progress*

When Jesus Christ declared that 'He [Moses] wrote of me' (John 5:46), he was undoubtedly referring to a fulness of meaning and variety of literary expression that far transcended any one explicit prophetic reference. J. C. Ryle expounds upon the sense of this verse as follows: 'At the very least we may conclude He meant that throughout the five books of Moses, by direct prophecy, by typical persons, by typical ceremonies, in many ways, in divers manners Moses had written of Him. There is probably a depth of meaning in the Pentateuch that has never yet been fully fathomed. We shall probably find at the last day that Christ was in many a chapter and many a verse, and yet we knew it not.'[2]

In the same way, John Bunyan too uses a variety of literary terminology, most of it taken from Scripture and expressed in biblical language, to describe this same Christ. *The Pilgrim's Progress* is more than a seamless robe of biblical truth; rather it is a full-orbed Christology. Richard Greaves accurately declares: 'Bunyan's thought as a whole was based on the doctrine of the grace of God revealed in Christ — a concept which permeated the whole of his writings and which was the focal point of his preaching and thinking.'[3] As we shall now see, this emphasis is well illustrated in the famous allegory in no less a degree than Bunyan's other writings. Of course, there is a degree of hiddenness inherent in the allegorical form, but this is intentional on Bunyan's part, and he expects us to 'lift the veil' and peer at the substance represented by the 'Lord of the Hill', the 'King' of glory, the 'Holy One', the 'Mighty One', the 'Prince', the 'Redeemer' — titles which are used over forty times in Part One.

'Yonder shining light'

When Evangelist directs the sight of Christian away from the City of Destruction and towards 'yonder shining light' in the distance, Bunyan intends that we should identify this situation with 2 Peter 1:19, where we read, 'We have also a more sure word of prophecy; whereunto ye do well that ye take heed, as

unto a light that shineth in a dark place, until the day dawn, and
the day star arise in your hearts' (AV). While the primary
reference of this passage of Scripture would seem to be to the
return of Jesus Christ at the end of this age[4] — that is, his
coming with brilliance and splendour — Bunyan appears to
apply it to the first dawning of the light of Christ in the heart of a
seeking unbeliever.

Christian is as yet too dim of sight to gain a clear view of the
Wicket-gate — that is, to perceive Christ as the exclusive way of
salvation — let alone the invitation inscribed over the gateway;
but he can make out something of Christ in 'the prophetic
word'. He has some light of the truth in the midst of a particularly squalid world. Early in *Grace Abounding to the Chief of
Sinners*, Bunyan relates how historical parts of the Bible first
appealed to him, and only later did Paul's epistles have any
attraction.[5] So Evangelist encourages Christian to pursue this
light which he only faintly perceives as yet, until it breaks forth
into the full glory of the gospel of Christ, which gives entry into
the narrow way.

The Wicket-gate complex

Just as John 10 presents Jesus Christ as 'the door' of the sheep
(vv. 7-9), 'the life-giver' for the sheep (v. 11) and 'the good
shepherd' of the sheep (vv. 11,14), so at the Wicket-gate this
same Christ is presented in a manifold way. It is what we might
call a Christocentric collage, a multifaceted representation of
Jesus Christ as the entrance to the narrow way (Matt. 7:13-14).

1. Christ as the Word

The first revelation of truth that Christian receives at the Wicket-
gate is the inscription over the entrance, which reads, 'Knock
and it shall be opened unto you' (Matt. 7:7). This word of
Christ, taken from the Sermon on the Mount, is a most

encouraging invitation that advises the earnest traveller to avail himself of the Son of God's gracious bidding.

2. Christ as Good-will

The porter Good-will, who is both a grave, or serious, and a welcoming person, is in fact the Son of God, as explained in chapter 6. Alexander Whyte adds: 'So much was Christian taken with the courtesy and the kindness of Good-will, that had it not been for his crushing burden, he would have offered to remain in Good-will's house to run his errands, to light his fires, and to sweep his floors. So much was he taken captive with Good-will's extraordinary kindness and unwearied attention.'[6]

3. Christ as the Wicket-gate

According to Bunyan's dream recounted in *Grace Abounding* (see chapter 6), the narrow gap through which he passes from darkness to sunshine is, in fact, 'Jesus Christ, who is the way to God the Father'.[7] In Part Two, when Christiana and Mercy come to the Keeper of the Gate, we read, 'Then Christiana made low obeisance, and said, Let not our Lord be offended with his handmaidens, for that we have knocked at his princely gate.'[8]

The Interpreter's-house complex

Since this is a depiction of the teaching ministry of the Holy Spirit, whose ministry is to focus on Christ (John 15:26; 16:13-14), all seven scenes here, either implicitly or explicitly, speak of Christ.

The implicit references are:

- The portrait of the godly pastor, who faithfully serves his Master.
- The distinction between the law and the gospel, in which the sprinkling represents the grace of Christ.
- The virtue of Patience contrasted with Passion, both of whom are subject to the pleasure of the Governor, that is, Christ.
- The valiant pilgrim who perseveres until he gains entrance into Christ's palace.
- The despairing reprobate in the iron cage, who spurns the mercy of the Son of the Blessed.

However, there are also two explicit references to Christ:

1. Christ as the one who maintains the work of grace in the heart

When Satan attempts to extinguish the fire that gospel grace has ignited in the heart of the true pilgrim, Christ provides the oil of grace that maintains the blaze. In other words, Christ continually intercedes for the child of God (Heb. 7:25) and strengthens the heart by grace (Heb. 13:8-9).

2. Christ as the Judge at the end of the age

For Bunyan, the great final assize at the end of this age will be executed by Jesus Christ in glory — that is, by the one who is identified four times as the 'Man' who sits upon the cloud (Acts 17:30-31; Rev. 14:14-16). This particular aspect of the work of Christ is constantly to be kept in sight by professing pilgrims as a sober reminder.

The Place-of-Deliverance complex

While the portrayal of Christ's saving work at this juncture is multifaceted, it has very much a singular focus — namely, on his atoning sacrifice. Furthermore, all that is revealed to Christian in this scene is to be recalled frequently for his ongoing edification.

Every benefit described here, whether experiential or declared, is rooted in Christ. We shall look at two in particular:

1. Christ as the burden-bearer

While it is not until Christian arrives at the Palace Beautiful that he specifically mentions the man who did 'hang bleeding upon the tree', nevertheless the praise of Christ is pre-eminent. The crucified Son of God grants rest, saves with power, supplies living water, forgives sin, imputes righteousness, sanctifies and secures.

2. Christ as the one who clothes with righteousness

Again, while it is not until Christian arrives at the Palace Beautiful that we learn that his new garment is a beautifully '*embroidered* coat', he rejoices that the one who strips away his filthy rags is also able to cover him with righteousness. So in praise of Christ he sings:

> Blest cross! blest sepulchre! blest rather be
> The man that there was put to shame for me![9]

The Palace-Beautiful complex

Christian is told by the porter at the Palace Beautiful that this edifice 'was built by the Lord of the Hill'.[10] Hence its beauty (Ps.

48:1-3) reflects its character as the Body of Christ, the church, while its every feature reflects the glory of Jesus Christ. In his *Discourse of the Building, etc., of the House of God* (a poem of 1310 lines), Bunyan describes the particular beauty of this spiritual building as follows:

> Lo her foundations laid with sapphires are;
> Her goodly windows made with agates fair,
> Her gates are carbuncles, or pearls; nor one
> Of all her borders but's a precious stone:
> None common, nor o' th' baser sort are here,
> Nor rough, but squar'd and polish'd everywhere.
> The doors, the walls, and pillars of this place;
> Forbidden beasts here must not show their face.
> With grace like gold, as with fine painting, he
> Will have this house within enriched be;
> Fig-leaves nor rags, must here keep out no cold,
> This builder covers all with cloth of gold,
> Of needle-work, prick'd more than once or twice
> (The oft'ner prick'd, still of the higher price)
> Wrought by his Son, put on her by his merit,
> Applied by faith, revealed by the Spirit.[11]

1. Christ as the Lord of the Hill

In other words, Jesus Christ is sovereign and Lord over the hill Difficulty upon which his church has been built'.[12] This person is the object of glad talk during suppertime, as well as the subject of discussion in the palace study, over which he reigns. In a similar pastoral sense he is the owner of the Delectable Mountains. In his triumphant resurrection, this Lord caused the wrath of man to praise him (Ps. 76:10; Acts 4:27-28). Thus, in partaking of the emblems of this Lord, both bread and wine, there is true feasting in the heart by faith; here is soul nourishment indeed; here Christian is satisfied with the true bread of life in the remembrance of this Lord (John 6:48-51,54-58).

2. Christ as the Warrior

His spiritual military rank and prowess, his great conquests, his subjection of his enemies, his dispersal of spoils to his subjects, his evident wounds, his triumphant enthronement, his whole recorded history — all delight the palace residents to such an extent that they share fellowship late into the night discussing these things (1 Cor. 15:25-28; Heb. 2:14-15; Rev. 19:11-16). Here Christian learns in particular of Christ's militant supremacy; this is timely in view of his impending encounter with Apollyon (Rom. 8:31-37).

3. Christ as the Saviour

He is especially devoted to the rescue of poor and beggarly pilgrims who, although corrupt in origin, yet are elevated to princely rank (1 Sam. 2:8; Ps. 113:7-8). The extent of this condescension is indicated by his being stripped naked and mortally wounded so that he might gather into his kingdom a multitude of royal citizens (Rev. 5:9-10). All this redeeming activity was for the adoption of sons 'according to the kind intention of his will, to the praise of the glory of his grace' (Eph. 1:4-6).

4. Christ as the Protector

As members of his body, the church, there is confidence expressed in intercessory prayer, by his subjects, that he will protect them (2 Tim. 4:18). As for the Head of this body, Bunyan elsewhere writes in *The Saint's Privilege and Profit* that '... his church is part of himself; it is his own concern, it is for our own flesh... Because we are part of himself, he cannot but care for us, nature puts him upon it; yea, and the more infirm and weak we are, the more he is touched with the feeling of our infirmities, the more he is afflicted for us.'[13]

5. Christ as the eternal Son

The records of great antiquity, kept in the palace library, show that the origins of the Lord of the Hill transcend time and can be traced back into eternity past. For he is the Son of God, the Son of 'the Ancient of Days' (Dan. 7:9,13-14). As such, his 'origin', or sonship. is by means of an 'eternal generation' (John 5:26).

The opponent of Apollyon

The great controversy here is between Apollyon and Christian's Prince. Christian himself is merely a pawn, albeit a significant one, in a struggle involving far greater stakes. Apollyon himself acknowledges this to be the case when he fiercely rages, 'I am an enemy to this Prince [Christian's Lord]; I hate this person, his laws, and people.'[14] In response, Christian speaks very knowledgeably of his King, acknowledging his own dependence on him: 'O thou destroying Apollyon! To speak the truth, I like his service, his wages, his servants, his government, his company, and country, better than thine; and, therefore, leave off to persuade me further; I am his servant, and I will follow him.'[15]

1. Christ as the King of princes

Christian's whole rebuttal of Apollyon's claims upon him concerns the reasons for his new allegiance to the 'King of princes'. The point here is that, whereas Apollyon has claimed to be the 'prince and god' of the City of Destruction, along with its evil alliances, Christian is now subject to one greater than this despot, namely the 'King of kings and Lord of lords' (1 Tim. 6:14-16; Rev. 19:11-16).

2. Christ as the merciful Prince

With regard to Apollyon's charge of evident sin and suffering in the course of Christian's earthly pilgrimage, two major rejoinders are offered. First, the King of princes is, unlike Apollyon, justly able to pardon offences, and especially those committed in the environment of the evil kingdom. Second, yes, it is true that the likes of Christian often suffer in their conflicts with Apollyon, but only for a period of probation, until their promised glory comes at the victorious appearance of their King.

The Conqueror of Moses

Faithful's inclination to yield to the desires of his flesh, in response to the overtures of Adam the First, earns for him not only the pain inflicted by the old man, but also the repeated assaults of Moses, who declares, 'I know not how to show mercy.'[16] But then comes one who is greater and stronger than Moses, who is identified as the pilgrims' Lord by the nail-prints in his hands and who commands the law-enforcer to forbear (John 1:17; Rom. 7:1-4; Heb. 3:1-3). So Moses flees and Faithful is then enabled to ascend the remainder of the hill Difficulty.

Concerning the role of the Mosaic law in the life of the Christian, Bunyan elsewhere writes, 'Whenever thou who believest in Jesus, dost hear the law in its thundering and lightening fits, as if it would burn up heaven and earth; then say thou, I am freed from this law, these thunderings have nothing to do with my soul ... when this law with its thunderous threatenings doth attempt to lay hold on thy conscience, shut it out with a promise of grace; cry, the inn is took up already, the Lord Jesus is here entertained, and here is no room for the law.'[17]

The one who passed through Vanity Fair

The necessity of all bona fide pilgrims passing through Vanity en route to the Celestial City brings to Bunyan's mind the thought that the Prince of princes passed this same way, although it would seem that, having descended from the Celestial City, he went in the opposite direction through Vanity towards the Place of Deliverance and from there was directly translated back to the glory from whence he had come. The point here is that pilgrims, in meditating on their Prince, are comforted by the knowledge that their Saviour has been touched with the feeling of their infirmities; as a consequence he has become a sympathetic High Priest who offers grace to help in time of need (Heb. 4:14-16).

Bunyan further explains in *The Saint's Privilege and Profit*: 'Are we tempted to distrust God? So was he [the Lord Jesus]: are we tempted to murder ourselves? So was he: are we tempted with the bewitching vanities of this world? So was he: are we tempted to commit idolatry, and to worship the devil? So was he (Matt. 4:3-10; Luke 4:1-13). So that herein we also were alike; yea, from his cradle to his cross he was a man of affliction throughout the whole course of his life.'[18] Hence, '… since he himself was tempted in that which he has suffered, he is able to come to the aid of those who are tempted' (Heb. 2:17-18).

The saving object of Hopeful's testimony

As a citizen of Vanity, Hopeful traded heavily at the fair. But Faithful's ominous preaching disturbed him and aroused conviction of sin which he sought to suppress. Increasingly tormented in his soul, he attempted religious self-reformation. Persistent inward conviction eventually caused him to seek counsel from Faithful, who told him his only hope was the obtaining of the righteousness of a perfectly righteous man. Thus Faithful declared Christ to Hopeful as follows:

1. Christ as the righteous Saviour

The Lord Jesus is revealed as the only sinless man who, having come from the right hand of the Most High God, is uniquely qualified as a justifier of those who believe in his substitutionary atonement (Rom. 3:21-26; 1 Tim. 2:5).

2. Christ as the willing Saviour

Hopeful doubts Christ's particular interest in him. But Faithful points out that the Lord Jesus died for others, not himself, and that he personally invites sinners to come and be welcomed by him (John 6:37; 7:37-39).

3. Christ as the revealed Saviour

As Hopeful recounts how he earnestly sought for salvation, Christian enquires whether Christ sovereignly revealed himself at that time (Luke 10:22). Hopeful replies that he was not immediately welcomed, yet he was prepared to die while seeking saving grace. Even so prevenient grace upheld him (Hab. 2:3) until such time as Christ was eventually, savingly revealed to him.

4. Christ as the embraced Saviour

Finally, light from heaven revealed the invitation, 'Believe on the Lord Jesus Christ, and thou shalt be saved ' (Acts 16:30-31, AV). Now the answers to Hopeful's objections flow directly from the Spirit of God through the Word, and are not mediated through Faithful (John 6:35-37; Rom. 4:5; 10:4; 2 Cor. 12:9; 1 Tim. 1:15; Heb. 7:24-25).

5. Christ as the transforming Saviour

Now Hopeful joyfully muses on the enlightenment and revelation that have come to his soul. Now he sees the world, God
and himself all in their true light (Rom. 6:17-18). Now his love
for Christ is full, personal and submissive.

The external object of Christian's testimony.

The closely disputed exchange between Christian and Ignorance concerns, not a vague and general understanding of 'faith
in Christ for justification', but rather a vital distinction between,
on the one hand, a subjective justification that works with and
in man and, on the other, a justification that is objectively a
work of God that originates from outside of man. When Ignorance scoffs at Christian's hope in 'what Christ in his own person
has done without [external to] us',[19] and the supposedly licentious implications of such a faith, he strikes at the very heart of a
right understanding of the doctrine of justification by faith. At
this point, it is perhaps most evident just how intensely Christ-
conscious Christian is as he travels the road. To say otherwise is
simply to indicate one's ignorance of the essential doctrine of
Bunyan's text.

The Lord of death

As Christian and Hopeful prepare to traverse the River of
Death, they are told that its apparent terror will be felt in proportion to the degree to which they 'believe in the King of the
place'.[20] As they are in transit, Christian despairs of being
welcomed on the other side. But Hopeful reassures his brother
with the confident assertion: 'Be of good cheer, Jesus Christ
maketh thee whole.' Then Christian's dullness vanishes as he
cries out, 'O I see him again, and he tells me, "When thou

passest through the waters, I will be with thee; and through the rivers, they shall not overflow thee" (Isa. 43:2).'[21] In every aspect of the Christian life Jesus Christ is the great forerunner (Heb. 6:20); that is, he has prepared the way ahead and made clear his steps in which we are to follow. And when we come to the last enemy, which is death, how comforting it is to understand that the Lord Jesus has gone ahead of us and prepared for our crossing of the bar (1 Cor. 15:26,54-57).

The Lord of glory

On the other side, Christian and Hopeful are by no means satisfied with their new-found immortality. Their conversation with the escorting angels is still of the glory of the heavenly Jerusalem just ahead of them. Certainly the anticipation of its citizenry and all its accoutrements is thrilling, yet supremely, they are told, 'you must ... enjoy the perpetual sight and vision of the Holy One, for 'there you shall see him as he is' (1 John 3:2).'[22] So they are eventually received into the Celestial City with the singing of, 'Enter ye into the joy of your Lord.' Then the new citizens join in singing, 'Blessing, and honour, and glory, and power, be unto him that sitteth upon the throne, and unto the Lamb for ever and ever' (Rev. 5:13, AV). Now journeying has culminated in arrival, and faith is supplanted by sight.

In Bunyan's *Dying Sayings* it is recorded: 'O! Who is able to conceive the inexpressible, inconceivable joys that are there [in heaven]? None but they who have tasted of them. Lord, help us to put such a value upon them here, that in order to prepare ourselves for them, we may be willing to forego the loss of all those deluding pleasures here. How will the heavens echo of joy, when the Bride, the Lamb's wife, shall come to dwell with her husband for ever? Christ is the desire of nations, the joy of angels, the delight of the Father; what solace then must that soul be filled with, that hath the possession of him to all eternity?'[23]

Conclusion

It hardly needs saying that Bunyan's writings in general simply pulsate with Christ. The contemplation of the Lord Jesus enthrals him at every turn. So he declares in a poem entitled, 'Of the Love of Christ':

The love of Christ, poor I! may touch upon;
But 'tis unsearchable. O! there is none
Its large dimensions can comprehend
Should they dilate thereon world without end.[24]

George Cheever further adds: 'In all things [connected with Bunyan's allegory] we are brought to Christ, and thrown upon him; and this is the sweet voice of the Pilgrim's Progress, as of the Gospel.'[25]

On the other hand, those who have neglected this aspect in their pursuit of lesser concerns in Bunyan studies have usually reflected a degree of impoverishment that is certainly rooted in the neglect of this passion for the Redeemer of sinners. And so it is the case with regard to *The Pilgrim's Progress* and its undoubted Christocentric emphasis. To study the allegory and avoid this vital core is likewise to be impoverished. On the other hand, to submit to Bunyan's fervent presentation of Christ is to experience a memorable encounter with the essence of the gospel of Paul and Luther.

The love of Christ

Christ is a person of no less quality than is [God the Father] that is, very God; so I say, not titularly, not nominally, not so counterfeitly, but the self-same in nature with the Father. Wherefore ... that a person so great, so high, so glorious, as this

Jesus Christ is, should have love for us, that passes knowledge. It is common for equals to love, and for superiors to be beloved; but for the King of princes, for the Son of God, for Jesus Christ to love man thus; this is amazing, and that so much the more, that man, the object of this love, is so low, so mean, so vile, so undeserving, and so inconsiderable, as he is described by the Scriptures every where to be. But to speak a little more particularly of this person.

1. *He is called God.*
2. *The King of glory, and the Lord of glory.*
3. *The Brightness of the glory of his Father.*
4. *The Head over all things.*
5. *The Prince of life.*
6. *The Creator of all things.*
7. *The Upholder of all things.*
8. *The Disposer of all things.*
9. *The Only Beloved of the Father.*

But the persons beloved of him are called transgressors, sinners, enemies, dust and ashes, worms, fleas, shadows, vapours, vile, sinful, filthy, unclean, ungodly, fools, madmen. And now is it not to be wondered at? And are we not to be affected herewith, saying, 'and wilt thou set thine eye upon such a one?' But how much more when he will 'set his heart' upon us? And yet this great, this high, this glorious person, verily, verily, loveth such!

John Bunyan
The Saints' Knowledge of Christ's Love,
Bunyan, *Works*, vol. II, pp.15-16

12.
Pastoral emphases in *The Pilgrim's Progress*

'Christians are like the
... flowers in a garden,
that have upon each of
them the dew of heaven,
which being shaken with
the wind, they let fall
their dew at each other's
roots, whereby they are
jointly nourished...'

(John Bunyan).

12.
Pastoral emphases in *The Pilgrim's Progress*

IN the course of seminar teaching on *The Pilgrim's Progress*, one pastor's comment has remained with me that has been of great encouragement. It was to the effect that because of the strong pastoral emphasis in the famous allegory, such teaching ought to be a mandatory study requirement for candidates entering the Christian ministry.

However, the perception of these emphases in *The Pilgrim's Progress* has not always been so readily forthcoming. Consider the following statement taken from B. R. White's article in the esteemed and learned collection of articles published under the title, *John Bunyan, Conventicle and Parnassus*. Under the heading of 'The Fellowship of Believers: Bunyan and Puritanism,' this Oxford scholar writes, 'Christian, Bunyan's pilgrim, was essentially a lonely figure. Admittedly he had counsellors such as Evangelist and the Interpreter and, importantly, friends on the way such as Faithful and Hopeful, but the sense of the surrounding presence of a church fellowship was almost completely absent.'[1]

It is the last comment that gives cause for concern since Part One of *The Pilgrim's Progress* is replete with references, both emphatic and indirect, which indicate the significant and edifying role of local church fellowship for earnest pilgrims. Yet in the nineteen pages of White's article, while there is detailed consideration of Bunyan Meeting, its origins, setting and distinctive characteristics, as reflected in an assortment of Bunyan's writings, apart from the introductory reference quoted above, *The Pilgrim's Progress* does not rate so much as a single considered mention — not even that magnificent and substantial portrayal of a faithful nonconformist church, the Palace Beautiful.

So in this chapter we take up the challenge that White's assessment presents, and illustrate how the doctrine of the church, or the roles of the pastor and the pastorate, are important themes in *The Pilgrim's Progress*, even as they were in the life and ministry of John Bunyan. This is obviously the position taken by Richard Greaves when, in his established doctrinal study of Bunyan, he devotes one of his six main subject divisions to the doctrine of the church under the heading, 'The Pilgrim's Stately Palace'.[2]

The problem of perception here is a matter of paying attention to Bunyan's introductory poetic exhortation to 'Put by the curtains, look within my veil,'[3] by which he clearly intends to indicate that some effort will be required. However, a certain pastoral sensitivity is also necessary. For this reason a comment made by the historian Christopher Hill ought to be challenged at this point. He states that 'I am neither a literary critic nor a theologian, the two persons best qualified to talk about Bunyan.'[4] With the greatest respect, the person best qualified to talk about Bunyan is that evangelical pastor who can, to a reasonable degree, enter into the spiritual animus that so dominated his esteemed mentor.

Pastor and pastorate in *The Pilgrim's Progress*

The ministry of Evangelist

It would be a fundamental error to impose upon Bunyan's character a modern understanding of the concept of an evangelist — that is, an itinerant, somewhat flamboyant, American-style preacher who pursues a decision-harvesting trail. Rather, Evangelist here represents a significant facet of the pastoral office which remains indissolubly related to the local church, whether or not it takes the form of an itinerant ministry.

To be more specific, it is most likely that Evangelist portrays the evangelistic emphasis of Pastor John Gifford, Bunyan's early mentor. In *Grace Abounding to the Chief of Sinners* Bunyan relates how, when he was burdened and searching for relief in his soul, 'About this time I began to break my mind to those poor people in Bedford, and to tell them my condition, which, when they had heard, they told Mr Gifford of me, who himself also took occasion to talk with me, and was willing to be well persuaded of me, though I think but from little grounds: but he invited me to his house, where I should hear him confer with others, about the dealings of God with the soul; from all which I still received more conviction, and from that time began to see something of the vanity and inward wretchedness of my wicked heart, for as yet I knew no great matter therein; but now it began to be discovered unto me, and also to work at that rate for wickedness as it never did before.'[5]

Each of Evangelist's three appearances reflects a distinctive aspect of the pastoral office.

His first appearance, in the City of Destruction, is as a *seeking evangelist/pastor* who is on the lookout for burdened sinners. The parchment-roll he gives to Christian, urging him to 'Fly from the wrath to come' (Matt. 3:7), represents his ministry of proclamation from the Word of God.

His second appearance is as a *guiding evangelist/pastor* who rescues wayward sinners. This follows after Mr Worldly-Wiseman has led Christian astray with a false gospel. Evangelist, as a faithful pastor, is the antithesis of a professional latitudinarian minister, as represented by Mr Worldly-Wiseman. The latter is probably based upon an Anglican vicar named Edward Fowler, later to become a bishop.

Evangelist's third appearance, just before the pilgrims reach Vanity Fair, is as a *shepherding evangelist/pastor* who nurtures saved sinners. This ongoing concern indicates pastoral integrity through the support of his spiritual offspring after they have been converted. He not only exhorts Christian and Faithful, but also takes on a prophetic role.

The House of Interpreter

This ministry is that which Good-will at the Wicket-gate has recommended to Christian. In other words, here is Christ's promised legacy of the Holy Spirit (John 14:16-18,26; 15:26; 16:7-11,13-14). These seven scenes all represent teaching which Bunyan considers to be necessary for a new convert, as well as reflecting that which he received at the Bedford nonconformist church under the pastoral ministry of John Gifford; here indeed was a godly mentor. Not surprisingly, it is the first scene that reveals the priority which Bunyan gives to the significance of the godly pastor.

1. The priority of the portrait of the godly pastor

This initial scene is declared by Bunyan, speaking through Interpreter, to be of primary importance: 'I have showed thee this picture first, because the man whose picture this is, is the only man whom the Lord of the place whither thou art going, hath authorized to be thy guide in all difficult places thou mayest meet with in the way.'[6] Pastoral nurture of this kind was only to be found within the confines of this man's residence — that is, at the Palace Beautiful and, at a later stage in the journey, the Delectable Mountains.

2. The reality depicted in the portrait of the godly pastor

Surely this must be, in part at least, a portrayal of Pastor Gifford, who was so influential in the early stages of Bunyan's own pilgrimage. In *Grace Abounding*, as quoted above, he describes how some Christian friends 'told Mr Gifford of me, who himself took occasion to talk with me, and ... invited me to his house, where I should hear him confer with others, about the dealings of God with the soul'. Following his conversion he expresses gratitude for 'holy Mr Gifford, whose doctrine, by God's grace, was much for my stability'.[7]

Bunyan's statue, erected at the corner of St Peter's Green, Bedford in 1874, is modelled on this portrait in the Interpreter's house, and rightly so. Everything about this pastor is rooted in the life of a faithful nonconformist church, especially his capacity to 'beget children, travail in birth with children, and nurse them himself when they are born ... his work is to know and unfold dark things to sinners'.[8] In other words, he acts as a spiritual midwife whose business is chiefly conducted in a suitable care-centre, the local church.

The Palace Beautiful

Here is an exquisitely beautiful and extensive portrayal of a faithful biblical local church, a nonconformist assembly, an outpost of the Celestial City, so necessary if sustained progress is to be maintained.[9] It is an interesting question why, in contrast, Faithful does not make a stop here, and we shall consider this matter in some detail in chapter 14.

A careful distinction is made here between Bunyan's belief in a separated church gathered out of sinful society and the comprehensive Church of England establishment that was wedded to the state, with the monarch as its head. In other words, local church membership in a nonconformist fellowship required a testimony to regeneration and personal salvation, in contrast with the merely nominal association with the Church of England to which the populace in general were admitted through the formal administration of the outward ritual of baptism.

Hence, Christian, arriving at the Palace Beautiful, portrays the new convert about to be carefully interviewed before membership in a separated church is granted. Notwithstanding this precautionary investigation, he perceives this edifice to be highly attractive, and a desirable spiritual oasis in the midst of the barren wilderness of this world.

1. Christian faces opposition on his approach to the palace

Here the savage opposition of civil and ecclesiastical tyranny, portrayed by two snarling lions, attempts to thwart pilgrims in their desire to associate with a nonconformist fellowship. However, Watchful, the porter (pastor) at the palace gate, like Gifford, encourages Christian to persevere in resisting the opposition, and attain edification and rest within God's spiritual retreat, a place built 'for the relief and security of pilgrims'.[10]

John Brown graphically describes this hostility towards nonconformists in his chapter entitled, 'The Church in the Storm'. He quotes instances of the most inhumane enforcement of penalties imposed upon people for being guilty of participation in an 'unlawful conventicle' (an unauthorized gathering for religious worship): 'Justices of the Peace and constables were empowered to break open doors in carrying out its provisions [i.e. those of the *New Conventicles Act*, consisting of "distraining", extracting money or goods in payment of penalties], and Lieutenants and Deputy-lieutenants of Counties were to disperse assemblies with horse and foot, if necessary... This resolute spirit of oppression was met, as is usual in the case of Englishmen, with an equally resolute spirit of resistance.'[11]

2. Christian faces initial examination at the palace

To begin with, the porter Watchful, then Discretion, followed by Prudence, Piety and Charity (perhaps reminiscent of the 'three or four poor women' whose godly conversation impressed Bunyan on a sunny day in Bedford),[12] all cautiously examine this new pilgrim. Entrance into church membership was not designed to be an easy process.

The investigation

The primary concern here is to discover whether the applicant is a legitimate pilgrim by virtue of his entrance through the Wicket-gate into the way, his persevering faith and his desire to reach the Celestial City. Personal testimony of conversion is a vital concern, since the palace residents, particularly the pastor and the four virtuous ladies, are well aware that the admission of an unconverted member would bring defilement to the whole community by its leavening effect (see 1 Cor. 5:5-8).

The pattern set by the Bunyan Meeting

Gordon Campbell comments: 'An examination of *The Church Book of Bunyan Meeting* shows that Bunyan drew the house rules of the Palace Beautiful from his own church, for it appears that those who desired to join the Bedford church had to wait outside till they were called in. The congregation decided "that such persons as desire to joyne in fellowship, if upon the conference of our friends with them ... our saide friends be satisfyed of the truth of the worke of grace in their heartes ... they shall desire them to come to the next church-meeting, and to waite neare the place assigned for the meeting, that they may be called in" (folio 17).' Bunyan himself was admitted to Gifford's church by such a process.[13]

3. Christian is examined for his edification

Following his reception into membership, there commences a most beautiful literary vignette portraying the ideal internal ministry of a faithful local church.

Equally attractive, though less well known, is Bunyan's depiction of local church life in a poem of 1,310 lines entitled, *A Discourse of the Building, Nature, Excellency, and Government of the House of God*. The following extract well illustrates the insightful teaching contained in it:

> Alas! Here's children, here are great with young;
> Here are the sick and weak, as well as strong.
> Here are the cedar, shrub, and bruised reed;
> Yea, here are such who wounded are, and bleed.
> As here are some who in their grammar be,
> So here are others in their A, B, C.
> Some apt to teach, and others hard to learn;
> Some see far off, others can scarce discern.
> Although this house thus honourable is,
> Yet 'tis not sinless, many things amiss
> Do happen here, wherefore them to redress,
> We must keep to our rules of righteousness;
> Nor must we think it strange, if sin shall be
> Where virtue is; don't all men plainly see
> That in the holy temple there was dust,
> That to our very gold, there cleaveth rust?
> This is the house of God, his dwelling place,
> 'Tis here that we behold his lovely face;
> But if it should polluted be with sin,
> And so abide, he quickly will begin
> To leave it desolate, and then woe to it,
> Sin and his absence quickly will undo it.[14]

Having gained entrance, Christian now finds his varied experiences coming under scrutiny. This illustrates the Puritan emphasis on 'cases of conscience' — that is, close examination of personal spiritual problems with a consideration of suitable scriptural remedies (cf. the writings of William Perkins, Richard Baxter, etc.)[15] This searching examination of Christian prepares him for participation in the supper (see 1 Cor. 11:28).

Questions concerning his journey to the palace

The new pilgrim is called on to recount his travel experiences thus far in the presence of a very sympathetic, though more mature, audience. Here Christian also reveals his inner desires, struggles, victories and delights. A local church is a place where the members of the body of Christ are concerned about the spiritual nurture of one another (1 Cor. 12:25).

Questions concerning his spiritual interests

Then follows more sensitive probing with regard to heart experience, in which Christian not only reveals problems, but also finds solutions that are sourced in faithful local church ministry. Of particular encouragement is the pilgrim's antici-pation of the Celestial City; such a perspective is given clearer focus within the assembly of God's people.

Questions concerning his family relationships

Even more sensitive questioning concerns the absence of Christian's wife and children, in response to which he explains the opposition they expressed to going on pilgrimage. Emphasis is placed upon the church member's responsibility to conduct himself before his family in a godly, virtuous and winsome manner (in contrast to Talkative whom he will meet later).

4. Christian receives enrichment at supper

Here is a precious jewel in Bunyan's allegorical casket. Following a period of examination, Christian shares in a banquet — that is, the Lord's Supper, which is a remembrance of the mercy and glories of Christ, as a Warrior, Saviour and Protector. There is nothing sacramental here, but rather rich remembrance, by means of spiritually nourishing emblems, concerning Christ's redeeming glory and generous, gracious benefits.

The discussion at the Lord's Table

As a Warrior, Christ triumphed over the prince of death, though he lost much blood in the process. As a Saviour, he determined to exalt poor pilgrims, even though they were born beggars and their nature originated from the dunghill. As a Protector, he became the sovereign guardian of the palace, resisting the one who had the power of death, that is, the devil (Heb. 2:14-15; cf. Matt. 16:18).

In *Christian Behaviour*, Bunyan writes, 'It is the ordinance of God, that Christians should be often asserting the things of God each to others; and that by their so doing they should edify one another (Heb. 10:24-25; 1 Thess. 5:11). The doctrine of the gospel is like the dew and the small rain that distilleth upon the tender grass, wherewith it doth flourish, and is kept green (Deut. 32:2). Christians are like the several flowers in a garden, that have upon each of them the dew of heaven, which being shaken with the wind, they let fall their dew at each other's roots, whereby they are jointly nourished, and become nourishers of one another. For Christians to commune savourily of God's matters one with another, it is as if they opened to each other's nostrils boxes of perfume.'[16]

The blessings of the Lord's Table

The resultant blessings are those of both peace and rest which Christian finds in his own heart as well as in the midst of corporate fellowship. The source of this peace and rest has been the focusing of the pilgrim's vision upon the gospel mercies of Jesus Christ. Here is the dynamic which causes 'all bitterness and wrath and anger and clamour and slander ... with all malice' to be done away with in local church life (Eph. 4:30 – 5:2). Thus participation in the Lord's Supper ought to be productive of peace, rest, refreshment and spiritual renewal for further travel.

It is not surprising that Christian wakes, as the next day dawns, with a new-found invigoration that expresses itself in joyful song. The words exult in the ecstasy of church fellowship, which may be likened to residing 'next door to heaven'.[17]

5. Christian receives instruction for his edification

The emphasis concerning local church activity now changes from one of fellowship in the truth to that of instruction in the truth — that is, 'the apostles' doctrine' (Acts 2:42), by means of 'pastors and teachers', so that the members might be 'edified' (Eph. 4:11-12). While Christian is as yet unaware of his impending contest with Apollyon, his palace guides seem to appreciate the need of every available means of grace. Thus he is equipped with personal information, fortification and vision. These remain abiding priorities for local church ministry.

The study

Here is a presentation of Bible truth that every pilgrim ought to know about, including the valiant acts of servants of the Lord, the mercies of the Lord towards great sinners, the history of the palace (church history), prophecies concerning their Lord, the nations and the climax of the ages.

The armoury

Here the supply of suitable weapons for vulnerable pilgrims is inexhaustible. There is also an encouraging display of memorabilia associated with valiant saints of the past.

In a later work, entitled *The House of the Forest of Lebanon*, Bunyan comments: 'The church also in the wilderness, even in her porch or first entrance into it, is full of pillars, apostles, prophets, and martyrs of Jesus. There also hang up the shields that the old warriors have used, and are plastered upon the walls the brave achievements which they have done. There are also such encouragements there for those that stand, that one would think none that came thither with pretence to serve there would, for very shame, attempt to go back again.'[18]

The rooftop vista

Christian's guides suggest an edifying rooftop perspective, having a heavenward focus, in the face of the pilgrim's eagerness to be on his way. While the view can sometimes be hazy, due to sin and dissension, on this occasion the closeness and unity of genuine fellowship have ensured that the way ahead may be viewed with breathtaking clarity. So the Delectable Mountains, another encouraging pastoral port of call, are recognized in the midst of Immanuel's Land, from where the Celestial City may be viewed.

6. Christian is equipped for his journey

The pilgrim is then personally equipped in the armoury with the weapons necessary for warfare, 'the full armour of God', as described in Ephesians 6:10-18. A supply of Christ's nourishing emblems, 'a loaf of bread, a bottle of wine, and a cluster of raisins', is also provided.[19] Thus Christian sets out from the protective and strengthening fellowship of a local church into the howling wilderness of this world.

Unfaithful pastors commended by By-ends and company

A devotee of the comfortable religion of mammon, By-ends unashamedly confesses that, as a citizen of the town of Fair-speech, he is also related to Mr Two-tongues, the local parson. The latter, like Mr Worldly-Wiseman, is probably intended to represent a Latitudinarian minister within the Church of England. After By-ends is joined by his three former school-friends, Mr Hold-the-World, Mr Money-love and Mr Save-all, the foursome commend the wily practices of a professional pastor who uses religion as a means for self-advancement. Doubtless Bunyan is portraying here establishment ministers who are ambitious for promotion and, in order to achieve this, are prepared to be flexible in their convictions and to accommodate the desires of the flesh. The view of the pastoral office portrayed here is the very antithesis of Bunyan's own biblical convictions and practice.

In particular, Mr Money-love enthuses about the hypothetical case of a minister who aspires to be appointed to a more prosperous church. As a consequence, he adjusts his preaching and principles in order to gain acceptance. He further propounds that a tradesman who attends church in order to profit materially as a result of marrying a wealthy lady is to be commended for his initiative. All four agree that these situations represent church life as it ought to be — only to find themselves on the receiving end of withering condemnation from Christian.

The awakening in Doubting Castle

While the weekdays spent in captivity under Giant Despair are arid and depressing for Christian and Hopeful, even to the point where Christian contemplates suicide, Saturday night introduces a change of circumstances. So we read, 'Well, on Saturday, about midnight, they began to pray, and continued in prayer till almost break of day. Now, a little before it was day, good Christian, as one half-amazed, brake out in his passionate speech: What a fool, quoth he, am I, thus to lie in a stinking dungeon, when I may as well walk in liberty! I have a key in my bosom, called Promise, that will, I am persuaded, open any lock in Doubting Castle.'[20]

The strong inference of Bunyan here is that, while the week up to and including Saturday had been parched and depressing, after a time of prayer early on the Lord's Day (worship on Sunday morning) suddenly the light of God's promises in his Word, proclaimed by the pastor, dispels the captivity and the paralysis of despair brought about by the preceding darkness.

In *The Jerusalem Sinner Saved*, Bunyan writes, 'Despair! When we have a God of mercy, and a redeeming Christ alive! For shame, forbear; let them despair that dwell where there is no God, and are confined to those chambers of death which can be quenched by no redemption... Oh! So long as we are where promises swarm, where mercy is proclaimed, where grace reigns, and where Jerusalem sinners [great sinners] are privileged with the first offer of mercy, it is a base thing to despair.'[21]

The fellowship at the Delectable Mountains

This episode provides us with another perspective of the nonconformist local church which Bunyan pastored at Bedford. However, John Kelman rightly points out that '... the former [the representation of the church at the Palace Beautiful] was elementary and preparatory: this is advanced enlightenment and guidance among spiritual heights. It is a place of contemplation such as is possible only after ripe experience.'[22]

The plurality of pastors comprises Knowledge, Experience, Watchful and Sincere, who exercise oversight from the tops of these peaks. They care for their flocks, which graze by the side of the highway. By means of their ministry to travelling pilgrims, both hope and fear are stimulated. In Part Two they welcome Mr Great-heart with his large company of pilgrims and, having invited both weak and strong to enjoy their hospitality, bring them 'to the palace door'.[23] Bunyan clearly identifies this gathering as a fellowship in association with the Palace Beautiful. Instruction, comfort and rest are to be found here. For these and other reasons true pilgrims find this place of residence to be exceedingly 'delectable' — that is, delightful to the taste of redeemed souls.

In *The Desire of the Righteous Granted*, Bunyan writes, 'Church fellowship, rightly managed, is the glory of all the world. No place, no community, no fellowship, is adorned and bespangled with those beauties as is a church rightly knit together to their head, and lovingly serving one another... Hence the church is called the place of God's desire on earth (Ps. 132:13-16).'[24]

At the Delectable Mountains the pilgrims are taken on a tour of the region that includes instruction from the heights designed to preserve them from the unholy depths of a shipwrecked faith.

I. The hill called Error

Below this peak are the remains of heretics who have been dashed to pieces, such as Hymenaeus and Philetus, who perverted the doctrine of the resurrection (see 2 Tim. 2:16-18). Commenting on this passage in 2 Timothy, William Hendriksen says, '[Hymenaeus and Philetus] resembled those present-day liberals who, while refusing to be caught saying, "There is no resurrection," allegorize the concept.'[25] These torn remains also represent the strewn wreckage of sectarian folly (Rom. 16:17), scholastic idolatry (2 Tim. 3:7) and fascination with doctrinal novelty (Acts 17:21).

2. The mountain called Caution

Here, in a sequel to Christian and Hopeful's earlier escape from Doubting Castle, they see blind men stumbling about amongst tombs, gashing themselves and apparently beyond rescue. To the mouth-stopping horror of the escorted pilgrims, these prove to be other doomed captives of Giant Despair. Not surprisingly we read, 'Then Christian and Hopeful shamefully looked upon one another, with tears gushing out, but yet said nothing to the Shepherds.'[26] Their gaunt and pallid expressions, accompanied by bodily tremors, testified to the inner unspoken chorus that 'There but for the grace of God go we' (see 1 Cor. 15:10).

3. The by-way to hell

In a valley adjoining an unnamed hill is a door to hell which, when opened, spews forth flame, sulphur fumes and the cries of tormented souls. Previous entrants by this door have included Esau, Judas, Alexander the blasphemer and Ananias and Sapphira. This sobering spectacle warns that many false pilgrims can persevere for great distances, even beyond this point. Thus Christian and Hopeful exclaim: 'We had need to cry to the Strong for strength.'[27]

4. The telescopic view from the hill Clear

By way of contrast we are presented with an encouraging vista, one which faithful pastors will always continue to offer to their flocks. From the hill Clear Christian and Hopeful are able to catch a glimpse of the glory of the Celestial City through the 'perspective glass' (telescope), even though the hands that hold it are still trembling on account of the sobering effect of the previous revelation. As a result of what they see they burst into song:

> Thus, by the Shepherds, secrets are reveal'd,
> Which from all other men are kept conceal'd.
> Come to the Shepherds, then if you would see
> Things deep, things hid, and that mysterious be.[28]

In Bunyan's poetic discourse concerning *The Building, Nature, Excellency, and Government of the House of God*, he describes this same pastoral priority on the part of a faithful seventeenth-century church that looks longingly from earth towards heaven:

> Such mountains round about this house do stand
> As one from thence may see the holy land.[29]

5. The parting pastoral exhortation

Each of the shepherds provides the pilgrims with his own distinctive piece of farewell counsel. Knowledge supplies a map of the way that lies before them. Experience warns of the Flatterer ahead. Watchful cautions against sleeping on the Enchanted Ground. Sincere prays that God will give them speed and safety. In yet another passage from *The Building, Nature, Excellency, and Government of the House of God*, Bunyan describes such shepherds/pastors in the following terms:

> This officer is call'd a steward too,
> 'Cause with his master's cash he has to do,
> And has authority it to disburse
> To those that want, or for that treasure thirst.[30]

The fellowship in Beulah Land

Here is the choicest of territory this side of the Celestial City. It is almost a suburb of heaven. The former terrors of the Valley of the Shadow of Death, Giant Despair and Doubting Castle cannot reach pilgrims in this region. Here is rich refreshment, by means of orchards and gardens, for pilgrims just prior to their crossing of the River of Death. Further, the King's gardener gives every assistance, including a personally escorted tour of the local features. He can probably be identified as representing another aspect of the pastoral office, as was the case with Evangelist. Here he cultivates nourishment and focuses upon comforting senior pilgrims as they anticipate the final stage of their journey.

Pastor Bunyan in *The Pilgrim's Progress*

It is abundantly clear that the whole pastoral vision of John Bunyan is interwoven throughout *The Pilgrim's Progress*. After the doctrine of the gospel, it appears to be the doctrine of the church and its administration according to biblical principles that most often occupies his thoughts.

The pastoral influences on John Bunyan

While the Bible dominated Bunyan's every consideration, there were also other factors that directed his thinking concerning the role of the local church and its shepherd. In a fraternal sense, there were the friendships of John Gifford, John Burton, William Dell and John Owen. All these men were thoroughly convinced concerning the matter of the church's independence from the state. From an opposite perspective, it was the non-conformist assessment, born of fearful experience, that the Church of England gave obvious evidence that its episcopal system was irreconcilable with the biblical pattern.

The pastoral influence of John Bunyan

Who can tell just how many at the pastoral level have themselves been nurtured by the ministry of John Bunyan? Pre-
eminent in this regard must surely be C. H. Spurgeon, whose
indebtedness to Bunyan will be dealt with in chapter 13.
However, numerous other Christian leaders have acknowledged their gratitude, not only for Bunyan's works in general,
but especially for *The Pilgrim's Progress*.

1. George Whitefield

Whitefield testifies: 'Perhaps, next to the first publishers of the
gospel of the blessed God, these sayings were never more
strongly exemplified in any single individual (at least in this, or
the last century) than in the conversion, ministry and writings of
that eminent servant of Jesus Christ, Mr John Bunyan, who was
of the meanest occupation, and a notorious sabbath-breaker,
drunkard, swearer, blasphemer, etc. by habitual practice; and
yet, through rich, free, sovereign, distinguishing grace, he was
chosen, called, and afterwards formed, by the all-powerful
operations of the Holy Spirit, to be a scribe ready instructed to
the kingdom of God. The two volumes of his works formerly
published [in 1736], with the success that attended them in
pulling down Satan's strongholds in sinners' hearts, when sent
forth in small detached parties, are pregnant proofs of this.
Some of them have gone through a great variety of editions.
His *Pilgrim's Progress*, in particular, has been translated into
various languages, and to this day is read with the greatest
pleasure, not only by the truly serious, of different religious
persuasions, but likewise by those to whom pleasure is the end
of reading. Surely it is an original, and we may say of it, to use
the words of the great Doctor Goodwin in his preface to the
Epistle to the Ephesians, that it smells of the prison. It was
written when the author was confined in Bedford gaol. And

ministers never write or preach so well as when under the cross: the spirit of Christ and of glory then rests upon them.'[31]

2. John Newton

Newton records, 'Soon after I returned from Yorkshire, I began to expound the *Pilgrim's Progress* in our meetings on Tuesday evenings; and though we have been almost seven months travelling with the pilgrim, we have not yet left the house Beautiful; but I believe we shall set off for the Valley of Humiliation in about three weeks. I find this book so full of matter, that I can seldom go through more than a page, or half a page at a time. I hope the attempt has been greatly blessed among us; and for myself, it has perhaps given me deeper insight into John Bunyan's knowledge, judgement, and experience in the Christian life, than I should ever have had without it.'[32]

3. J. Gresham Machen

Machen described 'that tenderest and most theological of books, the 'Pilgrim's Progress' of John Bunyan' as 'pulsating with life in every word'. [33]

Only in eternity will the full extent of Bunyan's ministry be estimated, when innumerable pastors will thank God for his biblical legacy and wise pastoral guidance. This is not to say that the life of this godly man was void of any indiscretion. The incident involving Agnes Beaumont, in which his behaviour was innocent but perhaps unguarded, provides an illustration of how necessary it is for a pastor to be circumspect at all times.[34] However, an elegy composed to mark Bunyan's death best conveys the measure of the man:

He in the pulpit preached truth first, and then
He in his practice preached it o'er again.[35]

13.
C. H. Spurgeon and
The Pilgrim's Progress

'Next to the Bible, the book that I value most is John Bunyan's "Pilgrim's Progress" ... it is ... the Bible in another shape. It is the same heavenly water taken out of this same well of the gospel'
(C. H. Spurgeon).

13.
C. H. Spurgeon and
The Pilgrim's Progress

THE most notable preacher of Victorian England was surely Charles Haddon Spurgeon, pastor of the Metropolitan Tabernacle located at Newington in the south-bank region of London. From the boy-preacher wonder aged nineteen to the seasoned Baptist leader of British nonconformity, with 6,000 regularly being packed into his Sunday services, this prince of the evangelical pulpit frequently acknowledged his indebtedness to John Bunyan, as to no other spiritual mentor. This is not mere speculation since his son Thomas once wrote, 'I am pretty sure that his answer to the query, "Who is your favourite author?" was, "John Bunyan". He has spoken of him over and over again as "my great favourite", and has left on record that he had read *The Pilgrim's Progress* at least one hundred times.'[1]

In *Grace Abounding to the Chief of Sinners*, Bunyan readily expresses his appreciation of his spiritual benefactor and counsellor, Pastor John Gifford. So, in like manner, Spurgeon seems to have sat at the feet of the Bedford tinker to the point where one can easily recognize a passion that both held in common — namely, for the saving grace of God to be earnestly pressed upon sinners of every kind. An example of this can be seen in Spurgeon's gospel tract, *Around the Wicket Gate*, which not only draws upon Bunyan's famous scene in *The Pilgrim's Progress* where Christian first becomes an authentic pilgrim, but also manifests a similar fervency in urging hesitating sinners to delay no longer; instead they are immediately to heed the welcoming call of the Lord Jesus Christ.

The feature of *The Pilgrim's Progress* which Spurgeon most admired probably was its seamless weaving of the Word of God into its very fabric, in such an appealing manner that he freely acknowledged it as ranking only second after the Bible in his opinion for that reason. Thus he is able to say, 'It [*The Pilgrim's Progress*] is a volume of which I never seem to tire; and the secret of its freshness is that it is so largely compiled from the Scriptures.'[2]

Spurgeon's formative years

1. The young lad in his grandfather's library

When living for several years with his grandfather, who was minister of an Independent church at Stambourne in Essex, the boy Spurgeon loved to spend time in a small, dark room, his grandfather's study, where there was a collection of books that greatly attracted him. Among many volumes representing classic English Protestantism, an illustrated version of *The Pilgrim's Progress* especially captured his attention. He recalls, following his conversion: 'John Bunyan could not have written as he did if he had not been dragged about by the devil for many years. I love that picture of dear old Christian. I know, when I first read *The Pilgrim's Progress*, and saw in it the woodcut of Christian carrying the burden on his back, I felt so interested in the poor fellow, that I thought I should jump with joy when, after he had carried his heavy load so long, he at last got rid of it; and that was how I felt when the burden of guilt, which I had borne so long, was for ever rolled away from my shoulders and my heart.'[3]

A boyhood friend also related that at the age of fifteen Spurgeon was heard to recite long passages from *Grace Abounding*.[4]

2. The young pastor meeting his future wife

In 1854, when Spurgeon first preached at New Park Street Chapel in London, there was a young lady named Susannah Thompson in attendance who would eventually become his beloved wife. (The marriage took place on 8 January 1856.) They first became acquainted through meeting at the home of deacon Thomas Olney, where Susannah was often a visitor, and where the young Spurgeon also came from time to time. Eighteen months before their marriage, Spurgeon gave this young lady an illustrated copy of *The Pilgrim's Progress* with the following inscription: 'Miss Thomson, with desires for her progress in the blessed pilgrimage, from C. H. Spurgeon, April 20, 1854.'[5] Years later Mrs Spurgeon writes, 'I do not think that my beloved had at that time any other thought concerning me than to help a struggling soul Heavenward; but I was greatly impressed by his concern for me, and the book became very precious as well as helpful.'[6]

Characteristics common to both Bunyan and Spurgeon

Both men were probably of French extraction. John Brown writes that 'In 1219 the form of the name [Bunyan] was Buignon, really an old French word... It is more probable that the Bunyans sprang from those Northmen who came to us through Normandy.'[7] Spurgeon was a descendant of the Protestant Huguenots who fled from persecution in France.[8]

Both were of Baptist convictions, believing in nonconformity and baptism by immersion upon confession of faith, although Bunyan was less rigid in not requiring baptism as a condition for church membership.

Both lacked formal university and theological education, though it is apparent that both were endowed with extraordinary natural ability which, in the providence of God, enabled them to learn from godly colleagues and pursue private study with intense earnestness.

Neither scorned the learning of godly men, yet both could be severe in their denunciation of the sterile religion of the established church that placed emphasis on the outward ritual of baptism and formality in worship rather than on the new birth and a transformation of the heart.

1. As pastors

Both were gifted *preachers* possessing great fluency and powers of expression. While Spurgeon drew immense crowds in London — as many as 24,000 at the Crystal Palace — Bunyan, who is said to have turned down invitations to pastor churches much larger than the Bedford Meeting, could draw 1,200 in London on a working day at 7 a.m. in the dark of winter with only twenty-four hours' notice; on a Sunday 3,000 would come to hear him.[9]

Both were gifted *writers* whose publications were circulated worldwide. If Bunyan could claim to have produced the second most widely published piece of literature after the English Bible, *The Pilgrim's Progress*, Spurgeon could claim to have produced the most widely circulated collection of sermons in the history of the Christian church, the *Metropolitan Tabernacle Pulpit*.

Both were beloved and able *pastors* whose pulpit and literary skills did not lead to isolation in study resulting in the neglect of shepherding their flocks. Admittedly Spurgeon had secretarial help and considerable financial support, but both were accessible. Bunyan in particular never forgot the pastoral encouragement given to him by John Gifford in the days when he was spiritually adrift. Spurgeon regularly counselled members of his congregation, enjoyed the company of orphans at the Stockwell Orphanage and invested much time in the lives of students at the Pastors' College, both during their training and in the course of their subsequent ministry as pastors, whether close by or in distant regions.

It is also important to remember that both Bunyan and Spurgeon were blessed with godly wives who provided unfailing support, as did their children also.

2. As Calvinists

However, the thing that most closely knit these two souls together undoubtedly was their passion for the gospel of the sovereign grace of God. In plain terms, Bunyan and Spurgeon were both thoroughgoing Calvinists, with Bunyan perhaps having a closer alignment with Luther.

Spurgeon recounts: 'Well can I remember the manner in which I learned the doctrines of grace in a single instant... I can recall the very day and hour when first I received those truths in my own soul — when they were, as John Bunyan says, burnt into my heart as with a hot iron; and I can recollect how I felt that I had grown on a sudden from a babe into a man.'[10]

Nevertheless this emphasis on the sovereignty of God was never merely cerebral or academic. Both Bunyan and Spurgeon were fervent in their proclamation of free grace through Christ, especially in doctrinal terms that were rooted in the Reformation. At the same time there was an immediacy on the part of both that pressed the gospel upon hesitating and burdened sinners with great urgency and experiential expectation; there was to be no delay on account of preparationism, nor did they make qualified and stilted offers of redemption based on reasonings concerning God's regard for the elect and non-elect. On the contrary, Bunyan declares in *Come and Welcome to Jesus Christ*, 'Coming sinner, see here the willingness of Christ to save; see here how free he is to communicate life, and all good things, to such as thou art. He complains, if thou comest not; he is displeased if thou callest not upon him.'[11] Similarly, Spurgeon writes in *Around the Wicket Gate*, after the manner of his mentor: 'It comes to this, my friend, as it did with John Bunyan; a voice now speaks to you, and says, "Wilt thou keep thy sin and go to hell? Or leave thy sin and go to heaven?" The point should be decided before you quit the spot. In the name of God, I ask you. Which shall it be — Christ and salvation, or the favourite sin and damnation?'[12]

The pulpit ministry

The formal preaching of C. H. Spurgeon at New Park Street Chapel and later at the Metropolitan Tabernacle spanned a period of over thirty-five years, from 1854-1891. A close study of this ministry reveals a pervasive influence by John Bunyan that not only confirms the opinion of his son Thomas quoted earlier that the Bedford pastor was his father's favourite author, but also that this seventeenth-century nonconformist was more influential on Spurgeon, to the very depths of his soul, than any other individual. Consider the following summary of information derived from *The New Park Street Pulpit* and the *Metropolitan Tabernacle Pulpit*, which are currently published in sixty-three volumes.[13]

1. Frequent references

Within the total of 3,561 published sermons that comprise Spurgeon's published pulpit ministry, the name of John Bunyan occurs 779 times, a figure which far exceeds references to numerous other revered saints such as Luther, Calvin, Owen, Baxter, Charnock, Henry, Whitefield, Gill, or Newton. Making certain allowances, this means that Spurgeon made reference to Bunyan, on average, in every sixth sermon that he preached over a period of thirty-five years. Other publications, including *Lectures to my Students*, *An All-Around Ministry*, *Morning and Evening*, *Spurgeon's Autobiography*, *The Treasury of David* and the monthly magazine *The Sword and Trowel,* all contain frequent references to Bunyan and his ministry.

2. Detailed exposition

Spurgeon manifests a profound understanding of *The Pilgrim's Progress* (both parts), *Grace Abounding* and *The Holy War.* All of these works are mentioned frequently, and often a reference to one incident or character will stimulate the recollection of another. The range of characters that Spurgeon cites is truly kaleidoscopic. Often a page of exposition and application will focus on a multiplicity of personalities derived from a notable allegorical scene, while aphorisms taken from Bunyan abound.

In particular there are six sermons that are devoted to specific allegorical situations:

- *Sermon 64, 1856,* 'The Enchanted Ground', on the text 1 Thessalonians 5:6. Believers are exhorted to beware of slumbering, just as Christian and Hopeful were warned by one of the shepherds at the Delectable Mountains. Supporting references include the hill Difficulty, the savage lions, Apollyon, Giant Despair and Beulah land.
- *Sermon 205, 1858,* 'A Lecture for Little-faith', on the text 2 Thessalonians 1:3. Little-faith is compared with Ready-to-halt, Mr Fearing, Mr Despondency, Miss Much-afraid, Mr Feeble-mind, Great-heart and Valiant-for-truth; Spurgeon also introduces characters of his own called Great-faith, Strong-faith and Mr Great-trouble.
- *Sermons 297-8, 1860,* 'Mr Evil Questioning Tried and Executed', on the text 2 Kings 5:12. Using imagery based upon *The Holy War,* Mr Evil-questioning is a Diabolonian with the deceitful alias of Honest-enquiring; he is married to No-hope and has children named Legal-life, Unbelief, Wrong-thoughts-of-Christ, Clip-promise, Carnal-sense, Live-by-feeling and Self-love. Having despised the work of

the Holy Spirit, he is judged guilty and hanged in Bad-
street.

- *Sermon 777, 1867,* 'Helps', on the text 1 Corinthians
12:28. The spiritual gift that Paul defines in this way is associated with Christian's rescuer at the Slough of Despond: '... "helps,' if I understand Bunyan aright, are
stationed all round the borders of the Slough of Despond,
and it is their business to keep watch all round and listen
for the cries of any poor benighted travellers who may be
staggering in the mire." ' [14]

- *Sermon 3449, 1870,* 'Buying the Truth,' on the text
Proverbs 23:23. The resistance of Christian and Faithful
to worldly overtures at Vanity Fair prompts their cry to
'buy the truth'. Spurgeon interprets this as preference for
biblical truth that is doctrinal, experiential and practical,
sourced in Christ and, therefore, 'without money and
without price'.

3. Distinctive reverence

Spurgeon's writings reveal a profound esteem for the author of
The Pilgrim's Progress that knows no other human parallel. For
instance, Bunyan is acclaimed as the 'half-inspired' master in
the realm of allegory.[15] Referring to the brilliant simplicity of his
style, Spurgeon asks the question: 'Why did John Bunyan
become the apostle of Bedfordshire, and Huntingdonshire, and
round about? It was because John Bunyan, while he had a
surpassing genius, would not condescend to cull his language
from the garden of flowers, but he went into the hayfield and
the meadow, and plucked up his language by the roots, and
spoke out in words that the people used in their cottages.'[16]

Spurgeon explains the reason for his singular devotion to
Bunyan when he says, 'Next to the Bible, the book that I value
most is John Bunyan's "Pilgrim's Progress", and I imagine I
may have read that through perhaps a hundred times; it is a
book of which I never seem to tire, but then the secret of that is,

that John Bunyan's "Pilgrim's Progress" is the Bible in another shape. It is the same heavenly water taken out of this same well of the gospel.'[17]

4. Identification with Bunyan's experience

Spurgeon could empathize with Bunyan since he found in the latter a kindred spirit in much the same way that Bunyan found one in Luther. So he refers affectionately to 'honest John', or 'Master John', and has no time for literary critics who opine that Bunyan was too self-absorbed: 'Southey, [the British poet laureate] in his "Life of Bunyan", seems at a difficulty to understand how Bunyan could have used such depreciating language concerning his own character. For it is true, according to all we know of his biography [*Grace Abounding*], that he was not, except in the case of profane swearing, at all so bad as the most of the villagers. Indeed, there were some virtues in the man which were worthy of all commendation. Southey attributes it to a morbid state of mind, but we rather ascribe it to a return of spiritual health. Had the excellent poet seen himself in the same heavenly light as that in which Bunyan saw himself, he would have discovered that Bunyan did not exaggerate, but was simply stating as far as he could a truth which utterly surpassed his powers of utterance.'[18]

Another instance of heartfelt loyalty concerns the flight from Doubting Castle by Christian and Faithful where, '… according to Master Bunyan, the key [Promise] turned in the great lock which locked the [outer] iron gate. To use John Bunyan's own words, he says, "That lock went damnable hard." In all the new editions of "Pilgrim's Progress," it is put, "That lock went desperate hard." That is the more refined way of putting it, but John Bunyan meant just what he said, and implied that there was a sense of the wrath of God upon the soul of man on account of sin, so that he felt as if he were near even to perdition itself. And yet, at such a time, the key did turn in the lock, and the iron gate was opened.'[19]

The lecture series

Following Spurgeon's death in 1891, the discovery was made of manuscripts of a series of addresses on *The Pilgrim's Progres* (both parts). These were probably given 'at Monday evening prayer-meetings with the special purpose of edifying such as had just begun to go on pilgrimage'.[20] Many of them were subsequently published in *The Sword and Trowel.* They all exude a spiritual enthusiasm that found in Bunyan's work a catalyst by which Spurgeon's evangelistic fervour could be ignited.

Commenting on Christian's jubilant response at his being delivered of his burden at the cross, Spurgeon declared:

> Well might poor Pilgrim, having lost his load, give three great leaps for joy and go on singing:
>
> Blest Cross! Blest sepulchre! Blest rather be
> The man that there was put to shame for me!
>
> Believer, do you recollect the day when your fetters fell off? Do you remember the place where Jesus met you and said, 'I have loved thee with an everlasting love; I have blotted out as a cloud thy transgressions, and as a thick cloud thy sins; they shall not be mentioned against thee any more for ever'? Oh! What a sweet season is that when Jesus takes away the pain of sin! When the Lord first pardoned my sin, I was so joyous that I could scarce refrain from dancing. I thought on my road home from the house where I had been set at liberty, that I must tell the stones in the street the story of my deliverance.[21]

14.
The companionship of Christian and Faithful

'What happiness it was for these Christians to meet each other! What delightful comparison of each other's experience, what strengthening of each other's faith and joy!'

(George Cheever).

14.
The companionship of Christian and Faithful

THERE is something very attractive and endearing about the warmth of spiritual friendship that develops between Christian and Faithful, fellow-citizens from the City of Destruction, when they eventually meet just beyond the Valley of the Shadow of Death. George Cheever describes this initial acquaintance as follows: 'What happiness it was for these Christians to meet each other! What delightful comparison of each other's experience, what strengthening of each other's faith and joy!'[1] This being so, it would seem difficult to ignore the real possibility that their relationship reflects a valued and intimate friendship enjoyed by Bunyan himself. But more of this speculation later on.

Christian leaves the City of Destruction first

Although Christian is deeply distressed at having to leave behind his wife and children, separation with regard to other social relationships in the City of Destruction does not appear to trouble him. Hence, knowing that Faithful is also residing in the same city at that time, we conclude that any knowledge they had of each other was relatively insignificant. The next incident that establishes some connection between these two as pilgrims, a considerable distance further on, concerns Christian's fearful experience of passing between the two savage lions and the relief which immediately follows when he is received at the Palace Beautiful, where he lodges for four nights.

Here Christian is informed by the porter that Faithful has recently passed by without stopping at the palace. Having passed through the Valley of Humiliation, where he faced conflict and trial, subsequently while passing through the Valley of the Shadow of Death, Christian hears Faithful cry out a short way ahead, 'Though I walk through the valley of the shadow of death, I will fear no evil, for thou art with me' (Ps. 23:4), though at that stage he does not know the identity of the speaker. Emerging from this terrible valley, he sees Faithful a short distance ahead and eventually catches up with him in circumstances that are both humiliating for him and comforting.

Faithful follows from the City of Destruction

In a testimony given later Faithful indicates that it was the influence of Christian's warning of imminent judgement, just before the latter's departure from the City of Destruction, that led to his own ensuing flight. His distinctive encounters with Madam Wanton, Adam the First, Moses, Discontent and Shame suggest a weakness of the flesh, but, on the other hand, he appears to lack Christian's tendency to pride.

On his approach to the Palace Beautiful Faithful discovers the lions to be asleep, and so passes between them without any harassment; he is then greeted by the porter of the palace, but on account of its being still only midday, he declines the invitation to seek accommodation there and join Christian. Instead Faithful resolutely presses on, avoiding Apollyon and the cave of Pope and Pagan. Indeed, he enjoys more in the way of sunshine than Christian did. Then he hears the cry of his friend who is trailing behind: 'Let me catch up, and I will be your companion.'[2]

The affectionate meeting of the two pilgrims

Here is a characteristic instance of Bunyan's ability simultaneously to amuse and edify. He portrays the determined Faithful as a pilgrim who will not for a moment halt in his journey, even when Christian does not lag too far behind and is hurrying to catch up with him. Then Christian races past, congratulates himself on overtaking his colleague and stumbles on account of his gloating. Cheever comments: 'Then did Christian vain-gloriously smile! Ah what a smile was that? But now see how he that exalteth himself shall be abased, and how surely along with spiritual pride comes carelessness, false security, and a grievous fall.'[3]

But without the slightest thought of offering a rebuke, the gentle Faithful raises his brother up, and so 'they went very lovingly on together'.[4] As Charles Wesley has written:

All praise to our redeeming Lord,
Who joins us by his grace,
And bids us, each to each restored,
Together seek his face.

He bids us build each other up;
And, gathered into one,
To our high calling's glorious hope
We hand in hand go on.[5]

The unresolved puzzle

Now while a truly memorable lesson has been taught here concerning Paul's admonition, 'Therefore let him who thinks he stands take heed that he does not fall' (1 Cor. 10:12), some obvious questions still remain unanswered. For instance, while we now understand how Faithful was able to get ahead of Christian, even so, what is Bunyan indicating here with regard to this avoidance by Faithful of the blessings of true local church fellowship available at the Palace Beautiful that were so greatly appreciated by Christian? Also, why were the lions angry with Christian, yet asleep when Faithful passed by? And again, assuming that Christian represents Bunyan, then whom might Faithful represent? Was there any known close acquaintance of Bunyan's whom we could specifically identify as being portrayed by Faithful?

Of one thing we can be sure, knowing Bunyan's intention to stimulate and arouse curiosity: these questions involve details that the author intends us to wrestle with and seek a resolution. And this we shall proceed to do.

The savage and the sleeping lions

In Part Two of *The Pilgrim's Progress*, Great-heart defends Christiana and her company in the Valley of the Shadow of Death against a prowling lion. This beast is identified by Bunyan, according to 1 Peter 5:8-9, as 'the devil'. However, most students of Bunyan are agreed that the two lions on either side of the narrow way, about a furlong before the Palace Beautiful, are to be otherwise identified. They are correctly recognized by Roger Sharrock, and most other commentators, as that marriage of church and state, that union of ecclesiastical and civil power, that found tyrannical expression in the English monarchy under Charles I and Charles II.[6] In his introduction to *Grace Abounding to the Chief of Sinners*, Bunyan describes himself as writing, while imprisoned, 'from the lions' dens'. He continues, 'I thank God upon every remembrance of you [believers in the

Bedford church]; and rejoice, even while I stick between the
teeth of the lions in the wilderness.'[7]

Christian is troubled

Clearly the lions are determined to prevent the pilgrim Christian, as epitomized by Bunyan, from reaching the security of the
Palace Beautiful — that is, a faithful nonconformist church.
Upon the accession of Charles II to the throne after the Restoration of the monarchy in 1660, opposition by independent
churches to legally mandated conformity led to Bunyan's
immediate imprisonment as well as the ejection of about 1,760
Dissenting ministers from their pastorates. Establishment
religion was exceedingly savage!

Faithful is not troubled

Following after Christian, in broad daylight, Faithful finds that
the lions are asleep. They probably sense that this pilgrim will
not seek accommodation at the Palace Beautiful; he is not in
such direct opposition to them as Christian was. If this is the
case, then what is Faithful's local church affiliation? There can
only be one possibility, and that is that he represents a Puritan
who remained in the established church, an Anglican Puritan
after the likes of the more moderate Richard Baxter and William
Gurnall.

The porter gains a guest and loses a guest

In seventeenth-century terms, John Bunyan was a thoroughgoing separatist and nonconformist. In other words, he evalu-
ated the established Anglican Church as being unbiblical in its

essential structure and, as such, beyond redemption. Hence, in the Palace Beautiful we see an attractively painted picture of the biblical ideal to which, no doubt, he desired that the nonconformist congregation in Bedford which he pastored should conform.

Therefore the porter's solicitation of both Christian and Faithful sets up an interesting matter for consideration since he is only successful with one of these genuine pilgrims. And we are also faced with the question whether Christian, the nonconformist, can still have true and intimate fellowship with Faithful, who remains within the established church.

Christian remains for several nights

To the trembling Christian, Watchful, the porter, gives great encouragement: 'Is thy strength so small? Fear not the lions, for they are chained, and are placed there for trial of faith where it is, and for discovery of those that have none. Keep in the midst of the path, and no hurt shall come unto thee.'[8] So, following careful investigation, the pilgrim enters into the bliss and blessing of genuine local church fellowship. Here edification is found to be many-faceted, substantial and faithful.

Faithful passes by

It seems most likely that the porter Watchful was just as solicitous in his conversation with Faithful, who passed on without stopping. Surely the porter must have mentioned the name of his recently arrived lodger. But Faithful was not sufficiently interested; he courteously declined the invitation and immediately commenced the descent into the Valley of Humiliation. Sad to say, members of the true body of Jesus Christ do not always adhere to the best earthly representation of that fellowship which is designated the Body of Christ. Often many traditional impediments get in the way.

Who then is Faithful?

From an overall point of view, he is just as admirable a saint as Christian. Richard Greaves proposes that he may represent Martin Luther,[9] though this seems rather unlikely since the German Reformer, in his own European setting, was definitely separated from the establishment, by means of his excommunication from the church of Rome. Faithful is somewhat beguiled by Talkative, yet his testimony at Vanity is triumphant, resembling that of Stephen (Acts 6:8-15; 7:54-60). Also, even though Faithful was a non-separatist, Bunyan, the nonconformist, clearly intends that we should appreciate the rich fellowship that developed between these two unlikely candidates. And why is this so? Because Bunyan himself entered into friendships with some Anglicans who remained within the fold of the established church. And the subject of one such pastoral relationship may well have been the person whom Faithful is intended to represent. His name is William Dell.

William Dell the Anglican

Dell was a native of Bedfordshire who became a Fellow of Emmanuel College, Cambridge, and was episcopally ordained. In 1642 he became the rector at Yelden, which is about eleven miles north of Bedford. Through the Earl and Countess of Bolingbroke, who sat under his ministry, Dell became influential amongst the Commonwealth leaders: 'In 1645-46 he was chaplain to the army under General Fairfax, and was the person appointed to bring the articles of the surrender of Oxford to Parliament. In 1649 ... he was made master of Gonville and

Caius College [Cambridge], still retaining his Bedfordshire rectory, and was one of the commissioners sent to attend Charles I before his execution … his sermons both before the House of Commons and in the country were matter of frequent debate in Parliament.'[10]

However, from an establishment point of view, Dell's opinions were regarded as tending towards radicalism, so that he was ejected from the Yelden pastorate in 1662. At heart he was more of an independent. Brown quotes his somewhat reactionary opinions as follows: 'In earthly governments there is no sameness … how much more evil it is to insist upon uniformity in the life of a Christian, and of the Churches of Christ, taking away all freedom of the Spirit of God, who, being one with God, works in the freedom of God… What wild and woeful work do men make when they will have the church of God thus and thus, and get the power of the magistrate to back theirs, as if the new heavens wherein the Lord will dwell must be the work of their own fingers, or as if the New Jerusalem must of necessity come out of the Assembly of Divines at Westminster.'[11]

William Dell the friend of John Bunyan

Although approximately twenty years older than Bunyan, Dell clearly appreciated the fraternal relationship that developed between the two men, for it appears that at heart they were in close agreement on many things, particularly with regard to church order and baptism, as well as esteem for Luther. Dell 'opposed kingship and tithes… He taught that "all churches are equal, as well as all Christians. Union with the church flows from our union with Christ, not vice versa."'[12]

Regardless of Cambridge dons who sneered at the tinker's aspiration to preach, the Yeldon rector was pleased to have Bunyan minister at his church on Christmas Day, 1659. In spite of some disgruntled parishioners, Dell responded that he would '"rather choose to be in fellowship with poor plain husband-men and tradesmen who believe in Christ ... than with the heads of universities and highest and stateliest of the clergy". He rejected the accepted idea that universities should be "the fountain of the ministers of the Gospel" ... His parishioners reported in 1660 that Dell had said Charles I "was no King to him, Christ was his King. A republic was good enough for Venice and Holland, why not England?"' [13]

Hence, it is highly likely that Bunyan was strongly influenced by his senior and more learned friend. Yet while Dell in many ways continued to maintain his Anglican connection — that is, until the establishment separated itself from him by ejection in 1662 — it may well be that as Faithful passed by the Palace Beautiful, he looked at its outward appearance with consider-able appreciation and longing. Yet for some unknown reason he could not bring himself to accept the porter's invitation.

Conclusions concerning Bunyan's ecumenicity

Upon the meeting of Christian and Faithful we read that '... they went very lovingly on together, and had sweet discourse of all things that had happened to them in their pilgrimage.' [14] The relationship between Bunyan and Dell appears to have been equally spiritually satisfying. While Bunyan had little time for broad and high churchmen, in the case of Dell we see that the tinker's views on those from other church backgrounds were not separatist in some cast-iron, second-degree-of-separation sense.

Bunyan the nonconformist fellowshipped with an Anglican

He offered companionship to a brother who had come along a pathway that differed considerably from his own. Dell was originally of the establishment mould. However, Bunyan's own separatist views notwithstanding, he profited from fellowship with Dell and probably learnt much from the relationship. In turn, upon Dell's ejection, who was better placed to offer comfort and encouragement than John Bunyan?

Bunyan the nonconformist preached for an Anglican

The fact that Bunyan agreed to preach at Yelden on Christmas Day, 1659, as a result of Dell's invitation, knowing that some of his congregation would be antagonistic, indicates the tinker's open-mindedness insofar as the uncompromising proclamation of the Word of God is concerned. So Vera Brittain can reasonably speculate concerning this occasion: 'At the end of the service, John accompanied William Dell to the Rectory to take Christmas dinner with him and his family... After dinner the two men sat alone over the table, discussing the local anti-Puritans and the state of the nation. The present anarchy could not continue.'[15] They probably sensed the imminent return of the monarchy and consequent intolerance of nonconformity.

Bunyan the nonconformist learned from an Anglican

That Bunyan, to some degree, embraced the terminology of covenant theology which was so prevalent during the seventeenth century is evident from his writings, and particularly from *The Doctrine of the Law and Grace Unfolded*, published in 1659.[16] However, as we noted earlier, he appears to equate the covenant of grace exclusively with the new covenant and not to superimpose it upon 'the covenants of promise' (Eph. 2:12) in some comprehensive sense (see chapter 8 for a more detailed consideration of this matter). Nevertheless, where Bunyan derived his understanding of the elements of this doctrinal system from remains a matter of conjecture. It is likely that he was not only guided in his reading by the recommendations of

Dell, not to mention Burton, Gifford and Owen, but frequently entered into discussion with these pastoral associates concerning such matters. Certainly he would have been stimulated by their learned discourse.

The extensive conversation between Christian and Faithful accentuates the distinctive experiences encountered by the two pilgrims, but also, more importantly, the spiritual profit that results from the sharing of testimony concerning these events. Doubtless Bunyan was particularly grateful for those times of fellowship with William Dell of Cambridge, as well as John Owen of Oxford, by means of which he became aware of pilgrimage experiences that differed significantly from his own.

The glory of right church fellowship

Church fellowship, or the communion of saints, is the place where the Son of God loveth to walk; his first walking was in Eden. Church fellowship rightly managed, is the glory of the world. No place, no community, no fellowship, is adorned and bespangled with those beauties as is a church rightly knit together to their head, and lovingly serving one another.

John Bunyan
The Desire of the Righteous Granted,
Bunyan, *Works*, vol. I, p.21

15.
The poems and songs of
The Pilgrim's Progress

'Who would true valour
see,
Let him come hither…
There's no discourage-
ment
Shall make him once
relent,
His first avow'd intent
To be a pilgrim'
(John Bunyan).

15.
The poems and songs of *The Pilgrim's Progress*

THOMAS GOODWIN, one of the classic Puritans of Cambridge and Oxford, writing during the early years of Bunyan's life, comments that while instrumental music was part of the Levitical form of worship for ancient Israel, yet 'Musical instruments are not to be in the worship of God now, no more than incense.'[1] The typical Puritan worship service was exceedingly simple; the only music was unaccompanied singing of the metrical psalms. Hence, because of this 'acappella singing in their churches, while Anglicans admitted instrumentalists, an idea has passed current that they were hostile to music. The truth is otherwise. Puritans produced the first Italian opera in England, Cromwell supported an orchestra at court, and [in America] music, both secular and sacred, was encouraged.'[2]

No doubt the banning of drama and a downplaying of the graphic arts in general may have contributed towards this false impression of a stilted approach to music. However, as Christopher Hill puts it, 'Myths have a way of living on long after they have been disproved. Some Puritans disliked certain types of music in church services, since they believed that polyphony or choral singing, for instance, or the playing of organs distracted the attention of auditors from the intellectual content of worship;

but under Puritan rule in the 1640s "music flourished as never before". Bunyan, like John Owen, played the flute, and the Bedford prisoner is said to have made himself a flute out of a chair-leg to play in jail. There survive a metal violin and a cabinet decorated with musical instruments which are believed to have belonged to him. The very title of *Grace Abounding* may come from a book of madrigals [part-songs]'.[3]

The metrical innovation of John Bunyan

Leaving aside John Milton, the Puritans in general made no effort to excel in poetry for the purpose of communicating divine truth. On the contrary, passionate pastoral prose always remained their forte.[4] However, John Bunyan was certainly an exception in this regard. Not only the forty or more poems and songs included in both parts of *The Pilgrim's Progress*, but his *Works* as a whole reflect a strong conviction that both poetic verse and hymns are suitable and arresting vehicles for the communication of the Word of God as well as being helpful stimuli for worship.

Examples of Bunyan's poetry

1. *Profitable Meditations* (756 lines, 1661)[5]

This first venture into verse commences with an apology reminiscent of the one which introduces *The Pilgrim's Progress*. Then follows doctrinal exhortation on a variety of subjects concerning man, sin, Christ, the church, death and judgement. The application is characteristically repeated and direct:

Take none offence, Friend, at my method here,
'Cause thou in Verses simple Truth dost see:

But to them soberly incline thine ear,
And with the Truth itself affected be.

'Tis not the Method, but the Truth alone
Should please a Saint, and mollifie his heart:
Truth in or out of Meeter is but one;
And this thou knowest, if thou a Christian art.

When Doctors give their Physick to the Sick,
They make it pleasing with some other thing:
Truth also by this means is very quick,
When by Faith it in their hearts do sing.

2. *Prison Meditations* (280 lines, 1663)[6]

In responding to a friend who had written a word of encouragement, Bunyan, writing from prison, expresses gratitude for his kindly counsel:

Thou dost encourage me to hold
My head above the flood,
Thy counsel better is than gold,
In need thereof I stood.

I am, indeed, in prison now
In body, but my mind
Is free to study Christ, and how
Unto me he is kind.

For though men keep my outward man
Within their locks and bars,
Yet by the faith of Christ I can
Mount higher than the stars.

3. *One Thing is Needful* (1190 lines, 1665)[7]

Bunyan describes this work as 'Serious meditations upon the four last things, death, judgement, heaven, and hell.' Thus he commences:

> These lines I at this time present
> To all that will them heed,
> Wherein I show to what extent
> God saith, Convert with speed.
>
> For these four things come on apace,
> Which we should know full well,
> Both death and judgement, and, in place
> Next to them, heaven and hell.

4. Ebal and Gerizim (870 lines, 1665)[8]

These two mountains, representing blessing and cursing (Deut. 11:29; 27:12-13), illustrate the mercy and severity of God.

> Thus having heard from Gerazim, I shall
> Next come to Ebal, and you thither call,
> Not there to curse you, but to let you hear
> How God doth curse that soul that shall appear
> An unbelieving man, a graceless wretch;
> Because he doth continue in the breach
> Of Moses' law, and also doth neglect
> To close with Jesus; him will God reject.

5. *A Caution to Stir up to Watch against Sin* (132 lines, 1684)[9]

Using a verse recommended to him, Bunyan then continues on the theme of the subtleties and deceitfulness of sin:

The first eight lines one did commend to me,
The rest I thought good to commend to thee:
Reader, in reading be thou rul'd by me,
With rhimes nor lines, but truths, affected be.

Sin will at first, just like a beggar, crave
One penny or one half-penny to have;
And if you grant its first suit, 'twill aspire
From pence to pounds, and so will still mount higher
To the whole soul: but if it makes its moan,
Then say, here is not for you, get you gone.
For if you give it entrance at the door,
It will come in, and may go out no more.

6. *A Book for Boys and Girls* (49 poems, 1686)[10]

Numerous editions, many with attractive engravings, have proved the popularity of this volume. It has an introduction by the author comprised of ninety-six lines.

Upon the frog

The frog by nature is both damp and cold,
Her mouth is large, her belly much will hold;
She sits somewhat ascending, loves to be
Croaking in gardens, though unpleasantly.

Comparison
The hypocrite is like unto the frog,
As like as is the puppy to the dog.
He is of nature cold, his mouth is wide
To prate, and at true goodness to deride.
He mounts his head as if he was above
The world, when yet 'tis that which has his love.
And though he seeks in churches for to croak,
He neither loveth Jesus nor his yoke.

7. A Discourse of the Building, Nature, Excellency, and Government of the House of God (1310 lines, 1688)[11]

Here is a delightful and comprehensive description of the doctrine of the Christian church that is strongly nonconformist:

> The builder's God, materials his Elect;
> His Son's the rock on which it is erect;
> The Scripture is his rule, plummet, or line,
> Which gives proportion to this house divine,
> His working tools his ordinances are,
> By them he doth his stones and timber square,
> Affections knit in love, the couplings are;
> Good doctrine like to mortar doth cement
> The whole together, schism to prevent.
>
> This place, as hospitals, will entertain,
> Those which the lofty of this world disdain:
> The poor, the lame, the maimed, halt and blind,
> The leprous, and possessed too, may find
> Free welcome here, as also such relief
> As ease them will of trouble, pain and grief.
>
> Art thou bound over to the great assize,
> For hark'ning to the devil and his lies;
> Art thou afraid thereat to show thy head,
> Fear thou then be sent unto the dead?
> Thou may'st come hither, here is room and place,
> For such as willingly would live by grace.

The development of Bunyan's poetic expression

Popular poetic resources were readily available to Bunyan in his youth in the form of ballads, broadsides (polemic pamphlets) and chap-books (pedlar's popular literature). In *Grace*

Abounding, Bunyan relates how he, as a newly married man, attended the Elstow parish church, 'and there should very devoutly, both say and sing as others did, yet retaining my wicked life'.[12] The version of the metrical psalms used at that time was probably the Sternhold and Hopkins edition dating back to 1563. Hill gives evidence for believing that Bunyan's earlier poetic form drew heavily upon Sternhold and Hopkins, while his later verse indicates a more free and developed style.[13] This fact seems especially evident when we consider the obviously superior verse composition that is found in Part Two of *The Pilgrim's Progress* when compared with that of Part One.

The development of Bunyan's hymnody

Bunyan's first recorded interest in instrumental music is his expressed delight in bell-ringing at the Elstow parish church following his attempt at outward religious reformation. However, he soon gave up this practice since it took on superstitious proportions and became in his mind a vain pursuit.[14]

The previous decade, which had been such a turbulent period for Bunyan, had witnessed an innovation in church life that became the cause of much controversy: 'Congregational hymn-singing flourished during the breakdown of ecclesiastical controls in the 1640s, when congregations could take their own decisions. Hymn-singing then was regarded by the authorities as potentially dangerous. It was associated with the lower classes, with Baptists and Muggletonians [apocalyptic, anti-trinitarians]... Among Baptists in particular the subject led to disagreements. There had been disputes over this in the Bedford church from its earliest days. Gifford warned against them in his deathbed letter.'[15]

Both Hanserd Knollys and Benjamin Keach were Baptists who encouraged congregational hymn-singing — the latter being pilloried and imprisoned for his trouble — and there is little doubt that John Bunyan was of the same opinion. In *Light for Them that Sit in Darkness* he writes of the 'peace of God' as follows: 'It is also expressed by "singing"; because the peace of God when it is received into the soul by faith putteth the conscience into a heavenly and melodious frame.'[16] That the author here intends that hymns be understood as the type of singing he has in mind is most obvious when the context of verse in *The Pilgrim's Progress* is understood.

The poems of *The Pilgrim's Progress*

The introductory poems of Part One and Part Two are of similar length and wholly comprised of rhyming couplets. Part One includes twenty verse sections, all rhyming couplets, of which twelve are specifically designated for singing. Part Two includes twenty-three verse sections, of which seven are couplets, fourteen are quatrains, and eight are designated for singing. Assuming a minimum of six years separating the writing of Parts One and Two of *The Pilgrim's Progress*, it is obvious that this period saw a considerable development in Bunyan's ability to compose poetic verse. Significantly, his most notable composition, in Part Two, 'Who would true valour see,' is the most complex in its construction.

Hill is certainly correct when he declares that '[Bunyan's] poems are enjoyable because he himself obviously enjoyed observing and writing them. He wrote with gusto and wit.'[17] But Louis Benson is much closer to the truth when he writes that Bunyan's verse 'is best described as being didactic rather than poetic in motive and accomplishment'.[18] The tinker was not interested in 'art for art's sake', but rather the poetic encapsulation of truth for the cause of effective evangelism and stimulating edification.

The songs of *The Pilgrim's Progress*

The twelve separate verse sections in Part One that enjoin singing must have been considered in Bunyan's time as a clear recommendation of congregational singing, especially since there is not so much as a single reference to a metrical psalm in the whole of *The Pilgrim's Progress*. Hill refers to a credible comment in this regard as follows: 'Tindall suggested that the songs in *The Pilgrim's Progress* were intended as propaganda on behalf of church singing.'[19] Sharrock is of the same opinion.[20] Notice that when Christian finds refreshment and rest at the Palace Beautiful, which, as we have seen, is a representation of a faithful nonconformist church, he wakes up the next morning and immediately bursts into song. Similarly in Part Two, when Christiana, her sons and Mercy feast at the House of Interpreter, they are entertained with minstrel music. Once again, at the Palace Beautiful, following a period of rest, they hear music which causes Mercy to exclaim: 'Wonderful! music in the house, music in the heart, and music also in heaven, for joy that we are here.'[21]

At the conclusion of Part One, like the strains of a finale, the welcoming music of 'the King's trumpeters' is heard and accompanies Christian and Hopeful to the very gates of the Celestial City. Once inside, they are given 'harps to praise withal ... then the bells in the city rang again for joy... I also heard the men themselves, that they sang with a loud voice, saying, "Blessing, and honour, and glory, and power, be unto him that sitteth upon the throne, and unto the Lamb, for ever and ever."'[22] Similarly at the conclusion of Part Two, several pilgrims cross the River of Death, including Christiana, Mr Valiant-for-truth and Mr Stand-fast, to find that the other side 'was filled with horses and chariots, with trumpeters and pipers, with singers and players on stringed instruments, to welcome the pilgrims as they went up'.[23]

The emphasis in Part One

The singing that is expressly stated as such commences with Christian's hymn of praise to Christ at the Place of Deliverance. Every other similar instance involves only the three principal pilgrims, Christian, Faithful and Hopeful. It is Christian and Hopeful who frequently sing together. As to the content, while several songs offer praise and thanksgiving, many more are concerned with exhortation, lament and warning:

- Christian sings in praise of Christ's saving benefits at the Place of Deliverance.
- Christian sings on waking after a night's rest at the Palace Beautiful.
- Christian sings after having traversed the Valley of the Shadow of Death.
- Faithful sings after he has resisted the persistent censure of Shame.
- Christian sings of Faithful's triumphant martyrdom at Vanity Fair.
- Christian sings to Hopeful when By-ends and his friends fall into the silver mine.
- Christian and Hopeful sing after they have been refreshed at the river of God.
- Christian and Hopeful sing after their escape from Doubting Castle.
- Christian and Hopeful sing after viewing the Celestial City through a telescope.
- Christian sings about the lesson of seeking more faith than Little-faith.
- Christian and Hopeful sing after they have been disciplined for heeding the Flatterer.
- Christian sings a song to Hopeful to keep him awake as they cross the Enchanted Ground.

The emphasis in Part Two

There is now a greater stress on singing in fellowship and the poetic quality of the songs is considerably improved. Three hymns in particular that have gained some degree of recognition, to the extent of being described by Graham Midgley as a 'lyrical breakthrough',[24] are listed below:

1. Mercy's hymn, 'Let the Most Blessed be my Guide'[25]

Benson suggests that this is most suitably sung at the admission of members to a church.[26]

Let the Most Blessed be my guide
If't be his blessed will;
Unto his gate, into his fold,
Up to his holy hill.

And let him never suffer me
To swerve or turn aside
From his free grace, and holy ways,
Whate'er shall me betide.

And let him gather them of mine
That I have left behind;
Lord, make them pray they may be thine,
With all their heart and mind.

2. The shepherd boy's hymn, 'He that is down needs fear no fall'[27]

This was the first hymn of Bunyan's to gain wide acceptance. It gives positive expression to life in the Valley of Humiliation:

He that is down needs fear no fall,
He that is low, no pride;

He that is humble ever shall
Have God to be his guide.

I am content with what I have,
Little be it or much;
And, Lord, contentment still I crave,
Because Thou savest such.

Fullness to such a burden is
That go on pilgrimage;
Here little, and hereafter bliss,
Is best from age to age.

3. Valiant-for-Truth's hymn, 'Who would true valour see.'[28]

Beyond dispute, this, Bunyan's most irregular hymn, has
become his most famous; it has found its way into the outstanding English hymnals of the past century. Furthermore, it
exquisitely reflects the essential pilgrim quality of *The Pilgrim's
Progress*, and for this reason deserves recognition as expressing
the theme of Bunyan's life:

Who would true valour see,
Let him come hither;
One here will constant be,
Come wind, come weather.
There's no discouragement
Shall make him once relent,
His first avow'd intent
To be a pilgrim.

Who so beset him round
With dismal stories,
Do but themselves confound,
His strength the more is;

No lion can him fright,
He'll with a giant fight;
But he will have the right
To be a pilgrim.

Hobgoblin nor foul fiend
Can daunt his spirit;
He knows he at the end
Shall life inherit.
Then fancies fly away,
He'll fear not what men say;
He'll labour night and day
To be a pilgrim.

Singing in the church

The songs sung in the temple were new, or such as were compiled after the manner of repeated mercies that the church of God had received, or were to receive. And answerable to this, is the church to sing now new songs, with new hearts for new mercies (Ps. 33:3; 40:3; 96; 144:9; Rev. 14:3). New songs, I say, are grounded on new matter, new occasions, new mercies, new deliverances, new discoveries of God to the soul, or for new frames of heart; and are such as are most taking, most pleasing, and most refreshing to the soul.

[These songs] also were called 'the songs of Zion,' and the 'songs of the temple' (Ps. 137:3; Amos 8:3). And they are so called as they were theirs to sing there; I say, of them of Zion, and the worshippers in the temple. I say, to sing in the church, by the church, to him who is the God of the church, for the mercies, benefits, and blessings which she has received from him. Zion-songs, temple-songs, must be sung by Zion's sons, and temple-worshippers.

To sing to God, is the highest worship we are capable of performing in heaven; and it is much if sinners on earth, without grace, should be capable of performing it, according to his institution, acceptably. I pray God it be done by all those that now-a-days get into churches, in spirit and with understanding.

John Bunyan
Solomon's Temple Spiritualized,
Works, vol. III, p. 496

16.
The Pilgrim's Progress and the seventeenth-century reader

'I have not so beautified my matter with acuteness of language as you could wish or desire... Sir, words easy to be understood do often hit the mark, when high and learned ones do only pierce the air'

(John Bunyan).

16.

The Pilgrim's Progress and the seventeenth-century reader

HAVING established that *The Pilgrim's Progress* deserves to be widely known and understood today, we must now consider in greater detail whether such faithful communication is really possible in a modern era that is so addicted to polychrome marketing of literary fast food. The content of Bunyan's allegory may well be timeless, yet its stylistic packaging may nevertheless be perceived as outdated and unappealing.

The famous eighteenth-century essayist Samuel Johnson, himself a High Church Tory and not a Calvinist, has been described as one 'who had no patience to read a book through', yet he is said to have 'found himself so fascinated by [*The Pilgrim's Progress*] ... that he could not put it down until it was finished'.[1]

In the next century, the historian and essayist Thomas Macaulay writes, 'In the wildest parts of Scotland *The Pilgrim's Progress* is the delight of the peasantry. In every nursery *The Pilgrim's Progress* is a greater favourite than Jack the Giant-killer. Every reader knows the straight and narrow path as well as he knows a road in which he has gone backward and forward a hundred times.'[2]

However, honesty compels us to admit that today there is no such spontaneous interest in Bunyan's allegory. To be sure, reprint sales remain steady worldwide. Nevertheless, in general there is only indifference and ignorance concerning *The Pilgrim's Progress*, as a survey in 1987 indicates. Christopher Hill relates that 'In the USA less than one in seven of a recent cross-section of 17-year olds could identify the book.'[3] At the same time the allegory is subjected to more direct opposition from the secular fringe of literary criticism.[4]

So what response is appropriate here? An immediate reply, certainly in tune with the ethos of this twenty-first century, would be the suggestion that Bunyan's product needs new packaging. And many evangelicals would join this chorus in calling for relevant communication. But before we respond to such a timely question without due thought, first let us consider the nature and purpose of seventeenth-century English Puritan literature as represented by Bunyan. For to neglect this fundamental matter is to be in danger of making an uninformed response that may lead us to venture into novel methods of communication that Bunyan would never have countenanced.

Seventeenth-century Puritan literature

To begin with, let us readily admit the prolixity of Bunyan's nonconformist contemporaries. Indeed, he himself could be wordy and intricate in some of his more polemical works, when compared with modern English, but he never used florid language in order to impress with his learning. In comparison with today's literary climate, representative writers of this Puritan era could be verbose in the extreme. Their sentences were long and circuitous, and their logic, although finely tuned, could stretch even an able mind to great lengths. J. I Packer lists: 'Joseph Caryl's 6,000 quarto pages on Job; 2,000 plus in folio on Hebrews from John Owen; Hildersam's 152 sermons on Psalm 51:1-7; over 800 pages of small print in all modern editions of William Gurnall's treatment of Ephesians 6:10-20, *The Christian in Complete Armour.*[5]

Yet on the other hand, who can read the last-mentioned work and not be impressed with Gurnall's legitimate exposition of his text, his masterful use of illustration and his constant practicality? Furthermore, we need to bear in mind that most secular writers of that period were equally wordy, and yet were well received. Furthermore, the writings of the Puritans were both avidly read and widely distributed, not only in Britain, but further afield in Europe, by means of various translations.[6] And, besides, is there not a place for some contemporary honesty here? Why are we today so critical of such 'ponderous' and 'heavy' tomes, when in fact it would seem more likely that the fault is largely our own? We ought to be able to read such literature with ease, but our present shallow roots in good literary soil, fostered by a revolution in the visual media, have weakened both our abilities and our interests.

In Bunyan's case, he is certainly easier to read than his scholarly friend John Owen,[7] and undoubtedly it was this unadorned, yet winsome, manner, equally evident in his popularity as a preacher, that helped to gain such broad approval for his writings. His adoption of this style was intentional, since he writes to his more learned readers: 'I have not so beautified my matter with acuteness of language as you could wish or desire... I have not given you, either in the line or in the margent, a cloud of sentences from the learned fathers... Sir, words easy to be understood do often hit the mark, when high and learned ones do only pierce the air... I honour the godly as Christians, but I prefer the Bible before them; and having that still with me, I count myself far better furnished than if I had without it all the libraries of the two universities. Besides, I am for drinking water out of my own cistern; what God makes mine by the evidence of his Word and Spirit, that I dare make bold with.'[8] Hence, in *The Pilgrim's Progress* there are no ornate literary flourishes, only plain prose that sparkles with the beauty of its purity and clarity. Here, then, is a work that is so composed as to be most suitable for communication to future generations.

The form of Puritan writings

Many of Bunyan's writings, like those of numerous prolific Christian writers — such as Luther, Calvin, Edwards, Spurgeon, Lloyd-Jones — and especially those of his Puritan contemporaries, Thomas Manton, Stephen Charnock and Richard Baxter, were probably the product of extensive and didactic preaching, including that which he performed in prison. It is likely that *The Pilgrim's Progress* incorporates many illustrations that were part of earlier sermons. This is even implied by the strange fact that in all of the three volumes of Bunyan's works edited by George Offor, there is only one designated sermon, that one being his last, the sermon based on John 1:13, delivered just twelve days before his death in August 1688.[9] However, along with his fellow-nonconformists, the Bedford pastor employed a communicative method that was characteristic of his time, and one which remains readily adaptable for the twenty-first century.

1. Bunyan was analytical

Like a dog with a bone, he wrestled with his text until every last vestige of meat was obtained from it. Take, for example, his manner of dealing with the text, 'So run, that ye may obtain' (1 Cor. 9:24, AV), published under the title of *The Heavenly Footman*. The whole concept of 'running' — that is, spiritual progress for the seeker and believer, is analysed with great penetration and discernment:

> All or every one that runneth doth not obtain the prize; there be many that do run, yea, and run far too who yet miss of the crown that standeth at the end of the

race. You know that all who run in a race do not obtain the victory; they all run, but one wins. And so it is here; it is not every one that runneth, nor every one that seeketh, nor every one that striveth for the mastery, that hath it (Luke 13).

Though a man do strive for the mastery, saith Paul, 'yet he is not crowned, except he strive lawfully'; that is, unless he so run, and so strive, as to have God's approbation (2 Tim. 2:5). What, do you think that every heavy-heeled professor will have heaven? What, every lazy one; every wanton and lazy professor, that will be stopped by anything, kept back by anything, that scarce runneth so fast heaven-ward as a snail creepeth on the ground? Nay, there are some professors do not go on so fast in the way of God as a snail doth go on the wall; and yet these think, that heaven and happiness is for them. But stay, there are many more that run than there be that obtain; therefore he that will have heaven must *run* for it.[10]

2. Bunyan was systematic

Puritans were often called 'precisians' because of their scrupulous lifestyles. And Bunyan was no exception in this respect. In other words, he was orderly and, like Manton, Charnock and Baxter, committed to following a thorough and detailed outline in his writing. Once again, *The Heavenly Footman* is a good illustration of this.[11] However, *The Pilgrim's Progress* is not so rigidly structured, although in this connection we should consider the careful arrangement of the description of Temporary: we are given four reasons why he departed from the faith, and nine progressive stages in his falling away are listed.[12]

3. Bunyan was illustrative

While his verbal illustrations are legion throughout his *Works*, he was not averse to using visual illustration in a supplementary capacity. His *Map Shewing the Order and Causes of Salvation* published in 1664[13] (which was similar to one produced earlier by William Perkins towards the end of the sixteenth century),[14] was certainly avant-garde for its time and easy to comprehend. Then again, Bunyan must evidently have approved of 'The Sleeping Portrait', as it is called, which was included in the third edition of *The Pilgrim's Progress* published in 1679 (see page 51).[15]

4. Bunyan was poetic

As we noted earlier, apart from Milton, the Puritans in general made no effort to excel in poetry for the purpose of communicating divine truth. Instead, passionate, though often ponderous, pastoral prose always remained their forte. Miller and Johnson write that 'It is as writers of prose that the Puritans' literary art finally must be judged. Prose was the vehicle of their finest thoughts.'[16] However, Bunyan was certainly an exception in this regard. Not only are there over forty poems and songs included in the two parts of *The Pilgrim's Progress*, but his *Works* as a whole reflect a strong conviction that both poetry and hymns are suitable vehicles for the communication of the Word of God. His *Book for Boys and Girls* especially demonstrates his fervent interest in this regard (see chapter 15, as well as volume VI of the Oxford University Press edition of *The Miscellaneous Works of John Bunyan*).[17]

5. Bunyan was not dramatic

While John Bunyan proved to be one of the ablest exponents of lively prosaic drama, he would undoubtedly have shunned any suggestion of a staged production of *The Pilgrim's Progress*. For him, the theatre was a favourite pastime of the inhabitants of Vanity; at their Fair all sorts of 'juggling, cheats, games, plays, fools, apes, knaves, and rogues' were to be found.[18] The Cromwellian interregnum was iconoclastic towards the stage:

'During the twenty years of Puritan rule at mid-century, most of the theatres were closed and hardly anything was written for the stage ... then the theatres were shut, abruptly and apparently for ever. When they opened in 1660, they were forced at first to rely on a backlog of twenty-year-old plays. But gradually they built up a repertoire of comedies (generally bawdy) and tragedies in the rhetorical declamatory manner.'[19]

The purpose of Puritan writings

There is little doubt that the overriding purpose in the writings of Puritans such as Bunyan was pastoral rather than professional. In other words, they were intensely concerned about spiritual shepherding and the welfare of redeemed children of God, both themselves and those committed to their care. Peter Lewis well describes this heart-possessing dynamic as follows:

> Puritanism was not merely a set of rules or a larger creed, but a life-force: a vision and a compulsion which saw the beauty of a holy life and moved towards it, marvelling at the possibilities and thrilling to the satisfaction of a God-centred life... Every area of life came under the influence of God and the guidance of the Word. Each day began and ended with searching, unhurried and devout personal and family prayer. Each task, whether professional or manual, was done to the glory of God and with a scrupulous eye to his perfect will.
>
> Every relationship, business or personal, was regulated by spiritual principles. Hours free from labour were gladly and zealously employed in the study of the Scriptures, attendance upon public worship, 'godly converse' or intense witness and every other means which contributed to the soul's good. In a word, the 'great business of godliness' dominated the ardent believer's ambitions and called forth all his energies. We may say that to a large

extent Puritanism succeeded where other more cloistered ideologies failed, because here men embodied true doctrine so that Puritanism was visible before men. Men saw on earth lives that were not earthly, lives that touched their own at so many points, yet which rolled on into a moral and spiritual continent of breathtaking landscape. Indeed, it is not too much to say that Puritans were Puritanism proper — for Puritanism was sainthood visible.[20]

It is for this reason that one might go so far as to suggest that J. I. Packer is guilty of tautology when he entitles a very fine chapter in his *A Quest for Godliness*, 'The Practical Writings of the English Puritans.'[21] In other words, we may well ask which writings, at least in any substantial sense, were *not* practical? At any rate, leaving this minor contention aside, let us turn to the chapter in question and make use of the author's excellent characterization, under five headings, of the practical purposes of Puritan writings, and especially as they are reflected through the pen of John Bunyan.[22]

1. Bunyan was a physician to the soul

According to Acts 20:28, he understood his first priority to be concern for his own relationship with God. Sensitivity in this regard permeates all his works, especially *Grace Abounding to the Chief of Sinners*, the concept of which is based on Psalm 66:16: 'Come and hear, all ye that fear God, and I will declare what he hath done for my soul.'

At the conclusion of this work he writes:

I find to this day seven abominations in my heart:

1. Inclinings to unbelief.
2. Suddenly to forget the love and mercy that Christ manifesteth.
3. A leaning to the works of the law.

4. Wanderings and coldness in prayer.
5. To forget to watch for that I pray for.
6. Apt to murmur because I have no more, and yet ready to abuse what I have.
7. I can do none of those things which God commands me, but my corruptions will thrust in themselves, 'When I would do good, evil is present with me.'

These things I continually see and feel, and am afflicted and oppressed with; yet the wisdom of God doth order them for my good.

1. They make me abhor myself.
2. They keep me from trusting my heart.
3. They convince me of the insufficiency of all inherent righteousness.
4. They show me the necessity of flying to Jesus.
5. They press me to pray unto God.
6. They show me the need I have to watch and be sober.
7. And provoke me to look to God, through Christ, to help me, and carry me through this world. Amen.[23]

As a consequence, Bunyan loved the souls of men, and especially those who were deeply conscious of being lost, even as he once was. Consider the following appeal that concludes his *Justification by an Imputed Righteousness*: 'Sinners, take my advice, with which I shall conclude... Call often to remembrance that thou hast a precious soul within thee; that thou art in the way to thy end... put thyself in thy thoughts into the last day thou must live in this world, seriously arguing thus... How if the first voice that rings tomorrow morning in my heavy ears be, "Arise, ye dead, and come to judgement?" ... O how serious should sinners be in this work of remembering things to come, of laying to their heart the greatness and terror of that notable day of God Almighty, and in examining themselves, how it is like to go with their souls when they shall stand before the Judge indeed! To this end, God make this word effectual. Amen.'[24]

2. Bunyan was an expositor addressing the conscience

Because the Bible was inerrant and truthful — that is, verbal and propositional revelation exhaled from the mouth of God (2 Tim. 3:16) who cannot lie (Heb. 6:18)[25] — such an authoritative foundation resulted in a homiletic method that gave unswerving commitment to the exposition of this sacred text. Here are a few examples:

- *The Greatness of the Soul,* based on Mark 8:37.[26]
- *The Strait Gate,* based on Matthew 7:13-14.[27]
- *The Pharisee and the Publican,* based on Luke 18:10-13.[28]
- *Paul's Departure and Crown,* based on 2 Timothy 4:6-8.[29]
- *An Exposition on the First Ten Chapters of Genesis.*[30]
- *The Heavenly Footman,* based on 1 Corinthians 9:24.[31]
- *The Holy City, or the New Jerusalem,* based on Revelation 21:10-27; 22:1-4.[32]

Moreover, Bunyan believed that the Word of God had a unique ability to lance the festering sores of the soul in such a way as to lead the person from conviction of conscience to repentance: 'Now when the hand of the Lord is with the Word, then it is mighty: it is "mighty through God to the pulling down of strong holds" (2 Cor. 10:4)... It sticks like an arrow in the hearts of sinners, to the causing of the people to fall at his foot for mercy (Heb. 4:12)... When seconded by mighty power, then the same is as the roaring of the lion, as the piercing of a sword, as a burning fire in the bones, as thunder and as a hammer that dashes all to pieces (Jer. 25:30; Amos 1:2; 3:8; Acts 2:37; Jer. 20:9; Ps. 29:3-9).'[33]

But what is the purpose of this convicting work? It is that, 'by [God's] breaking of the heart he openeth it, and makes it a receptacle of the graces of his Spirit; this is the cabinet, when unlocked, where God lays up the jewels of the gospel.'[34]

3. Bunyan was an educator of the mind

In today's existential, relational, subjective world governed by self-interest, sensuality and sentiment, this emphasis tends to be scoffed at on account of being unnecessarily cerebral and remote from contemporary reality or the hurting masses. At this point, Puritanism is in sharp conflict with the status-quo posture of contemporary evangelical Christianity.

Packer explains as follows: 'All the Puritans regarded religious feeling and pious emotion without knowledge as worse than useless. Only when the truth was being felt was emotion in any way desirable. When men felt and obeyed the truth they knew, it was the work of the Spirit of God, but when they were swayed by feeling without knowledge, it was a sure sign that the devil was at work, for feeling divorced from knowledge and urging to action in darkness of mind were both as ruinous to the soul as was knowledge without obedience. So the teaching of truth was the pastor's first task, as the learning of it was the layman's.'[35]

Bunyan would have been in full agreement with this point. His earliest two writings, *Some Gospel Truths Opened*[36] and *A Vindication of Gospel Truths*,[37] written to oppose the extreme interiorization of Christian truth by the Quakers, make plain that genuine subjective experience is grounded upon objective Scripture truth and that the knowledge of an indwelling Christ is rooted in a historic and external Christ seated at the right hand of the Father. He himself embodied what today might be called 'a walking Bible', except that he would not have allowed that there was any disjunction between the intellectual comprehension and the practical outworking of divine truth.

There is content and substance and doctrine in all that Bunyan writes; however, the strong meat is well seasoned with illustrations, full of vital spiritual nutrients, made readily digestible for assimilation by the soul, and strenuously recommended with great force of exhortation and evangelistic proclamation.

A good example of this is to be found in his catechism, *Instruction for the Ignorant* subtitled, 'A Salve to that Great Want [Lack] of Knowledge which so much Reigns both in Young and Old,' and especially in the section on 'Faith in Christ'. Here all sorts of spurious faith are distinguished from the true, which is described as 'faith [which] quickeneth to spiritual life, purifies and sanctifies the heart; and worketh up the man that hath it, into the image of Jesus Christ (Col. 2:12-13; Acts 15:9; 26:18; 2 Cor. 3:18)'.[38]

4. Bunyan was an enforcer of the truth

In other words, his manner of communication was intentionally unadorned with sophisticated terms or learned phraseology. The claims of the truth of God upon his life were far too important for literary flourish, homiletic performance, and pastoral posturing. So in his preface to *Grace Abounding*, Bunyan explains: 'I could also have stepped into a style much higher than this in which I have here discoursed, and could have adorned all things more than here I have seemed to do, but I dare not. God did not play in convincing of me, the devil did not play in tempting of me, neither did I play when I sunk into a bottomless pit, when the pangs of hell caught hold upon me; wherefore I may not play in my relating of them, but be plain and simple, and lay down the thing as it was.'[39]

Following the death of John Gifford in 1655, Bunyan's next pastor in Bedford was John Burton, who wrote a foreword to the new preacher's first published work, the polemical tract directed against the Quakers and Ranters mentioned earlier, with the title, *Some Gospel Truths Opened*. In this recommendation Burton writes, 'Reader, in this book thou wilt not meet with high flown airy notions, which some delight in, counting them high mysteries, but the sound, plain, common, (and yet spiritual and mysterious) truths of the gospel... Neither doth this treatise offer to thee doubtful controversial things, or matters of opinion, as some books chiefly do, which when insisted upon, the weightier things of the gospel have always done more hurt than good: But here thou hast things certain, and necessary to be believed, which thou canst not too much study... This man is not chosen out of an earthly, but out of the heavenly university, the church of Christ... And though this man hath not the learning or wisdom of man, yet through grace he hath received the teaching of God, and the learning of the Spirit of Christ, which is the thing that makes a man both a Christian and a minister of the gospel... He hath, through grace taken these three heavenly degrees, to wit, union with Christ, the anointing of the Spirit, and experience of the temptations of Satan, which do more fit a man for that mighty work of preaching the gospel, than all university learning and degrees that can be had.'[40]

Even though many of the Puritans were men of formal learning, they took as their example the similarly learned apostle Paul when he wrote to the Corinthians: 'And when I came to you, brethren, I did not come with superiority of speech or of wisdom, proclaiming to you the testimony of God... And my message and my preaching were not in persuasive words of wisdom, but in demonstration of the Spirit and of power' (1 Cor. 2:1,4). So the untutored Bunyan took the same stance as his fellow-Puritans; together they shunned 'pulpiteering' — that is, preaching in a grand and oratorical style — since, as Packer quotes John Flavel saying, 'A crucified style best suits the preachers of a crucified Christ.'[41]

5. Bunyan was a man of the Spirit

By this is meant that he was not only well endowed with spiritual gifts, but also that he was a pastoral exemplar of

spiritual graces. George Offor makes special mention of Bunyan's self-renouncing character as follows: 'The finest trait in
Bunyan's character was his deep, heartfelt humility. This is the
more extraordinary from his want of secular education, and his
unrivalled talent... He acknowledged to Mr. Cockayn [a London pastor and friend], who considered him the most eminent
man, and a star of the first magnitude in the firmament of the
churches, that spiritual pride was his easily besetting sin, and
that he needed the thorn in the flesh, lest he should be exalted
above measure... His self-abasement was neither tinctured with
affectation, nor with the pride of humility. His humble-
mindedness appeared to arise from his intimate communion
with Heaven.[42]

In other words, Bunyan's total submission to the Bible as
pure objective truth led to a subjective self-evaluation that is so
honestly recorded in *Grace Abounding*. There his transparency
is primarily before God. To be sure, the immediate experience
is withering humiliation, almost to the point of despair, yet the
ultimate end is the triumph and praise of sovereign grace.
Hence for the purpose of maintaining the house of the Lord or
the local church, he shares some 'of the spoils won in battles'.[43]

It is for this reason that, just as Bunyan declares, 'I preached
what I felt, what I smartingly did feel, even that under which my
poor soul did groan and tremble to astonishment,'[44] so he writes
with the same amalgam of revelation from God and intimate
encounter with God. There is no pretension, no scripting of
what others might have expected him to write, only a subdued
soul that, having been stripped naked of any sham, desires and
grasps for the gracious righteousness of God in company with
those of like mind.

He describes this quest as follows: 'For my part, I find it one
of the hardest things that I can put my soul upon, even to come
to God, when warmly sensible that I am a sinner, for a share in
grace and mercy. Oh! methinks it seems to me as if the whole
face of the heavens were set against me. Yes, the very thought
of God strikes me through, I cannot bear up, I cannot stand

before him, I cannot but with a thousand tears say, "God be merciful to me a sinner" (Ezra 9:15; Luke 18:13). At another time when my heart is more hard and stupid, and when his terror does not make me afraid, then I can come before him and talk of my sins, and ask mercy at his hand, and scarce be sensible of sin or grace, or that indeed I am before God: But above all, they are the rare times, when I can go to God as the Publican, sensible of his glorious majesty, sensible of my misery, and bear up, and affectionately cry, "God be merciful to me a sinner." ' [45]

Hence, it may be truly said of Bunyan that he never addressed hearers and readers with vital truth without having first addressed his own heart concerning the very same matter. Thus when Packer describes the Puritan contemporaries of the Bedford tinker, he at the same time precisely describes the tinker himself, for he also gave personal priority to 'conscientious faithfulness to the Bible; vivid perception of God's reality and greatness; inflexible desire to honour and please him; deep self-searching and radical self-denial; adoring intimacy with Christ; generous compassion manward; forthright simplicity, God-taught and God-wrought, adult in its knowingness while childlike in its directness'. [46]

As George Offor fittingly, lovingly, concludes his memoir, 'All the secret of Bunyan's vast usefulness, the foundation of all his honour, is, that the fear of God swallowed up the fear of man; that he was baptized into the truths of revelation, and lived to exemplify them.' [47]

The Pilgrim's Progress as Puritan literature

It is probably far more difficult for the Western mind in the twenty-first century to grasp the setting of communication in the Puritan seventeenth century than might at first be thought. It should be borne in mind that, as a teenager, Bunyan witnessed not only a civil war and the execution of the monarch, but also a resultant literary awakening that doubtless acted as a stimulant to his dawning imagination.

Christopher Hill explains: 'Before 1640 ordinary people had no share whatsoever in politics: they existed only to be ruled, an Elizabethan secretary of state said. There was a strict censorship. This broke down in 1640. So did the monopoly of the state church. What we feebly call "religious toleration" established itself. Suddenly ordinary men and women could gather in groups, under the chairmanship of a "mechanic preacher", a working artisan [Bunyan]. The collapse of the censorship saw a fantastic outpouring of books, pamphlets and newspapers. Before 1640 newspapers were illegal; by 1645 there were 722. Twenty-two books were published in 1640; over 2,000 in 1642... A starved public was hungry for ideas as well as for news, about life as well as about war.'[48]

Nevertheless, our view today of Puritan writings, influenced as it is by an orientation towards visual graphics and images, is likely to assess such literature as unattractive, verbose, dull, difficult to read, lacking in a sense of humour, boring, tedious, antiquated and highly moralistic. Yet how would a Puritan assess our writings today? The level of graphic presentation would undoubtedly amaze him for a while, as would the quality of printing and production. But with regard to content, apart from the numbing advance in technology, he would probably rate our books in general as juvenile, self-centred and in many cases trivial, quite apart from his obvious revulsion at the raw paganism and moral decadence of our culture.

So we may say that *The Pilgrim's Progress* remains a Puritan work that had great appeal in the seventeenth century, although it is also true that in some respects it was in advance of its time. What, then, can we say about it in preparation for considering how it should be communicated in this twenty-first century?

It addresses the reader through the printed word, not through visual images

By modern standards, the first edition of *The Pilgrim's Progress* was extremely plain and uninviting. No larger than 5½ inches by 4¼ inches (14 cm. by 11 cm.), it was printed in what to us would appear to be rough type, on yellowish-grey paper; it included instances of poor spelling and misprints and lacked a number of the narrative incidents that are included in the subsequent second and third editions. Bound in sheepskin, without any illustrations,[49] it consisted of 232 pages, not counting the author's apology and conclusion, and cost one shilling and sixpence. The circulation of thirteen editions published during Bunyan's lifetime was approximately 100,000.

In the light of its relatively plain, even tawdry, presentation, *The Pilgrim's Progress* presents a sharp contrast with the modern emphasis on visual imagery. This paperback-sized volume, printed in cold, black type and lacking the warmth and visual appeal of today's full-colour presentations, with their vivid illustrations and sophisticated layout, relies instead upon the alternative attractions of allegorical illustration, purity and simplicity of prose and the foundation of pervasive, authoritative biblical substance. Its appeal lies in its content rather than the visual presentation of the material.

It addresses the reader on the intellectual level

During the seventeenth century, the reader expected to be informed rather than impressed. He had no background of modern advertising that 'sells the sizzle, not the steak', of publishing that attracts by means of visual imagery rather than the presentation of objective truth, or of modern television that captures the interest by visual impression rather than conveying a message of truth.

However, a book composed of unadorned pages that are repetitively crammed with small type and large paragraphs did *not* present a problem for the literate English commoner. Why was this so? Neil Postman gives the answer, and even though he focuses upon the literacy of eighteenth-century America compared with today, his response is equally applicable to the literary acuity of the seventeenth-century Puritan and his audience in comparison with the relative dullness of evangelicals today with regard to intellectually acquired knowledge. He writes, 'The name I give to that period of time during which the American mind submitted itself to the sovereignty of the printing press is the Age of Exposition. Exposition is a mode of thought, a method of learning, and a means of expression. Almost all of the characteristics we associate with mature discourse were amplified by typography, which has the strongest possible bias toward exposition: a sophisticated ability to think conceptually, deductively and sequentially; a high valuation of reason and order; an abhorrence of contradiction; a large capacity for detachment and objectivity; and a tolerance for delayed response. Toward the end of the nineteenth century, for reasons I am most anxious to explain, the Age of Exposition began to pass, and the early signs of its replacement could be discerned. Its replacement was to be the Age of Show Business.'[50]

It addresses the reader with an allegory in order to convey reality

On the one hand, this modern age desperately attempts to escape reality and ultimate truth by means of Hollywood fantasy, television escapism, theme-park adventure, science-fiction make-believe, drug-induced hallucination and even the cosmetology of the funeral parlour. On the other hand, *The Pilgrim's Progress* uses allegory and an adventure format that are intended inevitably to lead the reader to confrontation with the reality of biblical truth and salvation. The allegorical adornment is merely a means to a substantial and objective end; it is *not* an end in itself.

In the same vein, this allegorical conveyance of reality concerns truth which alone can give rise to legitimate experience. The metaphorical road to reality leads from the truth of a wilderness world to the truth of citizenship in a holy heaven; from the truth of condemnation by God to the truth of saving grace from God; from the knowledge of this truth to the personal embrace of this truth. From the very beginning of *The Pilgrim's Progress*, Bunyan makes this intent quite clear:

> Would'st thou see a truth within a fable? …
> Would'st thou be in a dream, and yet not sleep?[51]

A word to the readers of 'Grace Abounding'

I have sent you here enclosed, a drop of that honey, that I have taken out of the carcass of a lion (Judges 14:5-9). I have eaten thereof myself also, and am much refreshed thereby. (Temptations, when we meet them at first, are as the lion that roared upon Samson; but if we overcome them, the next time we see them, we shall find a nest of honey within them.) The Philistines understand me not. It is something of a relation of the work of God upon my own soul …

I could have enlarged much in this my discourse, of my temptations and troubles for sin; as also of the merciful kindness and working of God with my soul. I could also have stepped into a style much higher than this in which I have here discoursed, and could have adorned all things more than here I have seemed to do, but I dare not. God did not play in convincing of me, the devil did not play in tempting of me, neither did I play when I sunk as into a bottomless pit, when the pangs of hell caught hold upon me; wherefore I may not play in my relating of them, but be plain and simple, and lay down the thing as it was. He that liketh it, let him receive it; and he that does not, let him produce a better. Farewell.

John Bunyan
Grace Abounding to the Chief of Sinners,
Bunyan, *Works,* vol. I, pp.4-5

17.
The Pilgrim's Progress and the modern reader

'Some will maintain that if
biblical principles are
presented, the medium
doesn't matter. That is
nonsense... Feeding people's
appetite for entertainment
only exacerbates the problems
of mindless emotion, apathy,
and materialism'

(John F. MacArthur, Jr.).

17.
The Pilgrim's Progress and the modern reader

To be transported rapidly from the literary culture of seventeenth-century England, and particularly the Puritan sermonic style of that period, with its emphasis on the printed word, to the ubiquitous multi-media jungle of the twenty-first century as it impacts evangelical Christianity, is to experience a truly Copernican revolution. To consider the 'advance' from the God of John Owen to the God of Robert Schuller, from Stephen Charnock to the drama and glamour of designer churches, from John Bunyan to the religious professionals of today who shamelessly promote the gospel using the marketing strategy of Vanity Fair, is to be confronted with a leap of quantum proportions. And this being the case, in our desire to communicate *The Pilgrim's Progress* effectively today, the vital question arises, to what degree can we make use of modern methods of communication without dishonouring God or disregarding Bunyan's expressed purposes? In other words, how can we employ modern means that transmit the truth — namely, a sacred message — and at the same time attain a holy, God-glorifying end? How can we uncompromisingly, and yet effectively, focus on the substance of this peerless allegory?

The legacy of the dominance of the printed word

It is no exaggeration to state that the two-hundred-year period following the publication of *The Pilgrim's Progress* in 1678 was dominated by, and increasingly saturated with, the printed page. This was really the only popular medium available. Neil Postman explains: 'From the seventeenth century to the late nineteenth century, printed matter was virtually all that was available, There were no movies to see, radio to hear, photographic displays to look at, records to play. There was no television. Public business was channelled into and expressed through print, which became the model, the metaphor and the measure of all discourse.'[1]

While advances were made in designing more efficient printing presses, in illustration and graphic design, in paper production and binding, the message imprinted by handset type was one to be mentally digested. Postman further characterizes this period as follows: 'From Erasmus in the sixteenth century to Elizabeth Eisenstein in the twentieth, almost every scholar who has grappled with the question of what reading does to one's habits of mind has concluded that the process encourages rationality... To engage the written word means to follow a line of thought, which requires considerable powers of classifying, inference-making and reasoning. It means to uncover lies, confusions, and over-generalizations, to detect abuses of logic and common sense. It also means to weigh ideas, to compare and contrast assertions, to connect one generalization to another... In a culture dominated by print, public discourse tends to be characterized by a coherent, orderly arrangement of facts and ideas.'[2]

It should also be kept in mind that during all this time, apart from the Bible, *The Pilgrim's Progress* was unquestionably the most widely read book in the English-speaking world. Further, in the realm of graphic layout considerable advance was made, and this is clearly demonstrated by the exquisite nineteenth-century illustration of Bunyan's masterpiece by Frederick Barnard, Charles H. Bennett, Harold Copping, George Cruikshank, Thomas Dalziel, J. D. Linton, Paolo Priolo, H. C. Selous, F. J. Shields, William Strang, J. D. Watson and the Rhead Brothers.

The dawning of audio-visual stimulation

Suddenly, as the nineteenth century drew to a close, alongside this surging torrent of the printed word, other very different forms of communication began to flood in, and it was not long before the two streams converged. This mingling of two strong currents, the typographic and the audio-visual media, was productive of greater variety of impression and style, of appeal to the senses as well as to the intellect, and provided increased choice for a human psyche that was all too ready for stimulation. The cumulative effect was overwhelming, with the result that the informative and educational process experienced a profound revolution. The table overleaf indicates the rapid succession of these new means of communication.

The invasion of new media

In addition we need to take account of recent developments such as ever larger digital screens and the imminent prospect of virtual reality. The greater influence of talk radio and cable news has also led to a shift away from the dominant influence of the major news networks. So, we ask, does this revolution in communications technology present a window of opportunity for a more welcome and clearer contemporary proclamation of *The Pilgrim's Progress*? Some would, with great creative enthusiasm, undoubtedly think so.

Medium	Inauguration	Comments
Print		
Flatbed	1450	Gutenberg
Rotary	1850	Letterpress only
Rotary — high speed	1920s	Letterpress, Gravure, Litho
Photography		
Film	1841	Negative/Positive copying
		Kodak
Digital cameras	1990	
Telegraphy	1845	Public Corp., Morse code
Telephone		
Wire	1878	Bell telephone
Radio	1927	Between U.S. and England
		A.T.& T. Bell Labs
Cellular	1977	Bell Telephone
Cordless	1980	
Phonograph	1877	Edison's first cylinder
Motion pictures		
Silent	1903	*The Great Train Robbery*
Colour	1922	*The Toll of the Sea*
Sound	1927	*The Jazz Singer*
Radio	1920	First scheduled broadcasts
Television		
Black and white	1936	Public broadcast, England
Cable	1949	Public broadcast, U.S.
Colour	1951	Public Broadcast, U.S.
HDTV	1990	FCC
Satellite	1962	Telstar
Personal computer	1983	Internet, email
	1983	Compact disc
	1997	DVD-Video

The widespread adoption of communication methods that appeal to the senses

What, then, has been the fallout effect of this new wave of communications technology upon print, the former prima donna of the cognitive world? Mitchell Stephens of the *Los Angeles Times* provides a good sitcom illustration: 'What's missing from these pictures? Three people sit in a doctor's waiting room. One stares at the television that rests on an end table, the second fiddles with a hand-held video game; the head of the third is wrapped in earphones. A couple of kids, waiting for bedtime, lie on the floor of a brightly painted room, busily manipulating the controls of a video game. Two hundred people sit in an airplane. Some have brought their own tapes, some doze, most stare up at a small movie screen. What is missing from these pictures, and increasingly from our lives, is the activity through which most of us learned much of what we know of the wider world. What's missing is the force that, according to a growing consensus of historians, established our patterns of thought and, in an important sense, made our civilization. What's missing is the venerable, increasingly dated activity that you ... are engaged in right now [reading].'[3]

However, these major contemporary media neophytes have taught the elder statesman (the printed word) a thing or two, though more by way of seduction than refinement of breeding. For the new generation of vehicles of communication, and television in particular, have distinguished themselves by offering expertise in suggestive imagery, sensual impression, disjointed immediacy, varnished reality and commercial profitability.

David Wells describes this distinctive capability as follows: 'Television entertainments tend to avoid problems that can't be solved by the end of an hour; in some ways they turn their backs on messy reality altogether, weaving a fiction of happy automatons with gleaming teeth, well-kept homes, shiny new cars, and hair that is never mussed for long... In television's fantasy world, gangsters are sophisticated and intelligent, and prostitutes are glamorous and healthy, untouched by the violence, manipulation, and fear that plagues the real world's mean streets. On the whole, television makes no pretence of having a social conscience. Its perspective on life is not moral. It is not even real... Television serves up a stream of fleeting images that ... are arranged more to produce a dramatic effect than to convey consistent ideas in a logical manner. It is of the very essence of television that it is impermanent. Viewers are meant to experience the programming, not to think about it.'[4]

As a result, the print media have not been slow to learn. Newspaper formats now present 'print-bites', rather than extended narrative or prose, supported by spot-colour layout and full-colour illustrations. *USA Today* has become the *CNN* of the press. Magazines and specialist newspapers place heavy emphasis on graphics and photography, almost to the point where the text has become of subsidiary importance. In children's literature, graphics, especially cartooning and vivid colour, have taken on a primary role in communicative method.

Yet has this shift of emphasis resulted in a resurgence of reading, even of the more popular sort? Has this mixture of television style and the printed word worked? In no way. Stephens explains: 'The Gulf War provided further evidence of how far the newspaper has fallen. According to a survey by Birch/Scarborough, a grand total of 8.9% of us [in the U.S.] said we kept up with the war news primarily through newspapers. The days when we found most of our news set in type on a page are long gone... Here is perhaps the most frightening of the statistics on books: According to the Gallup Poll, the number of Americans who admitted to having read no books during the past year — and this is not an easy thing to admit to a pollster — doubled from 1978 to 1990, from 8% to 16%.'[5]

Postman thoroughly agrees, though he is far more specific with regard to explaining not only why this conflict remains, but also why it offers no prospect of reconciliation: 'Television's way of knowing is uncompromisingly hostile to typography's way of knowing ... television's conversations promote incoherence and triviality ... the phrase "serious television" is a contradiction in terms ... television speaks in only one persistent voice — the voice of entertainment ... to enter the great television conversation, one American cultural institution after another is learning to speak its terms. Television, in other words, is transforming our culture into one vast arena for show business.'[6]

If this is the case, then ought the communication of *The Pilgrim's Progress* to this twenty-first-century generation include similar flirtation with the media-style of modernity? Should Bunyan's printed word be adapted to fit media which give the priority to imagery and immediate appeal to the senses?

The seductive power of communication that appeals to the senses

The seeming triumph of the phosphorous screen over the printed page, of the picture over text, of image over intellect, has far broader consequences that relate to human behaviour in general than merely a necessary change in communicative strategy. In Postman's *Amusing Ourselves to Death*, his title prophetically directs us to his main thesis that Western man's destiny, under the direction of the media, is one of blissful giddiness born of hedonistic intoxication. He writes, 'What I am claiming here is not that television is entertaining but that it has made entertainment itself the natural format for the representation of all experience... The problem is not that television presents us with entertaining subject matter but that all subject matter is presented as entertaining, which is another issue altogether... No matter what is depicted or from what point of view, the overarching presumption is that it is there for our amusement and pleasure... Everything about a news show tells us this — the good looks and amiability of the cast, their pleasant banter, the exciting music that opens and closes the show, the vivid film footage, the attractive commercials — all these and more suggest that what we have just seen is no cause for weeping. A news show, to put it plainly, is a format for entertainment, not for education, reflection or catharsis.'[7]

Postman further concludes that, because of this encroaching entertainment-orientated mind-set, Aldous Huxley's forecast of man's future direction in his *Brave New World* is far more probable than that of George Orwell in his *Nineteen Eighty-Four*. 'What Orwell feared were those who would ban books [in a police state]. What Huxley feared was that there would be no reason to ban a book, for there would be no one who wanted to read one [in an indulgent state]. Orwell feared those who would deprive us of information. Huxley feared those who would give us so much that we would be reduced to passivity and egoism. Orwell feared that the truth would be concealed from us. Huxley feared the truth would be drowned in a sea of irrelevance. Orwell feared that we would become a captive culture. Huxley feared that we would become a trivial culture, preoccupied with some equivalent of the feelies... In *1984*, Huxley added, people were controlled by inflicting pain. In *Brave New World*, they are controlled by inflicting pleasure... This book [*Amusing Ourselves to Death*] is about the possibility that Huxley, not Orwell, was right.'[8]

That Western society has moved in a more light-hearted direction, in parallel with its greater exposure to the audio-visual media, is not difficult to demonstrate. The trend is now, both in the workplace and in church life, towards a more relaxed atmosphere, informal protocol and casual dress. A recent syndicated newspaper article originating from Boca Raton, Florida, is headlined, 'Office laughter helps employees enjoy their work.' Author Amy Ellis explains that employers are finding 'that lightening up and encouraging their employees to do the same is an effective way to boost morale and worker productivity. "There's been a dramatic turn away from fear as a way to motivate the work force," says Bill Wood, president of the Delray Beach, Fla., Chamber of Commerce. "Things have loosened up at the workplace, and there's a general understanding that its OK to laugh and have a good time." Behind all the jocularity, however, there is a serious message. In his book, "Lighten Up," C. W. Metcalf maintains that "silliness in the face of seriousness is a mark of mental health, and the failure to find humour in threatening situations can indicate dullness, rigidity and sometimes even mental illness." ... Workers at Boca Raton First National Bank are encouraged to "dress down" on Fridays and "dress up" on major holidays. Staff members at Boca Raton Magazine relieve stress by starting water gun fights or playing with the company intercom.'[9]

If this tendency continues, it may well happen that the armed forces will be next to incorporate a philosophy of humour into their training for battle-preparedness! Even funerals are now euphemistically designated as 'celebrations of life'. So one may realistically wonder just how long it will take for grief therapy to incorporate clowning, and for the graveside ceremony to be reconstituted as a jovial 'ringing down of the curtain' upon the life of a person who entertained well. For after all, is not entertainment what life is all about?

The dilemma for the communicator with a serious message

That the print media are strong on stimulating retained understanding and weak on creating visual impression goes without need of further proof. That the audio-visual media, on the other hand, are strong on stimulating visual impression and weak on creating retained understanding is now a matter that is well supported by reliable evidence. In a *U.S. News & World Report* article entitled, 'What is TV Doing to America?', author James Mann writes, 'Until recently, there was little research on how the human brain absorbs information from TV. Many scholars long have been convinced that viewers retain less from television than from reading, but evidence was scarce. Now, a research project from Jacob Jacob, a Purdue University Psychologist, has found that more than 90 per cent of 2,700 people tested misunderstood even such simple fare as commercials or the detective series *Barnaby Jones*. Only minutes after watching, the typical viewer missed 23 to 36 per cent of the questions about what he or she had seen. One explanation is that TV's compelling pictures stimulate primarily the right half of the brain, which specializes in emotional responses, rather than the left hemisphere, where thinking and analysis are performed. By connecting viewers to instruments that measure brain waves, researcher Herbert Krugman found periods of right-brain activity outnumbering left-brain activity by a ratio of 2 to 1. Another difficulty is the rapid linear movement of TV images, which gives viewers little chance to pause and reflect on what they have seen. Scientists say this torrent of images also has a numbing effect, as measured electronically by the high proportion of alpha brain waves, normally associated with daydreaming or falling asleep. The result is shortened attention spans — a phenomenon increasingly lamented by teachers trying to hold the interest of students accustomed to TV.'[10]

So for the modern communicator who desires to get his message across in clear print, because he believes that understanding is of primary importance, a dilemma arises. On the one hand, the medium of the printed page will best accomplish his desired end, but at the same time it will only reach a diminishing audience that is unrepresentative of society in general. On the other hand, audio-visual media will reach a much wider audience, but, although it may succeed in impressing them to some degree, there will not be a high level of comprehension of the message it is intended to convey.

To focus even more closely on this problem, let us now consider the dilemma as it applies to the communication of *The Pilgrim's Progress* to a modern audience. Is the primary thrust to be the printed word, for the sake of imparting the truth faithfully to a comparatively limited audience, or is it appropriate to capitulate to the more in-vogue audio-visual media, for the sake of making a broad impression upon a wider audience? Is it perhaps possible to resolve this problem using a 'both-and' approach that effectively does away with the 'either-or' impasse? These questions will be specifically dealt with under the next heading, which also introduces a feature which is distinctively Christian — and that is the vital element of the Spirit of God that animates authentic proclamation of the truth of God to sinful mankind.

Of course, the dilemma just unfolded applies equally to the communication of the Word of God — that is, the Bible text. To consider it in parallel with *The Pilgrim's Progress*, while according to Scripture a reverence that no other book merits, will nevertheless help us in our quest how best to honour God through a correct presentation of Bunyan's classic allegory.

Christian literary communication in the present day

Of all the Christian literature published over the past two thousand years of church history, it would be hard to find a volume that lends itself to visual expression more than does Bunyan's *The Pilgrim's Progress*. Its literary imagery alone is quick to engrave indelible pictures on the mind. Hence, it is no surprise that those with an artistic and enterprising bent have attempted to employ audio-visual media of almost every kind for the purpose of communicating this vivid spiritual novel in an enhanced and more relevant way. Illustrations and other media styles, including cartooning, drama, music and film, have all been employed. However, the degree to which these means have been able to accomplish Bunyan's declared purposes, rooted as the latter are in expression through the printed word, still remains a most debatable point. And this being the case, it would seem that further reflection upon the conflicting principles involved may help to bring about a right resolution.

The modern trend for audio-visual indulgence

In general, contemporary Christianity, whether liberal, moderate, or conservative, has readily bought into the overtures of opportunity marketed by the audio-visual media. We recall the statement of Postman that '... to enter the great television conversation, one American cultural institution after another is learning to speak its terms'. [11] That Postman includes the Christian church as a major contributor to this trend is beyond doubt, especially when he goes on to devote one whole chapter to American Christianity's romance with 'showbiz' communication. His conclusion, which is apparently not that of a conservative evangelical, is frank and to the point. It is cause for serious reflection: 'First ... on television, religion, like everything else, is presented, quite simply and without apology, as an entertainment. Everything that makes religion an historic, profound and sacred human activity is stripped away; there is no ritual, no dogma, no tradition, no theology, and above all, no sense of spiritual transcendence. On these shows, the preacher is tops. God comes out as second banana.'[12] In other words, television cannot be tamed or subdued, though it does transform and subdue those who would attempt to sanctify its secularity. It does wed well with its own kind.

Coleen Cook, an evangelical Christian and former TV news presenter, comments: 'One reason Charismatics dominate much of Christian TV is that charismatic expression is simply more theatrical and visual than the worship style of some other Protestant groups. Charismatic theology also tends to be less preoccupied with complex theological concepts and systematized theology. Since it is less complicated, it tends to work better on television.'[13]

1. The case of *Christianity Today*

In David Wells' *No Place for Truth*, he carefully documents the effect of the audio-visual media, over a thirty-year period, upon evangelical Christianity's best-known magazine, originally a classic medium of the printed word:

> *Christianity Today* was born in 1956 at almost exactly the moment when Americans entered the Age of Television; 1955 was the year when 50 per cent of Americans owned television sets, and by 1960 the overwhelming majority had purchased passports to the new Promised Land of video experience. The early years of *Christianity Today*, perhaps out of financial exigency, showed no recognition of the new Age that had dawned, but as black and white sets increasingly gave way to colour, so too did *Christianity Today*. The cheap, pulpy paper on which it had begun its life gave way to bright, colourful coated stock in the 1970s...
>
> By 1989, then the transition had been completed. *Christianity Today* now looked like a poor cousin to *Time* magazine, basically a news magazine that was simply a little more pious and a little less interesting than the genuine article. And, like *Time*, it has repackaged its content for the video age, using abbreviated stories and lots of colour graphics to encourage a leisurely, recreational reading of the magazine. This is not a particularly happy development in the pages of a magazine covering the secular fabric of society, but it is a cause for considerably graver concern when the Christian faith is used as a matter for our distraction and entertainment.[14]

However, even more disturbing for Wells is his discovery of a shift of emphasis with regard to content, from the doctrinal to the relational, from the objective to the subjective, from essays to more segmentation: 'By 1989, gone was the vision in which the magazine was born, gone was its moral and intellectual fibre, and gone was its ability to call the evangelical constituency to greater Christian faithfulness. Reflecting the nostrums of the therapeutic society had been transformed from a vice into a virtue, and popularity had been transformed from something incidental to Christian truth to something central to it.'[15]

2. The case of Marvel Comics' *The Pilgrim's Progress*

A review article in the issue of *Christianity Today* for 19 July 1993 describes a joint publishing venture between Thomas Nelson Publishers and Marvel Comics. They had just released an all-colour comic-strip version of *The Pilgrim's Progress* which the reviewer hails as the first in a series of Christian classics. We are told that '... the primary difference in story line between the comic-book and the original is that the story has been updated to the twentieth century'.[16] In other words, we are to expect the application of audio-visual media principles of communication to a text-only medium in such a way that image-focused teens, who only dimly comprehend the printed word, can more easily understand the essential truth of Bunyan's biblical allegory. So to what degree is this goal faithfully accomplished?

Image adaptation is vivid in the extreme, as is characteristic of comic-strip style. Christian, Faithful and Hopeful are frequently shown bare-chested and all give the appearance of being on high-protein diets and preoccupied with body-building. Scenes of conflict are portrayed in a manner which is grotesque and carried to extremes. Heaven is represented in galactic terms, while the discourses which are so rich in substantial biblical content are totally missing. The supreme virtue would appear to be virility, rather than the meek and humble spirit that Bunyan so epitomized.

The level of truth content confronts us with far more serious problems and, indeed, with perversion of catastrophic proportions. We are not considering here merely the use of contemporary expressions for the sake of relevance, but obvious revisionism.

- In a slough of industrial waste, Christian is rescued by a man (presumably meant to be a modern version of Help) who is labelled 'Our Earth Ecology, Inc.'.
- In the original text the man in the iron cage describes himself as once a 'fair and flourishing professor' (in other words, he once made a profession of faith and gave every appearance of going on well). This meaning is, however, totally lost on the reviser, who has the man say, 'I was once a flourishing scholar.'
- Then, in total contradiction of what Bunyan actually wrote, the despairing man goes on to explain, not, that 'God himself hath shut me up in this iron cage', but that 'I have built this cage to live in. Here, I can hide and be safe from troubles.'[17]
- When a demon attacks Christiana and Mercy and exclaims, 'Hahh!! They're just women!!,' to the rescue comes a nubile Great-heart clad in shapely armour — in other words, the man-servant of Interpreter has been turned into a woman.
- Also, since the gospel is portrayed more synergistically, greater emphasis is placed upon faith itself than upon faith's atoning object, thus ignoring Bunyan's overwhelming interest in the latter. The truth of justification by faith in Christ's personal substitutionary righteousness, as represented by Christian's embroidered coat, is omitted, no doubt on account of the theology being considered too complex for the reader.
- Not surprisingly, Mr Valiant-for-truth is not even mentioned.

Surely the tinker of Bedford would cry out in dismay at such a travesty of his work, 'And as I slept I dreamed a dream … and behold it has now been turned into a nightmare!'

The challenge posed by capitulation

From the outset, it should be made clear that what is proposed in the following paragraphs, although strongly critical of popular 'Christian' communications theory, is nevertheless not a call to blind obscurantism, or to the avoidance of change for the sake of the preservation of historic tradition. The social status quo of the present day must be honestly addressed, and not merely some unattainable ideal. However, the case that follows is, without apology, a call for the resistance of any overtures on the part of communications theory that, even with the best of intentions, have the effect of revising the truth, diluting the truth, demeaning the truth, or that employ media which are in conflict with the truth.

Admittedly, the whole contemporary media culture spends enormous amounts of energy in soliciting participation in the stimulating delights it has to offer. And the Christian church has in no way been immune from feeling the tremendous force of this industry's siren-like argument — namely, that if you want to reach the world, then you must communicate using the world's language. However, to this proposition two additional truths must be added.

Firstly, the language of this world is primarily moulded and transmitted by the audio-visual media, and this means that its essential thrust is entertainment, which certainly takes priority over the dissemination of truth.

Secondly, we must take into account in this connection the results of research by George Barna concerning the basic focus of most Americans. He concludes: 'Two out of three adults (63%) concur that the purpose of life is enjoyment and personal fulfilment. They have little sense that we have been placed on earth with a higher mission, or to fulfil the goals of an omnipotent and omniscient God.'[18] In other words, even at a religious level, most Americans are primarily interested in entertainment, in being made to feel good, in egocentricity. So that, in the absence of some prophetic jeremiad to jolt them into awareness, some awakening pulpit fire from a modern-day John the Baptist, then perhaps the only alternative is capitulation to the allurement and agenda of the visual media.

1. Visual performance as a means of attracting interest

Unfortunately, some Christians seem ready to yield to the beckoning call of, if not the primary electronic media, at least the kindred means of audio-visual communication that similarly engage interest through entertainment.

To quote Coleen Cook again, she thoroughly agrees with Postman's analysis of television, and especially its identification as an entertainment genre.[19] She even adds: 'I know that television is best at creating illusions, not at communicating truth. Since Jesus was in the truth business, television might have presented some very perplexing problems for him.'[20] However, her conclusion in *All that Glitters* leads us in a change of direction, almost a complete about-turn, when she recommends church drama as a means of reaching baby-boomers and seekers.

What rationale does she give for this proposal? 'The church must recognize that this new breed of church seeker has been subliminally conditioned to the look and feel of television information and will be unconsciously drawn to church initially by the style of presentation, not by the substance of the teaching. This is not to suggest that there should be no substance in what we present during church, but that we need to adapt our style of presentation to the conditioned expectations of the audience — especially the unchurched — if we are to reach them.'[21]

That is to say, the church must offer the unbeliever the enticement of the medium to which he is accustomed. If the world is attracted by the mode of entertainment, then the church is to clothe the substance of its message in the guise of entertainment. But, to draw upon Postman's essential conviction, what happens to the substance that Cook wants to convey by such a medium? Surely it transpires that the communication of that substance by means of an entertainment medium results in the substance itself being identified by the congregation *as* entertainment. The medium inevitably intrudes upon the message. In this way the truth becomes polluted.

Cook continues: 'The church can learn from "preachers" such as Norman Lear [the humanist producer of the television series *All in the Family*] — people today accept information more readily if they are being entertained.'[22] But it appears that the intention here is not merely to entertain as a prelude to imparting truth, but to package the gospel itself in a manner that makes it more digestible. Thus Cook explains: 'I believe that the church is standing at a crossroads in communicating the gospel. We are faced with the difficult, but not impossible, task of drawing secular people to the point of faith by first recognizing where their frame of reference is. Bowing to the demands of a TV-conditioned culture and being contemporary in our approach can give a face-lift to the gospel presentation that is a starting point but not the ending.'[23]

This sort of reasoning would have been unthinkable for the apostles of the early church, even though they encountered cultural diversity of no lesser proportions than exist today, especially when one considers the variations between Hebrew, Greek and Roman life-styles. They would have considered such reasoning as bordering on heresy, and particularly the suggestion that the gospel needed an updated dress, one that would appeal to the world.

John MacArthur, Jr., addresses this capitulation of the evangelical church in America very plainly in his book, *Ashamed of the Gospel*. We need many more forthright preachers of his courageous stance, instead of pastoral executives whose expertise is marketing and communications strategy. He writes, 'Some will maintain that if biblical principles are presented, the medium doesn't matter. That is nonsense. If an entertaining medium is the key to winning people, why not go all out? Why not have a real carnival? A tattooed acrobat on a high wire could juggle chain saws and shout Bible verses while a trick dog balanced on his head. That would draw a crowd. And the content of the message would still be biblical... What's wrong with that? For one thing, the church has no business marketing its ministry as an alternative to secular amusements (1 Thess. 3:2-6). That corrupts and cheapens the church's real mission... Moreover, instead of confronting the world with the truth of Christ, the market-driven megachurches are enthusiastically promoting the worst trends of secular culture. Feeding people's appetite for entertainment only exacerbates the problems of mindless emotion, apathy, and materialism. Quite frankly, it is difficult to conceive of a ministry philosophy more contradictory to the pattern our Lord gave us.'[24]

2. The emptiness of visual performance

It is significant to contemplate that the numerous visual / dramatic presentations of *The Pilgrim's Progress*, virtually without exception, have been characterized by extravagant form while at the same time lacking much of the original substance. This is especially true with regard to the considerable pruning of the discourse sections. For instance, the long, though significant, discourse during the crossing of the Enchanted Ground especially suffers in this regard. It seems that when the visual/dramatic mode takes control, it cannot tolerate any content that might call for serious thought and thus detract from its appeal to the senses.

A theme-park parody

I must say I find it surprising that, to date, no one appears to have suggested that a commercial theme park should be developed based upon *The Pilgrim's Progress*. It is mind-boggling to imagine the various rides and exhibits that could be constructed. At the park entrance, a roller-coaster would whisk visitors away at high speed from solicitous hucksters and furrow its way through the parting sludge of the Slough of Despond. More athletic types could attempt the impossible by trying to climb the snow-capped hill of Mount Sinai, beyond which can be seen the shimmering lights of the illuminated village of Morality. A variety of Disney-style characters, some admirable, others seductive or disgusting, would mingle with the crowd readily agreeing to be photographed with tourists, both young and old.

The tour of the House of the Interpreter — all seven dazzling rooms — would elicit screams of both delight and horror. At the wayside Place of Deliverance Chapel, there would be an opportunity for meditation, or wedding ceremonies could be performed. Then, after passing through a lane of caged lions, one would reach the glittering Palace Beautiful with its flowing fountains, martial-arts demonstrations, full-service restaurant and overnight accommodation. A high-tech exhibit, employing the very latest in robotic engineering, would pit Christian in shining armour, complete with laser sword, against a lumines-cent green Apollyon, belching fire and curses. Then would follow the fiendish Doubting Castle, complete with shrieks of despair, and ghoulish dramatizations of Bible stories, also available on video. At Beulah Land, a theatre in the round would project dazzling vistas of the Celestial City. The River of Death would be crossed just before the exit by means of a pleasant boat-ride leading to a reception by winged angels who would bid the pilgrims farewell with gospel tracts and discount coupons for passing on to friends. Of course, the declared purpose of this whole enterprise would be — perish the thought that it could be mercenary or otherwise! — the presentation of the gospel in the modern idiom. After all, is not audio-visual communication, garnished with entertainment, the only way to go?

Surely the response to the scenario posited above, on the part of anyone who takes seriously the essential character of biblical Christianity, must be an emphatic repudiation. Such a disturbing parody, reflective though it may be of much contem-porary evangelism, must conjure up a sense of revulsion in the heart of the earnest child of God. And why is this so? Because the audio-visual-entertainment mix not only attempts to use unholy means to attain a holy end, which leads to contamination, but it is also grossly deficient in truth content.

Stage and drama presentations

The same problems arise if a dramatic stage presentation of *The Pilgrim's Progress* is envisaged. The medium remains an audio-visual-entertainment mix that is in essential conflict with Bunyan's sacred purposes, and with even his allegorical style. Postman comments: 'Most Americans ... have difficulty accepting the truth, if they think about it at all, that not all forms of discourse can be converted from one medium to another... Moreover, the television screen itself [and, we may add, the stage] has a strong bias toward a psychology of secularism. The screen [and the stage] is so saturated with our memories of profane events, so deeply associated with the commercial and entertainment worlds that it is difficult for it to be created as a frame for sacred events.'[25]

Furthermore, the dramatic stage, like television, will, by its very nature, dethrone the priority of truth content and supplant it with the priority of entertainment. Truth will by no means be absent, but it will be subservient to the interests of presentation, impression, sensual experience and satisfaction.

In this same vein, we can be sure that Bunyan would in no way have approved of a presentation of *The Pilgrim's Progress* in the style of a musical oratorio which, even though the most accomplished of instrumentalists and soloists were employed, eviscerated the text of eighty per cent of its content and rearranged the remaining twenty per cent. Such a work has indeed been produced by the eminent English composer Ralph Vaughan Williams. Given the simple title of *The Pilgrim's Progress*, it was first performed in four acts in 1951 at the Royal Opera House, Covent Garden, London, and lasted approximately two and a half hours. The production was well received, especially in America, but the medium, as entertainment, overshadowed the very diminutive role accorded to truth.[26]

Especially revealing in this regard is the composer's response, in the course of correspondence with a friend, to the comment: 'By the way, your Pilgrim seems to be afraid of his Christian name.' To this Vaughan Williams replied, 'I on purpose did not call the pilgrim "Christian" because I want the idea to be universal and apply to anybody who aims at the spiritual life [as a pilgrimage] whether he is Xtian, Jew, Buddhist, Shintoist, or 5th Day Adventist.'[27] Thus the essential Christian purposes of Bunyan were of no concern to this composer. In plain terms, the result is revisionism, something to which all writers and composers object when their own works are the subject of it, and which is particularly serious when it leads to the distortion of truth.

3. The essential issue

This then brings us to the parting of the ways, the point at which the purposes of Bunyan, so clearly expressed in *The Pilgrim's Progress,* diverge from those of the modern apologists for the audio-visual-entertainment media. Bunyan's overriding concern in composing *The Pilgrim's Progress* was objective, biblical truth, doctrinal truth, gospel truth, truth that transforms lives. At the same time he was not afraid to incorporate subsidiary embellishments, whether these take the form of allegorical style, occasional instances of droll humour, or even interpretive illustrations. But the important point here is that these elements most definitely remain subsidiary. They do not distort or overwhelm the message.

However, in the case of enthusiasts for the use primarily of audio-visual-entertainment media, the reverse is true. For these people, whether or not there is an element of religious investment, their first interest is in stimulating the senses, promoting contentment and gaining the approval of men, even at the expense of truth. They fear giving offence; they are concerned about being responsible for inducing boredom; they worry about being rejected. So, to eliminate any such risk, they change the original presentation and contextualize, or to be more precise, modify, the facts to suit the audience. This kind of attitude is the very reverse of being prophetic, especially in a biblical sense.

Hence we may conclude that to be faithful today to Bunyan's purposes for the proclamation of *The Pilgrim's Progress*, those media which best communicate truth ought primarily to be employed. Audio-visual support media may be incorporated, but only in a secondary sense and only as long as they remain supportive and do not lead either to the diminution of truth or to conflict with it.

The lesson from divine revelation

The God of the Bible has made himself known to mankind; that is, he has disclosed or revealed himself in ways of his determining. Thus God has established communication with man, and he has determined specific media by which the infinite God might inform finite man; the eternal God might be known by temporal man; the spiritual God might have fellowship with material man; and the heavenly God might reach down to earthly man. However, our specific concern here is both the identification and analysis of these divine media, most commonly designated as general and special revelation, and especially their relationship to the relative usefulness of human audio-visual media, on the one hand, and that of the printed word on the other, which evangelical Christianity has as its disposal today.

Although it is true that God has implanted some knowledge of himself within the soul of man (Rom. 2:14-15), original sin, and its universal inheritance, has caused that understanding to be thoroughly perverted (Rom. 1:21-23). However, external to man, God has mediated the truth about himself principally by means of general or natural revelation — that is, the created order (Ps. 19:1-6; Acts 14:15-17; Rom. 1:18-21) — and special or personalized revelation — that is, the written Word of God and the incarnate appearing of the Lord Jesus Christ (Ps. 19:7-14; John 1:14; 2 Tim. 3:16-17; Heb. 1:1-2).

That God was most particular in his design for man to receive a true self-disclosure of his person is evident by the fact that he utterly forbade, on pain of death (Deut. 17:2-5), any attempt by man to make a visual or substantial representation of himself. Postman presses home this point in a very relevant way: 'In studying the Bible as a young man, I found intimations of the idea that forms of media favour particular kinds of content and therefore are capable of taking command of a culture. I refer specifically to the Decalogue, the Second Commandment of which prohibits the Israelites from making concrete images of anything. "Thou shalt not make unto thee any graven image, or likeness of any thing that is in the heaven above, or that is in the earth beneath, or that is in the water beneath the earth." I wondered then, as so many others have, as to why the God of these people would have included instructions on how they were to symbolize, or not symbolize, their experience. It is a strange injunction to include as part of an ethical system unless the author assumed a connection between forms of human communication and the quality of a culture.'[28]

As has already been stated, God has seen fit to communicate himself in a variety of ways. Nevertheless, he has mandated against *man's* having this same freedom and flexibility with regard to selecting media for the human communication of God. Even so, in God's self-disclosure, he has evidently chosen certain media and excluded others for very definite purposes. And these purposes seem to indicate clear guidelines for the Christian church's selection of appropriate media for the proclamation of the truth of God.

1. God's medium of his creation

Here is God's audio-visual communication involving impressive orchestration concerning the glory of his sovereignty, intricate providence and transcendence. So Calvin writes, 'We must therefore admit in God's individual works — but especially in them as a whole — that God's powers are actually represented as a painting.'[29] Yet he concludes: 'It is therefore in vain that so many burning lamps shine for us in the workmanship of the universe to show forth the glory of its author. Although they bathe us wholly in their radiance, yet they can of themselves in no way lead us into the right path ... we have not the eyes to see this unless they be illumined by the inner revelation of God through faith.'[30]

Why is this so? Because although the man of this world patronizes the painting, he scorns the Painter. And, besides, the painting of creation does not instruct man with regard to his insulting and proud attitude, nor does it specify the remedy of saving grace. While creation proclaims the awesome character of God by its imagery, it cannot provide the essential truth concerning man's predicament and God's remedy. Here is mouth-stopping spectacle divorced from specific, applicatory truth.

2. God's medium of his revealed Word

In contrast, here is objective, propositional, tangible revelation concerning the moral state of the universe and the moral character of God. This was to be the appointed means for the disclosure of the heart of God, as distinct from his handiwork. Postman adds: 'The God of the Jews was to exist in the Word and through the Word, an unprecedented conception requiring the highest order of abstract thinking. Iconography thus became blasphemy so that a new kind of God could enter a culture. People like ourselves who are in the process of converting their culture from word-centred to image-centred might profit by reflecting on this Mosaic injunction.'[31]

Even the coming of the incarnate Son of God, the 'Word made flesh' (John 1:14), did not alter this priority of the word over other media. With this superior manner of revelation (Heb. 1:1-2), the truth was objectively incorporated and personified to a supreme degree, and then maintained as before through the permanent record of Holy Scripture (2 Peter 1:17-19).

What, then, does this divine mandate for the priority of the printed word over audio-visual media suggest? Again, that any reversal of this order will continue to produce disastrous consequences, especially for evangelical Christianity. As we shall now see, in *The Pilgrim's Progress* itself Bunyan was quite insistent on this priority.

The lesson from Vanity Fair

The arrival of Christian and Faithful at the town of Vanity, with its notorious fair, is in reality another manifestation of the City of Destruction which now parades itself in a more festive and embellished manner. The spirit of this community is one of gaiety, indulgence of the senses, amusement and novelty — or, in a word, entertainment. Now, by representing it in this way, Bunyan instructs us concerning the nature of this world, whether that of his day or of our own, that there is no essential difference in terms of its basic interests. That is to say, unbelieving man has always craved for pleasurable stimulation in a primary and selfish sense. And at Vanity Fair, as in this present modern age, there is always that same narcissistic and sensual pursuit.

However, in terms of communication, what media does Bunyan indicate as being those that both Christian and Faithful are to employ in their witness as pilgrims in transit through the town? Negatively, there is no suggestion that they should incorporate the lifestyle of Vanity into their methodology; they are not to reach out with the media that are so popular in Vanity. But, positively, they are to focus upon one medium only, the individual pilgrim, who is to transmit upon three different wavelengths:

1. The witness of evident holiness

Christian and Faithful were distinguishable by means of their unusual clothing, or close identification with Christ, even to the point of being regarded as fools (1 Cor. 4:10), their uncommon speech, and in particular its biblical and heavenly quality (Col. 4:6), and their genuine disinterest in merchandise on offer in Vanity Fair (Matt. 6:19-20) — that is, worldly possessions. It was their holy distinctiveness that testified of their holy God, not an unholy adoption of the attributes or methods of the world — not even as a witnessing style.

2. The witness of truth as revealed in Scripture

Both for import and for export, their only stock-in-trade was the objective Word of God. They sought the truth by crying out, 'We buy the truth' (Prov. 23:23), and at the same time proclaimed the truth, as Faithful did, and did effectively, in his witness to Hopeful. They freely marketed the produce of divine truth that, when digested, nourishes and invigorates the soul (John 17:17). They did not offer sugar-coated platitudes that prove to be a bitter pill, or temporary roller-coaster thrills that must inevitably come down to the harsh reality of earth.

3. The witness of manifest graciousness

They showed kindness in exchange for malice directed towards them, and bore with patience the abuse inflicted on them (Rom. 12:20-21; 1 Peter 3:8-9), thereby gaining a sympathetic following. Later in the account of Part Two, when Mercy, along with Christiana, resides at Vanity in the house of Mr Mnason, she shows such care for the poor that they call her blessed. By these means, the names of Faithful and Christian, which were formerly cursed, come to be admired by many. As a result of the combined testimony of the pilgrims as a whole, a small fellowship is gradually established in Vanity that gains some honourable recognition.[32]

Again we see the priority, for Bunyan, of truth proclaimed over visual exhibitions of the type which Vanity-Fair was well equipped to stage. In this situation, it is particularly the uncluttered consistency of the truth, its uncompromising proclamation, even unto death, that begins to make inroads into Satan's entrenched domain.

The call for a return to the word/truth priority

While the distinctive mix of *The Pilgrim's Progress* as a literary whole is readily admitted, yet, as has been cumulatively demonstrated, the great passion of its author is the truth of God as revealed in the Bible. The various component parts of allegory, occasional humour, intrigue, adventure, contrast and continuity, beauty of expression, human interest and poetic interlude are all no more than subsidiary embellishments superimposed on the supremely important, concrete foundation of divine revelation which is external to man.

Now the reason for propounding this evaluation of Bunyan in such definite terms is to be found in the contemporary climate — not excluding certain trends in the Christian church — which has moved this focus of Bunyan's away from outward, concrete assertion towards inward and sensual stimulation; that is, from objective reality towards subjective relativism. Throughout the 1970s Francis Schaeffer warned evangelical Christendom of this insidious development. In one of his later writings he challenged Christians: 'We must not finally even battle [against humanism] on the front for freedom, and specifically not only our freedom. It must be on the basis of Truth. Not just religious truths, but the Truth of what the final reality is. Is it impersonal material or is it the living God?'[33]

More recently, another voice appeared similarly to warn us of the further progress of corrosive modernity in humanizing, and therefore destroying, the solid foundation of biblical Christianity. In his book already mentioned, *No Place for Truth*, David Wells concludes: 'The bottom line for our modernized world is that there is no truth; the bottom line for Christian consciousness is precisely the opposite. The Christian predisposition to believe in the kind of truth that is objective and public and that reflects ultimate reality cuts across the grain of what modernity considers plausible... Today, reality is so privatized and relativized that truth is often understood only in terms of what it means to each person. A pragmatic culture will see truth as whatever works for any given person. Such a culture will interpret the statement that Christianity is true to mean simply that Christianity is one way of life that has worked for someone, but that would not be to say that any other way of life might not work just as well for someone else... The contraction of reality into the self, whether in its Liberal or evangelical versions, introduces nothing more or less than the reordering of reality by our modernized world, and the first casualty of this reordering, with respect to the mind, is the belief that truth is something that should be found outside of our own subjective consciousness.'[34]

Hence, it is my firm contention that, in conformity with Bunyan's primary intention to communicate biblical substance while employing the secondary means of allegorical form,[35] the priority of the word and of truth in *The Pilgrim's Progress* must be reclaimed, while by no means jettisoning the appropriate use of visual imagery in a supporting role. To do otherwise would be to capitulate to modernity and subordinate the fundamental importance of rational discourse to more subjective visual impression. For biblical Christianity there can be no yielding whatsoever at this point.

In our increasingly unrighteous society, the primary need is for a revival of manifest righteousness that is clearly sourced in the God of all righteousness. However, such a moral revolution cannot result, whatever claims may be made on behalf of a relational/subjective gospel, unless the roots of truth, in channelling understanding through the trunk and branches of proclamation, bring about the flowering of ethical godliness. It is for this reason that Isaiah declared, 'Truth has stumbled in the street, and uprightness cannot enter' (Isa. 59:14). The parallelism here clearly suggests that 'truth' is productive of 'righteousness'. In other words, the truth of God must have priority in proclamation, or else a moral community cannot be born, sustained and flourish (Ps. 85:11).

Apart from the Bible, then, what better vehicle of Bible truth could there be for worldwide consumption than *The Pilgrim's Progress*? The medium has already proved its universal and timeless appeal. All that now needs to be accomplished is for its true message to be more widely made known. It is not enough for *The Pilgrim's Progress* simply to be made available on the shelves of bookstores. Certainly that is one way that it can reach seeking people. But, in accord with its author's original intention, it also needs to be expounded as never before. In his concluding poem Bunyan writes:

> Now, Reader, I have told my dream to thee;
> See if thou canst interpret it to me,
> Or to thyself, or neighbour...[36]

In other words, readers of *The Pilgrim's Progress* are to proclaim its message to their neighbours. They are to use the book as helpful and interesting literature both for adult evangelism and for edification, as a narrative compendium of the truth of God revealed only in Holy Scripture. These modern times desperately call for those who have a sense of prophetic urgency concerning the truth of Scripture and who, like their Old and New Testament mentors, while directed by God to communicate with a variety of suitable media, will never veer from the bottom line of giving priority to verbal proclamation of the truth.

The solution for making *The Pilgrim's Progress* known today

In summary, the following principles are suggested for the proper communication and teaching of *The Pilgrim's Progress* to this present modern generation. In all of this, it should go without saying that it is the truth of the Word of God that is to prevail in terms of the message being declared.

Be faithful to Bunyan's original purposes

Frequently review Bunyan's purposes in writing his allegory, as expressed in both the introductory apology and the concluding poem of Part One of *The Pilgrim's Progress*. Consider how faithfully Bunyan fulfilled these purposes in his own pastoral ministry. Encourage the reading of other non-allegorical writings by this author.

Give the priority to verbal proclamation of the truth

Aim at guiding people back to a word/truth priority that first engages the mind, then brings weight to bear upon the conscience and persuasively invites submission. Encourage the supplementary reading, where appropriate, of relevant extracts from the writings of Schaeffer, Postman and Wells, etc., which expose the distinctive cultural biases and fallacies of the present day.

Beware of the impressionism created by the modern media

Encourage people to be critical of the contemporary trend to give priority to visual imagery which, by appeal to the senses and subjectivism, has the effect of subordinating the mind to impression and feeling, and thus — whether consciously or not on the part of the individual — is in direct opposition to the priority of biblical absolutes.

Proclaim the message of *The Pilgrim's Progress* with personal conviction

The truth embodied in *The Pilgrim's Progress* must first become a personal stimulus through careful study; then interest can be aroused in others through communication and teaching, using direct exposition of the narrative that continuously draws attention to the revealed Word of God.

Encourage the reading of *The Pilgrim's Progress*

Make use of, and recommend, an edition of Part One of *The Pilgrim's Progress* that is faithful to the original, as well as the reading of other related works of Bunyan, including, for instance, Part Two, *Grace Abounding to the Chief of Sinners*, *The Holy War* and *The Heavenly Footman*.

Maintain Bunyan's truth content

Always pay heed to Bunyan's exhortation to 'look within my veil, turn up my metaphors'; in other words, continually dig for the Bible truth that is buried below the surface of the allegory. Give special emphasis to the teaching of the discourse sections.

Endeavour to understand Bunyan's doctrinal emphases

Draw particular attention to Bunyan's teaching on the gospel, sanctification, the pastorate and reaching heaven. Communicate this truth according to its integral relationship to the allegorical framework rather than by means of systematic formulations.

Employ well-structured outlines

As an equivalent to the media sound-bites with which society is so familiar, do not hesitate to employ an outline of the text of *The Pilgrim's Progress*. At the same time be careful to maintain the order of the narrative and the truth taught through it.

Use visual imagery only in a supplementary capacity

Supplement *The Pilgrim's Progress* with visual images, such as suitable illustrations, that faithfully correspond to, but never overwhelm, the original text. The use of such imagery is certainly not mandatory, though the times and audience may require it.

A word of advice

1. *Dost thou love thy own soul? Then pray to Jesus Christ for an awakened heart, for a heart so awakened with all the things of another world, that thou mayest be allured to Jesus Christ.*

2. *When thou comest there, beg again for more awakenings about sin, hell, grace, and about the righteousness of Christ.*

3. *Cry also for a spirit of discerning, that thou mayest know that which is saving grace indeed.*

4. *Above all studies apply thyself to the study of those things that show thee the evil of sin, the shortness of man's life, and which is the way to be saved.*

5. *Keep company with the most godly among professors.*

6 *When thou hearest what the nature of true grace is, defer not to ask thine own heart if this grace be there.*

John Bunyan
The Strait Gate,
Works, vol. I, p.390

18.
Modern assessments of *The Pilgrim's Progress*

'[Bunyan's] doctrine was the doctrine of the best and strongest minds in Europe... In them it was a fire from heaven shining like a sun in a dark world. With us the fire has gone out; in the place of it we have but smoke and ashes...'

(J. A. Froude).

18.

Modern assessments of
The Pilgrim's Progress

IN discussion and analysis of *The Pilgrim's Progress* since its publication in 1678, there has been an increasing tendency for interest in Bunyan's classic to be channelled along two distinct lines, thus creating a disjunction between the literary / historical and biblical / theological aspects of the work. At the allegory's inception, and on into the eighteenth century of evangelical awakening, although literary/historical considerations were matters of serious interest, they were unquestionably subordinated to an overwhelming regard for biblical / theological truth.

While C. Stephen Finley's comments relate particularly to the nineteenth century, they also have relevance to this earlier period: 'John Bunyan benefited, as much as any figure associated with the dramatic Puritanism of the seventeenth century, from the Evangelical majority culture of the Victorians. Indeed, for many of the Victorian faithful, including many of the men and women who were to go on to greatness in Victorian literary and religious circles, Bunyan played a role in their religious formation and in their personal mythologies of quest and development second only to that of the Bible itself. A complete list of such persons would be very long indeed, but would include, to cite only the literary, Macaulay, Carlyle, Ruskin, Froude, [and] Charlotte Brontë.'[1]

However, for all of this 'Evangelical majority culture', the Victorian era increasingly witnessed a reversal of interest in *The Pilgrim's Progress* that resulted in the ascendancy of literary / historical concern over that of biblical/theological truth, certainly in parallel with an increasing secularization of society as a whole.

As a result, by the time of the publication of J. A. Froude's *John Bunyan* in 1880, he could write, '[Bunyan's] doctrine was the doctrine of the best and strongest minds in Europe. It had been believed by Luther, it had been believed by Knox... Few educated people use the language of it now. In them it was a fire from heaven shining like a sun in a dark world. With us the fire has gone out; in the place of it we have but smoke and ashes... Unfortunately, parents [now] do not read Bunyan, he is left to the children... The conventional phrases of Evangelical Christianity ring untrue in a modern ear like a cracked bell.'[2]

George Offor's definitive three-volume edition of Bunyan's *Works*, published in 1854, was a scholarly product that equally exuded warm evangelical sympathy for its author. However, by the turn of the century comparable enthusiasm for the truth of *The Pilgrim's Progress* is difficult to find, at least in academic circles.

In 1905 Robert Bridges, poet and man of letters, writes, 'Bunyan's chief merit ... is his prose style, which is admired by all who prefer the force of plain speech to the devices of rhetoric... It is pleasanter to write about Bunyan without reference to his theology ... his theology needs so much allowance that anything which isolates him from his time does him vast injury; and this some of his warmest friends do not perceive, when they Victorianize his spelling and parade his Calvinism on shiny paper.'[3]

So as the twentieth century progressed, it increasingly came to be expected that the correct procedure in Bunyan studies required a writer to be scrupulously dispassionate — except when it was a question of expressing disagreement with the tinker's literalist hermeneutic concerning the Bible or his Calvinistic doctrine.

However, if the Bedford pastor were alive today, he would undoubtedly reprimand those who only offer their literary patronage, and would exhort them to repent and humble themselves under the righteous hand of God and seek his mercy. It is in this sense that the last century has proved to be a wilderness period since, for all that there have been a considerable number of academic contributions in the field of Bunyan studies, these have studiously avoided focusing on the passion for the saving grace of the Lord Jesus Christ which lies at the very heart of Bunyan's work, and as a result, they have only helped to augment the spiritual sterility of the present day. Froude's comment remains profoundly true: 'The fire has gone out; in the place of it we have but smoke and ashes.'[4]

Twentieth-century analyses of Bunyan

Academic interest in John Bunyan since the beginning of the twentieth century divides itself into five areas of specialization that, for the most part, have two features in common: a secular approach and a lack of sympathy with Bunyan's essential purposes. To some degree, conservative Christianity is to blame for this trend, in neglecting the adult character of *The Pilgrim's Progress*, since this has left the way open for a number of academics to adopt the Bedford tinker for themselves, treating him very much as an adult, but at the same time denuding him of his vital gospel dress.

Let us take a moment, then, to consider these distinctive subdivisions of twentieth-century investigation, while always keeping in focus Bunyan's biblical and gospel passion, which would certainly have been the basis for any judgement that he himself would have brought to bear on his critics.

Literary criticism

The principal contribution in the field of modern Bunyan studies comes from lecturers and professors in university English
departments. In *The Pilgrim's Progress, Critical and Historical
Reviews*, edited by Vincent Newey and published in 1980, all
fourteen essays are by authors employed in university English
departments. Over half of the collection of twelve essays to
commemorate Bunyan's tercentenary published in 1988 under
the title, *John Bunyan, Conventicle and Parnassus*, and edited
by N. H. Keeble, are by university English specialists. Of the
nine scholars who contributed to another collection of tercentenary essays, *Bunyan in our Time*, which was published in 1989
and edited by Robert G. Collmer, eight are English lecturers or
professors. Amongst all the contributors to these three volumes,
it would be difficult to recognize even one author who shows
himself to be clearly in sympathy with Bunyan's specific presentation of the gospel. At the same time, secular and theologically liberal sympathies are evident throughout these collections.

While one might be tempted to accept this emphasis as only
to be expected, in view of the formative role played by Bunyan
in the field of English composition, it needs to be clearly understood that the author of *The Pilgrim's Progress* never intended
that his work should be honoured for its literary form and development without regard to its evangelical truth. Granted that
he intended a plainness of style in his magnum opus, which the
scholars seem incapable of reproducing in their writing about
him, it is nevertheless sadly significant that his principal area of
concern, that of Bible truth, has today undoubtedly been relegated to a position of relative insignificance.

The distinctly secular and surgical character of twentieth-
century analysis of Bunyan in the field of literary and historical
criticism is especially noticeable in the light of the intentional
detachment of the researchers from any evangelical sympathy
in this pursuit. The exception here is when the author cannot
refrain from expressing polite disparagement and adopting a

patronizing manner towards seventeenth-century theology from the vantage-point of these more 'enlightened' times.

Certainly the new Oxford University Press publication of Bunyan's works has been an outstanding achievement that has employed many scholars who are both accomplished and dedicated in their fields of either English or history. Yet, by itself, this product will simply be assessed as a notable academic monument, an admirable anachronism, unless the heart-warming truth of Bunyan is once more given its rightful place of prominence.

Admittedly, it is clear that Bunyan intends that the reader should carefully delve into his allegory and thus 'look within [his] veil', but it is his design that that this method should lead to the discovery of 'the substance of my matter', not to finding ever more original, not to say bizarre, nuances, many of which are couched in terms of reference that only the scholastically initiated can understand.

Historical investigation

After university English department personnel, the most prolific contributors to contemporary Bunyan studies are undoubtedly specialist historians with a particular focus on seventeenth-century England. On the matter of historical background, no one would deny how vast and helpful is Christopher Hill's comprehension of Bunyan's era, notwithstanding the necessity to filter his conclusions through Marxist presuppositions, social-class consciousness and a decidedly materialist perspective. Similarly, Richard Greaves has offered a constant stream of judicious and perceptive writings that have been most illuminating; his doctrinal sensitivity in this regard has greatly enhanced his contribution.

But still, as far as Bunyan is concerned, we are dealing with a matter which, though important, is only secondary. Of course, the historical foundation of biblical Christianity is a matter of vital concern, but even research into that area must yield second place to the understanding and interpretation of those events as revealed in Scripture, notably the apostle Paul's passionate emphasis upon the saving grace of God offered to great sinners such as himself. In the same way, when it comes to understanding *The Pilgrim's Progress*, it is that same truth from the pen of Paul, and passed on from him through Augustine and Luther at a human level, that is of supreme importance. To investigate the history surrounding Bunyan and his allegory, and yet at the same time to repudiate his central message of gospel truth, is like playing around with the skeleton of an animal that has been slaughtered for human consumption while people nearby are starving and in desperate need of the nourishment the meat has to offer.

Psychological analysis

One of the most appealing characteristics of John Bunyan is the sheer honesty of his writing, warts and all, and this is particularly evident in *Grace Abounding to the Chief of Sinners*. This being so, it is not surprising that students of human psychology, whether professional or otherwise, have found in *Grace Abounding* — as in other writings of a confessional nature — a happy hunting-ground for conjecture. A classic, though clinically secular estimate is that provided by William James who, as a psychologist focusing on religious experience, describes Bunyan's post-conversion troubles in terms that border on ascribing to him a psychotic frame of mind.[5]

A more recent analysis is that of another university English lecturer, John Stachniewski, who in *The Persecutory Imagination*, stridently opposes the Calvinistic biblicism of which Bunyan was so representative, alleging that it was responsible for leading a generation to excesses of despair. Even Roger Sharrock cannot resist the temptation to attempt a diagnosis that is symptomatic of modern psychoanalysis.[6]

However, it is difficult to avoid the conclusion that so much of this type of investigation, of which the examples quoted above are typical, is based upon a subjective and humanistic estimate that has not the faintest understanding of what it is to be deeply convicted of sin according to biblical standards.

In this respect we can draw a parallel with the secular critics and analysts who foist their own standards upon a gullible public, and come up with similar analyses of the apostle Paul and his conversion on the road to Damascus. One such case is that of Dr William Sargant's book *Battle for the Mind*, published in 1957, in which he explains Paul's experience in terms of 'total collapse, hallucinations and an increased state of suggestibility due to exhaustion', followed by the 'implanting of new beliefs and imposed indoctrination' by Ananias. Dr. D. Martyn Lloyd-Jones, who was both a highly qualified physician and Christian minister, gives an able refutation of this whole naturalistic approach.[7]

It seems that Bunyan himself anticipated this type of criticism. In his introduction to *Grace Abounding*, written after he had already spent six years in Bedford county jail, he specifically addresses in his preface those whom he calls 'My dear children' — that is, the nonconformist congregation of which he was a member and whom he yearned to encourage. So he keeps his account 'plain and simple', encouraging the believers to profit from recalling 'the very beginnings of grace in their souls'. Then he adds, 'The Philistines understand me not... He that liketh it, let him receive it; and he that does not, let him produce a better.'[8]

Political and sociological theory

In terms of remoteness from John Bunyan's essential purposes in writing, it is probably this field of investigation that is the most distressing, since it is a deliberate exercise in using the Bedford preacher to serve a particular literary end in a way that he himself would have strenuously denounced. It is typical of the times in which we live that a disjunction is made between idealism and reality. Hence when Bunyan is viewed through socialist / materialist spectacles, a fascination with his social environment leads to extrapolation concerning his proletarian courage and literary inventiveness, accompanied by a total rejection — a loathing even — of his passionate and predominant biblical convictions. One of the foremost exponents of this methodology is Christopher Hill, whose Marxist, and therefore materialist, beliefs undergird his whole exposition of Bunyan, and are dealt with in more detail later in this chapter.

In this same vein, we will pause for a moment to consider David Herreshoff's essay, 'Marxist Perspectives on Bunyan', which focuses on an array of Marxists who have, in a variety of ways, admired the Bedford tinker's social role and allegorical skills, though definitely not his evangelical doctrine. Consequently they have attempted to baptize him with their socialist ideology. The author even goes so far as to raise the question: 'Is Bunyan "ours" or "theirs", or perhaps both?' In other words, does Bunyan belong to 'secular and proletarian' or 'Christian and bourgeois' interests?[9]

Marxist talk using biblical / Bunyanesque expressions abounds: 'The revolution is the work of a conscious class incarnating an idea, the proletariat as collective messiah... Another reason for Marxists' being attracted to Bunyan is that he is seen by them as a guide who can show them to a wicket gate beyond which they can get a clear view into the political landscape of the English Revolution and its aftermath... Readers of recent Marxist Bunyan scholarship will discover that the ideological clothing metaphor is alive and well in the prose of some [Is this a reference to Christian's embroidered coat?]... If the Puritan revolutionaries could see their world only through a glass, darkly, the proletarian revolutionaries will see historical reality face to face'[10] (an allusion to 1 Cor. 13:12?).

The agenda for those involved in this incongruous relationship is evident from Herreshoff's reference to the German

Marxist, Georg Seehase: 'Aware that German editions of *The Pilgrim's Progress* which serve the cause of Christian propaganda continue to appear, Seehase believes it is feasible to prepare an edition at least of the First Part to serve the needs of socialist publishing policy. It would be provided with a suitable and appealing commentary... If one concedes that Bunyan is ineradicably possessed of a religious false consciousness, however, *The Pilgrim's Progress* can only be understood as, at the most, a belles-lettristic tract [a literary essay read primarily for its aesthetic qualities] illustrative of the Bible. Seehase wants more for the book than that; he wants to annex it to the domain of the socialist heritage.'[11] The only fitting response to such blatant revisionism is the assessment that it is representative of a system that has no objective morality and therefore does not blush or so much as raise an eyebrow when literary rape is proposed.

Theological appreciation

In contrast with the categories listed above, any serious and sympathetic consideration of Bunyan's doctrinal stance is difficult to find, even within conservative Christendom. Exceptions in this respect are Richard Greaves' *John Bunyan* and Pieter de Vries' *John Bunyan on the Order of Salvation,* both of which are reviewed later in this chapter.

U. Milo Kaufmann's *The Pilgrim's Progress and Traditions in Puritan Meditation* is certainly insightful, but hardly sympathetic towards Bunyan's evangelicalism. He writes, 'No religious awakening is likely to be an awakening of a seventeenth-century Puritan sensitivity and a recovery of its categories. Too much has happened in the meantime. A more rewarding course, it seems to me, is to affirm that *The Pilgrim's Progress* offers us the handsomely-articulated structure of literature's basic plot: the career of a human life.'[12]

Similarly, there is former seminary principal Gordon Wakefield's *Bunyan the Christian,* also reviewed in this chapter.

Although his work reflects affection for Bunyan, his interpretation of the Bedford pastor's writings is evidently based upon liberal presuppositions and twentieth-century Arminianism, both of which are the complete opposite of what Bunyan believed.

While, on the one hand, a deep evangelical appreciation of Bunyan is sadly lacking, at the same time we find that children's versions of *The Pilgrim's Progress* abound in ever more simplistic forms which are undoubtedly leading to a misrepresentation of the allegory amongst adults in general. Seminar experience in teaching *The Pilgrim's Progress* to adults has repeatedly proved this assertion to be true. Time and time again, people who have been led through the allegory have freely confessed their previous ignorance and misunderstandings in this regard. It is also probable that, in an age that has become so addicted to visual stimulation, it is more difficult for people today to move beyond Bunyan's imagery to the deeper levels of objective, biblical truth.

One of the features of George Offor's edition of Bunyan's *Works* is the obvious loving regard which he felt, not only for the person of the Bedford pastor, but also for his doctrine. And it is this quality that will continue to endear his devoted contribution to lovers of Bunyan, whatever his scholastic shortcomings may be. The same could also be said of John Brown's biography; clearly this author profoundly loved his subject.

But when one considers, by comparison, two more recent and parallel works, the Oxford University Press edition of Bunyan's *Works* on the one hand, and Michael Mullett's *John Bunyan in Context* on the other, there is a notable absence of that warmth and affection that was so evident in the works mentioned earlier. No doubt this would be justified in the name of impartial scholarship. Be that as it may, while expressing a measure of gratitude, we ought not to be too fulsome in our praise of works that are more sterile, even if more learned, than those of earlier writers. It would be better if we returned to 'heart work', as Bunyan calls it, as a matter of primary concern, although, of course, this is not in any way to suggest that we

should neglect the importance of an accurate text and historical
enlightenment.

The recognition of presuppositions

In Iain Murray's biography *Jonathan Edwards*, published in
1987, he commences with a most necessary introduction, which
he calls 'On Understanding Edwards'.[13] His concern is that
some of the more recent scholarly writings on the life of Edwards, such as those by Ola Winslow and Perry Miller, fail to
acknowledge their own naturalistic presuppositions which are
doctrinally alien to those of the Bible and of early eighteenth-
century Calvinism in New England.

So Murray explains: 'Those who consider that modern enlightenment has superseded the possibility of the supernatural
and displaced the Bible as a revelation from a living God, ought
at least to have considered the alternative reason which Edwards proposes for disbelief [namely deadness and darkness of
the soul through pride]. Instead, they simply assume that Christianity is "discovered to be fictitious". And they proceed to write
about Edwards as though this makes no difference to any
genuine understanding of his life and thought. They never address themselves to the question, What would follow if Edwards' religion is in accord with Christ and the Bible and if it be
true? Any references which they make to the Bible at all are
commonly as superficial as that of Henry Churchill King who at
the Edwards' Bicentenary regretted that Edwards lacked
"Christ's wonderful faith in men".'[14]

The same applies today with regard to modern estimates of
The Pilgrim's Progress and of Bunyan. He died only fifteen years
before the birth of Edwards and the mishandling to which he is
subjected is not at all unlike that of the Massachusetts divine as
described by Murray. And the reason for this is not hard to discover. The plain fact is that, like Edwards, Bunyan believed the

Bible to be truthful and without error. It is not surprising, then, to discover that, in spite of their very different educational levels, these two choice saints were in close agreement regarding essential Christian doctrine.

However, when the modern biographer of Bunyan, Gordon Wakefield, is confronted with this biblical world-view, he raises a very appropriate point: 'The chief question for our time is whether Bunyan's view of the universe has any meaning for us.'[15] In real and objective terms for this liberal scholar, the answer, not only with regard to the universe, but also to Bunyan's view of God, the Bible, sin and the gospel, must surely be negative. Nevertheless, in subjective terms Wakefield gives a positive response — that is, when an existential and relativistic extrapolation is applied.

In a manner consistent with his theology, it is this latter course for which Wakefield opts. He briefly describes Bunyan's 'Map Shewing the Order and Causes of Salvation and Damnation'. Then he illustrates: 'Some people are helped by maps even if they do not correspond to the actual terrain to be traversed. In *Bugles and a Tiger* John Masters told of a Gurkha prisoner of the Japanese in Burma, who managed to escape and made his way by an arduous journey through the Burmese jungle back to base. They asked him how he had done it. He said he had a map. Astonished and eager they asked to see it. He produced it. It was a street map of London.'[16]

Wakefield readily admits that *The Pilgrim's Progress* is a more popular guide than Bunyan's 'Map', but he concludes that 'There are those who may live good and Christian lives and attain health and peace of soul according to a plan of salvation which does not bear any relation to what seem to most people to be the objective and believable realities of God and the world. And though it may be fearsome it may lead, as with Bunyan, to a life of integrated fulfilment and at any rate a sight of journey's end.'[17] In other words, though the famous allegory clearly presents a very specific conservative biblical theology,[18] it is possible to approach the theological framework and in some way incorporate into it a contrary theology, and still travel to a journey's end. The fact that it is possible to travel in this manner, according to Bunyan, and in so doing to resemble Ignorance — a character for whom Wakefield has sympathy —[19] does not strike the author as contradicting this interpretation. Yet Bunyan would have seen such an imposition upon his dream as nothing short of error to be condemned, much like the false teaching of the Latitudinarian, Edward Fowler.

The point, then, is that, as Murray warns, it is vital that the underlying bias of modern Bunyan scholars should be recognized. For instance, in spite of Christopher Hill's encyclopaedic understanding of seventeenth-century England and his modest style, yet, as a confessed Marxist, his obsession with viewing the work from a proletarian and materialist stance needs to be understood since it inhibits him from entering into the same kind of spiritual camaraderie with Bunyan as George Offor does.

Eight modern Bunyan scholars

The following eight vignettes are representative of various shades of modern Bunyan scholarship. The field as a whole is broad, though, sad to say, almost totally lacking in evangelical warmth. This is not meant to demean the positive contribution of predominantly textual, stylistic and historical study. Nevertheless, it remains true that most of the studious investigations in this area come from scholars who are decidedly opposed to Bunyan's doctrine, and this, it would seem, militates against a faithful presentation of Bunyan's total and essential message.

It is my firm conviction that when we are dealing with the author of *The Pilgrim's Progress*, it is this aspect of authoritative Bible truth at an experiential level that ought to be our prime concern.[20] To deny this is to treat the classic allegory more as a literary cadaver suitable only for dispassionate dissection or for the exercise of the most advanced cosmetic skills. However, this will never bring back the life of God to this corrupt and apathetic generation, in the way that Bunyan intended for the people of his own day. Rather, we must heed his exhortation: 'Do thou the substance of my matter see.' In other words, we must return to the gospel he so fervently proclaimed, the gospel of Luther and the apostle Paul, the one and only gospel of the sovereign grace of God.

Roger Sharrock

Sharrock, who was formerly professor of English at King's College, University of London, probably ranks as the foremost Bunyan scholar of the twentieth century. His monumental contribution was not only in his role as General Editor of the Oxford University Press edition of the full works of Bunyan which was intended to replace the standard three-volume set produced during the nineteenth century by George Offor, but also as the particular editor of the 1960 revision of the critical text of *The Pilgrim's Progress* which had originally been edited by J. B. Wharey in 1928. This volume, also published by Oxford University Press, contains not only the definitive text of the famous allegory, with full critical apparatus, but also a mine of information that includes a supplementary commentary.

Also significant in this respect is Sharrock's editorship of *Grace Abounding*, Bunyan's spiritual autobiography, published in 1962. Sharrock's numerous other books and articles of a textual, literary and historical nature, including a biography of Bunyan, have always been regarded, from the point of view of his areas of expertise, as judicious and insightful, drawing upon a profound knowledge of seventeenth-century England and the best available primary sources.

A representative sample of Sharrock's writing can be found in his introductory essay to the Penguin edition of *The Pilgrim's Progress*.[21] He repeatedly acknowledges the foundational role of the Bible in the allegory. It is Bunyan's 'reliance on the literal text of the Bible which is the prime motive of the autobiography [*Grace Abounding*]' (p.11), and, we may add, of *The Pilgrim's Progress*. He goes on to state that '*The Pilgrim's Progress* is soaked in the imagery of the Bible and deeply pervaded by the Puritan belief that the Bible provided a key to every problem of life and thought' (p.23). Moreover — and Sharrock's lack of sympathy with Bunyan seems to show through here — 'Bunyan's intense, *peculiar* reading of Scripture has guided the very structure of his narrative' (p. 25, emphasis added).

In the same subjective vein we read: 'Puritanism has been misconceived as restrictive moral prohibitions, weighed down by sexual guilt; in the mid seventeenth century it was a fiery religious and social dynamic resembling Marxism more than modern Fundamentalism' (p.13). But surely this is a very inappropriate parallel. True, the revolution under Cromwell was militant, social as well as religious, though these elements were definitely subordinate to an authoritative Bible that was very much revered in a manner similar to that of twentieth-century biblical fundamentalism. Bunyan would have abominated dialectical materialism, that is the philosophic root of Marxism derived from Feuerbach and Hegel.

However, Sharrock provides a good description of the heart of Christian's quest. In parallel with Luther, '... it is his tremendous need to find a righteousness not his own by which to be saved, which is the force irresistibly driving Christian along the road to his final entry into the Celestial City' (p. 11).

Sharrock's explanation, for the benefit of the reader who is new to Bunyan, of an extremely important principle concerning Bunyan's multi-layered style is also helpful: 'For the modern reader, the human working compromise between realism and allegory is likely to conceal the firm outlines of the theological structure which were more obvious to Bunyan's contemporaries and especially to his fellow-Nonconformists. What is on the surface an episodic series of adventures, a folk-tale of ups and downs such as Bunyan himself enjoyed in the popular romances of his unregenerate youth, has a tough skeleton of which each articulated joint precisely indicates a stage in the Puritan psychology of conversion' (p.18).

On the other hand, one must raise an objection to the suggestion that, following Christian's fierce engagement with Apollyon, during which he made use of various weapons, his subsequent recourse to a distinctive weapon named 'All-prayer' while passing through the Valley of the Shadow of Death is allegorical inconsistency, 'clumsiness', a 'gaffe' and a 'blunder' (p.17). The truth is that Bunyan is being consistent with Scripture when he moves from a reference to 'the sword of the Spirit' to the need for 'all prayer', following the order in which both are mentioned in Ephesians 6:17-18. Bunyan is also true to his own experience, for he relates that at times the Bible could be for him 'as dry as a stick'. Yet such an experience of barrenness would press him 'to pray unto God'.[22]

Nevertheless, Sharrock has left us with a legacy of textual, literary and historical clarification that will greatly profit students of Bunyan and his writings for many generations to come.

Christopher Hill

As the pre-eminent modern historian in the field of seventeenth-century English history, with an ability to communicate his conclusions in an appealing manner, Christopher Hill has particularly focused his attention upon the time of the Civil War and Commonwealth. It was towards the close of this period that John Bunyan's pen first began to be exercised with such creative effect. Hill, a former Master of Balliol College, Oxford, published in 1989 an acclaimed study of 'John Bunyan and his Church, 1628-1688', the American edition of which has the title, *A Tinker and a Poor Man*. It continues to be acknowledged as both innovative in much of its interpretation and encyclopaedic with regard to the sources it references.

It is not surprising that Hill, as a humanistic Marxist and former member of the Communist Party of Great Britain, views

Bunyan and his environment in a secular and social context. This is in no way meant to depreciate his vast understanding of Bunyan's times, which he unveils with such fascinating detail. Hill comprehends the Bedford pastor's doctrinal stance in a formal sense, though it is not difficult to perceive that he has no sympathy whatsoever with this biblical world-view. Even so, it is readily acknowledged that Hill's style is peaceable.

Christopher Hill's grand thesis is that, if one peels away the prominent top layers of Christian doctrine and the use of allegory as a means of holding the reader's interest, a careful analysis of Bunyan and his writings provides a fascinating scenario of social and class tension in the light of the pervasive Puritan economic dynamic. He states: 'We must therefore be alert to the devices of allegory, use of Biblical myths, parable, metaphor, and irony which Bunyan regularly employed. His main themes are simple, clear, and straightforwardly expressed: but their application contains a wealth of overt and covert allusions, some of which I have tried to bring out. There are risks in trying to read between the lines. But there was a chasm between Bunyan's thinking and that of the JPs who sent him to jail; between him and the Latitudinarian clergy, the more liberal wing of the Church of England. I am not suggesting that Bunyan's interests were primarily political; far from it... But the mere fact of being a protestant dissenter forced political decisions on him.'[23]

So while the author is well aware of the priority for Bunyan of spiritual and gospel truth, he is content to concentrate on the backdrop scenery and ignore the performance on centre stage. Thus, when we come to the chapter on *The Pilgrim's Progress*, the focus upon the social context is heavy indeed, to the intentional avoidance of Christian's main problem, which is the burden of personal sin. So we read:

> Running through *The Pilgrim's Progress* is a strong sense of the superiority of the poor to the rich... The pilgrim, like the whole book, is firmly set in a lower-class ambience... When we first see him the Pilgrim is in rags

— allegorical rags, to be sure, but they also represent real poverty... The Pilgrim is a 'labouring man', of 'base and low estate and condition'... Undesirable characters in *The Pilgrim's Progress*, as later in *The Holy War*, are almost obsessively labelled as lords and ladies, gentlemen and gentlewomen.

In the most helpful analysis of *The Pilgrim's Progress* I have read for a long time, James Turner describes Bunyan as 'a despised itinerant manual worker, excluded from land-ownership, exposed to the rigours of the open road as he travelled and the violence of property-owners [Giant Despair] if he deviated; yet he was a householder and artisan, descended from yeomen and small traders.'[24] ... In Emmanuel's Land, on the Delectable Mountains and in Beulah, lands and their produce are 'rent free', 'common ... for all the pilgrims'. In the Celestial City, it is said, pilgrims have houses of their own [but surely this is a reference to John 14:2]... The burden [on Christian's back] is sin, the product of centuries of unequal society [not according to Bunyan's doctrine!][25]

So with a great socialist and revisionist flourish, Hill concludes: 'Puritanism, tenacious especially in defeat, combined to make *The Pilgrim's Progress* not only a foundation document of the English working-class movement but also a text which spoke to millions of those poor oppressed people whom Bunyan ... wished to address.'[26]

Again, it is worth repeating that Hill provides a wealth of intriguing and helpful background information concerning Bunyan and his writings. But 'background' rather than 'foreground' is precisely the right term to be used in this analysis. The author admittedly plays with the skeleton and flesh rather than the heart or soul of his topic. But then, as a materialist, Hill would not believe that there is such an entity as a 'soul', nor in the existence of original sin, or a redeeming Christ, or a truthful Word of God. He is as likely to arrive at a right understanding of the inner core of Bunyan as a camel is to pass through the eye of a needle.

Neil H. Keeble

A professor of English at Stirling University in Scotland, Neil Keeble has focused his studies on seventeenth-century Puritanism in England with considerable emphasis being given to a literary focus on the life and times of John Bunyan. At the time of writing he is President of the International John Bunyan Society. In 1980 he published an essay entitled 'Christiana's Key: The Unity of *The Pilgrim's Progress*',[27] in which he well demonstrates the diversity within unity in the relationship between Parts One and Two. He puts it this way, alluding to 1 Corinthians 13:13: 'If Part I had handled faith and hope, Part II turns to charity... He "who would true valour see" had best read the whole of *The Pilgrim's Progress*.'[28]

Keeble's most substantial contribution appears to be *The Literary Culture of Nonconformity in Later Seventeenth Century England*, published in 1987.[29] Whereas there has been a tendency to isolate Bunyan and *The Pilgrim's Progress* in their Puritan setting, Keeble here presents the Bedford pastor as an integral part of the literary scene and nonconformist struggle within Restoration England.

In 1988 he edited a notable volume called *John Bunyan, Conventicle and Parnassus*. This was a collection of essays dedicated to the tercentenary of the death of the Bedford tinker. Keeble's own contribution, '"Of him thousands daily Sing and talk": Bunyan and his reputation'. is an excellent and detailed description of the growth of influence and circulation of *The Pilgrim's Progress* since its first publication in 1678.[30] The outline of this essay describing the development of the reception accorded to Bunyan is worthy of mention here:

- *The Seventeenth-century Bunyan*. While the common people heard him gladly, the educated considered him vulgar.
- *The Augustan Bunyan*. Improving regard and acceptance find Dr Samuel Johnson giving his approval along with the disguised recognition of William Cowper. However, Edmund Burke considers him degraded and David Hume in bad taste.
- *The Evangelical Bunyan*. As the darling of the Great Awakening, there is high regard from the leaders, such as John Wesley, George Whitefield and, later, John Newton.
- *The Romantic Bunyan*. A period of heightened taste and aesthetics provides the approval of Robert Southey, William Blake, Charles Lamb, Sir Walter Scott, Lord Macaulay and Samuel Taylor Coleridge.
- *The Victorian Bunyan*. Now he makes impression upon the works of Nathaniel Hawthorne, Charlotte Brontë, William Thackeray and Louisa M. Alcott. Scholarly affection flows from George Offor and John Brown.
- *The Modern Bunyan*. Roger Sharrock, William York Tindall, Christopher Hill and U. Milo Kaufmann give social and literary analysis.

Of special note is Keeble's editorship of the Oxford University Press edition of *The Pilgrim's Progress* in The World's Classics series, published in 1984, the actual text of which is that of the 1960 Wharey and Sharrock edition. While his indebtedness to Sharrock is acknowledged, a distinctive contribution is made here in terms of commentary. The introductory essay follows closely the twentieth-century mode in giving considerable emphasis to nuances of style, culture, history and motives, while avoiding the specifics of Bunyan's supreme passion for gospel grace and truth. The comment that 'Puritanism was a preeminently social movement whose considerable literature was characterized by a fascinated interest in the actual experiences of men,'[31] is far too removed from the heart of the matter. It would be more correct to say that Puritanism was a conservative Christian movement born of a desire for reformation within Anglicanism, though doubtless with social consequences, and one which was rooted in a thoroughly authoritative Bible and Reformation theology.

Richard Greaves

Richard Greaves, the Robert O. Lawton Distinguished Professor of History and Courtesy Professor of Religion at Florida State University, obtained his Ph.D. degree from the University of London for his research into Puritan theology as represented by John Bunyan. An edited version of his doctoral thesis was published in 1969 under the simple title, *John Bunyan*. However, the scarcity of such a study within the vast array of investigative literature into Bunyan, focusing as it does on historical theology, makes it to be of distinct importance. For this reason, a modified outline of the main chapters is given below:

A. The pilgrim's God
   1. Divine wrath and grace
   2. Divine extension of grace
   3. Necessity of satisfaction
   4. Extent of grace

B. The pilgrim's call
   1. Predestination and election
   2. Predestination and reprobation
   3. Free will
   4. Divine call

C. The pilgrim's response
1. Faith
2. Repentance
3. Justification
4. Forgiveness
5. Sanctification
6. Perseverance

D. The pilgrim's covenant
1. Covenant of works
2. Covenant of grace — the divine aspect
3. Covenant of grace — the human aspect
4. Covenant of grace — the legal aspect

E. The pilgrim's stately palace
1. Church
2. Ministry
3. Sacraments
4. Christian life

This is an excellent study that appears to be free of liberal nuances, secular dominance and preoccupation with social issues, although one could wish for at least a hint of passion on the part of the author, since the grasp of Bunyan's belief here ought surely to result in more than a mere acknowledgement of correctness. It is strange that the Bedford pastor's high view of Scripture, which is so foundational to his doctrine and such a thorn to modern critics, is neglected, or perhaps assumed. The chapter on Bunyan's covenant theology is open to some question, since the tendency is to associate it with the prevailing understanding of the distinctive systematic doctrine at that time. However, although Bunyan does frequently use the term 'covenant of grace' in his *Doctrine of the Law and Grace Unfolded*,[32] yet it is intended to describe chiefly the new covenant according to the influence of Luther, and not an overarching covenant under which many administrations are subsumed, according to the definition of *The Westminster Confession of Faith*. Further, it is noteworthy that Bunyan does not use covenant terminology at all, or even hint at it, in *The Pilgrim's Progress*, a point confirmed by Greaves' admission that he failed in his attempt to derive such an association.

Concerning the tinker's Calvinism, Greaves gives a very fine analysis of Bunyan's understanding of divine sovereignty; again it is rooted more in Luther's predestinarian appreciation of grace than in the Westminster divines' teaching on God's eternal decree. Greaves suggests that this is the reason for Bunyan's distinctive vibrancy. So he concludes: 'Always there remained that motivating force of transforming grace which neither maturity nor theological awareness diminished. This, coupled with his skill "in the direct colloquial expression of truth", was the key to the success which he achieved as a writer and a preacher. '[33]

Mention should also be made of Greaves' substantial editorial involvement with the completed publication by Oxford University Press of Bunyan's *Miscellaneous Works*; this includes his editorship of volumes II, VIII, IX and XI within that series. Another collection of stimulating essays under the title, *John Bunyan and English Nonconformity*, includes his cautious opinion, in agreement with that of Sharrock, that *Reprobation Asserted* is a spurious work.[34] In addition, Greaves has published *An Annotated Bibliography of John Bunyan Studies* (84 pp.) and, together with James Forrest, *John Bunyan — A Reference Guide* (478 pp.).

However, perhaps this author's crowning scholarly achievement is the thematic biography, *Glimpses of Glory: John Bunyan and English Dissent*. In harmony with the blandness of contemporary Bunyan studies, here is a volume that will not appeal to the enquiring soul who longs for encouraging exposition of the grace that Bunyan himself found. In dispassionate, analytical terms there is extensive investigation of Bunyan's depressed psyche, as well as historic, literary, social and religious categories. There is intricate dissection, but not the slightest concern for allowing Bunyan to speak authoritatively, even evangelistically.

The concluding paragraph sufficiently reflects this detachment, using abstract terms which Bunyan, who was always so passionately specific about the saving grace of Christ, would never have considered to be a true reflection of his pulsating heart: 'Bunyan's literary success ultimately rests on his extraordinary ability to rouse the imaginations of his readers — an ability rooted in his intense spirituality and powerful creativity, and given emotive force by his deep sympathy for the poor and oppressed and his fierce commitment to the principle that truth must be free... No less significant was his triumph over the debilitating, harrowing depressive moods that plunged him into the depths of black despair in the 1650s and early 1660s, leaving him with a keen sensitivity to the importance of light, warmth, and love, all of which ultimately helped him to hold back the dark. In the end his potent creativity enabled him to turn his experiences into a gripping autobiography and two major allegories that attest to his triumph over crippling despair and a repressive government.'[35]

Gordon Campbell

As a professor of Renaissance literature at the University of Leicester, Campbell is worthy of inclusion here for two particular reasons.

First, he has contributed essays on Bunyan in two significant scholarly volumes in the realm of Bunyan studies. They are, 'The Theology of *The Pilgrim's Progress*,' in *The Pilgrim's Progress, Critical and Historical Views*, published in 1980 and edited by Vincent Newey; and, 'Fishing in Other Men's Waters: Bunyan and the Theologians' in *John Bunyan, Conventicle and Parnassus*, the collection of essays edited by N. H. Keeble mentioned earlier.

Second, both of these essays are obviously concerned with Bunyan's theological beliefs and sources, and this emphasis is very much related to our concerns in this present volume.

Now it is readily acknowledged that Campbell appreciates the problem of confronting a Puritan biblicist faith: 'Because Bunyan's theology impinges to some extent on *The Pilgrim's Progress*, students of literature too often dismiss it as a book which champions a faith to which they feel hostile, if they are non-believers, or which they find distastefully evangelical, if they subscribe quiescently to a liberal form of Christianity.'[36] However, because it is obvious that Campbell himself is troubled with such unabashed evangelicalism, an approach is suggested that is certainly not novel in the modern arena of Bunyan studies. It is simply ideological extrapolation that pushes to one side the doctrinal specifics: 'But the redeeming literary quality of *The Pilgrim's Progress* resides in the fact that Bunyan's imagination transcends his theological convictions, in much the same way that his energetic pursuit of souls shows a compassion for the fate of the dispossessed which arises from his cold theological conviction that an overwhelming proportion of humanity has been consigned irrevocably to hell.'[37]

Hence, Campbell's essays soon reveal an unabashed bias away from Bunyan's evangelical doctrine that colours the whole of his writings. He declares: 'Puritans deemed the Bible to be the sole and sufficient source of doctrine. In practice, however, the process of exegesis did not consist in teasing doctrines out of the Bible, but rather in reading doctrines in which they already believed into the Bible. The Bible is not, after all, a theological work, but rather a collection of narratives and epistles from which, at best, doctrines can be inferred; even the relatively explicit teaching of the apostle Paul stands in need of strenuous explication if it is to be transformed into the dogmas of the Christian faith... His [Bunyan's] affirmation of the Trinity is a good example of a belief which cannot be traced to the Bible for the simple reason that there is no biblical doctrine of the Trinity. It is possible on biblical evidence to mount an argument of some respectability for the divinity of Jesus, but it is a long step from that doctrine to a belief in a triune godhead.'[38]

Surely the overbearing dismissal of one of the cardinal doctrines of the Christian faith is not only breathtaking, but also little short of bigotry. Therefore we will consider just one notable instance in which the Bedford tinker comes under scrutiny which quickly discards his faith on the grounds that it is traditional rather than really biblical, when in fact the criticism is born of doctrinal antipathy and misrepresentation.

In one of Bunyan's earliest publications, *Some Gospel-Truths Opened according to the Scriptures*, he poses a rhetorical question to the nominal Christian: 'But when did God shew thee that thou wert no Christian? When didst thou see that: And in the light of the Spirit of Christ, see that thou wert under the wrath of God because of original sin? (Rom. 5:12).'[39] Campbell claims that because Romans 5:12 is quoted in support here, Bunyan's doctrine must have been based upon a faulty translation of the second part of this verse, which gave the rendering, 'in whom [presumably Adam] all sinned' instead of the more correct, 'because all sinned'. On this basis he declares, 'The fact that the doctrine of original sin rested on a mistranslation did not impede its influence, and it became a central doctrine of the faith. Bunyan believed it, and believed it to be biblical.'[40] Thus the impression clearly conveyed, based upon references to J. N. D. Kelly's *Early Christian Doctrines*,[41] is that the doctrine of original sin has rested principally upon a mistranslation of Romans 5:12b by Ambrosiaster in *c.* 375 A.D., with the subsequent support of Augustine, who was no expert in the biblical languages. So he claims that a longstanding doctrine has in fact no biblical basis and as a consequence the uneducated Bunyan has been misled by poor exegesis.[42]

To begin with, to read Kelly is to discover that he is not so reckless as to claim that a whole doctrine arose in Christendom on account of Ambrosiaster's poor exegesis at this one point, though he does see it as significant, even pivotal and influential where Augustine was concerned. There were other Scriptures used for proof at that time.[43] Campbell's inference that, had Romans 5:12b been correctly interpreted, the doctrine of original sin would never have arisen, cannot be supported. Further, while the prevailing contemporary opinion is that Romans 5:12b should be translated 'because all sinned', those who would translate it in this way include several conservative scholars such as Moo, Morris and Shedd.[44] who are nevertheless committed to the orthodox doctrine of original sin. Even so, it is simplistic to sweep aside the alternative 'in whom all sinned' when F. W. Danker, E. Stauffer, Nigel Turner and W. Manson are in essential agreement with it.[45] Turner significantly comments: 'I am bound to say that this [*in whom* all men sinned] seems more consistent with the apostle's main argument when one reads the epistle to the Romans *as a whole*' (emphasis added).[46] Very much so, and it is for this reason that when Bunyan makes a further comment concerning original sin he quotes in support another significant reference: 'He [Adam] did not only leave them a broken covenant, but also made them himself sinners against it. He made them sinners — "By one man's disobedience many were made sinners" (Rom. 5:19)... Not only so, but also before he left them [the sons of Adam] he was the conduit pipe through which the devil did convey off his poisoned spawn and venom nature into the hearts of Adam's sons and daughters, by which they are at this day so strongly and so violently carried away, that they fly as fast to hell, and the devil, by reason of sin, as chaff before a mighty wind.'[47]

John Stachniewski

A former professor of English at Manchester University, John Stachniewski gained considerable limelight in the area of Puritan and Bunyan studies on account of writing *The Persecutory Imagination*, published by Oxford University Press in 1991. Subtitled 'English Puritanism and the Literature of Religious Despair', its main thesis is that seventeenth-century English

Puritanism, on account of its preoccupation with an oppressive God derived from Calvinism and a literalist interpretation of the Bible, generated excessive symptoms of despair sometimes resulting in suicide.

The author states: 'Puritans, for my purposes, were people whose minds appear to have been captured by the questions whether or not they were members of the elect, and how the life of an elect (and elect community), in contradistinction to that of a reprobate, should be ordered. In principle they took a literalist view of the Bible and were either vociferous and vigorous in their attempts to purify the Church of England of perceived accretions to the practices of the primitive church or split off into sects which they thought conformed to these most closely.'[48]

Of the various Puritan writers whom he cites in support of this analysis, the greatest attention is given to John Bunyan and in particular to *Grace Abounding* and *The Pilgrim's Progress.* Christopher Hill raises this matter in his book,[49] and Stachniewski's thesis appears to be substantially another, though more strident, expression of the same allegation.

That the Puritans, genuine representatives of biblical Christianity though they were, had some serious failings, is beyond doubt. Lloyd-Jones gets to the heart of the matter when he says that they were 'too much influenced by the analogy of the Old Testament and of Israel, and applying it to England. Was not that the real error? In the Old Testament and under that Dispensation the State (of Israel) was the church (Acts 7:38), but the State of England in the sixteenth century was not the church. In the Old Testament the two were one and identical. But surely in the New Testament we have the exact opposite. The church consists of the "called out" ones, not the total state.'[50]

Now, this being so, it must be admitted that many Puritans — though Bunyan was not one of their number — did place legal requirements on the people resembling those which even the apostles described as 'a yoke which neither our fathers nor we have been able to bear' (Acts 15:10).[51] Yet Stachniewski does not concern himself with this aspect at all. He has a different target in his sights. Nor is he a dispassionate commentator, for he openly admits, 'I see no point in seeking to conceal, by a wholly impersonal tone, the reflexes of my own value system.'[52] Hence, with this object in view, he not only expresses his considerable distaste for Bunyan's beliefs and experience, but goes on to describe his alleged mental state as 'a phenomenon as bizarre as belief in the Calvinist God'.[53]

So, for this reason, he musters substantial evidence to prove that an epidemic of despair hung over Bunyan's generation. Thus he writes, '*The Pilgrim's Progress* evolves under similar pressures, except that here the psychic persecution is more fully amplified in its social dimensions. Bunyan's allegory provided the aptest literary vehicle for the persecutory imagination, uniting the physical, psychological, and social levels on which it was simultaneously experienced.'[54]

Using a style that could learn much from the more temperate, though no less committed, writing of Christopher Hill, Stachniewski provides a vast array of seventeenth-century literary evidence concerning individual introspective preoccupation with the eternal purposes of God. Admittedly, the atmosphere which prevailed at that time was certainly quite different from the almost carnival spirit of today. However, even if there is some evidence supporting his claim of such a welter of depression, the cause is more broadly based than the author's thesis will allow. Not surprisingly, Hill suggests economic factors, though he also allows for perceived sin and Calvinism; then he concludes: 'It would be useless to speculate which was the more operative cause.'[55]

However, the great issue that Stachniewski does not in any way prove is whether the incidence of depression and suicide in this modern era, one which is definitely not dominated by Calvinism, is comparatively any less than that of seventeenth-century Puritan England. It would be a brave person who would answer in the affirmative, although this is the response to be expected in support of the author's basic thesis, but it would hardly be realistic. As a matter of fact, The World Health Organization released a prediction in 1997 that in the twenty-first century, depression will rise to the first place as the most disabling condition, in terms of its impact on the individual, taking precedence over road accidents, heart disease and war.[56]

Gordon Wakefield also comes to the same conclusion: '[Stachniewski's book] is a valuable corrective to the over-eager and selective admiration of Puritanism, which I recognize as a danger in some of my own work... Yet the reaction goes too far... Despair is not confined to Protestantism, nor its literature to Stachniewski's period [of concern]. If Calvinism may have aggravated his [Bunyan's] despair, did it not also deliver him from falling into the abyss of religious aberrations? Some of us may have presented the Puritan divines in too attractive a guise. But in Bunyan above all there is a tenderness as well as a humility which engages our affections still.'[57]

Pieter de Vries

This Dutch scholar obtained a Ph.D. in Theology from the University of Utrecht, the title of his thesis being *John Bunyan on the Order of Salvation*. A revised English version was published in 1994.[58] A particularly noteworthy feature of this work is the delightful discovery that here we have another study of Bunyan's doctrine after the manner of Richard Greaves' doctoral dissertation, though in this instance the author is less restrained in making clear his personal commitment to Bunyan's doctrinal stance; and his scholarship in no way suffers on this account. At the conclusion we read: 'Those who cherish the Reformed standards of faith will be conscious of a heart-felt union with Reformed Baptists like John Bunyan... May the Lord use this study to build his church. The church professes that God has blessed her with all spiritual blessings in Christ. It is the Christian's comfort that the same God who has predestinated him to be conformed to the image of his Son, has also called him, and justified him, and will some day glorify him. How good it is to serve and praise this God. Amen.'[59]

Here Bunyan's convictions are considered according to the *ordo salutis* (order of salvation) with a lapsarian focus, although these technical terms were not coined until after Bunyan's era. Here, then, is a study of the Bedford pastor's distinctive brand of Puritanism and his kinship with European Reformed doctrine as it is reflected in the 'golden chain' of Romans 8:28-30. However, the Englishman's distinctiveness is not lost: 'Bunyan was a preacher of free grace. In answering the question how man might flee from the wrath to come, he did not refer to human properties or duties to be performed. He powerfully taught that we can only stand in the judgement of God if we are clothed with Christ's righteousness. The foundation on which we can stand before God is entirely outside of us in the work of Christ. In the history of the church law and gospel have time and again been mixed up. Christ has repeatedly been seen to be transformed into a new Moses, delineated as a taskmaster rather than a Saviour.'[60]

In this thesis, unlike a considerable proportion of Bunyan studies today, there is so much that is good, clarifying and edifying that a short review such as this will be forced to leave a substantial part unmentioned. Nevertheless, even though the author reflects a very affectionate regard for Bunyan and his ministry — an attitude which has been especially evident among the Dutch — he does raise several matters that are open to question.

For instance, he makes the comment: 'R. L. Greaves' conclusion that Bunyan displayed Antinomian tendencies is in my opinion incorrect.'[61] However, the consequences of Bunyan's later belief that the Sabbath was not a creation ordinance, but rather ordained for Israel, would be considered by many today as grounds for making the charge of antinomianism. The same charge is sometimes made with regard to his belligerent terminology concerning Moses (see chapter 8).

Then there is the identification of Bunyan's use of the terms 'covenant of works' and 'covenant of grace' with the more formulated statements.[62] Classic definitions of the 'covenant of grace' speak of an overarching covenant under which are subsumed the specific administrations, or biblically stated covenants. Bunyan, however, uses the term 'the covenant of grace' in a more narrow sense, according to which it is identical with, rather than inclusive of, 'the new covenant'. As detailed in chapter 8, this 'covenant of grace' was transacted in heaven between the Father and the Son, and did not involve any participation on the part of God's elect. It was not a derived and comprehensive covenant according to the usage of this term in confessions such as *The Westminster Confession of Faith*.

Michael A. Mullett

This professor of history at Lancaster University, in England, has published extensively on religious history, with biographies of Luther, Calvin and studies of nonconformity. More recently he has written what will be regarded for many, at least in the intellectual arena, as one of the most significant analyses of Bunyan and his world. *John Bunyan in Context* is a scholarly study of the allegorist's historical setting, life and writings, and is exhaustively referenced. This is not a book for the layman on account, not only of its decidedly prolix and circuitous style, but also of the nuances that presuppose much in the realm of historic background, literary composition and even theological expression.

It is refreshing to read of a call that directs us back to the more classic Bunyan whose involvement in political matters, notwithstanding the secularist emphases of William York Tindall and, more recently, Christopher Hill, is relatively minor: 'It is worth noting that, of his nearly sixty published works, none directly concerns politics, and that one early production, the 1663 *Christian Behaviour* "illustrates the conservatism of Bunyan's social views" [quoting Hill]. Conservative or not, there is every indication that Bunyan was not deeply interested in political questions, in view of the overwhelming priority of spiritual and religious issues in his scheme of things.'[63]

Mullett repeats this thought by concluding that in the attempted political reconstruction of the allegorist, particularly 'the Tindall-Hill image of a "turbulent, seditious and factious" plebeian, subversively addressing the political issues of his day, lies a truth about Bunyan. But, hard though this may be for the twentieth-century *homo politicus* searching for the political element in all forms of discourse to digest, the authentic Bunyan may actually be closer to the Victorian version.'[64]

The breadth of Mullett's task, including some degree of commentary on a large proportion of Bunyan's writings, has inevitably resulted in instances of imbalance and skimpiness that leave the reader unfulfilled in certain areas. For instance, there is an exceedingly detailed consideration of Bunyan's arrest, trial and imprisonment, and the space devoted to this topic substantially exceeds the whole of the single chapter apportioned to consider Part One of *The Pilgrim's Progress*. As might be expected, there is much that calls for investigation from a historical perspective, such as the claim that 'Bunyan took a royalist line' following the Restoration of the monarchy,[65] the fact of Bunyan's medieval inheritance in relation to the matter of his literary dependency[66] and the intriguing parallels between Luther and Bunyan which only reinforce the fundamental point concerning the substantial influence of the German theologian upon the English nonconformist.[67]

But it is in the chapter devoted to Part One of *The Pilgrim's Progress* that inadequate coverage becomes especially obvious. The treatment at this point, as in other chapters, is most eclectic. To begin with, there is the statement that 'it [*The Pilgrim's Progress*] became a children's classic,' and the suggestion is made that this could have been Bunyan's original purpose.[68] (See chapter 19 for a more detailed response to this misunderstanding.) No one would argue against the fact that the allegory is more substantially a discourse than an itinerary, but why take several pages to prove this? The exposition on the subject of Pope and Pagan is certainly enlightening, though out of proportion. More significant is the elucidation of the fact that the Palace Beautiful is a representation of the Bedford congregation. So he writes, '*The Pilgrim's Progress*, then, is a Puritan book, and concerned with the life of the gathered churches.'[69]

A particularly disappointing omission is that of any consideration of the issues of despair, suicide and their remedy, according to Bunyan's portrayal through the imagery of Doubting Castle. In a similar vein, and from an evangelical perspective — which was surely also that of Bunyan — the most unsatisfactory feature of the book as a whole is the doctrinal leanness that is so representative of much contemporary Bunyan scholarship. This lack simply betrays a spiritual void concerning a passionate appreciation of Reformation truth.

For example, we read, 'Yet, although Bunyan rejected a soteriology of self-assurance which he ascribed to Fowler [the latitudinarian whom Bunyan characterized elsewhere in *Pilgrim's Progress*], he himself, especially in his repudiation of the inactive and verbal religion of Talkative, seems again to move away from a Reformation doctrine of justification by faith alone, and to place confidence in the role, not of the individual's election or saving faith, but in his or her moral actions and works.'[70] This comment demonstrates a failure to understand Bunyan at the doctrinal level, especially the relationship between justification and inevitable sanctification. With regard to Talkative, the confrontation that took place between him and Faithful was obviously not a gospel presentation. It was intended to facilitate exposure, to bring Talkative to repentance concerning his blindness to his own sin; should this have happened, then the truth of justification by faith would have been presented to him just as plainly as it was, later on, by Faithful to Hopeful.

Like so much of modern Bunyan scholarship, this writing is heavy on historical discovery and light on theological/biblical/ experiential matters. Certainly Mullett is a historian, but his theological comment, which is hardly of an evangelical character, is of secondary concern, and such a priority does fundamental disservice to Bunyan. It is this poverty of emphasis that betrays the reason for the cool character of modern academic investigation devoid of spiritual commitment and enthusiasm. The overwhelming theme of John Bunyan, in *The Pilgrim's Progress* as elsewhere, is the free saving grace of God through the Lord Jesus Christ that is offered to great sinners. If a writer does not know anything of this soul-enthralling truth, it seems as though it is impossible for him to do justice adequately to the essential Bunyan. In the light of this fact, the most faithful book by a modern commentator on the real objectives of Bunyan has yet to be written.

Conclusion

It is abundantly clear that the non-evangelical, theologically insipid, biblically liberal and secular spirit of the present time, which seems to dominate scholarly literary analysis, is not comfortable with the doctrine of John Bunyan. Of course, the same could be said with regard to the beliefs of Luther, Calvin, Edwards, etc. However the literati like the company of the truly great Christians, even if in their hearts they spurn their doctrine. With the arrogance of this modern age, they convince themselves that, had the fruits of contemporary textual criticism with regard to the Bible been available to our spiritual forefathers, they too would have come to the enlightened, albeit soul-debilitating conclusions of today. So older writings, such as *The Pilgrim's Progress*, are patronized for their literary and historical merit only, while the literal Bible teaching contained in them is at best regarded as passé.

Thus Vincent Newey, a professor of English at the University of Leicester, has concluded 'that the assumptions in which *The Pilgrim's Progress* is rooted are no longer generally assumed [a fact which] allows us broader sympathies. But the collapse of the work's controlling beliefs — whether we think of religion itself or of the more precise Calvinist scheme of salvation — can account only for a shift in attitude towards such figures, and not for the vividness of their continuing presence. What gives them "immortality" is Bunyan's creativity, appetite for life, and instinctive embrace of experience. He was restricted by his creed but was not its victim.'[71]

Of course, this is simply a reiteration of the views of Sharrock, Hill, Campbell and Stachniewski, with regard to their rejection of the esteem in which Bunyan held the Bible. This is the bottom-line issue from which so much of a certain brand of appreciation of *The Pilgrim's Progress* is derived.

This chapter commenced, quite unapologetically, with the assertion that, in the realm of Bunyan studies, and in consideration of the Bedford tinker's most passionate concerns, the last hundred years have proved to be a relative wilderness period. The fact is that detailed literary analysis, novel historical interpretation and avant-garde psychological investigation have not been able to obscure a fundamental poverty of appreciation concerning what, for Bunyan, were by far the most important issues of all. Bold confession of detachment from Bunyan's biblicist and Calvinist faith notwithstanding, the end result is a soulless and sterile contribution that will do nothing for any burdened sinner. Luther scholar Gordon Rupp perceives this problem when he explains 'why a Protestant Christian can understand things about Bunyan that are hidden from the innumerable literary critics who have written some very foolish pages about the measurement of Bunyan's sins, and failed altogether to understand either what it means to have a '"bruised conscience" or justification by faith'.[72]

George Offor sympathetically understood this truth, but then his style is now regarded as 'quaint' on this account. One thing is certain: Bunyan himself would have regarded the literary, historical, sociological and psychological speculations of those who reject the plain truth of Scripture as the greatest imaginable folly.

19.
The Pilgrim's Progress for young people

'[Bunyan's] language is everywhere level to the most ignorant reader... there is a homely reality about it; a nursery tale is not more intelligible in its manner of narration, to a child' (Robert Southey).

19.
The Pilgrim's Progress for young people

IF the communication of *The Pilgrim's Progress* to adults requires that priority be given to the word and truth, then a serious case can also be made for the argument that the communication of Bunyan's allegory to children and young people equally requires a similar priority. Unfortunately, the present deluge of fantasy-oriented and audio-visual presentations has tended to militate against such a concept. The media thrust has become so powerful that, unless children are fortified with solid doses of objective truth conveyed in words, they tend to subject reality to fantasy and impose fantasy upon reality.

Coleen Cook well illustrates this point as follows: 'The powerful effect of some of these artificial memories [fantasies] is vividly illustrated by a phenomenon some fire fighters call the "Darth Vader Syndrome". Increasingly, masked fire fighters are noticing that many small children caught in burning homes are running from, hiding from, or furiously fighting and resisting rescuers instead of co-operating with them in the middle of life-threatening situations. Subsequent interviews with small survivors pinpoint the problem. "I thought you were a spaceman," or "I thought you were Darth Vader," they confess.'[1]

The rise of audio-visual education

Of course, related to this problem is its alignment with the audio-visual model of learning so prevalent in adult communication. Even more so with children, the argument has arisen that to make the learning process visually exciting and fun is to enhance learning. However, we need to enquire what precisely is learned by means of this 'fun'? One thing is certain: a young person exposed to this hedonistic philosophy learns to be dependent on media which arouse emotion and create subjective impressions, and to spurn those which require the intellectual apprehension of cold facts. Thus Neil Postman explains: 'As a television show, and a good one, "Sesame Street" does not encourage children to love school or anything about school. It encourages them to love television.'[2]

However, the intention here is not to depreciate the proper place of imagination and fantasy in relation to audio-visual media since, at this point, we touch upon that which is so precious and memorable in childhood — in past centuries no less than today. Rather, the purpose of this chapter is to uphold the subsidiary role of these elements as a means of communication, in relation to the primary role of those media that present truth and reality by means of verbal communication and the thought-processes.

The rise of audio-visual versions of *The Pilgrim's Progress*

This now brings us to the specific point of how *The Pilgrim's Progress* ought to be communicated to young people today, and the obvious thrust of the foregoing paragraphs has established a basic principle. This is that, as in the case of adults, media which present the truth in words must be the primary means of communication and audio-visual media must occupy a secondary role. It needs to be stressed once again that what is proposed is not being presented in an either/or fashion.

However, the widespread marketing of some questionable modern versions of *The Pilgrim's Progress* aimed at the younger generation calls for the adopting of a definite stance on this issue.

In John Brown's classic biography of Bunyan, he lists thirty-two 'Editions of *The Pilgrim's Progress* for Children and Young People', the earliest being *Bunyan Explained to a Child*, published in 1825.[3] Two editions published by separate authors both had the title, *The Pilgrim's Progress in Words of one Syllable*. From a further study of copies of these earlier versions for young people held at the Bedford Public Library and the Evangelical Library in London, it would appear that, in the main, while illustrations adorned some editions of *The Pilgrim's Progress* from its third edition in 1679 onwards,[4] designated versions for children did not appear in reasonable numbers until the early nineteenth century. Even then, a preponderance of these early versions in fact consisted of the full text with the added attraction of numerous appealing illustrations. However, during the twentieth century there was an increasing tendency to publish versions that were strong in graphic representation but weak — if not actually perverse – when it comes to the editing and alteration of the text.

In this regard, it is surprising to find Bunyan scholar Michael Mullett making the following comment: 'Whether or not it [*The Pilgrim's Progress*] was aimed at children — as, expressly, was his *A Book for Boys and Girls* (1684) — it became a children's classic... In the Romantic era, the book's apparent suitability for and appeal to children allowed for its reclassification — in terms of approval, given the Romantics' general admiration for childhood — as a children's book.'[5]

Proof is then offered in support of this claim that includes the early nineteenth-century recommendations of its use for children made by Robert Southey and George Crabbe, although they were doubtless referring to the full text and not to simplified versions. However, Southey does not in fact suggest that *The Pilgrim's Progress* is chiefly suitable for children; rather he indicates its 'general popularity; — his [Bunyan's] language is everywhere level to the most ignorant reader, and to the meanest capacity: there is a homely reality about it; a nursery tale is not more intelligible, in its manner of narration, to a child'.[6] Certainly Macaulay and Coleridge, who were also of that period, regarded Bunyan's magnum opus as being more than just a novel primarily intended for young people.

It needs to be reiterated that, as stated in chapter 1, *The Pilgrim's Progress*, according to Bunyan's purposes, is primarily an adult book; yet at a basic level it also has great appeal for children. Its substance, though presented in the most delightful manner, portrays adult situations throughout. For example, consider the character of Madam Wanton, the criticism from Shame, the appeal to the flesh of Adam the First, the worldliness of By-ends and his friends, the subject matter dealing with despair and suicide at Doubting Castle and the substantial doctrine contained in the discourse entered into while the pilgrims are traversing the Enchanted Ground.

A selection and review of contemporary versions

The selection of reviews that follow is intended to be representative of the large number of versions of *The Pilgrim's Progress* that continue to flood the market. It should be evident from the following examples that parents who want to teach their children the truth of Bunyan's allegory, in the way he intended, need to be very careful in selecting a suitable version.

Oliver Hunkin, *Dangerous Journey*, illustrations by Alan Parry (Grand Rapids: Wm. B. Eerdmans, 1990)

This version was originally produced for Yorkshire Television, in England, in 1985. A video-cassette version of this series, professionally produced, is currently available, and is comprised of nine fifteen-minute episodes. The book, in large format, was published at the same time, and presumably intended for children, though this is not stated. The main focus is on Part One of *The Pilgrim's Progress*, but a very condensed version of Part Two is also included.

To begin with, the illustrations by Alan Parry are magnificently British and undoubtedly the strength of this version. Nevertheless, the drastically edited text leaves much to be desired. From beginning to end, what little is left of Bunyan's doctrinal content is emptied of its specific quality and replaced with a more ecumenical brand. The encounter with Simple, Sloth and Presumption is shunted back to before Christian's arrival at the Wicket-gate. In the same vein, and contrary to the original text, Pope is dead while Pagan is still alive and Pope's stiff joints and nail-biting frustration are attributed to him instead.

The lengthy discussion during the crossing of the Enchanted Ground concerning Hopeful's conversion, Ignorance's false gospel and Temporary's apostasy has been completely eliminated, and herein lies the heart of the problem. Virtually all the substantial discourse sections have been excluded. With this version we are confronted with impressive graphics but, at best, a very sentimentalized portrayal of doctrine.

The Pilgrim's Progress, illustrations by Albert Wessels (Harpenden, England: The Bunyan Press, 1993).

Here is a handsome and full presentation of the original text of Part One of *The Pilgrim's Progress* that, while not specifically marketed as a version for young people, is to be highly recommended. Published in 1993, it is typographically very readable, though the highlight is the illustrative skill of the Dutch painter, Albert Wessels. His colourful renderings of over seventy scenes draw upon many older engravings that are given new life, particularly in their depiction of the facial features. Several of the illustrations incorporate considerable detail derived from the text, and add an interpretive touch.

The Pilgrim's Progress, retold by Dan Larsen, illustrated by Al Bohl (Uhrichsville, OH: Barbour & Company, 1989).

The opening sentences of this racy version, which covers both Parts I and II, hardly seem designed to encourage the reader to read on, as we are told, 'The man stood in the field outside the City of Destruction and cried out in terror, "What shall I do!"' Omissions from Part I include five of the seven scenes at the house of the Interpreter, Pope and Pagan, the meeting with By-ends and his friends, the narratives concerning Little-faith and Temporary and the concluding scene involving Ignorance.

Now while simplification of the text may be justified, it seems to me that omissions are another matter and tend to underestimate the capacity of young people to comprehend the full panorama of Bunyan's story. If length is a problem, then why not divide the whole account into a number of separate episodes? This version, like so many others of its type, also omits all the poetic passages and thus denies the reader an introduction to Bunyan's use of poetry as a means of stimulating understanding of truth.

Little Pilgrim's Progress, Helen L. Taylor, illustrated by W. Lindsay Cable (Chicago: Moody Press, n.d).

The cover indicates that over 350,000 copies of this version, designated as suitable for ages seven to twelve, have been sold. The distinctive feature here is the adaptation of *The Pilgrim's Progress* into the world of children by means of characterization, vocabulary and juvenile concepts. So the rather bland commencement reads: 'Little Christian lived in a great city called Destruction. Its streets were full of boys and girls who laughed and played all day long. This was in the summertime when the sun was shining and the city looked bright and pleasant. On the rainy days in winter the children did not feel so happy, and they would sometimes be glad to sit down quietly and listen to stories.' This is pure sentimental misrepresentation.

Does communication for the young require that all the adult settings be eliminated or recast into a youthful frame of reference? Again, simplification may have a place, yet, much as children enjoy fantasy, they also aspire to the world of adults, which is so meaningfully portrayed by Bunyan's allegory. Normal childhood is always progressive, never static.

Besides this edition also includes revision, not mere simplification. For instance, why is Apollyon renamed 'Self'? By all means change the name to the simpler 'Satan'. But Bunyan is most definitely portraying this foul fiend as a personal devil, and not merely in terms of internal conflict! At the conclusion, and in reversal of the order of events in the text, Ignorance faces his final destiny first, after which Little Christian gains entrance to the Celestial City — doubtless to give the story a happier ending.

Pilgrim's Progress, retold by Mack Thomas, illustrated by Keith Criss (Sisters, OR: Gold 'n' Honey Family Classics, 1996).

We are told on the jacket of this revision of Part One, 'Many contemporary editions of *Pilgrim's Progress* shorten the story, eliminating important details. Others retain the seventeenth-century English that children find difficult to understand. But this vivid retelling of *Pilgrim's Progress* offers a full text that remains faithful to the dramatic, dream-like simplicity of Bunyan's original version, while carefully presenting the story in understandable, modern English.' In terms of this stated goal, it is on the whole well achieved since all the major events and most of the characters are included.

However, this version does omit a number of literary touches and expressions which Bunyan uses and which, in my opinion, ought to be taught to young people. For instance, the classic beginning reads, 'As I walked through the wilderness of this world, I lighted on a certain place, where there was a den; and I laid me down in that place to sleep: and as I slept I dreamed a dream.' Certainly this introduction could be made to read more smoothly, perhaps on the following lines: 'As I walked through the wilderness of this world, I came upon a certain place, where there was a den; and I lay down in that place to sleep; and as I slept I dreamed a dream.' However, this version has omitted altogether the concepts of the world as a wilderness and life as a journey through it. Instead it simply reads: 'While walking in a forest I found a cave, where I lay down to sleep. And as I slept, I dreamed a dream.' The impact of the original seems to me to have been completely lost.

Furthermore, Pope is identified merely as 'Pompous', and Hopeful's detailed and substantial testimony of his conversion, while traversing the Enchanted Ground, is reduced to a sentence of only fifteen words. Similarly, the extended encounter with Ignorance which discusses the heart of the gospel is shortened to a mere eight sentences, and there is no mention of Temporary.

Attractively published in a large format with many coloured illustrations, this version is better than many, yet by no means ideal. Rather parents should aim at teaching the complete version of *The Pilgrim's Progress* to their children as soon as is possible, using initiative and the simplification of some expressions. With a minimum of effort, such a goal is certainly achievable.

The Pilgrim's Progress, retold by Martin Powell, illustrated by Seppo Makinen (New York: Marvel Comics, 1992)

Reference has already been made to this version in chapter 17. In my opinion it is one of the most objectionable and revisionist versions that have become available in recent years. From a literary point of view, *The Pilgrim's Progress* is thoroughly eviscerated of its essential content. The writer understands little of what Bunyan is about. From the point of view of graphics, a comic world perspective imposes, not a contemporary under-standing, but a degenerate portrayal of sexual nuances, physical exposure, gross misrepresentation and identity with comic unreality rather than biblical reality.

The Game of Pilgrim's Progress, created by Marla Hershberger. (Bozeman, MT: Family Time, Inc., 1994).

This is a modern, professionally produced, fully-fledged board game which the publisher commends as follows: 'We hope that this game will not only be fun, but that it will also be used as a devotional tool. This game was purposefully designed to stimulate thoughtful discussion and generate a greater aware-ness of biblical principles and spiritual truths. We want to challenge each player to live a life of purity and holiness in obedience to Jesus Christ (Colossians 3:17).'

Nevertheless, while having enjoyed many a board game with my own children, and anticipating doing so in future with the grandchildren, I have to say I find it impossible to recom-mend a game such as this where salvation is obtained by means of the throw of dice! The salvation of a soul ought never to be presented in such a way that it is considered as a 'fun thing', in much the same way as a game of Monopoly is enjoyed. It could never be said of Bunyan that he composed *The Pilgrim's Progress* in a similar way; his presentation of the gospel is in deadly earnest, even though some situations contain an ele-ment of humour.

Furthermore, in the actual structure of the game several very serious problems arise. First, contrary to Bunyan's intention as explained in chapter 6, salvation is associated with the Place of Deliverance rather than the Wicket-gate. Secondly, landing on any one of six cross squares brings salvation; there are four at the Place of Deliverance, and two scattered apart much further ahead. We are told, 'It is possible to miss landing on a 'Cross' square. In that case, the pilgrim must proceed with his burden on.' Thus it is quite possible for a player to enter the Celestial City still carrying his burden!

The author comments: 'We created *The Game of Pilgrim's Progress* to stimulate greater learning of the truths set forth in the book.' One thing is certain: this game presents a false representation of the biblical gospel and Bunyan's allegorical description of it.

Conclusion

It gives me no pleasure to be, on the whole, more critical than complimentary with regard to these reviews. As a five-year-old, I well remember my own first encounter with a coloured-lantern-slide presentation of *The Pilgrim's Progress* at an after-school meeting in a local Baptist church. In fact it is my hope in the future to produce a comparable visual presentation that would be suitable for projection, though probably via a CD-ROM disc. However, such a production would include the full revised text and thus maintain Bunyan's truth content and emphases. Supporting graphics and sound effects would enhance, but not overwhelm, the intended dominance of truth conveyed through words. Production design would allow for a variety of episodic and segmented presentations.

We need to remember that, as indicated earlier, as a general rule versions of *The Pilgrim's Progress* for young people did not appear till nearly 150 years after its first publication, and even then these most often contained the full, unabridged text. It was not until the latter part of the twentieth century that a plethora of condensed versions began to appear. The fact is that today's generation is not so well able to read Bunyan's classic because of a comprehension disorder that has arisen as a result of the audio-visual media orientation described more fully in chapter 17. Presenting a visually projected version of *The Pilgrim's Progress* to young children is one thing, but neglecting to encourage the understanding of the full text by older children and young teens is quite another.

Are Christian parents today simply going to capitulate to the pressures and siren-like overtures of the vast audio-visual media conglomerate? They must not if they want their children to grasp truth, especially Bible truth. Instead, they need to coach and encourage them with books such as *The Pilgrim's Progress*, and not yield to the vogue of pruning and contemporizing in such a way that the author's original purposes are lost.

Instead I would propose the following guidelines:

- As early as possible, present a child or young person with the full text of *The Pilgrim's Progress*, spread over a number of episodes, rather than a pared-down version in a short space of time.

- By all means use a full version of the text of The Pilgrim's Progress that reads in a more contemporary style, provided that it in no way compromises the truth as Bunyan intended it. For example, my own revised edition, published under the title, *The Pilgrim's Progress, Accurate Text Revision*,[7] contains the complete text of Part One with no omissions whatsoever. A number of archaic expressions in the original are retained, but contemporary equivalents and other explanatory comments are included. Biblical references in the text are identified in the footnotes. The format also includes the division of the text into thirty-six chapters, and illustrations depicting the principal characters.

- By all means use illustrative material to enhance the text, but avoid any version that allows visual presentation to dominate to the extent of detracting from the communication of the truth. In other words, the child needs to appreciate that the text is the primary point of reference.

- Where visual aids are employed in addition to the text, make sure that these are faithful to the text and not revisionist in their representation of it, or culturally in conflict with Bunyan's setting.

• Lead the child on from the adventurous allegorical form to the substance of doctrinal truth in such a way that he or she enjoys the discovery.

A penny loaf

Thy price one penny is, in time of plenty;
In famine doubled, 'tis from one to twenty.
Yea, no man knows what price on thee to set,
When there is but one penny loaf to get.

Comparison

This loaf's an emblem of the word of God,
A thing of low esteem, before the rod
Of famine smites the soul with fear of death:
But then it is our all, our life, our breath!

John Bunyan
Divine Emblems, or Temporal Things Spiritualized,
Bunyan, *Works*, vol. III, p. 759

20.
Conclusion

`I am more glad than I
can say for what
Puritans like Bunyan
and Baxter have taught
me about dying; I needed
it, and the preachers I
hear these days never
get to it, and modern
Christian writers seem
quite clueless about it´
(J. I. Packer).

20.
Conclusion

THE purpose of this work has been to address themes and issues that arise from a serious study of *The Pilgrim's Progress* in such a way as to offer a vigorous apologetic from a conservative evangelical perspective. While it should be abundantly clear that John Bunyan was of this same evangelical opinion — and fervently so — the last hundred years have presented formidable obstacles to the comprehension of his distinctive writings, notwithstanding the previous centuries in which he received unparalleled recognition. As already demonstrated, an increasingly secular mentality has gained control of the media marketplace with the result that communication of sacred truth, shrouded in allegorical form, appears to have become increasingly difficult. At the same time the world has attempted to ape the allegorical format, often employing great visual skills, while investing it with an alien gospel message. One final example of this beguiling literary stratagem will, it is hoped, stimulate the reader to a better appreciation of the superiority of Bunyan's allegorical representation of Bible truth.

John Bunyan and L. Frank Baum

It would not be true to say that this present generation has entirely lost sight of the concept of life being represented in terms of a journey, or a pilgrimage. However, what is disturbing is the transformation of the itinerary from spiritual to merely earthly categories. Consider the following illustration of this decline in Western society.

Originally published in 1900 as *The Wonderful Wizard of Oz* by L. Frank Baum, the 1939 film adaptation by MGM of *The Wizard of Oz* has been ranked as the sixth most significant film ever produced in America. Without a doubt, today more young people and adults would recognize the characters and incidents of this fairyland pilgrimage than they would those of *The Pilgrim's Progress*, and this fact ought to be a matter for great concern, especially when comparisons are made and the contrast between the secular, on the one hand, and the sacred, on the other, is highlighted.

- To begin with, Baum was a Theosophist, while Bun-yan was a Christian.
- Dorothy's travelling companions in her dream are the Scarecrow, the Tin Woodman and the Cowardly Lion. Those of Christian, also in the context of a dream, are Faithful and Hopeful. Other pilgrims are also mentioned, such as Little-faith.
- Dorothy's pilgrimage is directed by Glinda, the Good Witch of the North, along the Yellow Brick Road, from Munchkin Land, which had been captured by the Wicked Witch of the West, to the Wizard of Oz in the Emerald City. Christian's pilgrimage is directed by Evangelist along the Narrow Way, from the City of Destruction, which is captive to Beelzebub, to the Lord of the Celestial City.
- Along the Yellow Brick Road Dorothy is snared by sleeping in the poppy field, confronted by the Wicked Witch of the East and imprisoned in her castle. Along the Narrow Way Christian is confronted by Apollyon, incarcerated in Doubting Castle and then warned against sleeping on the Enchanted Ground.

- However, in stark contrast, Dorothy eventually returns to her heart's desire, which is being with Uncle Henry and Aunt Em in Kansas because 'There is no place like home!' On the other hand, Christian is received into the Celestial City to be with Christ in heaven. Baum can only offer worldly sentimentality while Bunyan's hope is of 'a better [heavenly] country' (Heb. 11:16).

Thus instead of Western society being taught biblical reality through allegory, it has been seduced by unreal fantasy through allegory. Kansas has now become more important than heaven! Hence there is a desperate need to return to Bunyan, to instil his itinerary into the hearts and minds of a generation that has been shaped by Hollywood. But only those who resonate with Bunyan's fervent evangelical faith are really qualified to carry out this task.

Bunyan and scholasticism

As has already been emphasized, the Bedford tinker's zealous evangelicalism has not been so widely appreciated from the second half of the twentieth century onwards as it was in former times, and that in spite of the continuing obsession on the part of academics with Bunyan studies. However, there is not the slightest doubt as to how Bunyan would have addressed this situation in which we find ourselves today, for in his time he encountered academia on a number of occasions. In the light of his genuine friendship with John Owen and William Dell on a common basis of Christian fellowship, it could never be said that he was anti-intellectual. However, when Bunyan encountered a disjunction between a merely cerebral awareness of evangelical truth and a heart-embrace of that same truth, then his rebuke could be severe. And it would be the same today, because a similar disjunction exists — one with which scholasticism is content to live.

In the case of Talkative in *The Pilgrim's Progress*, we see a clear portrayal of Bunyan's attitude towards those who, although they may be very articulate on the subject of truth (whether secular and sacred), are strangers to any genuine experience of that about which they so fluently converse.

At Bunyan's death, as has already been mentioned, an elegy was written about him which well expresses this consistency between truth and life which he himself so faithfully embodied:

> He in the pulpit preached truth first, and then
> He in his practice preached it o'er again.[1]

A deficiency in modern Bunyan studies

For all the emphasis placed by the modern Bunyan studies movement upon literary form and historic background, there has at the same time been an increasing neglect of the most important aspects of all — namely, gospel truth, sanctifying truth and pastoral truth at an adult level, born of an authoritative Bible. It is important that we should not yield this ground to a scholarly obsession with the fields of literature, history, psychology, sociology, or political science that distances itself from the experiential embrace of the saving grace of God.

A final illustration of this contemporary problem comes from an essay by Roger Sharrock entitled 'Bunyan Studies Today: An Evaluation'. To begin with, it is only partly true that 'Forty years have seen a revolution in our midst in our attitude to seventeenth-century Puritanism, and for that matter to the Christian tradition in general and even to Christian belief. Bunyan scholarship has benefited from this cultural and hermeneutic transformation.'[2] Certainly our understanding of Puritanism has been refined and improved, though the movement has not always been portrayed accurately, as secular caricature of it indicates. Failures in arriving at a correct assessment can be ascribed to the influence of liberal and moderate (or what in

Bunyan's day would have been called latitudinarian) scholastic presuppositions.

Furthermore, the proposal that there has been a hermeneutic advance in our understanding of what Sharrock rather loosely terms 'the Christian tradition in general' is most questionable. A much better case can be made for a regression.

Moreover, his further opinion that this supposed advance in understanding can to some degree be attributed to Barth's commentary on Romans and the writings of Kierkegaard is doubtful, to say the least, although his reference to the influential contributions of Perry Miller and William Haller with regard to renewed interest in Puritanism has some plausibility.[3] Even so, what of the resurgence of interest in Puritan works promoted by evangelical book publishers such as the Banner of Truth Trust?

In relation to Bunyan studies, Sharrock also mentions W. Y. Tindall's *John Bunyan: Mechanick Preacher*, in which he was portrayed as 'a typical, competitive, scurrilously controversial mechanick preacher'.[4] While this was in fact a misrepresentation,[5] it nevertheless became a catalyst for more secular and political analyses.

Not surprisingly, there then follows a glowing celebration of Christopher Hill's writings on the subject of seventeenth-century sectarianism: 'His inquiry into the role of radical movements like the Levellers and the Diggers has been found relevant to the background of the artisan Bunyan, as has his analysis of the social and economic pressures on Puritanism and on the Puritan household and family.'[6]

It is in fact this emphasis on 'background' that is the principal cause for concern here, since in reality 'background' has become 'foreground'. In the whole of Sharrock's essay, the emphasis is predominantly upon the various aspects of 'background', whereas the matter of biblical truth, which constituted Bunyan's overwhelming passion, receives scant mention. There is a brief appreciative comment relating to Richard Greaves' contribution in 'admirably defining his [Bunyan's] theological position in relation to that of other Restoration Nonconformists', but this is merely referred to in passing, while the essay as a whole is dominated by these matters of 'background'.

At the risk of sounding repetitive, it is freely acknowledged that the literary and historical movement has certainly contributed much that is helpful. However, this movement detracts from its usefulness when it moves outside its proper sphere of expertise, when it overemphasizes its own importance and when its secular preoccupations take pride of place, rather than remaining subservient to higher spiritual priorities.

This remains an ongoing problem, and one which is clearly demonstrated when we find scholars pontificating in the realm of Christian truth, while at the same time having no more qualifications in this matter than the average unbeliever, or Christian, in society in general. Certainly, like anyone else, they are entitled to their opinions; but their specialized scholastic qualifications are in no way to be considered as conferring an imprimatur upon any comments that they make on biblical topics. For instance, Roger Sharrock writes, 'Not all the pictures in the Interpreter's House are biblical, but all are supported by texts. The Interpreter may be the Holy Spirit.'[7] Such an opinion is not only entirely arbitrary, but reflects presuppositions that are hardly grounded upon the evangelicalism that Bunyan has represented for over three centuries.

Elsewhere, this same author is simply out of his depth in attempting to understand Bunyan's Calvinism. Consider in this connection his reasoning that, because of the security which the certificates which they have received afford to Christian and Hopeful, '... this might seem to confirm the view that for the ordinary reader Calvinism drains away all dramatic interest from the Christian life in the world... How can a progress of which the end is foreordained keep the interest of a novel? ... One literary consequence of Bunyan's theology is that there is no possibility of a treatment of the full life of man like that in Catholic allegory, or even in Spenser. The power of final perseverance granted to the pilgrims in election limits the range of human experience Bunyan can deal with.'[8] All that needs to be said in response is that history has overwhelmingly invalidated these concerns; though we might also go on to ask whether Sharrock's own Catholicism is intruding here.

The dangers in this issue of academic research, in matters relating to Christian doctrine, overriding and displacing biblical truth and experience, are not new. The apostle Paul warns of those who are 'always learning and never able to come to the knowledge of the truth' (2 Tim. 3:7). In other words, there is always the problem of toying with the truth, of enjoying the pursuit of truth rather than embracing it for oneself. In romance we find those who seem to enjoy the chase rather than the prospect of actual marriage. So in the realm of learning, there are those like Gotthold Lessing, a leader in eighteenth-century German 'enlightened rationalism', of whom John Hurst writes, 'He was honest in his love of truth, but he loved the search for it more than the attainment. The key to his whole life may be found in his own words: "If God should hold in his right hand all truth, and in his left the ever-active impulse and love of search after truth, although accompanied with the condition that I should ever err, and should say, 'Choose!' I would choose the left with humility, and say, 'Give, Father! Pure truth belongs to thee alone!'"'[9]

Torpor in Bunyan studies

So, in the realm of current Bunyan studies, the predominant emphasis seems to have become the artistry of the Bedford tinker's great composition, in terms of style and setting, in such a way that it is divorced from life, and especially as the allegory defines it. G. M. Trevelyan rightly perceives this disabling distinction as follows: 'None of the people who talk about "art for art's sake" and "the distracting influence of a moral purpose in art", have ever yet produced art on a par with Milton's or Bunyan's, and they never will. The greatest artists are even more interested in life than art. Art seems to them as something given, by which to interpret the significance of life.'[10] This is exactly so today where the endless secular dissection of the allegorist and his pen is studiously divorced from the life of Bunyan's redeemed soul that gave birth to his extraordinary writings.

To further illustrate this point, let us pause a moment to consider the confession of the Dutch scholar and theologian, Herman Bavinck, as recounted by William Hendriksen: '"My learning does not help me now; neither does my Dogmatics; faith alone saves me." These remarkable words, uttered by one of the greatest Reformed theologians, Dr Herman Bavinck, should not be misinterpreted. They were uttered on his death-bed and did not imply that this humble child of God retracted anything that he had written or that he was trying to express regrets. The statement simply means that a system of doctrine, however necessary and valuable, is of no avail in and by itself. It must be translated into Christian living. There must be genuine faith in the Triune God as manifested in Jesus Christ.'[11]

It should by now be obvious that John Bunyan was of the same opinion as Bavinck. In *Grace Abounding to the Chief of Sinners* the pursuit of truth is not enough. His struggles as a young believer, though definitely not an experience to be advocated, were a terrifying transitional stage before he came to a place of relative stability and rest as a result of embracing the truth concerning Jesus Christ's substitutionary righteousness, something which he repeatedly and passionately commends to his readers.

However Bunyan's ultimate and dominant goal lies beyond the struggles of the Christian pilgrimage. At the conclusion of the preface to *Grace Abounding* we read the encouragement: 'My dear children, the milk and honey is beyond this wilderness. God be merciful to you and grant that you be not slothful to go in to possess the land.'[12] Similarly, the predominant emphasis in *The Pilgrim's Progress* is not on departure from the City of Destruction, nor even on the journey itself, with its attendant trials and blessings, but on arrival at the Celestial City, resulting in unclouded fellowship with the Lord of that city. It is for this reason that, when Christian and Hopeful have entered through the gates of the Celestial City, Bunyan adds his editorial comment: 'I wished myself among them.'[13]

Here is the reason for the spiritual sterility of so many modern Bunyan studies; there is no soul-longing for the biblical prospect of heaven according to the terms of entrance that the Bible defines. J. I. Packer demonstrates his appreciation of this vital matter when he writes, 'As I move through my own seventh decade, in better health than can possibly last, I am more glad than I can say for what Puritans like Bunyan and Baxter have taught me about dying; I needed it, and the preachers I hear these days never get to it, and modern Christian writers seem quite clueless about it.'[14]

Bunyan and grace for sinners

For Bunyan, truth must be personally appropriated; Jesus Christ must be not only studied, but embraced experientially and consummately; the pursuit of salvation must lead to nothing short of being saved by great grace that results in jubilation of soul. And in emphasizing such a vital point, it is proposed that the personal discovery of this spiritual leitmotif is the only way that a right appreciation of the person and writings of this very useful servant of God can be obtained.

If ultimate proof of this overall assertion needs to be demonstrated, it will be found at the conclusion of so many of Bunyan's writings; there he repeatedly, and with great animation, exhorts his readers to act upon what he has written, to commit, to yield, to embrace this welcoming Saviour. In conclusion, ponder the following examples.

The Jerusalem Sinner Saved

'Christ is Jacob's ladder that reacheth up to heaven; and he that refuseth to go by this ladder thither, will scarce by other means get up so high. There is none other name given under heaven, among men, whereby we must be saved. There is none other sacrifice for sin than this; he also, and he only, is the Mediator that reconcileth men to God. And, sinner, if thou wouldst be saved by him, his benefits are thine; yea, though thou art a great and Jerusalem transgressor.'[15]

The Greatness of the Soul, and Unspeakableness of the Loss Thereof

'Sinners, would I could persuade you to hear me out! A man cannot commit a sin, but, by the commission of it, he doth, by some circumstance or other, sharpen the sting of hell, and that to pierce himself through and through, and through, with many sorrows (1 Tim. 6:10)… I will yet add to all this; how will the fairness of some for heaven, even the thoughts of that, sting them when they come to hell!'[16]

Come and Welcome to Jesus Christ

'Coming sinner, the Jesus to whom thou art coming is lowly in heart, he despiseth not any. It is not thy outward meanness, nor thy inward weakness; it is not because thou art poor, or base, or deformed, or a fool, that he will despise thee: he hath chosen the foolish, the base, and despised things of this world, to confound the wise and mighty. He will bow his ear to thy stammering prayers, he will pick out the meaning of thy inexpressible groans; he will respect thy weakest offering, if there be in it but thy heart (Matt. 11:29; Luke 14:21; Prov. 9:4-6; Isa. 38:14-15; S. of S. 5:15; John 4:27; Mark 12:33-34; James 5:11). Now, is not this a blessed Christ, coming sinner?'[17]

Justification by an Imputed Righteousness, or No Way to Heaven but by Jesus Christ

'Sinners, take my advice, with which I shall conclude this use — Call often to remembrance that thou hast a precious soul within thee; that thou art in the way to thine end, at which thy precious soul will be in special concerned, it being then time to delay no longer, the time of reward being come. I say again, bring thy end home; put thyself in thy thoughts into the last day thou must live in this world, seriously arguing thus — How if this day were my last? How if I never see the sun rise more? How if the first voice that rings tomorrow morning in my ears be, "Arise, ye dead, and come to judgement?" Or how, if the next sight I see with mine eyes be the Lord in the clouds, with all his angels, raining floods of fire and brimstone upon the world? ... Will my profession, or the faith I think I have, carry me through all the trials of God's tribunal?'[18]

The Strait Gate

'Dost thou love thine own soul? Then pray to Jesus Christ for an awakened heart, for a heart so awakened with all the things of another world, that thou mayest be allured to Jesus Christ... When thou comest there, beg again for more awakenings about sin, hell, grace, and about the righteousness of Christ... Cry also for a spirit of discerning, that thou mayest know that which is saving grace indeed... Above all studies apply thyself to the study of those things that show thee the evil of sin, the shortness of man's life, and which is the way to be saved... Keep company with the most godly among professors... When thou hearest what the nature of true grace is, defer not to ask thine own heart if this grace be there.'[19]

The Doctrine of the Law and Grace Unfolded

'O, therefore, let all this move thee, and be of weight upon thy soul to close in with Jesus, this tender-hearted Jesus. And if yet, for all that I have said, thy sins do still stick with thee, and thou findest thy hellish heart loath to let them go, think with thyself in this manner — Shall I have my sins and lose my soul? Will they do me any good when Christ comes? Would not heaven be better to me than my sins? And the company of God, Christ, saints, and angels, be better than the company of Cain, Judas, Balaam, with the devils in the furnace of fire?'[20]

John Bunyan's last sermon, on John 1:13

'If you are the children of God, live together lovingly; if the world quarrel with you, it is no matter; but it is sad if you quarrel together; if this be amongst you, it is a sign of ill-breeding; it is not according to the rules you have in the Word of God. Dost thou see a soul that has the image of God in him? Love him, love him; say, This man and I must go to heaven one day; serve one another, do good for one another; and if any wrong you, pray to God to right you and love the brotherhood.

Lastly, if you be the children of God, learn that lesson — Gird up the loins of your mind, as obedient children, not fashioning yourselves according to your former conversation; but be ye holy in all manner of conversation. Consider that the holy God is your Father, and let this oblige you to live like the children of God, that you may look your Father in the face, with comfort, another day.'[21]

The Heavenly Footman

'That you may be provoked to run with the foremost, take notice of this. When Lot and his wife were running from cursed Sodom to the mountains, to save their lives, it is said that his wife looked back from behind him, and she became a pillar of salt; and yet you see that neither her practice, nor the judgement of God that fell upon her for the same, would cause Lot to look behind him.

'I have sometimes wondered at Lot in this particular; his wife looked behind her, and died immediately, but let what you would become of her, Lot would not so much as look behind to see her. We do not read that he did so much as once look where she was, or what was become of her; his heart was upon his journey, and well it might: there was the mountain before him, and the fire and brimstone behind him; his life lay at stake, and he had lost it if he had but looked behind him. Do thou so run: and in thy race remember Lot's wife, and remember her doom; and remember for what that doom did overtake her; and remember that God made her an example for all lazy runners, to the end of the world.'[22]

A Few Sighs from Hell

'Have a care thou receive not this doctrine in notion only, lest thou bring a just damnation upon thy soul, by professing thyself to be freed by Christ's blood from the guilt of sin, while thou remainest still a servant to the filth of sin. For I must tell you, that unless you have the true and saving work of the faith and grace of the gospel in your hearts, you will either go on in a legal holiness, according to the tenor of the law; or else through a notion of the gospel, the devil bewitching and beguiling thy understanding, will, and affections, thou wilt, Ranter-like, turn the grace of God into wantonness, and bring upon thy soul double, if not treble damnation, in that thou couldest not be contented to be damned for thy sins against the law, but also to make ruin sure to thy soul, thou wouldest dishonour the gospel, and turn the grace of God, held forth and discovered to men by that, into licentiousness.'[23]

John Bunyan's purpose in preaching

In my preaching I have really been in pain, and have, as it were, travailed to bring forth children to God; neither could I be satisfied unless some fruits did appear in my work. If I were fruitless it mattered not who commended me; but if I were fruitful, I cared not who did condemn. I have thought of that, "He that winneth souls is wise" (Prov. 11:30)…

It pleased me nothing to see people drink in opinions if they seemed ignorant of Jesus Christ, and the worth of their own salvation, sound conviction for sin, especially for unbelief, and an heart set on fire to be saved by Christ, with strong breathing after a truly sanctified soul; that it was that delighted me; those were the souls I counted blessed.

John Bunyan
Grace Abounding to the Chief of Sinners,
Bunyan, *Works*, vol. I, pp. 43-4

Study questions on
The Pilgrim's Progress

THESE questions are designed to stimulate further research into the overall legacy of John Bunyan — that is, his times, person, writings, and especially *The Pilgrim's Progress*, although with the presumption of the allegorist's firm evangelical convictions. This book as a whole offers much in terms of guidance as to the general direction such investigation should take, though many questions require study in outlying fields.

The level of study involved here would equate to high school and college standards. However, the student ought constantly to keep in mind Bunyan's biblical purposes and not be satisfied with merely detached and academic answers. The author would be glad to interact with those who earnestly desire to study these issues from an evangelical perspective.

Introductory considerations

1.   Explain why *The Pilgrim's Progress* ought to be taught and made known today. Be specific in your reasoning.

2.   'Because the Bible is incomparable as the inspired Word of God, we ought not to elevate a mere uninspired human work such as *The Pilgrim's Progress* to even the supposed rank of "the second best book in all the world".' Critique this statement, especially in the light of Bunyan's expressed intentions in publishing the allegory, its essential character and its significant involvement in the history of the Christian church.

3.   '*The Pilgrim's Progress* is principally a book designed for adults rather than children.' Discuss the degree to which this statement is true. Support your opinion from the text.

4.   What were Bunyan's purposes in writing *The Pilgrim's Progress*? Consult in particular the introductory apology and concluding poem.

Explain why these purposes are important for the communication of the allegory today.

5. Where in the Bible does Bunyan derive his concept of 'journeying' or 'pilgrimage' from?

6. In Bunyan's poem concluding Part One, he warns against 'playing with the outside of my dream'. What is the 'inside' of his dream? How will the proper communication of *The Pilgrim's Progress* avoid a misunderstanding of this expressed purpose?

7. To what degree do Bunyan's introductory apology and concluding poem in Part One of *The Pilgrim's Progress* provide an adequate response to the conflicting assessments of it that were forthcoming at the time of initial publication, and to those made during its subsequent history?

8. On the title page of the first edition of *The Pilgrim's Progress*, Bunyan quotes Hosea 12:10, 'I have used similitudes,' as justification for his allegorical method. Discuss the legitimacy of his line of reasoning here.

9. Samuel Taylor Coleridge described *The Pilgrim's Progress* as 'incomparably the best *Summa Theologiae Evangelicae* [summary of evangelical theology] ever produced by a writer not miraculously inspired'. Comment on the truthfulness of this assessment.

Bunyan's personal experience

10. Compare *Grace Abounding to the Chief of Sinners* with *The Pilgrim's Progress*. In what ways are they related, and how does *Grace Abounding* help in the interpretation of *The Pilgrim's Progress*?

11. Relate the trial of Christian and Faithful at Vanity Fair to Bunyan's own arrest, trial and imprisonment. To what degree is such satire legitimate in Christian witness? Is there biblical justification for such an approach?

12. How does the encounter of Christian and Hopeful with Giant Despair of Doubting Castle reflect certain trials experienced by Bunyan himself? Contrast this scene with the despair of Christian in the Slough of Despond.

13. Several modern estimates of Bunyan consider his self-analysis, such as that in *Grace Abounding*, to be too extreme and the product of a severe seventeenth-century Calvinistic environment. Assess the validity of this opinion.

14. Compare Christian's experiences in the Valley of Humiliation and the Valley of the Shadow of Death with those of Faithful. To what degree are Christian's struggles a reflection of Bunyan's own experiences described in *Grace Abounding*?

15. Compare the conversions of Christian and Hopeful in *The Pilgrim's Progress* with that of Bunyan described in *Grace Abounding to the Chief of Sinners*. Compare these contrasting perspectives with the terms that are considered normative in describing evangelical conversion at the commencement of this twenty-first century.

16. Bunyan's formal education was less than modest. Compare this initial level of education with his apparent breadth of knowledge in later years. How did this improvement come about? How widely did Bunyan read? What was his overall attitude to a university education and the learned?

17. What do we know of Bunyan as a family man? Consider the circumstances of his two marriages. How is his appreciation of family life reflected in both parts of *The Pilgrim's Progress*?

18. What were the major influences on Bunyan's religious development, both before and after his conversion? Consider individuals, national events and movements such as various sects, as well as the pervasive presence in his environment of the Church of England.

19. Discuss the impact of the opening paragraph of Part One of *The Pilgrim's Progress*, and compare it with the closing paragraph, which has sometimes been awarded a less favourable estimate.

Assessments of individual characters and events

20. Bunyan's portrayal of Christian as leaving his wife and children behind could be misunderstood, especially when one considers the tinker's own family life. Discuss this problem with regard to both Parts One and Two of *The Pilgrim's Progress*.

21. John Kelman writes, 'On the whole, Obstinate is a better and more hopeful man than Pliable. Perverse though he be, and boorish beside this other, yet there is character in him, and more can be made of him.' Discuss why you agree or disagree with this statement.

22. Considering that Christian's name before his conversion is Graceless — as we are told at the Palace Beautiful — why does Bunyan refer to the pilgrim as 'Christian' while he is still unconverted — that is, before his entrance through the Wicket-gate?

23. In the early sequence of events in *The Pilgrim's Progress*, what is the significance of placing the Slough of Despond before the Wicket-gate is reached? Consider the 'bedaubing' of Pliable and of Christian. What distinguishes the despondency at this scene from that which Christian experiences subsequent to his conversion?

24. Describe the essential differences between Christian and Pliable, especially with regard to motives, as they travel and converse with each other and then tumble into the Slough of Despond.

25. What is the essence of Mr Worldly-Wiseman's gospel? What seventeenth-century and modern representations of him can we identify? Give special attention to the distinctive doctrinal features of these movements and also to those which they have in common.

26. The Wicket-gate is not only the place where Christian becomes an authentic pilgrim, but also a scene of intense conflict between Christ and Satan. Expand upon this thought, as it is described in other parts of the allegory. How do the experiences of Christian, Faithful and Christiana, along with Mercy, differ at this point?

27. In *The Pilgrim's Progress* Jesus Christ is portrayed by several different characters and situations. Identify as many of these in Part One as you can, and comment on their individual and collective significance.

28. Expand upon the significance of the house of Interpreter as it relates both to John 14-16 and to the fact of Christian's recent conversion.

29. How do the seven scenes portrayed at the house of Interpreter, and especially the first scene depicting the portrait of the godly pastor, reflect Bunyan's own pastoral priorities?

30. Expound upon Bunyan's portrayal of the despairing reprobate in the iron cage. What historic precedents might he be drawing upon? What is his purpose here? What is Bunyan's view of reprobation in his other writings?

31. Carefully consider the point at which Christian encounters Simple, Sloth and Presumption, and speculate as to where they may have come from.

32. Describe the differences between Christian as an authentic pilgrim and Formalist and Hypocrisy as counterfeits. In *The Pilgrim's Progress*, what essentially distinguishes a true pilgrim?

33. How does confrontation with the hill Difficulty affect the journey of four distinguishable pilgrims? What major lessons are learned in this regard?

34. Consider the symbolic meaning of the two savage lions close to the entrance to the Palace Beautiful. Explain the relevance of what they represent to Bunyan's own experience, and in particular to the confrontation with savage opposition that nonconformist pilgrims in general encountered. Also consider Faithful's contrasting experience in the same circumstances.

35. To what degree is the Palace Beautiful a faithful biblical representation of a local church? Relate your answer to other passages in Bunyan's writings which deal with pastoral matters.

36. Analyse the assault of Apollyon upon Christian so as to discover the different stratagems that he uses. Then describe the pilgrim's responses which effectively repel this foul enemy.

37. What is the real character of the Valley of Humiliation? Consider the contrasting experiences of Christian in Part One and Christiana in Part Two.

38. Consider Bunyan's estimate of Pope and Pagan with regard to the times in which he lived and also in the light of subsequent centuries to date. To what degree was Bunyan influenced by history?

39. Explain the exposure of Talkative's hypocrisy, especially the strategy employed. What, then, is Bunyan's teaching concerning the validation of a person's claim to be a Christian?

40. While Christian sets off from the City of Destruction before Faithful, Faithful later passes by the Palace Beautiful and so moves ahead of Christian. What does Bunyan intend by this?

41. Compare Bunyan's portrayal of Evangelist in *The Pilgrim's Progress* with the latter's counterpart today. Consider Evangelist's continuing interest in, and his post-conversion involvement with, the status of the pilgrims.

42. What similarities and differences are there with regard to the City of Destruction and the town of Vanity? What other localities are mentioned that have related characteristics?

43. Explain the continuity of thought that Bunyan intends when he relates the successive events concerning By-ends and his friends, Demas and the silver mine at the Hill Lucre, and the monument to Lot's wife.

44. Elaborate upon the significance of the fruit and leaves that Christian and Hopeful partake of when they are refreshed beside the River of the Water of Life. How does this experience relate to their subsequent complaining?

45. In Doubting Castle, Christian and Hopeful are encouraged by Giant Despair and his wife to commit suicide. Evaluate the interaction that takes place between the two prisoners on this subject. Why does Bunyan inject this topic into his allegory?

46. What is the significance of the fact that Christian and Hopeful, having been imprisoned in Doubting Castle from Wednesday until Saturday evening, escape from Giant Despair on Sunday morning?

47. What solutions does Bunyan offer for depression/despair in the scene at Doubting Castle? Relate these solutions to his own experiences described in *Grace Abounding*.

48. Expound upon the similarities and contrasts that Bunyan establishes between Little-faith, Turn-away and Temporary. What pastoral insights does this teaching suggest?

49. Explain the non-negotiable nature of Little-faith's jewels when compared with his stolen petty cash, especially in biblical terms. Consider Bunyan's biblical illustrations which uphold his reasoning at this point.

50. Assess the distinction that Bunyan makes between Little-faith and Great-grace, especially in pastoral terms. Then contrast Little-faith and Hopeful.

51. Atheist claims to have been seeking for the Celestial City for the past twenty years. In what ways might this pursuit have been misdirected?

52. What specifically are the snares of the Enchanted Ground and their remedy? Relate these remedies to the three distinct scenes that are portrayed during the crossing of this region.

53. Comment on the contrasting characteristics of Hopeful, Ignorance and Temporary as they are consecutively portrayed by Bunyan in the discourse during the traversing of the Enchanted Ground.

54. To what extent do Christian and Hopeful portray a normative and mature biblical attitude when they enjoy the delights of the land of Beulah?

55. Expound upon the contrasting experiences of Christian and Hopeful at the River of Death. Also relate this to the later crossing of Ignorance at this same place.

56. Give reasons why you agree or disagree with Bunyan's portrayal of Christian and Hopeful as crossing the River of Death in company rather than alone.

57. What, for Bunyan, are the terms of entrance into the Celestial City? Relate this to the expectations of contemporary evangelicalism.

58. Consider the Celestial City, the repeated emphasis on it in *The Pilgrim's Progress* and further descriptions of this heavenly home in Bunyan's other writings.

59. 'The concluding contrast between the destiny of Christian and that of Ignorance is both awesome and breathtaking!' Comment on this opinion. Why did Bunyan not conclude the first part of *The Pilgrim's Progress* with a happy ending?

60. The three leading pilgrims in Part One of *The Pilgrim's Progress* are Christian and his two successive companions, Faithful and Hopeful. Assuming that Christian portrays Bunyan the author, what other close

friends of Bunyan might be represented, to some degree, by Faithful and Hopeful? Who were the tinker's intimate spiritual acquaintances?

61. Discuss the contrasts that Bunyan portrays by means of a variety of true and false pilgrims. Relate this to Bunyan's pastoral experience as well as his other writings.

Doctrinal issues

62. What is Bunyan's attitude towards the Bible, specifically with regard to his understanding of inspiration and inerrancy? How does he interpret it?

63. Nominate and discuss the five most important doctrinal emphases in *The Pilgrim's Progress*.

64. Discuss the significance of Dr J. Gresham Machen's description of *The Pilgrim's Progress* as 'that tenderest and most theological of books ... pulsating with life in every word'.

65. '*The Pilgrim's Progress* is firstly about Christian sanctification and secondly about salvation.' Discuss the degree to which this statement is true.

66. Of what significance is the doctrine of justification by faith to John Bunyan, as represented in *The Pilgrim's Progress*? Explain his biblical teaching and include reference to his other writings.

67. To what extent was the ministry of Martin Luther influential in the spirit and doctrine of *The Pilgrim's Progress*? Consider the overall influence of the Reformer on Bunyan, especially with regard to the nature of the gospel.

68. Compare Bunyan's teaching on sanctification, as illustrated by Christian's spiritual growth in *The Pilgrim's Progress*, with various 'holiness' and evangelical convention emphases that are rooted, directly or indirectly, in the historic Keswick, Higher Life and Victorious Life movements.

69. Compare Bunyan's teaching on sanctification, as illustrated by Christian's spiritual growth in *The Pilgrim's Progress*, with that of the modern charismatic movement.

70. What does Bunyan teach us in *The Pilgrim's Progress* concerning the Christian doctrine of assurance?

71. In what ways does *The Pilgrim's Progress* reflect a seventeenth-century, nonconformist understanding of the nature and function of the church?

72. What evidence is there of Bunyan's Calvinism in *The Pilgrim's Progress*? Relate this to his pastoral ministry and other writings.

73. 'As a Calvinist, Bunyan gives a balanced emphasis on the doctrines of divine sovereignty and human responsibility.' Indicate from *The Pilgrim's Progress* to what degree this assessment is true.

74. At what stage in *The Pilgrim's Progress* is Christian converted? Give reasons for your answer. Consider Bunyan's own experience, especially as it is related in *Grace Abounding to the Chief of Sinners*.

75. Explain the biblical basis and individual significance of the benefits which Christian receives from the three Shining Ones at the Place of Deliverance. Consider the ongoing importance of these items.

76. Expound upon the Palace Beautiful so as to indicate how many facets of the doctrine of the local church are represented by this portrayal.

77. Expound upon the importance which Bunyan places on a pilgrim's being well equipped with spiritual weapons, and especially with regard to Christian's encounter with Apollyon and passage through the Valley of the Shadow of Death.

78. Comment on the doctrinal significance of Ignorance's response to Christian: 'What! Would you have us trust to what Christ in his own person has done without us?'

79. Explain the doctrinal relationship that Bunyan portrays in *The Pilgrim's Progress* with regard to Adam the First, Moses and Christ. Give scriptural support, paying particular attention to the passages which Bunyan appears to draw upon.

80. Explain the characteristics that distinguish true and counterfeit faith in *The Pilgrim's Progress*.

81. What are the major points of doctrine that are fundamental to Hopeful's conversion testimony? With these in mind, what essentially is the gospel in this testimony?

82. Expound upon the essential distinction that Bunyan makes in *The Pilgrim's Progress* between the hope of Ignorance's false gospel and the gospel hope of Christian and Hopeful. What historic movement(s) does Ignorance represent?

83. Expound on Bunyan's understanding of the role of women in Part One of *The Pilgrim's Progress*, while also drawing upon Part Two and his other writings.

84. What is the role of prayer in *The Pilgrim's Progress*? Refer to all instances.

85. To what degree does Bunyan portray the future glory of heaven as a fundamental goal of the authentic pilgrim? Contrast this with the emphases of contemporary evangelicalism with regard to being heavenly-minded.

86. Expound upon the important role that Esau plays in *Grace Abounding to the Chief of Sinners* and *The Pilgrim's Progress*.

87. Designate and consider the main genuine, or progressing, pilgrims and the principal false, or regressive, pilgrims. What characteristics distinguish these two groups?

88. Describe those areas in *The Pilgrim's Progress* where Bunyan writes as a classic Puritan, and other areas where he seems to veer away from this norm.

89. Richard Greaves writes in his doctrinal study of John Bunyan that the antecedents of the Bedford tinker's understanding of the sovereignty of God were derived more from Luther's understanding of grace than from Calvin's views of predestination by decree. Give a critique of this opinion, and consider Bunyan's friendship with John Burton, John Gifford, John Owen and William Dell.

90. Assess Bunyan's representation of covenant theology, especially as described in *The Doctrine of the Law and Grace Unfolded*, and then in his subsequent writings.

91. Was Bunyan an antinomian to any degree? Define antinomianism, especially in terms of the seventeenth century, and relate your answer to Bunyan's understanding of the role of Moses and the law of God.

Christian experience

92. What incentives does Bunyan repeatedly offer in *The Pilgrim's Progress* for pilgrims such as Christian, Faithful and Hopeful, so that they might persevere towards the Celestial City rather than regress?

93. Consider the characteristics and experiences which are common to Christian, Faithful and Hopeful, and those which are distinctive to each. To what extent do spiritual gifts and graces provide an explanation for the differences? What stimulus for Christian fellowship is there here?

94. What instances of discouragement and depression in the lives of pilgrims are included in *The Pilgrim's Progress*, and what remedies does Bunyan recommend for these ailments?

95. What emphasis does Bunyan give in *The Pilgrim's Progress* to the problem of worldliness for a pilgrim? What dangers are encountered? How is deliverance described?

96. Expound upon Bunyan's understanding of separation from the world, through which we travel, as illustrated in *The Pilgrim's Progress*. Consider both negative and positive aspects.

97. What lessons does Vanity Fair teach concerning the relationship that exists between the world and biblical Christianity? What distinctive experiences does Bunyan draw upon that are incorporated in this scene?

98. Expound upon the world-view of By-ends and his friends, especially as its religious tone may find expression in twenty-first-century churches.

99. What are the grounds for Christian and Hopeful's being disciplined following their yielding to the Flatterer's enticement? Are these grounds biblical? What is the fruit of this chastisement?

100. To what extent is Bunyan concerned about covetousness on the part of pilgrims in *The Pilgrim's Progress*?

101. Explain Bunyan's concept of 'conversion' and 'progress' in *The Pilgrim's Progress*. Relate biblical conversion and progress to the modern conception of a Christian 'going on pilgrimage'.

102. How would you respond to someone who commented that *The Pilgrim's Progress*, by virtue of being Puritan literature over three hundred years old, is not relevant to our contemporary society?

103. Where is there exhortation to both hope and fear in *The Pilgrim's Progress*? To what degree does Bunyan communicate a balance between hope and fear in pastoral guidance to progressing pilgrims?

104. Relate instances of the pilgrims' experiences being recalled and mused over in *The Pilgrim's Progress*. For what reasons does Bunyan make this emphasis?

Pastoral concerns

105. What pastoral influences came upon Bunyan and in turn influenced his composition of *The Pilgrim's Progress*?

106. Summarize Bunyan's understanding of faithful pastoral oversight as depicted in *The Pilgrim's Progress*.

107. In what ways does Bunyan illustrate, in Part One of *The Pilgrim's Progress*, the crucial importance of Christian fellowship, both individual and corporate?

108. Describe the major pastoral emphases that are evident in Christian and Hopeful's encounter with By-ends and his three friends.

109. In *Grace Abounding to the Chief of Sinners*, Bunyan writes that a former pastor and mentor in Bedford, John Gifford, 'made it much his business to deliver the people of God from all those false and unsound rests that, by nature, we are prone to take and make to our souls'. In what ways did Bunyan fulfil this same responsibility in his own ministry, especially as indicated in *The Pilgrim's Progress*?

110. Concerning *The Pilgrim's Progress*, George Whitefield wrote, 'Surely it is an original, and we may say of it, to use the words of the great Doctor Goodwin in his preface to the Epistle to the Ephesians, that it smells of the prison. It was written when the author was confined in Bedford jail. And ministers never write or preach so well as when under the cross: the spirit of Christ and of glory then rests upon them [1 Peter 4:14].' Discuss and illustrate from the allegory, as well as the life of its author, the truth of this statement.

111. In what ways does *The Pilgrim's Progress* reflect life in a seventeenth-century nonconformist church, especially with regard to the character of the Palace Beautiful?

112. How does the Palace Beautiful reflect the requirements for membership in a seventeenth-century nonconformist church?

113. Establish Bunyan's homiletical method in terms of sermon arrangement and delivery, as far as this can be ascertained from his writings and reputation. What sort of preacher was he?

114. Assess Bunyan's faithfulness as a pastor, and especially relate this to the pastoral ideals of *The Pilgrim's Progress*.

Literary criticism

115. Assess the Bunyan-studies movement of the twentieth and twenty-first centuries. Especially relate this evaluation to Bunyan's expressed purposes.

116. Many modern assessments of *The Pilgrim's Progress* have tended to admire Bunyan's style and at the same time unashamedly distance themselves from his biblical emphasis. Further, they have attempted to make secular use of this disjunction. Assess the morality and success of this movement.

117. In the introductory apology and concluding poem of Part One of *The Pilgrim's Progress*, Bunyan employs eight terms to describe his style — namely 'allegory', 'similitude', 'metaphor', 'parable', 'figure', 'type', 'fable' and 'shadow'. Consider the distinguishing meanings of each of these terms and establish to what extent Bunyan generally or specifically incorporates these into his style.

118. '*The Pilgrim's Progress* is an allegory of continuity, comparisons and contrasts.' Demonstrate the degree to which this statement is true.

119. Discover and assess some particular examples of criticism brought against Bunyan's literary and allegorical style in *The Pilgrim's Progress*.

120. Examine Bunyan's style of English expression in *The Pilgrim's Progress* and compare it with other notable examples of English literature. To what extent has Bunyan's literary style contributed towards the popularity of this, the most famous of all of his writings?

121. Compare the purpose, doctrine, impact and style of *The Pilgrim's Progress* with those of John Milton's *Paradise Lost*.

122. Compare the purpose, doctrine, impact and style of *The Pilgrim's Progress* with Dante Alighieri's medieval counterpart, *The Divine Comedy*.

123. Compare the purpose, doctrine, impact and style of *The Pilgrim's Progress* with the religious allegorical intent of Daniel Defoe's *Robinson Crusoe*.

124. Compare the purpose, doctrine, impact and style of *The Pilgrim's Progress* with what is regarded as Bunyan's intended sequel, *The Life and Death of Mr Badman*.

125. Provide a careful book review of the definitive and critical text of *The Pilgrim's Progress* edited by Wharey and Sharrock and published by Oxford University Press in 1960.

126. Read Part Two of *The Pilgrim's Progress* and describe instances where it illuminates certain teaching and events in Part One.

127. Assess the novelty, quality, importance and character of the poems and songs included in Parts One and Two of *The Pilgrim's Progress*.

128. How has regard for *The Pilgrim's Progress* at various levels of society changed from its inception up to the present?

129. Review two modern assessments of *The Pilgrim's Progress*. To what degree is there doctrinal sympathy with Bunyan? What most concerns these assessments in the light of Bunyan's stated purposes?

130. It is commonly suggested that in Bunyan's writing of *The Pilgrim's Progress*, in varying proportions, he draws upon his extensive Bible knowledge, his personal experience as a Puritan and other literature of his time. Which of these three factors do you think is the principal contributor? How do the other two factors relate to your opinion? Are there any other significant contributing factors?

131. Critically assess the engravings and illustrations embodied in *The Pilgrim's Progress* since the inclusion of the 'sleeping portrait' in the third edition up to the present time.

132. Bunyan acknowledges that *The Pilgrim's Progress* 'may put thee into a laughter or a feud'. Critically assess the degree to which the allegory is witty and serious. To what extent is this style consistent with biblical and Puritan ideals?

133. Roger Sharrock has written concerning Puritanism, with which Bunyan so closely identified, that '... it was a fiery religious and social

dynamic resembling contemporary Marxism more than modern Fundamentalism'. Critique this statement.

134. Critique Christopher Hill's political/social assessment of John Bunyan in his *A Tinker and a Poor Man*.

135. Summarize the incident relating to Agnes Beaumont, drawing upon her autobiographical account, and reflect on Bunyan's role here as a pastor.

Historical background

136. Bunyan's life spans the end of the English monarchy at the execution of King Charles I, the establishment of the Commonwealth under Oliver Cromwell and the Restoration of the monarchy under King Charles II. How does *The Pilgrim's Progress* reflect this turbulent period in English history?

137. A significant influence on Bunyan's early Christian life was Pastor John Gifford of Bedford. Provide a summary of Gifford's life and estimate his influence upon Bunyan.

138. Bunyan's friends included two notable, learned and contrasting Puritans, William Dell and John Owen. Describe these relationships, and comment on the extent to which they may have influenced the author of *The Pilgrim's Progress*.

139. Assess Bunyan's attitude towards the monarchy and the Cromwellian revolution.

140. Define 'latitudinarianism' as it existed in seventeenth-century England, with reference to its modern manifestations, and describe how Bunyan confronted this deviant pastoral philosophy. In what ways do certain characters in *The Pilgrim's Progress* reflect this latitudinarianism?

141. Why was Bunyan so opposed to the Quaker movement? How did he respond?

142. What sectarian movements were contemporary with Bunyan? In particular, which ones does he mention in his writings? To what extent was he influenced or aroused by them?

143. Describe the structure and life of the Bedford congregation that Bunyan pastored.

Communication

144. In his introductory poetic apology, Bunyan uses four successive illustrations concerning dark clouds, a fisherman, a fowler and a pearl. Explain these emblematic scenes and consider their relevance for making *The Pilgrim's Progress* known today.

145. How should *The Pilgrim's Progress* be communicated to children and young people? What are the guiding principles behind your opinion?

146. In this modern era, several film, dramatic and musical versions of *The Pilgrim's Progress* have been produced. Discuss their degree of success, effectiveness, faithfulness and conformity to Bunyan's purposes.

147. Examine Bunyan's introductory poetic apology, and especially his justification of his allegorical and appealing style. Are there limits to the communication of biblical truth using a variety of contemporary means? If so, what are these limiting principles?

148. Assess Ralph Vaughan Williams' oratorio *The Pilgrim's Progress* in the light of Bunyan's stated allegorical purposes, and the related question of the communication of truth in a way that is suitable to this twenty-first century.

149. Critically assess Neil Postman's estimate, in his *Amusing Ourselves to Death*, that we have moved from the mind-set of previous generations, where the dominant influence was the printed word, to a present age of entertainment and sensory indulgence through imagery. Relate your answer to the effective contemporary communication of *The Pilgrim's Progress*.

150. Review a selection of four recently published children's versions of *The Pilgrim's Progress*.

Notes

The writings of John Bunyan

1. John Bunyan, *The Works of John Bunyan*, ed. George Offor (Edinburgh, The Banner of Truth Trust, 1991 [first published 1854]), vol. II, pp.742-3. John Brown likewise expressed considerable doubt concerning the authenticity of this work (John Brown, *John Bunyan: His Life, Times and Work*. London: Hulbert Publishing, Tercentenary Edition, 1928, pp.433-4).

2. Brown, *John Bunyan*, pp.161-2.

3. *Ibid.,* p.228.

4. Richard Greaves, *John Bunyan and English Nonconformity* (London: The Hambledon Press, 1992), p.185. In this essay Greaves also responds to an article by Paul Helm in *The Baptist Quarterly*, XXVIII, April 1979, pp.87-93, which, with considerable persuasion, attempts to defend Bunyan's authorship of *Reprobation Asserted* (See chapter 9, pp.212-19 for a more detailed discussion).

5. Bunyan, *Works,* vol. II, p.386.

6. John Bunyan, *The Miscellaneous Works of John Bunyan*, 'The Poems,' ed. Graham Midgley (Oxford University Press), vol. VI, pp.xxii-xxv.

Chapter 1 — Why *The Pilgrim's Progress* is a book for our time

1. Bunyan, *Works,* vol. III, p.169.

2. W. R. Owens, 'The reception of *The Pilgrim's Progress* in England,' *Bunyan in England and Abroad*, eds. M. van Os and G. J. Schutte (Amsterdam: VU University Press, 1990), pp.91-2.

3. N. H. Keeble, '"Of him thousands daily Sing and talk": Bunyan and his reputation,' *John Bunyan, Conventicle and Parnassus*, ed. N. H. Keeble (Oxford University Press [Clarendon], 1988), p.245.

4. William Cowper, *The Poetical Works of William Cowper* (London: T. Nelson, 1852), p.308. It is noteworthy that in this poem, entitled 'Tirocinium; or a Review of Schools', the author recommends the popular allegory as part of his preferred curriculum in providing Christian private tuition, a method of education which he recommends in preference to attendance at relatively less edifying schools open to the general public.

5. Lord Macaulay, *Macaulay's Lives of Bunyan and Goldsmith* (Darby, PA: Arden Library, 1979), p.22.

6. G. M. Trevelyan, 'Bunyan's England,' *The Review of the Churches*, July 1928, pp.319, 325.

In 1912 a whole window of stained-glass panels at Westminster Abbey was devoted to *The Pilgrim's Progress*. At the dedication it was declared that 'This window is not only a valuable addition to the art which enriches and distinguishes this temple of fame, it also commemorates one of the most powerful books written by one of the greatest saints. But chiefly this work is a memorial of one of the saints who through "Grace abounding to the chief of Sinners" still continues his ministry to man, and will from this spot witness to the vital truths of the Gospel to the fundamental facts of Christian experience, and to the growing catholicity of Christian men all over the world' (Brown, *John Bunyan*, p. 491).

7. David Wallechinsky, Irving Wallace and Amy Wallace, *The Book of Lists*, pp.218-19.

8. Diane Ravitch and Chester E. Finn, Jr., *What do our 17-years-olds know?* (New York: Harper & Row, 1987), cited by Christopher Hill, *A Tinker and a Poor Man* (New York: Alfred A. Knopf, 1989), pp.372-3.

9. Gordon Rupp, *Six Makers of English Religion, 1500-1700* (London: Hodder & Stoughton, 1957), p.98.

10. J. Gresham Machen, *Christianity and Liberalism* (London: Victory Press, 1925), p.46.

11. Bunyan, *Works,* vol. III, p.167.

12. C. H. Spurgeon, *C. H. Spurgeon's Autobiography* (London: Passmore & Alabaster, 1897), vol. IV, p.268.

13. Bunyan, *Works,* vol. III, p.94.

14. M. H. Abrams. ed., *The Norton Anthology of English Verse* (New York: Norton, 1993), vol. I, pp.1857-8.

15. N. H. Keeble writes, 'No other seventeenth-century text save the King James Bible, nothing from the pen of a writer of Bunyan's social class in any period, and no other puritan, or, indeed, committed Christian work of any persuasion, has enjoyed such an extensive readership' (John Bunyan, *The Pilgrim's Progress*, ed. N. H. Keeble. Oxford: Oxford University Press, The World's Classics, 1989, p.ix). See also Keeble's excellent review of Bunyan's rise in popularity in, '"Of him thousands daily sing and talk"', pp.241-63. In the eighteenth century Benjamin Franklin writes that *The Pilgrim's Progress* 'has been more generally read than any other book, except perhaps the Bible' (Benjamin Franklin, *The Autobiography of Benjamin Franklin,* Philadelphia: American Baptist Publications Society, 1845), p.53.

16. John Bunyan, *The Pilgrim's Progress,* ed. Roger Sharrock (Harmondsworth, England: Penguin Books, 1965), p.7.

17. A. R. Ward and A. R. Waller, *The Cambridge History of English Literature,* (New York: Macmillan, 1949), vol. VII, p.177.

18. Nathaniel Hawthorne, *The Celestial Railroad* (Harrisonburg, VA: Sprinkle Publications, 1990), 20 pp.

19. George Sampson, *The Concise Cambridge History of English Literature* (Cambridge: Cambridge University Press, 1941), p.375.

20. Bunyan, *Works,* vol. III, p.85.

21. Beyond any doubt, Bunyan was a strict Calvinist, yet on the other hand here we note his innovative approach to the communication of the truth of God. For a more detailed consideration of this matter see chapters 16-17.

22. Bunyan, *Works,* vol. III, p.8.

23. Roger Sharrock, ed., *Bunyan, The Pilgrim's Progress, A Casebook* (London: Macmillan, 1976), p.53.

24. Bunyan, *Works,* vol. I, paras. 129-30, pp.40-41.

25. Sharrock, ed., *The Pilgrim's Progress, A Casebook,* p.54.

26. See J. C. Ryle, *Holiness* (James Clarke, 1956) and B. B. Warfield, *Perfectionism* (Philadelphia: Presbyterian & Reformed Publishing, 1967).

27. Rupp, *Six Makers of English Religion,* p.101.

Chapter 2 — Biblical reality through allegory

1. R. E. Allen, ed., *The Concise Oxford Dictionary* (Oxford University Press, 1991), p.30.

2. Posthumously published in 1698 and based on 1 Corinthians 9:24, this small work similarly uses the pilgrimage motif to represent the Christian as being encouraged to avoid dallying and rather to run with preparation towards heaven.

3. Bunyan, *Works,* vol. III, p.85.

4. John Bunyan, *The Pilgrim's Progress,* eds. James Blanton Wharey and Roger Sharrock (Oxford University Press, 1960), p.312.

5. Bunyan, *Works,* vol. III, p.86.

6. Richard Greaves explains: 'Those admitted to church membership, according to Bunyan, were those who were "for separating from the unconverted and open prophane, and for building up one another an holy Temple in the Lord, through the Spirit"' (Richard L. Greaves, *John Bunyan.* Grand Rapids: Wm. B. Eerdmans, 1969, p.127).

7. Sharrock, ed., *Bunyan, The Pilgrim's Progress, A Casebook,* p.68.

8. Bunyan, *Works,* vol. III, p.166.

9. *Ibid.,* p.87.

10. *Ibid.,* p.128.

11. *Ibid.,* p.1.

12. *Ibid.,* p.87.

13. *Ibid.,* vol. I, pp.4, 5.

14. *Ibid.,* vol. III, p.166.

15. Sharrock, *Pilgrim's Progress, A Casebook,* p.20.

16. However, William Perkins had published a similar diagram in the previous century.

17. Bunyan, *The Pilgrim's Progress*, eds. Wharey and Sharrock, pp.xxxviii-xxxix, 353-4.

18. Hill, *A Tinker and a Poor Man*, p.198.

19. Brown, *John Bunyan*, p.251.

20. Christopher Hill, 'Bunyan's Contemporary Reputation,' *John Bunyan and his England, 1628-88*, eds., A. Lawrence, W. R. Owens and S. Sim (1990), p.15.

21. Keeble, *Conventicle and Parnassus*, pp.247, 248.

22. Cowper, *Poetical Works*, p.308.

23. Keeble, *Conventicle and Parnassus*, p.249.

24. John Newton, *The Works of John Newton* (Edinburgh: Banner of Truth Trust, 1988), vol. VI, pp.37-8.

25. Keeble, *Conventicle and Parnassus*, p.254.

26. J. A. Froude, *Bunyan* (London: Macmillan, *English Men of Letters* series, 1880), pp.154-5.

27. Sharrock, *Pilgrim's Progress, A Casebook*, pp.114-15.

28. *Ibid.*, pp.69-70.

29. Bunyan, *The Pilgrim's Progress*, ed. Keeble, p.275.

30. Bunyan, *Works*, vol. I, p.50.

31. Brian Nellist, '*The Pilgrim's Progress* and Allegory,' *The Pilgrim's Progress: Critical and Historical Views*, ed. Vincent Newey (Liverpool: Liverpool University Press, 1980) pp.140-41.

32. Christian simply declares: 'I think verily I know the meaning of this,' without any unfolding of this meaning being given (Bunyan, *Works*, vol. III, p.100).

33. Gordon Wakefield, *Bunyan the Christian* (London: HarperCollins, 1992), p.89.

34. *Ibid.*, pp.48-9,76.

35. Bunyan, *Works*, vol. III, p.167.

Chapter 3 — The Bible and *The Pilgrim's Progress*

1. Froude, *John Bunyan*, p.4.

2. Bunyan, *The Pilgrim's Progress*, ed. Sharrock, pp.11, 25.

3. Roger Sharrock, *John Bunyan* (London: Hutchinson House, 1954), p.64.

4. *Ibid.* Sharrock also footnotes a reference to William James' secular analysis of Bunyan's conversion testimony in his *Varieties of Religious Experience* (New York: Collier Books, 1961), pp.136-8. It is worth noting that Sharrock converted to Roman Catholicism in 1951.

5. Greaves, *John Bunyan and English Nonconformity*, pp.30-31. Monica Furlong takes a similar approach when, somewhat patronizingly, she comments: 'The more relaxed way he [Bunyan] talks of God and of scripture later in his life, together with what little we know of the religious development of individuals, suggests a move away from literalism into a deeper understanding

of the deeper truth of metaphor' (Monica Furlong, *The Puritan's Progress: A Study of John Bunyan*. London: Hodder and Stoughton, 1975, p.147).

6. Greaves does make reference to Owen's profession of verbal inspiration, though not to his substantial work entitled, 'Three Treatises Concerning the Scriptures' (John Owen, *The Works of John Owen*. Edinburgh: T. & T. Clark, 1862, vol. XVI, pp.281-476).

7. This is precisely how Emil Brunner regards the Bible: 'Everyone has seen the trade slogan "His Master's Voice". If you buy a gramophone record you are told that you will hear the Master Caruso. Is that true? Of course! But really his voice? Certainly! And yet — there are some noises made by the machine which are not the master's voice, but the scratching of the steel needle upon the hard disc. But do not become impatient with the hard disc! For only by means of the record can you hear "the master's voice". So, too, is it with the Bible. It makes the real Master's voice audible — really His voice, His words, what He wants to say. But there are incidental noises accompanying, just because God speaks His word through the voice of man... Therefore the Bible is all His voice, notwithstanding all the disturbing things, which, being human, are unavoidable' (Emil Brunner, *Our Faith,* pp.19-20).

8. See J. I. Packer, 'John Owen on Communication from God' in relation to Barth's view of Scripture (J. I. Packer, *A Quest for Godliness.* Wheaton: Crossway Books, 1990, pp.81-96).

9. Bunyan, *Works,* vol. I, p.59.

10. *Ibid.,* p.386.

11. References to John 10:35 include: *Works,* vol. I, paras. 195, 209, 245, pp.31, 33, 37-8. Other references to his belief in the authority of Scripture include: vol. I, paras. 96-7, 186, pp.17, 29-30; also vol. II, p.601.

12. *Ibid.,* vol. III, p.767.

13. Norman L. Geisler, ed., *Inerrancy* (Grand Rapids: Zondervan, 1980), p.496.

14. Bunyan, *Works,* vol. I, p.695.

15. Hill, *A Tinker and a Poor Man,* p.169.

16. Bunyan, *Works,* vol. I, pp.50-62.

17. Bunyan, *Pilgrim's Progress,* ed. Sharrock, p.23.

18. Bunyan, *Works,* vol. III, p.708.

19. *Ibid.,* vol. II, p.574.

20. G. B. Harrison, *John Bunyan: A Study in Personality* (Garden City, N.Y.: Doubleday, 1928), pp.11, 13, 185.

21. Bernard Ramm, *Protestant Biblical Interpretation* (Grand Rapids: Baker Book House, 1956), pp.54, 58.

22. Packer, *A Quest for Godliness,* p.101.

23. Bunyan, *Works,* vol. I, p.53. The subjective and selective use of the literal principle here is not totally consistent with the essential Protestant principle that *all* Scripture be interpreted literally (See Ramm, *Protestant Biblical*

Interpretation, pp.89-96; J. I. Packer, *'Fundamentalism' and the Word of God.* London: Inter-Varsity Fellowship, 1960, pp.102-6).

24. Bunyan, *Works,* vol. III, p.462.

25. John R. Knott, Jr., ' "Thou must live upon my Word": Bunyan and the Bible,' Keeble, ed., *Conventicle and Parnassus,* p.162. U. Milo Kaufmann makes the same point about Bunyan's hermeneutic (U. Milo Kaufmann, *The Pilgrim's Progress and Traditions in Puritan Meditation.* New Haven: Yale University Press, 1966, pp.25-41).

26. Bunyan, *Works,* vol. I, para. 3, p.6.

27. *Ibid.,* para. 10, p.7.

28. *Ibid.,* para. 29, p.9.

29. *Ibid.,* para. 46, p.11.

30. *Ibid.,* para. 96, p.17.

31. *Ibid.,* para. 115, p.20 (See chapter 6 for a more detailed consideration of Bunyan's conversion).

32. *Ibid.,* paras. 204, 206, p.32.

33. *Ibid.,* para. 230, p.36.

34. *Ibid.,* p.50.

35. Knott, 'Bunyan and the Bible,' p.165.

36. Bunyan, *Works,* vol. III, p.12.

37. *Ibid.,* vol. I, para. 45, p.11.

38. *Ibid.,* pp.97-8.

39. These ladies probably represent those saints who gave Bunyan early guidance, not feminine leadership (*Works,* vol. I, paras. 37-41, pp.10-11).

40. Bunyan, *Works,* vol. III, pp.398-9.

Chapter 4 — The concept of progress in pilgrimage

1. Bunyan, *Works,* vol. III, p.89.

2. *Concise Oxford Dictionary,* p.902.

3. William Haller, *The Rise of Puritanism* (New York: Harper & Row, 1957), p.190.

4. Philip Edwards, 'The Journey in *The Pilgrim's Progress,*' *The Pilgrim's Progress, Critical and Historical Views,* ed. Vincent Newey (Liverpool: Liverpool University Press, 1980), p.111.

5. Bunyan, *Works,* vol. III, p.161.

6. *Ibid.,* p.144.

7. This patronage has brought forth a wide variety of themes that are remote from Bunyan's expressed purposes. A few examples include the class struggles and sectarian conflicts of the seventeenth century, historical investigation into a turbulent era, Puritan studies, feminism, the psychology of conversion and despair, literary structure and linguistic analysis, etc.

8. Wakefield, *Bunyan the Christian,* pp.48-49, 76.

9. *Ibid.,* pp.72-3.

10. Bunyan, *Works,* vol. III, p.374.

11. *Ibid.*, vol. I, p.7. This popular presentation of gospel truth underwent twenty editions during the period between1600 and 1640. It is comprised of discussion between Theologus (a divine), Philagathus (an honest man), Asunetus (an ignorant man) and Antilegon (a caviller, or petty objector).

12. *Ibid.*, vol. III, pp.44, 45.

13. *Ibid.*, p.30.

14. Hill, *A Tinker and a Poor Man*, p.201.

15. Greaves, *John Bunyan* (a published doctoral thesis). A more recent doctoral thesis by Pieter de Vries has been published under the title of *John Bunyan on the Order of Salvation* (New York: Peter Lang, 1994). This work is highly recommended for briefly and correctly assessing Bunyan's high view of Scripture; its heartfelt sympathy for Bunyan's overall doctrine is refreshing while uncommon.

16. Hill, *A Tinker and a Poor Man*, p.169.

17. Bunyan, *Works*, vol. III, p.716.

18. Bunyan, *The Pilgrim's Progress*, ed. Sharrock, pp.10-11.

19. Hill, *A Tinker and a Poor Man*, pp.206-7.

20. Brainerd P. Stranahan upholds the primary significance of Hebrews in 'Bunyan and the Epistle to the Hebrews: His Source for the Idea of Pilgrimage in *The Pilgrim's Progress*,' *Studies in Philology* 79 (1982), pp.279-96. See also Stranahan, 'Bunyan's Satire in its Biblical Sources' in Robert G. Colmer, ed., *Bunyan in our Time* (Kent, Ohio: The Kent State University Press, 1989), pp.35-60.

21. Bunyan, *Works*, vol. III, p.164.

22. *Ibid.*, pp.89, 90, 108, 137.

23. *Ibid.*, p.94.

24. *Ibid.*, p.97.

25. *Ibid.*, p.117.

26. *Ibid.*, p.136.

27. *Ibid.*, p.138.

28. *Ibid.*, p.139.

29. *Ibid.*, p.144.

30. *Ibid.*, p.151.

31. *Ibid.*

32. *Ibid.*, p.115.

33. *Ibid.*, p.190. In Part II, at the Place of Deliverance, Great-heart explains to Christiana and her company the atoning deed that is displayed before them: 'The pardon that you and Mercy, and these boys have obtained, was obtained by another, to wit, by him that let you in at the gate; and he hath obtained it in this double way. He has performed righteousness to cover you, and spilt blood to wash you in.'

34. *Ibid.*, p.127.

35. *Ibid.*, p.380.

36. Bunyan, *The Pilgrim's Progress*, eds. Wharey and Sharrock, p.xxxii.
37. Bunyan, *Works*, III, p.31.

Chapter 5 — The gospel in *The Pilgrim's Progress*

1. Bunyan, *Works*, vol. III, p.158.
2. The expression 'Lord of the Hill' is used on eight occasions and in context refers to the hill Difficulty, upon which the Palace Beautiful was situated and down which pilgrims descended into the Valley of Humiliation (*Ibid.*, pp.105-7, 109-10, 143).
3. *Ibid.*, p.108.
4. Greaves, *John Bunyan*, p.36.
5. Bunyan, *Works*, vol. I, paras. 229-30, pp.35-6.
6. *Ibid.*, vol. III, pp.154-5.
7. *Ibid.*, p 156.
8. *Ibid.*, p.104.
9. Christopher Hill describes 'Latitudinarians' as 'liberal, rational, middle-of-the-road men'. He explains that, in Edward Fowler's *The Design of Christianity*, this Anglican moderate not only rejected the doctrine of imputed righteousness, but also propounded that 'A holy and a moral life was possible for everyone, because the principles of such a life were written in the hearts of all men' (Hill, *A Tinker and a Poor Man*, p.130).
10. de Vries, *John Bunyan on the Order of Salvation*, pp.147, 148.
11. Bunyan, *Works*, vol. III, p.158.
12. *Ibid.*
13. Bunyan uses 'without' in the archaic sense of 'external to', rather than the modern 'exclusive of'' (See *The Oxford English Dictionary*). Further support for this usage is found in Bunyan's *Some Gospel Truths Opened* where he distinguishes between a subjective and an objective atonement, even though in this instance he is opposing Quaker doctrine: 'The new, false Christ, is a Christ crucified within, dead within, risen again within, and ascended within, in opposition to the Son of Mary, who was crucified without, dead without, risen again without, and ascended in a cloud away from his disciples into heaven without them (Acts 1:9-11)' (*Works*, vol. II, pp.134-5).
14. Bunyan, *Works*, vol. III, p.158.
15. *Ibid.*, p.96.
16. *Ibid.*, p.180.
17. *Ibid.*, vol. III, p.99.
18. *Ibid.*, vol. II, p.28.
19. *Ibid.*, vol. III, p.100.
20. *Ibid.*, p.109.
21. *Ibid.*
22. *Ibid.*
23. *Ibid.*, p.146.
24. *Ibid.*, p.166.

25. *Ibid.*, vol. I, p.505.
26. *Ibid.,* vol. II, p.166.
27. *Ibid.*, p.512.
28. *Ibid.*
29. 'It is no error to say, that a man naturally has Will, and a Power to pursue his will, and that as to his salvation [his own way]. But it is a damnable error to say that he hath will and power to pursue it, *and that in God's way*' (*Ibid.,* p.241, emphasis added; cf. also pp.312, 756).
30. *Ibid.,* p.134.
31. *Ibid.,* vol. I, paras. 129-30, p.22.
32. *Ibid.*, paras. 229-30, p.72.
33. Martin Luther, *Luther's Works,* vol. 27, pp.22, 27. Cf. a similar comment on Galatians 2:15-16, p.225.
34. Greaves, *John Bunyan,* p.155.
35. Hill, *A Tinker and a Poor Man,* pp.157-60.
36. Bunyan, *Works,* vol. III, p.94.
37. *Ibid.*, vol. I, pp.492-575.
38. *Ibid.,* p.7.
39. Greaves, *John Bunyan,* pp.156-7.
40. *Ibid.,* pp.51-61.
41. *Ibid.,* pp.41-5.
42. Sharrock, ed., *Bunyan, The Pilgrim's Progress, A Casebook,* p.54.
43. Bunyan, *Works,* vol. III, p.113.
44. *Ibid.,* p.132.
45. *Ibid.,* p.101.
46. *Ibid.,* p.143.
47. *Ibid.,* pp.155, 156.
48. *Ibid.,* pp.155, 158.
49. *Ibid.,* pp.709-10.
50. Greaves, *John Bunyan,* pp.159-60.

Chapter 6 — The conversion of Christian

1. Bunyan, *Works,* vol. III, p.97.
2. *Ibid.,* p.100.
3. *Ibid.,* p.103.
4. *Ibid.,* p.146.
5. *Ibid.,* p.180.
6. *Ibid.,* p.190.
7. *Ibid.,* vol. I, paras. 53-6, pp.12-13.
8. Bunyan, *The Pilgrim's Progress,* eds. Wharey and Sharrock, p.315.
9. Bunyan, *Works,* vol. I, para. 55, pp.12-13.
10. *Ibid.,* p.365.
11. *Ibid.*

12. C. H. Spurgeon, *Around the Wicket Gate, The C. H. Spurgeon Collection* (Albany, OR: Ages Software, 1998), p.3.

13. Richard L. Greaves, *Glimpses of Glory: John Bunyan and English Dissent,* (Stanford: Stanford University press, 2002), p.230.

14. de Vries, *John Bunyan and the Order of Salvation,* p.207.

15. *Ibid.,* p.206.

16. Bunyan, *Works,* vol. III, p.174.

17. *Ibid.,* p.106.

18. de Vries, *John Bunyan and the Order of Salvation,* p.208.

19. Bunyan, *Works,* vol. II, p.580.

20. *Ibid.,* vol. III, pp.278-83, 289, 292, 295-7, 299, 302-3.

21. While having the most affectionate regard for Bunyan's ministry, and specifically for his literary magnum opus, I too would disagree with one feature of *The Pilgrim's Progress*. It is that at the River of Death Christian and Hopeful cross over together; indeed Hopeful is very much a helping companion to Christian as they encounter this fearful trial. However, for the Christian, death is always a solo experience. Perhaps Hopeful is here intended to represent that loving assistance and encouragement which an earthly friend in Christ can offer to a departing saint.

22. C. H. Spurgeon, *Metropolitan Tabernacle Pulpit,* vol. XLVI, pp.211-12. See also similar criticism by Spurgeon in a sermon on 1 Corinthians 12:28 (*Metropolitan Tabernacle Pulpit,* vol. XIII, p.593).

23. Bunyan, *Works,* vol. I, pp.7-36.

24. John Stachniewski, *The Persecutory Imagination: English Puritanism and the Literature of Religious Despair* (Oxford University Press, 1991), pp.1-216. But how does one account for the remarkable ongoing popularity of Bunyan's testimony? A new Christian, having just read *Grace Abounding,* was once heard to comment: 'Why, pastor, that book is about me!'

25. Bunyan, *Works,* vol. I, pp.7-36. Paragraph numbers only follow in this section.

26. *Ibid.,* para. 115, pp.19-20.

27. *Ibid.,* p.10. This heading incorporates paras. 37-116.

28. John Kelman, *The Road,* vol. I, p.47. Many new Christians, whose sins have been dealt with at the Wicket-gate, unnecessarily carry a burden representative of uncertainty concerning their forgiveness.

29. Bunyan, *Works,* vol. I, para. 117, p.20.

30. *Ibid.,* vol. I, paras. 117-228, pp.20-35.

31. George Cheever, *Lectures on The Pilgrim's Progress* (Glasgow: William Collins, 1860), p.162.

32. Bunyan, *Works,* vol. I, paras. 237, 239, p.37.

33. *Ibid.,* para. 243, p.37.

34. *Ibid.,* vol. III, p.102.

35. *Ibid.,* vol. I, para. 114, p.19.

36. *Ibid.,* paras. 244-52, pp.37-8.

37. de Vries, *John Bunyan on the Order of Salvation*, pp.193, 197-9.

38. *'I Will Pray with the Spirit'; The Doctrine of the Law and Grace Unfolded* Bunyan, *Miscellaneous Works.*, ed. Richard L. Greaves, vol. II, p.xxxv.

39. Bunyan, *Works*, vol. I, pp.548-50.

40. Spurgeon, *Autobiography*, vol. I, pp.97-115.

41. Bunyan, *Works*, vol. I, paras. 114-16, pp.19-20.

42. *Ibid.*, vol. III, pp.153-6.

Chapter 7 — Sanctification in *The Pilgrim's Progress*

1. A more recent representation of this teaching is to be found in Ruth Paxon's *Life on the Highest Plane*, where the believer is to obey Romans 6:13 and thus, '"Yield" "*yield*," "YIELD" — by a definite, intelligent, voluntary act of the will the believer must choose Christ as his new Master and yield himself to Him as Lord' (p.237). I can well remember attending a number of Keswick conventions in Australia and England many years ago where, after the customary exposition of Romans 5-8, Christians were prompted to come forward to signify their decisive yielding and surrender to the Holy Spirit so that he might live the Christian life for them and in them. The call was to 'let go and let God' by an act of faith in divine enabling, to the neglect of emphasizing the biblical responsibility of believers to use appointed means of grace.

2. For a good survey of this 'Higher Life movement', see D. M. Lloyd-Jones, *The Puritans: Their Origins and Successors* (Edinburgh: Banner of Truth Trust, 1987), pp.316-25. For greater detail refer to Warfield, *Perfectionism*, pp.216-311.

3. Ryle, *Holiness*, pp.xvii-xviii.

4. *Ibid.*, pp.xvi-xvii. Ryle also points out that '… the expression "yield yourselves" is only to be found in one place in the New Testament, as a duty urged upon believers. That place is in the sixth chapter of Romans, and there within six verses the expression occurs five times. (See Romans 6:13-19.) But even there the word will not bear the sense of "placing ourselves passively in the hands of another". Any Greek student can tell us that the sense is rather that of actively "presenting" ourselves for use, employment, and service. (See Rom. 12:1.)' (*Ibid.*)

5. *Ibid.*, p.xvii.

6. Bunyan, *Works*, vol. I, paras. 229-32, pp.35-6.

7. *Ibid.*, vol. I, paras. 114, 244-52, pp.19, 37-8.

8. For a detailed consideration of 'definitive sanctification' and its distinctive relationship with regard to 'progressive sanctification', see John Murray, *Collected Writings of John Murray* (Edinburgh: Banner of Truth Trust, 1976), vol. II, pp.277-317.

9. Ryle, *Holiness*, p.16.

10. *Ibid.*, pp.16-24.

11. Bunyan, *Works*, vol. III, p.102.

12. *Ibid.*, p.103.

13. *Ibid.*, p.112.
14. *Ibid.*, p.106.
15. *Ibid.*, pp.106-7.
16. *Ibid.*, pp.122-3.
17. *Ibid.*, p.125.
18. *Ibid.*, p.161.
19. *Ibid.*, p.111.
20. *Ibid.*, p.118.
21. *Ibid.*, p.137.
22. *Ibid.*, p.165.
23. *Ibid.*, p.102.
24. *Ibid.*, p.165.
25. *Ibid.*, p.162.
26. *Ibid.*, vol. II, p.507.
27. *Ibid.*, vol. III, p.124.
28. *Ibid.*, p.104.
29. *Ibid.*, p.156.
30. *Ibid.*, p.158.
31. Ryle, *Holiness*, p.21.
32. Bunyan, *Works*, vol. III, p.105.
33. *Ibid.*, p.91.
34. *Ibid.*, p.111.
35. *Ibid.*, p.162.
36. *Ibid.*, p.89.
37. *Ibid.*, p.90.
38. *Ibid.*, p.104.
39. *Ibid.*, p.111.
40. *Ibid.*
41. Packer, *A Quest for Godliness*, pp.69-70.
42. Bunyan, *Works*, vol. I, paras. 234-5, p.36.
43. *Ibid.*, vol. III, p.103.
44. *Ibid.*, p.156.
45. *Ibid.*, p.103.
46. *Ibid.*, p.132.
47. *Ibid.*, p.138.
48. *Ibid.*, p.206.
49. *Ibid.*, p.100.
50. *Ibid.*, p.101.
51. *Ibid.*, p.102.
52. *Ibid.*, p.145.
53. *Ibid.*, p.151.
54. *Ibid.*
55. *Ibid.*, p.104.
56. *Ibid.*, p.114.

Chapter 8 — Law and grace in *The Pilgrim's Progress*

1. Dennis Michael Swanson, *Charles H. Spurgeon and Eschatology: Did he Have a Discernible Millennial Position?* Unpublished dissertation, The Master's Seminary, California, 1996. Internet sourced. The claim of Dr Peter Masters for amillennialism and that of Erroll Hulse for postmillennialism are here thoroughly refuted.

2. 'No single theological label without careful qualification will fit Bunyan. He was bitterly opposed both to Arminianism and to Quakerism, and he was neither a moderate Calvinist nor a true Antinomian, although at certain points his doctrine was harmonious with Antinomian tenets. His foundation principles were basically Lutheran, but much of his theology was in full accord with the orthodox Calvinism of his period. His doctrine of the church and sacraments was neither Calvinist nor Lutheran but a heritage from the Independent-Baptist tradition, particularly the segment of that tradition of which he was a part' (*John Bunyan*, p.159).

3. Richard Greaves states, 'In *Law and Grace* Bunyan ... on occasion ... evinces Antinomian influence.' He also documents the claims that Richard Baxter and Anthony Burgess more strongly judged Bunyan's particular treatise here as Antinomian (John Bunyan, 'I Will Pray with the Spirit,' p.xxxv). On the other hand Pieter de Vries writes, 'R. L. Greaves' conclusion that Bunyan displayed Antinomian tendencies is in my opinion incorrect... He rejected both Anti- and Neonomianism' (*John Bunyan and the Order of Salvation*, p.160).

4. John Owen moved from Anglicanism and the repudiation of Presbyterianism to Congregationalism. A treatise on *The Dominion of Sin and Grace*, based on Romans 6:14 and published posthumously in 1688, seems to indicate his arrival at a view regarding law and grace much closer to that of Bunyan than might have been the case in his earlier years. He gives four reasons why the Christian is not under law:

> 1. The law *giveth no strength against sin* unto them that are under it, but grace doth...
>
> 2. The law *giveth no liberty of any kind*; it gendereth unto bondage, and so cannot free us from any dominion...
>
> 3. The law *doth not supply us with effectual motives and encouragements* to endeavour the ruin of the dominion of sin in a way of duty... It works only by fear and dread, with threatenings and terrors of destruction...
>
> 4. *Christ is not in the law*; he is not proposed in it, not communicated by it — we are not made partakers of him thereby. This is the work of grace, of the gospel... He [Christ] alone ruins the kingdom of Satan, whose power is acted in the rule of sin

> (Owen, *Works*, vol. VII, pp 542-51).

5. William Dell, Master of Gonville and Caius College, Cambridge, and rector of Yelden until ejected in 1662, was a pastoral friend of Bunyan's who eventually embraced Independency and probably exerted considerable influence on the Bedford preacher. He was an antinomian, according to Christopher Hill (*A Tinker and a Poor Man,* p.167).

John Brown records a typical strong opinion: 'If two or three Christians in the country, being met in the name of Christ, have Christ Himself with His Word and Spirit among them, they need not ride many miles to London to know what to do… What wild and woeful work do men make when they will have the Church of God thus and thus, and get the power of the magistrate to back theirs, as if the new heavens wherein the Lord will dwell must be the work of their own fingers, or as if the New Jerusalem must of necessity come out of the Assembly of Divines at Westminster' (Brown, *John Bunyan,* p.75).

6. Michael A. Mullett, *John Bunyan in Context* (Pittsburgh: Duquesne University Press, 1997), p.48.

7. Bunyan, *Works,* vol. I, p.498. The antithetical 'covenant of grace' is the new covenant or bargain established by the blood of Christ (*Ibid.,* pp.522-3), which is more reflective of Luther's law/gospel antitheses than those of the Westminster divines.

8. *Ibid.,* p.498.

9. *Ibid.,* p.499.

10. *Ibid.,* vol. II, pp.363, 365, 366.

11. *Ibid.,* p.379.

12. Greaves, *John Bunyan,* p.118.

13. Bunyan, *Works,* vol. I, p.543.

14. *Ibid.,* vol. III, p.119.

15. *Ibid.,* pp.94,96.

16. *Ibid.,* vol. I, p.494.

17. *Ibid.,* vol. III, p 98.

18. *Ibid.,* pp.98-9.

19. *Ibid.,* pp.99-100.

20. *Ibid.,* p.99.

21. *Ibid.,* pp.118-19.

22. *Ibid.,* p.382.

23. *Ibid.,* vol. I, p.560.

24. *Ibid.,* vol. II, p.386.

25. *Ibid.,* pp.387-8. Compare a similar explanation in *The Saint's Knowledge of Christ's Love,* also published in 1692. Here Bunyan warns of 'not suffering the law to rule but over my outward man, not suffering the gospel to be removed one hair's breadth from my conscience. When Christ dwells in my heart by faith (Eph. 3:17), and the moral law dwells in my members (Col. 3:5), the one to keep up peace with God, and the other to keep my conversation in a good decorum: then am I right, and not till then. But this will not be done without much experience, diligence, and delight in Christ. For there is nothing

that Satan more desireth, than that the law may abide in the conscience of an awakened Christian, and there take up the place of Christ, and faith' (*Ibid.,* p.29).

26. *Ibid.,* vol. I, p.360.

27. Bunyan, *The Pilgrim's Progress,* ed. Keeble, p.267. See also Bunyan's definition of grace that incorporates 'good-will' in *Works,* vol. I, p.644.

28. Bunyan, *Works,* vol. III, p.91.

29. *Ibid.,* vol. III, pp.180, 190.

30. *Ibid.,* p.96.

31. *Ibid.,* p.121.

32. *Ibid.,* p.155.

33. *Ibid.,* p.158.

34. *Ibid.*

35. *Ibid.,* pp.98-100.

36. Luther comments on Galatians 3:25: 'If therefore ye look unto Christ and that which he hath done, there is now no law. For he, coming in the time appointed, verily took away the law. Now, since the law is gone, we are not kept under the tyranny thereof any more; but we live in joy and safety under Christ, who now so sweetly reigneth in us by his Spirit... As long then as we live in the flesh, which is not without sin, the law oftentimes returneth and doth his office, in one more and in another less, as their faith is strong or weak, and yet not to their destruction, but to their salvation... If I behold Christ, I am altogether pure and holy, knowing nothing at all of the law; for Christ is my leaven' (*A Commentary on St Paul's Epistle to the Galatians,* pp.336-8). This comment certainly has the flavour of Bunyan about it, especially as he writes in 'Of the Law and a Christian,' *Works,* vol. II, pp.386-8.

37. In *The Westminster Confession of Faith,* the law is not merely for times of carnality, but rather it is a revelation and code for the stimulation of righteousness, of 'moral duties'. That is, '... as a rule of life, informing them [true believers] of the will of God and their duty, it [the law of the Ten Commandments] directs and binds them to walk accordingly;' it 'encourageth ... a man's doing good' (Philip Schaff, *The Creeds of Christendom.* Grand Rapids: Baker Book House, 1969, vol. III, pp.640-43). In response to this, both Luther and Bunyan would claim that now, by means of a faith union, the Lord Jesus Christ is supremely and transcendently to be our code of moral duty, our rule of life and our encouragement for good.

38. Schaff, *The Creeds of Christendom,* vol. III, pp.616-18.

39. *Ibid.,* vol. I, pp.493, 499-500.

40. *Ibid.,* p.520.

41. *Ibid.,* p.522.

42. *Ibid.,* p.538.

43. *Ibid.,* p.544.

44. *Ibid.,* pp.4-5.

45. *Ibid.,* para. 118, p.20.

46. *Ibid.*, para. 175, p.28.
47. *Ibid.*, para. 206, pp.32-3.
48. *Ibid.*, para. 252, p.38.
49. So, '... works and grace, as I have showed, are in this matter opposite each to other; if he be saved by works, then not by grace; if by grace, then not by works (Rom. 11)' (*Ibid.*, p.356).
50. *Ibid.*, p.349.
51. *Ibid.*, pp.351, 355.
52. *Ibid.*, p.346.
53. Brown, *John Bunyan*, p.297.
54. *Ibid.*, pp.296-7.
55. Bunyan, *Works*, vol. I, pp.341-2.
56. *Ibid.*, p.351.
57. *Ibid.*, p.644.
58. Bunyan, 'I will pray in the Spirit,' pp.xxxiv-xxxv.
59. Bunyan, *Works*, vol. I, para. 129, p.22.
60. Gordon Rupp, *The Righteousness of God* (London: Hodder & Stoughton, 1953), p.347.
61. See 'The Westminster Confession of Faith,' Chapter VII (Schaff, *The Creeds of Christendom*, vol. III, pp.616-18); Herman Witsius, *The Economy of the Covenants Between God and Man* (Escondido, CA: den Dulk Christian Foundation, 1990 [first published 1677]), vol. I, pp.291-324.
62. Bunyan, *Works*, vol. I, p.498.
63. *Ibid.*, vol. I, pp.363, 365, 366.
64. *Ibid.*, pp.522-3.
65. Greaves, *John Bunyan*, pp.106-7.
66. Bunyan, *Works*, vol. II, p.594.
67. Hill, *A Tinker and a Poor Man*, p.86.
68. Walter J. Chantry seems to suggest this antinomian tendency when he writes, obviously in defence of *The Westminster Confession of Faith*'s understanding of the Christian sabbath, 'It would be difficult to endorse all of his [Bunyan's] specific arguments [against seventh-day Christians] in this article' (*God's Righteous Kingdom*. Edinburgh: Banner of Truth Trust, 1980, p.138).
69. D. Martyn Lloyd-Jones, *Romans, The New Man, Exposition of Chapter 6* (Grand Rapids: Zondervan, 1973), pp.8-10.

Chapter 9 — Sovereignty, election and free will

1. Bunyan, *Works*, vol. III, p 86.
2. J. C. Ryle, *Old Paths* (Cambridge: James Clarke, 1972), p.473.
3. Bunyan, *The Pilgrim's Progress, A Casebook*, ed. Roger Sharrock, p.53.
4. Bunyan, *Works*, vol. III, p.96. Greaves sees electing grace here since, 'No would-be pilgrim had the ability to open the gate' (*John Bunyan and English Nonconformity*, p.197).

5. Good-will represents Christ (see ch. 6, pp.125-6).

6. John Bunyan, *The Pilgrim's Progress* — notes and memoir by James Inglis (London: Gall and Inglis, n. d.), p.22.

7. Bunyan, *Works,* vol. III, p.101.

8. *Ibid.,* p.113.

9. *Ibid.,* p.132.

10. *Ibid.,* p.149.

11. *Ibid.,* p.143. See also Stuart Sim, ' "Safe for Those for Whom it is to be Safe": Salvation and Damnation in Bunyan's Fiction', *John Bunyan and his England, 1628-88,* eds. Lawrence, Owens, Sim (London: The Hambledon Press, 1990), pp.149-60.

12. *Ibid.,* pp.155-6.

13. *Ibid.,* pp.158-9.

14. *Ibid.,* vol. I, p.549.

15. *Ibid.,* vol. I, paras. 12-13, p.7.

16. *Ibid.,* paras. 58-61, p.13.

17. *Ibid.,* paras. 68, 104, 143, 185, 201, 206, pp.14-32.

18. *Ibid.,* vol. II, pp.598-9.

19. *Ibid.,* vol. I, pp.163-4.

20. *Ibid.,* p.519.

21. *Ibid.,* vol. II, p.756.

22. *Ibid.,* vol. III, p.383.

23. *Ibid.,* vol. II, p.652.

24. *Ibid.,* p.312.

25. Greaves, *John Bunyan,* p.59.

26. Bunyan, *Works,* vol. II, p.335; vol. III, p.763. Charles Doe had been a personal friend of Bunyan who, in 1691, published a catalogue of the Bedford pastor's works that included a short biographical sketch under the title, *The Struggler.*

27. Greaves, *John Bunyan and English Nonconformity,* p.186.

28. *Ibid.,* pp.185-6. It would be helpful if more details of Sharrock's investigation and conclusions in this regard were made available.

29. Brown, *John Bunyan,* p.228.

30. *Ibid.*

31. Greaves, *Bunyan and English Nonconformity,* p.185.

32. *Ibid.,* p.188.

33. *Ibid.,* pp.189-90.

34. *Ibid.,* p.191. Would a Particular Baptist uphold a general atonement?

35. Henri Talon, *John Bunyan: The Man and his Works* (Cambridge: Harvard University Press, 1951), p.261n.

36. Harrison, *John Bunyan: A Study in Personality,* pp.125-6.

37. By the term 'general atonement' is generally meant God's sincere offer of salvation through Christ to all men who, in spite of being sinners, retain an autonomous and decisive capacity to believe or not believe.

38. Paul Helm, 'Bunyan and *Reprobation Asserted*,' *The Baptist Quarterly*, Vol. XXVIII, April 1979, p.88.

Pieter de Vries does not agree with Greaves that we have a doctrinal conflict here since the author of *Reprobation Asserted*, unlike Bunyan, expresses belief in universal redemption (*John Bunyan on the Order of Salvation*, p.73).

39. Helm, 'Bunyan and *Reprobation Asserted*,' pp.88-9.

40. Bunyan, *Works*, vol. II, p.349.

41. Helm, 'Bunyan and *Reprobation Asserted*,' p.91.

42. Greaves, *John Bunyan and English Nonconformity*, pp.190-91.

43. This charge of a fraudulent or insincere offer is that which Hyper-Calvinists have brought against Calvinists such as John Owen, who taught the free offer of the gospel to all while believing in a limited atonement. This led to the Hyper-Calvinist belief in a proclaimed gospel that does not invite, with the expectation that only the elect would respond (See Peter Toon, *The Emergence of Hyper-Calvinism in English Nonconformity*. London: Olive Tree, 1967, pp.70-103, 134-5).

44. Helm, 'Bunyan and *Reprobation Asserted*,' p.91.

45. Bunyan, *Works*, vol. II, p.348.

46. *Ibid.*, pp.348-9, 352.

47. *Ibid.*, p.355.

48. *Ibid.*, p.358.

49. In *The Death of Death in the Death of Christ*, John Owen counsels on this vital matter: 'A minister is not to make enquiry after, nor to trouble himself about, those secrets of the eternal mind of God, namely, — whom he purposeth to save, and whom he hath sent Christ to die for in particular. It is enough for them to search his revealed will, and thence take their *directions*, from whence they have their *commissions*... They command and invite all to repent and believe; but they know not in particular on whom God will bestow repentance unto salvation, nor in whom he will effect the work of faith with power' (*Works*, vol. X, p.300).

Chapter 10 — The despairing reprobate in the iron cage

1. John Kelman, *The Road* (Edinburgh: Oliphant Anderson and Ferrier, 1912), vol. I, p.64.

2. Bunyan, *Works*, vol. III, p.101.

3. *Ibid.*, p.102.

4. *Ibid.*, p.184.

5. *Ibid.*, p.101.

6. *Ibid.*, pp.579-85.

7. Cheever, *Lectures on The Pilgrim's Progress*, p.174.

8. Robert Maguire, *Lectures on Bunyan's Pilgrim's Progress* (London: The London Printing and Publishing Company, 1859), p.40.

9. Kelman, *The Road*, vol. I, p.67.

10. Bunyan, *Works,* vol. III, pp.577-8.
11. *Ibid.,* pp.72-3.
12. Brown, *John Bunyan,* pp.120-21.
13. Bunyan, *The Pilgrim's Progress,* ed. Keeble, p.268.
14. Stachniewski, *The Persecutory Imagination,* pp.199-200n.
15. Bunyan, *Works,* vol. I, p.118.
16. *Ibid.,* para. 163, pp.25-6.
17. *Ibid.,* para. 179, p.28.
18. *Ibid.,* vol. III, pp.382-3.
19. *Ibid.,* p.582.
20. *Ibid.,* p.101.
21. *Ibid.,* vol. I, p.118.
22. *Ibid.,* vol. III, p.583.
23. *Ibid.,* pp.128-9, 131-2.
24. *Ibid.,* p.579.
25. Bunyan, *Works,* vol. III, pp.560-85.
26. *Ibid.,* vol. I, paras. 147-8, p.24.
27. *Ibid.,* vol. I, para. 140, p.23.
28. *Ibid.,* p.566. See George Butler, 'The Iron Cage of Despair and "The Unpardonable Sin" in The Pilgrim's Progress,' *English Language Notes,* XXV, Sept. 1987, pp.34-8.
29. Bunyan, *Works,* vol. III, pp.100-101.
30. *Ibid.,* vol. I, pp.102-3.
31. *Ibid.,* vol. III, pp.579-85.
32. *Ibid.,* pp.577-9.
33. *Ibid.,* p.661.

Chapter 11 — Images of Jesus Christ in *The Pilgrim's Progress*

1. Brian Nellist, 'The Pilgrim's Progress and Allegory,' p.150.
2. J. C. Ryle, *Expository Thoughts on John* (Edinburgh: Banner of Truth Trust, 1987), vol. I, p.324.
3. Greaves, *John Bunyan,* p.159.
4. Charles Bigg, *contra* Joseph B. Mayor.
5. Bunyan, *Works,* vol. I, paras. 29, 46, pp.9, 11.
6. Alexander Whyte, *Bunyan Characters* (Grand Rapids: Baker Book House, 1981), vol. I, p.69.
7. Bunyan, *Works,* vol. I, para. 55, p.13.
8. *Ibid.,* vol. III, p.179.
9. *Ibid.,* p.103.
10. *Ibid.,* p.107.
11. *Ibid.,* vol. II, p.578.
12. See chapter 5, note 2, p.466 above.
13. *Ibid.,* vol. I, p.674.
14. *Ibid.,* vol. III, p.113.

15. *Ibid.*, p.112.
16. *Ibid.*, pp.118-19.
17. *Ibid.*, vol. II, p.388.
18. *Ibid.*, vol. I, p.673.
19. *Ibid.*, vol. III, p.158.
20. *Ibid.*, p.163.
21. *Ibid.*, p.164.
22. *Ibid.*
23. *Ibid.*, vol. I, p.66.
24. *Ibid.*, vol. III, p.760.
25. George Cheever, *Lectures on The Pilgrim's Progress,* p.vi.

Chapter 12 — Pastoral emphases in *The Pilgrim's Progress*

1. B. R. White, ' "The Fellowship of Believers": Bunyan and Puritanism,' *John Bunyan, Conventicle and Parnassus,* ed. Keeble, p.1.
   Pieter de Vries takes a similar line when he writes that 'In *The Pilgrim's Progress* the church plays a very modest role' (*John Bunyan on the Order of Salvation,* p.80).
2. Greaves, *John Bunyan,* pp.123-51.
3. Bunyan, *Works,* vol. I, p.167.
4. Christopher Hill, 'John Bunyan and the English Revolution,' *The John Bunyan Lectures 1978* (Bedford: Bedfordshire Education Service, 1978), p.15.
5. *Ibid.*, vol. I, para. 77, p.15.
6. *Ibid.*, vol. III, p.98.
7. *Ibid.*, vol. I, paras. 77, 117, pp.15, 20.
8. *Ibid.*, vol. III, p.98.
9. Greaves, *John Bunyan,* p.123. C. H. Spurgeon devotes two chapters to this matter in his *Pictures from Pilgrim's Progress,* pp.113-29.
10. Bunyan, *Works,* vol. III, p.106.
11. Brown, *John Bunyan,* p.204.
12. Bunyan, *Works,* vol. I, paras. 37-8, p.10.
13. Gordon Campbell, 'The Theology of *The Pilgrim's Progress,*' *The Pilgrim's Progress, Critical and Historical Views,* ed. Vincent Newey (Liverpool: Liverpool University Press), pp.251-2.
14. *Ibid.*, vol. II, pp.583, 587.
15. One of Bunyan's later writings is entitled, *A Case of Conscience Resolved,* in which he considers the appropriateness of women conducting their own separate prayer meetings and the like (Bunyan, *Works,* vol. II, pp.658-74).
16. Bunyan, *Works,* vol. II, p.570. Offor's praise of this delightful picture is richly deserved.
17. *Ibid.*, vol. III, p.110.
18. *Ibid.*, vol. III, p.535.
19. *Ibid.*, p.111.

20. *Ibid.*, p.142.

21. *Ibid.*, vol. I, p.92.

22. Kelman, *The Road*, vol. II, p.67.

23. Bunyan, *Works*, vol. III, p.230.

24. *Ibid.*, vol. I, pp.757-8.

25. William Hendriksen, *I & II Timothy and Titus* (Edinburgh: Banner of Truth Trust, 1972), p.265.

26. Bunyan, *Works*, vol. III, p.145.

27. *Ibid.*, p.145.

28. *Ibid.*

29. *Ibid.*, vol. II, p.579.

30. *Ibid.*, p.581.

31. John Bunyan, *The Works of that Eminent Servant of Christ, Mr John Bunyan* (London: E. Gardiner, 1736-1737), vol. I, pp.v-vi.

32. Newton, *Works*, vol. VI, pp.37-8.

33. Machen, *Christianity and Liberalism*, p.46.

34. In 1674, when Agnes Beaumont, a single woman aged twenty-one, urgently needed a ride from her brother's farmhouse to a Bedford church meeting at Gamlingay, on seeing Pastor Bunyan approach on horseback, she pressed him to take her up with him on his horse. He reluctantly agreed. However, Agnes' father was enraged at the sight of his daughter riding away in this manner and so he locked her out of his house that evening. Though Agnes was soon allowed back home, within a week her father died suddenly. As a result, opponents of Bunyan started rumours concerning unfounded allegations in this regard. Eventually John was fully cleared of all blame, but he must have regretted ever having given her that ride (See Brown, *John Bunyan*, pp.225-7; John Bunyan, *Grace Abounding to the Chief of Sinners*, ed. Roger Sharrock. Oxford: Oxford University Press [Clarendon], 1962, pp.176-80).

35. Bunyan, *Works*, vol. I, p.lxxiv.

Chapter 13 — C. H. Spurgeon and *The Pilgrim's Progress*

1. Thomas Spurgeon, Editor's Introduction, C. H. Spurgeon, *Pictures from Pilgrim's Progress* (Pasadena, TX: Pilgrim Publications, 1973), p.5.

2. Spurgeon, *Pictures from Pilgrim's Progress*, p.11.

3. C. H. Spurgeon, *C. H. Spurgeon's Autobiography* (London: Passmore and Alabaster, 1897), vol. I, p.103.

4. *Ibid.*, pp.53-4.

5. *Ibid.*, vol. II, pp.6-7.

6. *Ibid.*, p.7.

7. Brown, *John Bunyan*, p.19.

8. Charles Dargan, *A History of Preaching* (New York: Hodder & Stoughton, 1905), vol. II, pp.534-5.

9. Charles Doe, 'The Struggler,' Bunyan, *Works*, vol. III, pp.766-7.

10. Spurgeon, *Autobiography,* vol. I, pp.181-2.

11. Bunyan, *Works,* vol. I, p.298. Andrew Fuller rejected the denial of gospel invitations by Hyper-Calvinists: 'I had read pretty much of Dr Gill's Body of Divinity, and from many parts of it had received considerable instruction. I perceived, however, that the system of Bunyan was not the same with his; for that while he maintained the doctrines of election and predestination, he nevertheless held with the free offer of salvation to sinners without distinction' (*The Complete Works of the Rev. Andrew Fuller.* Philadelphia: American Baptist Publications Society, 1845, vol. I, p.15).

12. Spurgeon, *Around the Wicket Gate,* p.36.

13. These sixty-three volumes were accessed using *The C. H. Spurgeon Collection*, a compact disc published by Ages Digital Library (Albany, OR; Ages Software, 1998). All page numbers refer to this edition.

14. Spurgeon, *Metropolitan Tabernacle Pulpit,* vol. 13, p.729.

15. *Ibid.,* vol. 9, p.293; vol. 11, p.93.

16. *Ibid.,* vol. 3, p.99.

17. *Ibid.,* vol. 47, pp.259-60.

18. *Ibid.,* vol. 14, p.185. This same opinion is repeated in vol. 15, p.601; vol. 26, p.911. Like Southey, Richard Greaves expresses a similarly doubtful estimate (*John Bunyan and English Nonconformity,* p.194).

19. *Ibid.,* vol. 59, pp.472-3.

20. Thomas Spurgeon, introduction to Spurgeon, *Pictures from Pilgrim's Progress,* p.4.

21. Spurgeon, *Pictures from Pilgrim's Progress,* p.85.

Chapter 14 —The companionship of Christian and Faithful

1. Cheever, *Lectures on The Pilgrim's Progress,* p.230.

2. Bunyan, *Works,* vol. III, p.116.

3. Cheever, *Lectures on The Pilgrim's Progress,* p.230.

4. Bunyan, *Works,* vol. III, p.117.

5. *The Methodist Hymn-Book,* p.648.

6. Bunyan, *The Pilgrim's Progress,* eds. Wharey and Sharrock, p.320.

7. Bunyan, *Works,* vol. I, p.4.

8. *Ibid.,* vol. III, p.106.

9. Bunyan, *The Doctrine of the Law and Grace Unfolded,* p.xviii.

10. Brown, *John Bunyan,* pp.74-5. See also Eric C. Walker, *William Dell, Master Puritan* (Cambridge: W. Heffer & Sons, 1970), 238 pp.

11. *Ibid.,* p.75.

12. Hill, *A Tinker and a Poor Man,* p.167.

13. *Ibid.,* pp.166-7.

14. Bunyan, *Works,* vol. III, p.117.

15. Vera Brittain, *In the Steps of John Bunyan* (London: Rich & Cowan, 1987), p.180.

16. Bunyan, *Works,* vol. I, pp.520-34.

Chapter 15 — The poems and songs of *The Pilgrim's Progress*

1. Thomas Goodwin, *The Works of Thomas Goodwin* (Edinburgh: James Nichol, 1866), vol. III, p.215.

2. Perry Miller and Thomas H. Johnson, eds., *The Puritans — A Source-Book of Their Writings* (New York: Harper & Row, 1965), vol. II, p.394.

3. Hill, *A Tinker and a Poor Man*, p.261. The quotation is from Scholes, *The Puritan and Music.*

4. Miller and Johnson, eds., *The Puritans*, vol. I, pp.77-9.

5. Bunyan, *Miscellaneous Works*, vol. VI, ' The Poems,' pp.1-35.

6. Bunyan, *Works*, vol. I, pp.63-6.

7. *Ibid.,* vol. III, pp.726-37.

8. *Ibid.,* pp.737-45.

9. *Ibid.,* vol. II, pp.575-6.

10. *Ibid.,* vol. III, pp.746-62.

11. *Ibid.,* vol. II, pp.577-90.

12. *Ibid.,* vol. I, para. 16, p.7.

13. Hill, *A Tinker and a Poor Man*, pp.266-7.

14. Bunyan, *Works*, vol. I, paras. 33-4, p.10.

15. Hill, *A Tinker and a Poor Man*, pp.262-4.

16. Bunyan, *Works*, vol. I, p.424.

17. Hill, *A Tinker and a Poor Man*, p.272, quoting Tindall's *John Bunyan: Mechanick Preacher.*

18. Louis Benson, *The Hymns of John Bunyan* (New York: The Hymn Society, 1930), p.3.

19. Hill, *A Tinker and a Poor Man*, p.264.

20. Bunyan, *The Pilgrim's Progress*, eds. Wharey and Sharrock, pp.343-4.

21. Bunyan, *Works*, vol. III, pp.188, 198.

22. *Ibid.,* pp.165-6.

23. *Ibid.,* p.244.

24. Bunyan, *Miscellaneous Works*, vol. VI, pp.lvi-lvii.

25. Bunyan, *Works*, vol. III, p.178.

26. Benson, *Hymns of John Bunyan*, pp.5-6.

27. Bunyan, *Works*, vol. III, p.206.

28. *Ibid.,* p.235.

Chapter 16 — *The Pilgrim's Progress* and the seventeenth-century reader

1. Ezra S. Tipple, 'Pilgrim's Progress a Book for Preachers,' *Methodist Review,* July 1908, p.591.

2. Quoted in *Bunyan, The Pilgrim's Progress, a Casebook*, ed. Roger Sharrock, p.67.

3. Christopher Hill, *A Tinker and a Poor Man*, pp.372-3.

4. L. R. Gardiner, in noting the literary hostility of the 1960s towards evangelical religion, quotes the pungent criticism of *The Pilgrim's Progress* by Brophy,

Levey and Osborne in their *Fifty Works of English (and American) Literature we Could do Without* (Ian Breward, ed., *John Bunyan — A Commemorative Symposium*. Melbourne: The Uniting Church Historical Society, 1988, p.2).

More recently Bunyan has been subjected to sharp, historical psychoanalysis by John Stachniewski. The author of *The Pilgrim's Progress* is said to have suffered from a severe persecution complex on account of his belief in an oppressive God derived from Calvinism and a literalist interpretation of the Bible (Stachniewski, *The Persecutory Imagination*, pp.1-84, 127-216). By way of response, we may quote Bunyan's terse prefatory comment in *Grace Abounding* that 'The Philistines understand me not' (Bunyan, *Works*, vol. I, p.4). George Offor adds: 'He [Bunyan] lived in an atmosphere, and used a language, unknown to the wisdom of this world... His mind was deeply imbued with all that was most terrific, as well as most magnificent in religion. In proportion as his Christian course became pure and lovely, so his former life must have been surveyed with unmitigated severity and abhorrence. These mental conflicts are deeply interesting; they arose from an agonized mind — a sincere and determined spirit roused by Divine revelation, opening before his astonished but bewildered mind, solemn, eternal realities. He that sits in the scorner's seat may scoff at them, while he who is earnestly enquiring after the way, the truth, and the life, will examine them with prayerful seriousness' (Bunyan, *Works*, vol. III, p.10).

5. Packer, *A Quest for Godliness*, p.73.

6. *Ibid.*, pp.62-3.

7. C. H. Spurgeon makes a delightful comparison between Bunyan and Owen: 'Dr John Owen said that he would give all his learning to be able to preach like the tinker, John Bunyan... Owen's discourses [were] profound, solid, weighty, and probably heavy, suited [to] a class of persons who could not have received Bunyan's delightfully illustrated preaching of the plain gospel... Dr Owen, you had better remain Dr Owen, for we could by no means afford to lose that mine of theological wealth which you have bequeathed to us. You would have looked very awkward if you had tried to talk like the marvellous dreamer, and he would have played the fool if he had imitated you' (*Eccentric Preachers*. Pasadena, TX; Pilgrim Publications, 1978, p.33).

8. Bunyan, *Works*, vol. III, p.398.

9. On occasion Bunyan does admit that a particular piece of writing is based upon sermons previously delivered.

10. Bunyan, *Works*, vol. III, pp.381-2.

11. *Ibid.*, p.380.

12. *Ibid.*, pp.160-61.

13. *Ibid.*, inserted between p.559 and p.560, but excluded from the recent Banner of Truth reprint.

14. Stachniewski, *The Persecutory Imagination*, pp.196-7.

15. Bunyan, *The Pilgrim's Progress*, eds. Wharey and Sharrock, pp.151-4.

16. Miller and Johnson, eds., *The Puritans — A Sourcebook,* vol. I, pp.77-9.

17. Bunyan, *Miscellaneous Works* (Oxford: Oxford University Press, 1980), vol. VI, *'The Poems'* (470 pp.)

18. Bunyan, *Works,* vol. III, p.127.

19. Abrams, ed., *The Norton Anthology of English Verse,* vol. I, pp.1055-6.

20. Peter Lewis, *The Genius of Puritanism* (Haywards Heath: Carey Publications, 1975), p.12.

21. Packer, *A Quest for Godliness,* p.49.

22. *Ibid.,* pp.64-77.

23. Bunyan, *Works,* vol. I, p.50.

24. *Ibid.,* p.334.

25. See chapter 3.

26. *Ibid.,* pp.104-50.

27. *Ibid.,* pp.362-90.

28. *Ibid.,* vol. II, pp.215-77.

29. *Ibid.,* vol. I, pp.721-2.

30. *Ibid.,* vol. II, pp.413-502.

31. *Ibid.,* vol. III, pp.375-94.

32. *Ibid.,* pp.395-459.

33. *Ibid.,* vol. I, p.694.

34. *Ibid.,* p.709.

35. Packer, *A Quest for Godliness,* p.70.

36. Bunyan, *Works,* vol. II, pp.129-74.

37. *Ibid.,* pp.176-214.

38. Bunyan, *Works,* vol. II, p.686.

39. *Ibid.,* vol. I, p.5.

40. *Ibid.,* vol. II, 140-41.

41. Packer, *A Quest for Godliness,* p.75.

42. Bunyan, *Works,* vol. I, p.lxxvii.

43. *Ibid.,* para. 339, p.49.

44. *Ibid.,* para. 276, p.42.

45. *Ibid.,* vol. II, p.261.

46. Packer, *A Quest for Godliness,* p.77.

47. Bunyan, *Works,* vol. I, p.lxxix.

48. Hill, 'Bunyan's Contemporary Reputation,' p.6.

49. This assumes the conclusion of Sharrock that the 'Sleeping Portrait' was not included until the third edition (Bunyan, *The Pilgrim's Progress,* ed. Sharrock, pp.xxxviii-xxxix.) While illustrated versions, especially for children, were forthcoming, it was the use of verbal imagery, rather than pictures, that brought rapid popularity.

50. Neil Postman, *Amusing Ourselves to Death* (New York: Penguin Books, 1985), p.63.

51. Bunyan, *Works,* vol. III, p.87.

Chapter 17 —*The Pilgrim's Progress* and the modern reader

1. Neil Postman, *Amusing Ourselves to Death,* p.41.

2. *Ibid.,* p.51.

3. Mitchell Stephens, 'The Death of Reading,' *Los Angeles Times* magazine, 22 September 1991, p.10.

4. David F. Wells, *No Place for Truth* (Grand Rapids: Wm. B. Eerdmans, 1993), pp.200-201.

5. Stephens, 'The Death of Reading,' p.12.

6. Postman, *Amusing Ourselves to Death,* p.80.

7. *Ibid.,* pp.87-8.

8. *Ibid.,* pp.vii-viii.

9. Amy Ellis, 'Office laughter helps employees enjoy their work,' *Escondido Times Advocate,* 26 September 1993, pp.G2-3.

10. James Mann, 'What is TV Doing to America?', *U.S. News & World Report,* 2 August 1982, p.28.

11. Postman, *Amusing Ourselves to Death,* p.80.

12. *Ibid.,* pp.116-117,121. In response to Postman's pessimistic appraisal of television in terms of its being a relative failure, as a medium of serious religious communication, is *Redeeming Television* by Quentin Schultze. Writing from a Reformed perspective, and that of the cultural mandate, Schultze argues for the redemption of television as a useful means of communication through the employment of certain principles:

> 1. Christians are to become discerning viewers.
> 2. Christians need to be educated concerning television.
> 3. Christians should help to redeem television institutions.
> 4. Christians should cultivate commercial alternatives.
> 5. Christians should encourage informed media criticism (Quentin Schulze, *Redeeming Television.* Downers Grove: Inter-Varsity Press, 1992, pp.165-80).

However, I would still side with the view of Postman that television, because of its essential visual, image-and-entertainment character, cannot supplant the priority of truth communicated through the printed word.

13. Coleen Cook, *All that Glitters* (Chicago: Moody Press, 1992), p.195.

14. Wells, *No Place for Truth,* pp.207, 210-11.

15. *Ibid.,* p.211.

16. Ross Pavlac, 'Bang! Zow! Christian Comic Books Join Fight for Teens,' *Christianity Today,* 2 July 1993, p.48.

17. John Bunyan-Martin Powell, *The Pilgrim's Progress,* Marvel Comics.

18. George Barna, *What Americans Believe* (Ventura: Regal Books, 1991), p.30.

19. Cook, *All that Glitters,* pp.241-3.

20. *Ibid.,* p.202.

21. *Ibid.,* p.262.
22. *Ibid.,* p.264.
23. *Ibid.,* p.264. The author musters several arguments to support her case. New Testament evidence of any sort is conspicuous by its absence:

> *1. In the Old Testament, both tabernacle and temple worship were audio-visual in nature and appealed to all five senses.*
>
> However, in the New Testament these matters are described as part of 'the weak and worthless things' (Gal. 4:3,9) which, for Christians, have been superseded by worship 'in spirit and truth' (John 4:21-24).
>
> *2. The illiterate medieval church resorted to passion and morality plays.*
>
> However, the remedy for this situation was the Reformation, when the truth of God's Word initiated earth-shaking revival and supplanted ineffectual drama with the glories of the gospel.
>
> *3. The Old Testament prophets proclaimed truth using a variety of visual media.* Presumably Jeremiah's visit to the potter (Jer. 18:1-6), Ezekiel's depiction of the siege of Jerusalem on a tile (Ezek. 4:1-4), and Amos' vision of the Lord's plumb line (Amos 7:7-9) are in mind here.
>
> However, most emblems of this sort were beheld in visions; they, together with the relatively few tangible items, were undoubtedly revealed to the prophets for the purpose of being recorded for all time in the pages of Scripture. It should be remembered that *verbal* imagery, as opposed to *visual* imagery, plays a significant part in Scripture. This is also the case with *The Pilgrim's Progress.*

24. John F. MacArthur, Jr., *Ashamed of the Gospel* (Wheaton: Crossway Books, 1993), pp.69, 71.
25. Postman, *Amusing Ourselves to Death,* pp.117, 119.
26. R. Vaughan Williams, *The Pilgrim's Progress* (New York: Oxford University Press (Inc.), 1968), pp.i-vii.
27. Michael Kennedy, *The Works of Ralph Vaughan Williams* (New York: Oxford University Press (Inc.), 1994), pp.312-14.
28. Postman, *Amusing Ourselves to Death,* p.9.
29. John Calvin, *Institutes of the Christian Religion* (Philadelphia: The Westminster Press, 1960), I, V, 10.
30. *Ibid.*
31. Postman, *Amusing Ourselves to Death,* p.9.
32. Bunyan, *Works,* vol. III, pp.132, 224-5.
33. Francis Schaeffer, *A Christian Manifesto* (Westchester: Crossway Books, 1981), p.54. It is ironic that this very book, in making a plea for the recovery of truth, should suffer so much at the hands of error. Carol Flake reports that '… although *A Christian Manifesto* outsold Jane Fonda's *Workout Book* by two to

one in May 1982, Fonda was number one on *The New York Times'* best-seller list and Dr Schaeffer "was relegated to ignominious oblivion"' (Carol Flake, *Redemptorama* (Garden City, NY: Anchor Press, 1984), p.165.
34. Wells, *No Place for Truth,* pp.280-81.
35. Bunyan, *Works,* vol. III, p.167.
36. *Ibid.*

Chapter 18 — Modern assessments of *The Pilgrim's Progress*
1. C. Stephen Finley, 'Bunyan Among The Victorians: Macaulay, Froude, Ruskin', *Journal of Literature & Theology,* Vol. 3, No. 1, March 1989, pp.77-94.
2. Froude, *John Bunyan,* pp.49-50, 55-56, 62, 29.
3. Robert Bridges in Sharrock, ed., *The Pilgrim's Progress, A Casebook,* pp.112-15.
4. Froude, *John Bunyan,* pp.55-6.
5. 'He was a typical case of the psychopathic temperament, sensitive of conscience to a diseased degree, beset by doubts, fears and insistent ideas, and a victim of verbal automatisms, both motor and sensory. These were usually texts of Scripture which, sometimes damnatory and sometimes favourable, would come in a half-hallucinatory form as if they were voices, and fasten on his mind and buffet it between them like a shuttlecock. Added to this were a fearful melancholy, self-contempt and despair' (William James, *The Varieties of Religious Experience.* New York: Collier Books, 1961, p.136).
6. 'Bunyan speaks in the autobiography of being troubled in childhood by fearful dreams and visions. It may be that there was a pathological side to the nervous intensity of these fears; in the religious crisis of his maturity his guilty terrors took the form of hallucinations and auditory and tactile delusions' (Bunyan, *Grace Abounding to the Chief of Sinners,* ed. Roger Sharrock, p.xiii).
7. D. Martyn Lloyd-Jones, *Knowing the Times* (Edinburgh: Banner of Truth Trust, 1989), pp.61-89.
8. Bunyan, *Works,* vol. I, pp.4-5.
9. David Herreshoff, 'Marxist Perspectives on Bunyan,' *Bunyan in our Time,* ed. Robert G. Collmer (Kent, Ohio: The Kent State University Press, 1989), pp.161-2.
10. *Ibid.,* pp.162-3.
11. *Ibid.,* p.183.
12. Kaufmann, *The Pilgrim's Progress and Traditions in Puritan Meditation,* p.vi.
13. Iain Murray, *Jonathan Edwards* (Edinburgh: Banner of Truth Trust, 1987), pp.xix-xxxi.
14. *Ibid.,* p.xxvi.
15. Wakefield, *Bunyan the Christian,* p.125.
16. *Ibid.*

17. *Ibid.,* p.126.

18. *Ibid.,* pp.34-6.

19. *Ibid.,* p.89.

20. George Marsden has vainly attempted to call secular scholarship back to an inclusion of an experiential Christian emphasis, and doubtless his plea will go unheeded by an audience that in general is fundamentally opposed to historic evangelical truth and resultant experience; that is, unless an unorthodox twist on experience is offered. His solution, the validity of which is hardly demonstrated in the history of Christian revival, is explained as follows: 'Religious-political conservatives who complain about the establishment of "secular humanism" are partially correct... The religious right does not help by suggesting, in effect, that we go back to a Christian establishment. That is not the only alternative and it is not a desirable one. Rather, we should recognize that we are dealing with an over-correction and look for a way to restore a better balance among both religious and non-religious voices' (*The Outrageous Idea of Christian Scholarship,* New York: Oxford, 1997, p.24).

21. Bunyan, *The Pilgrim's Progress,* ed. Sharrock, pp.7-26.

22. Bunyan, *Works,* vol. I, p.50.

23. Hill, *A Tinker and a Poor Man,* pp.14-15.

24. James Turner, 'Bunyan's Sense of Place,' *The Pilgrim's Progress, Critical and Historical Views,* ed. Vincent Newey (Liverpool: Liverpool University Press, 1980), p.97.

25. Hill, *A Tinker and a Poor Man,* pp.212-13, 215, 219-20, 377.

26. *Ibid.,* p.380.

27. N. H. Keeble, 'Christiana's Key: The Unity of The Pilgrim's Progress,' *The Pilgrim's Progress, Critical and Historical Views,* ed. Newey, pp.1-20.

28. *Ibid.,* pp.14, 18.

29. N. H. Keeble, *The literary culture of nonconformity in later seventeenth-century England* (Athens: University of Georgia Press, 1987), 356 pp.

30. Keeble, 'Of him thousands daily Sing and talk', pp.241-64.

31. Bunyan, *The Pilgrim's Progress,* ed. Keeble, pp.xii-xiii.

32. John Bunyan, 'I will pray in the Spirit,' pp.xxxiv-xxxv.

33. Greaves, *John Bunyan,* p.160.

34. Greaves, *John Bunyan and English Nonconformity,* pp.185-91.

35. Greaves, *Glimpses of Glory,* p.634.

36. Gordon Campbell, 'Fishing in Other Men's Waters: Bunyan and the Theologians,' *Conventicle and Parnassus,* ed. Keeble, p.150.

37. *Ibid.*

38. *Ibid.,* pp.137-8, 144.

39. Bunyan, *Works,* vol. II, p.166.

40. Campbell, 'Fishing in Other Men's Waters', p.138.

41. J. N. D. Kelly, *Early Christian Doctrines* (New York: Harper, 1958), pp.354, 363.

42. It is interesting to note that Campbell, with some justification, suggests that Bunyan's reliance upon an English text of the Bible was most likely that of the Geneva version, at least with regard to his earlier writings ('Fishing in Other Men's Waters', p.138). Yet this version's translation of Romans 5:12 does not follow that of Ambrosiaster or Augustine. It reads: 'Wherefor, as by one man sinne entred into the worlde, and death by sinne, and so death went over all men: for as muche as all men have sinned.'

43. Kelly refers to the use of Psalm 51:5 by Ambrose. Concerning Augustine he writes, 'So Augustine has no doubt of the reality of original sin. *Genesis* apart, he finds Scriptural proof of it in *Ps. 51*, *Job* and *Eph.* 2:3, but above all in *Rom.* 5:12 (where, like Ambrosiaster, he reads "in whom") and *John* 3:3-5' (*Early Christian Doctrines*, pp.355, 363).

44. Douglas J. Moo, *The Epistle to the Romans* (Grand Rapids: Wm. B. Eerdmans, 1996), pp.314-29; Leon Morris, *The Epistle to the Romans* (Grand Rapids: Wm. B. Eerdmans, 1997), pp.227-32; William G. T. Shedd, *Commentary on Romans* (Grand Rapids: Baker Book House, 1980), pp.119-30.

45. Moo, *Romans*, p.322n.

46. Nigel Turner, *Grammatical Insights into the New Testament* (Edinburgh: T & T. Clark, 1965), p.116.

47. Bunyan, *Works*, vol. I, p.505.

48. Stachniewski, *The Persecutory Imagination*, p.11.

49. Hill, *A Tinker and a Poor Man*, pp.184-7.

50. Lloyd-Jones, *The Puritans*, pp.64-5.

51. An overly romantic estimate of Puritan New England needs to consider Alice Morse Earle's *The Sabbath in Puritan New England* (New York: Scribner's, 1900). For example: In '1670 two lovers, John Lewis and Sarah Chapman, were accused of and tried for "sitting together on the Lord's Day under an apple tree in Goodman Chapman's Orchard"... In Plymouth a man was "sharply whipped" for shooting fowl on Sunday... Captain Kemble of Boston was in 1656 set for two hours in the public stocks for his "lewd and unseemly behaviour", which consisted in his kissing his wife "publicquely" on the Sabbath Day, upon the doorstep of his house, when he had just returned from a voyage and absence of three years... In 1760 the legislature of Massachusetts passed the law that "any person able of Body who shall absent themselves from publick worship of God on the Lord's Day shall pay ten shillings fine"' (pp.246, 247, 250).

52. Stachniewski, *The Persecutory Imagination*, p.14.

53. *Ibid.*

54. *Ibid.*, p.7. However, see John R. Knott, *Discourses of Martyrdom in English Literature, 1563-1694* (New York: Cambridge University Press, 1993), p.195, where it is suggested that Bunyan's persecutory imagination was derived from his admiration of the Marian martyrs as described in *Foxe's Book of Martyrs*.

55. Hill, *A Tinker and a Poor Man*, p.185.

56. Philip Mitchell and Greg Clarke, 'Comprehending the darkness,' citing the World Health Organization and *New Scientist, The Briefing,* 2 April 1997, p.9.

57. Gordon Wakefield, review of Stachniewski's *Persecutory Imagination, Journal of Theological Studies,* Oct. 1992, pp.749-53.

58. de Vries, *John Bunyan on the Order of Salvation,* p.234.

59. *Ibid.,* pp.220-21.

60. *Ibid.,* p.218.

61. *Ibid.,* p.160.

62. 'The Puritans, and Bunyan is no exception, were decidedly covenant theologians' (*Ibid.,* p.98). This is a confusing statement since Bunyan was not classically covenantal within the mainstream of English Puritanism, notwithstanding the covenantal terminology especially used in *The Doctrine of the Law and Grace Unfolded* (see chapter 8).

63. Mullett, *John Bunyan in Context,* pp.52-3.

64. *Ibid.,* p.284.

65. *Ibid.,* p.110.

66. *Ibid.,* p.192.

67. *Ibid.,* pp.10-12, 15-16, 35-6, 48.

68. *Ibid.,* pp.191-2.

69. *Ibid.,* p.202.

70. *Ibid.,* p.200.

71. Vincent Newey, 'Bunyan and the Confines of the Mind,' *The Pilgrim's Progress, Critical and Historical Views,* ed. Newey, p.44.

72. Rupp, *Six Makers of English Religion,* p.94.

Chapter 19 — *The Pilgrim's Progress* for young people

1. Cook, *All that Glitters,* p.142.

2. Postman, *Amusing Ourselves to Death,* p.144.

3. Brown, *John Bunyan,* p.482.

4. The third edition of *The Pilgrim's Progress,* published in 1679, appears to have been the first one to be printed with any illustrations. It included what is now known as 'the Sleeping Portrait' (see p.51).

5. Mullett, *John Bunyan in Context,* p.191.

6. Sharrock, ed., *Bunyan, The Pilgrim's Progress, A Casebook,* p.57.

7. Barry E. Horner, *The Pilgrim's Progress, Accurate Text Revision* (Lindenhurst, NY: Reformation Press, 1999).

Chapter 20 — Conclusion

1. Bunyan, *Works,* vol. I, p.lxxiv.

2. Roger Sharrock, 'Bunyan Studies Today: An Evaluation,' *Bunyan in England and Abroad,* eds. M. Van Os and G. J. Schutte (Amsterdam: VU University Press, 1990), p.45.

3. *Ibid.,* pp.45-6.

4. *Ibid.,* p.53.

5. Mullett, *John Bunyan in Context,* p.284; also Greaves, *John Bunyan and English Nonconformity,* pp.42-5, 101-26.

6. Sharrock, 'Bunyan Studies Today,' p.52.

7. Sharrock, *John Bunyan,* p.79.

8. *Ibid.,* pp.87-9.

9. John F. Hurst, *History of Rationalism* (New York: Nelson & Phillips, 1865), p.155.

10. Trevelyan, 'Bunyan's England,' July 1928, p.319.

11. Herman Bavinck, *The Doctrine of God,* translation ed. William Hendriksen (Grand Rapids: Baker Book House, 1985), p.5.

12. Bunyan, *Works,* vol. I, p.5.

13. *Ibid.,* vol. III, p.166.

14. Packer, *A Quest for Godliness,* p.14.

15. Bunyan, *Works,* vol. I, p.103.

16. *Ibid.,* p.150.

17. *Ibid.,* p.297.

18. *Ibid.,* p.334.

19. *Ibid.,* p.390.

20. *Ibid.,* p.575.

21. *Ibid.,* II, p.758.

22. *Ibid.,* vol. III, p.394.

23. *Ibid.,* p.724.

Bibliography

Works by John Bunyan

The Works of John Bunyan, ed. George Offor, 3 vols. (Edinburgh: The Banner of Truth Trust, 1991; first published 1854)

The Miscellaneous Works of John Bunyan, general ed. Roger Sharrock, 13 vols. (Oxford: Oxford University Press [Clarendon], 1975-94)

The Works of that Eminent Servant of Christ, Mr John Bunyan, 2 vols. (London: E. Gardiner, 1736-1737)

The Pilgrim's Progress, ed. N. H. Keeble (Oxford: Oxford University Press [The World's Classics], 1989)

The Pilgrim's Progress, ed. Roger Sharrock (Harmondsworth: Penguin Books, 1965)

The Pilgrim's Progress, eds. James Blanton Wharey, Roger Sharrock (Oxford: Oxford University Press [Clarendon], 1960)

The Pilgrim's Progress, ed. James Inglis (London: Gall and Inglis, n.d.)

Grace Abounding to the Chief of Sinners, ed. Roger Sharrock (Oxford: Oxford University Press [Clarendon], 1962)

General references

Abrams, M. H., ed. *The Norton Anthology of English Verse* (New York: Norton, 1993)

Allen, R. E., ed. *The Concise Oxford Dictionary* (Oxford: Oxford University Press [Clarendon], 1991)

Barna, George. *What Americans Believe* (Ventura: Regal Books, 1991)

Bavinck, Herman. *The Doctrine of God,* trans. William Hendriksen (Grand Rapids: Baker Book House, 1985)

Benson, Louis. *The Hymns of John Bunyan* (New York: The Hymn Society, 1930)

Boardman, J. Harold and John, Ivor B., eds. *Macaulay's Lives of Bunyan and Goldsmith* (London: Adam and Charles Black, 1914)

Breward, Ian. *John Bunyan, A Commemorative Symposium* (Melbourne: The Uniting Church Historical Society [Victoria], 1988)

Brittain, Vera. *In the Steps of John Bunyan* (London: Rich and Cowan, 1987)

Brown, John. *John Bunyan: His Life, Times and Work* (London: Hulbert Publishing [Tercentenary Edition], 1928)

Calvin, John. *Institutes of the Christian Religion*, 2 vols. (Philadelphia: The Westminster Press, 1960)

Campbell, Gordon. 'Fishing in Other Men's Waters: Bunyan and the Theologians', *John Bunyan, Conventicle and Parnassus*, ed. N. H. Keeble (Oxford: Oxford University Press [Clarendon], 1988)

'The Theology of The Pilgrim's Progress', *The Pilgrim's Progress: Critical and Historical Views*, ed. Vincent Newey (Liverpool: Liverpool University Press, 1980)

Chantry, Walter J. *God's Righteous Kingdom* (Edinburgh: Banner of Truth Trust, 1980)

Cheever, George. *Lectures on The Pilgrim's Progress* (Glasgow: William Collins, 1860)

Collmer, Robert G., ed. *Bunyan in Our Time* (Kent, Ohio: The Kent State University Press, 1989)

Cook, Coleen. *All that Glitters* (Chicago: Moody Press, 1992)

Cowper, William. *The Poetical Works of William Cowper* (London: T. Nelson, 1852)

Dargan, Charles. *A History of Preaching*, 2 vols. (New York: Hodder & Stoughton, 1905)

de Vries, Pieter. *John Bunyan on the Order of Salvation* (New York: Peter Lang, 1994)

Earle, Alice Morse. *The Sabbath in Puritan New England* (New York: Scribner's, 1900)

Edwards, Philip. 'The Journey in The Pilgrim's Progress', *The Pilgrim's Progress, Critical and Historical Views*, ed. Vincent Newey (Liverpool: Liverpool University Press, 1980)

Flake, Carol. *Redemptorama* (Garden City, N. Y.: Anchor Press, 1984)

Franklin, Benjamin. *The Autobiography of Benjamin Franklin* (Philadelphia: Henry Altemus, 1895)

Froude, A. J. *Bunyan, English Men of Letters* (London: Macmillan, 1880)

Fuller, Andrew. *The Complete Works of the Rev. Andrew Fuller*, 3 vols. (Philadelphia: American Baptist Publications Society, 1845)

Furlong, Monica. *The Puritan's Progress: A Study of John Bunyan* (London: Hodder and Stoughton, 1975)

Geisler, Norman L., ed. *Inerrancy* (Grand Rapids: Zondervan, 1980)

Goodwin, Thomas. *The Works of Thomas Goodwin,* 12 vols. (Edinburgh: James Nichol. 1866)

Greaves, Richard L. *Glimpses of Glory: John Bunyan and English Dissent* (Stanford: Stanford University Press, 2002).

    John Bunyan (Grand Rapids: Wm. B. Eerdmans, 1969)

    John Bunyan and English Nonconformity (London: The Hambledon Press, 1992)

Haller, William. *The Rise of Puritanism* (New York: Harper & Row, 1957)

Harrison, G. B. *John Bunyan: A Study in Personality* (Garden City, N.Y.: Doubleday, 1928)

Hawthorne, Nathaniel. *The Celestial Railroad* (Harrisonburg, VA: Sprinkle Publications, 1990)

Hendriksen, William. *I & II Timothy and Titus* (Edinburgh: Banner of Truth Trust, 1972)

Herreshoff, David. 'Marxist Perspectives on Bunyan', *Bunyan in Our Time,* ed. Robert G. Collmer (Kent, OH: The Kent State University Press, 1989)

Hill, Christopher. *A Tinker and a Poor Man* (New York: Alfred A. Knopf, 1989)

    'Bunyan's Contemporary Reputation', *John Bunyan and His England, 1628-88,* eds. Anne Lawrence, W. R. Owens, and Stuart Sim (London: Hambledon Press, 1990)

    'John Bunyan and the English Revolution', The *John Bunyan Lectures 1978* (Bedford: Bedfordshire Education Service, 1978)

Hurst, John F. *History of Rationalism* (New York: Nelson & Phillips, 1865)

James, William. *The Varieties of Religious Experience* (New York: Collier Books, 1961)

Kaufmann, U. Milo. *The Pilgrim's Progress and Traditions in Puritan Meditation* (New Haven: Yale University Press, 1966)

Keeble, N. H. 'Christiana's Key: The Unity of The Pilgrim's Progress', *The Pilgrim's Progress: Critical and Historical Views,* ed. Vincent Newey (Liverpool: Liverpool University Press, 1980)

    '"Of him thousands daily Sing and talk": Bunyan and his reputation', *John Bunyan, Conventicle and Parnassus,* ed. N. H. Keeble (Oxford: Oxford University Press [Clarendon], 1988)

    The literary culture of nonconformity in later seventeenth-century England (Athens: University of Georgia Press, 1987)

Keeble, N. H., ed. *John Bunyan, Conventicle and Parnassus* (Oxford: Oxford University Press [Clarendon], 1988)

Kelly, J. N. D. *Early Christian Doctrines* (New York: Harper, 1958)

Kelman, John. *The Road,* 2 vols. (Edinburgh: Oliphant Anderson and Ferrier, 1912)

Kennedy, Michael. *The Works of Ralph Vaughan Williams* (New York: Oxford University Press (Inc.), 1994)

Knott, John R. *Discourses of Martyrdom in English Literature, 1563-1694* (New York: Cambridge University Press, 1993)

Knott, John R., Jr. '"Thou Must Live upon My Word': Bunyan and the Bible', *John Bunyan, Conventicle and Parnassus,* ed. N. H. Keeble (Oxford: Oxford University Press [Clarendon], 1988)

Lawrence, Anne, Owens, W. R., and Sim, Stuart., eds. *John Bunyan and his England 1628-1688* (London: Hambledon Press, 1990)

Lewis, Peter. *The Genius of Puritanism* (Haywards Heath: Carey Publications, 1975)

Lloyd-Jones, D. Martyn. *Knowing the Times* (Edinburgh: Banner of Truth Trust, 1989)

   Romans, The New Man, Exposition of Chapter 6 (Grand Rapids: Zondervan, 1973)

   The Puritans: Their Origins and Successors (Edinburgh: Banner of Truth Trust, 1987)

Luther, Martin. *A Commentary on St Paul's Epistle to the Galatians* (Cambridge & London: James Clarke, 1972)

   Luther's Works, 56 vols. (Saint Louis: Concordia Publishing House, 1972)

MacArthur, John F., Jr. *Ashamed of the Gospel* (Wheaton: Crossway Books, 1993)

Machen, J. Gresham. *Christianity and Liberalism* (London: Victory Press, 1925)

Maguire, Robert. *Lectures on Bunyan's Pilgrim's Progress* (London: The London Printing and Publishing Company, 1859)

Marsden, George. *The Outrageous Idea of Christian Scholarship* (New York: Oxford, 1997)

Methodist Hymn-Book, The (London: Methodist Conference Office, 1938)

Miller, Perry and Johnson, Thomas H., eds. *The Puritans – A Sourcebook of Their Writings,* 2 vols. (New York: Harper & Row, 1965)

Moo, Douglas. *The Epistle to the Romans* (Grand Rapids: Wm. B. Eerdmans, 1996)

Morris, Leon. *The Epistle to the Romans* (Grand Rapids: Wm. B. Eerdmans, 1997)

Mullett, Michael A. *John Bunyan in Context* (Pittsburgh: Duquesne University Press, 1997)

Murray, Iain. *Jonathan Edwards* (Edinburgh: Banner of Truth Trust, 1987)

Murray, John. *Collected Writings of John Murray,* 4 vols. (Edinburgh: Banner of Truth Trust, 1976)

Nellist, Brian. 'The Pilgrim's Progress and Allegory', *The Pilgrim's Progress, Critical and Historical Views,* ed. Vincent Newey (Liverpool: Liverpool University Press, 1980)

Newey, Vincent. 'Bunyan and the Confines of the Mind', *The Pilgrim's Progress, Critical and Historical Views,* ed. Vincent Newey (Liverpool: Liverpool University Press, 1980)

Newey, Vincent., ed. *The Pilgrim's Progress: Critical and Historical Views* (Liverpool: Liverpool University Press, 1980)

Newton, John. *The Works of John Newton,* 6 vols. (Edinburgh: Banner of Truth Trust, 1988)

Owen, John. *The Works of John Owen,* 17 vols. (Edinburgh: T. & T. Clark, 1862)

Owens, W. R. 'The reception of *The Pilgrim's Progress* in England', *Bunyan in England and Abroad,* eds. M. van Os and G. J. Schutte (Amsterdam: VU University Press, 1990)

Packer, J. I. *A Quest for Godliness* (Wheaton: Crossway Books, 1990)
  Fundamentalism and the Word of God (London: Inter-Varsity Fellowship, 1960)

Paxon, Ruth. *Life on the Highest Plane* (Grand Rapids: Kregel, 1996)

Postman, Neil. *Amusing Ourselves to Death* (New York: Penguin Books, 1985)

Ramm, Bernard. *Protestant Biblical Interpretation* (Grand Rapids: Baker Book House, 1956)

Ravitch, Diane, and Finn, Chester E., Jr. *What do our 17-years-olds know?* (New York: Harper & Row, 1987)

Ray, Charles. 'Mrs Spurgeon', *The C. H. Spurgeon Collection* (Albany: Ages Software, 1998)

Rupp, Gordon. *Six Makers of English Religion* (London: Hodder and Stoughton, 1957)
  The Righteousness of God (London: Hodder and Stoughton, 1953)

Ryle, J. C. *Expository Thoughts on John,* 3 vols. (Edinburgh: Banner of Truth Trust, 1987)
  Holiness (London: James Clarke, 1956)
  Old Paths (Cambridge: James Clarke, 1972)

Sampson, George. *The Concise Cambridge History of English Literature* (Cambridge: Cambridge University Press, 1941)

Schaeffer, Francis. A. *A Christian Manifesto* (Westchester: Crossway Books, 1981)

Schaff, Philip. *The Creeds of Christendom,* 3 vols. (Grand Rapids: Baker Book House, 1969)

Schultze, Quentin. *Redeeming Television* (Downers Grove: Inter-Varsity Press, 1992)

Sharrock, Roger. 'Bunyan Studies Today: An Evaluation', *Bunyan in England and Abroad,* eds. van Os, M. and Schutte, G. J. (Amsterdam: VU University Press, 1990)

   John Bunyan (London: Hutchinson House, 1954)

Sharrock, Roger., ed. *Bunyan, The Pilgrim's Progress, A Casebook* (London: Macmillan, 1976)

Shedd, William G. T. *Commentary on Romans* (Grand Rapids: Baker Book House, 1980)

Sim, Stuart. '"Safe for Those for Whom it is to be Safe": Salvation and Damnation in Bunyan's Fiction', *Bunyan and his England, 1628-88.* eds. Lawrence, Anne; Owens, W. R.; and Sim, Stuart (London: The Hambledon Press, 1990)

Spurgeon, C. H. 'Around the Wicket Gate', *The C. H. Spurgeon Collection* (Albany, OR: Ages Software, 1998)

   Eccentric Preachers (Pasadena, TX: Pilgrim Publications, 1978)

   Metropolitan Tabernacle Pulpit, 63 vols. (Albany, OR: Ages Software, 1998)

   Metropolitan Tabernacle Pulpit, 63 vols. (Pasadena, TX: Pilgrim Publications, 1980)

   Pictures from Pilgrim's Progress (Pasadena, TX: Pilgrim Publications, 1973)

   C. H. Spurgeon's Autobiography, 4 vols. (London: Passmore and Alabaster, 1897)

   The C. H. Spurgeon Collection (Albany: Ages Software, 1998)

   'The Great Change — Conversion', *The C. H. Spurgeon Collection* (Albany: Ages Software, 1998)

Spurgeon, Thomas. 'Editor's Introduction', *Pictures from Pilgrim's Progress* (Pasadena, TX: Pilgrim Publications, 1973)

Stachniewski, John. *The Persecutory Imagination: English Puritanism and the Literature of Despair* (Oxford: Oxford University Press [Clarendon], 1991)

Swanson, Dennis Michael. *Charles H. Spurgeon and Eschatology: Did he Have a Discernible Millennial Position?* (Unpublished dissertation, The Master's Seminary, CA, 1996. Internet sourced)

Talon, Henri. *John Bunyan: The Man and his Works* (Cambridge: Harvard University Press, 1951)

Toon, Peter. *The Emergence of Hyper-Calvinism in English Nonconformity* (London: Olive Tree, 1967)

Turner, James. 'Bunyan's Sense of Place', *The Pilgrim's Progress: Critical and Historical Views,* ed. Vincent Newey (Liverpool: Liverpool University Press, 1980)

Turner, Nigel. *Grammatical Insights into the New Testament* (Edinburgh: T. & T. Clark, 1965)

van Os, M. and Schutte, G. J., eds. *Bunyan in England and Abroad* (Amsterdam: VU University Press, 1990)

Walker, Eric C. *William Dell, Master Puritan* (Cambridge: W. Heffer & Sons, 1970)

Wakefield, Gordon. *Bunyan the Christian* (London: HarperCollins, 1992)

Wallechinsky, David, Wallace, Irving, and Wallace, Amy. *The People's almanac presents the book of lists* (New York: Morrow, 1977)

Ward, A. R. and Waller, A. R. *The Cambridge History of English Literature,* 15 vols. (New York: Macmillan, 1949)

Warfield, B. B. *Perfectionism* (Philadelphia: Presbyterian and Reformed Publishing, 1967)

Wells, David F. *No Place for Truth* (Grand Rapids: Wm. B. Eerdmans, 1993)

White, B. R. '"The Fellowship of Believers": Bunyan and Puritanism', *John Bunyan, Conventicle and Parnassus,* ed. N. H. Keeble (Oxford: Oxford University Press [Clarendon],1988)

Whyte, Alexander. *Bunyan Characters* (Grand Rapids: Baker Book House, 1981)

Williams, R, Vaughan. *The Pilgrim's Progress* (New York: Oxford University Press (Inc.), 1968)

Witsius, Herman. *The Economy of the Covenants Between God and Man,* 2 vols. (Escondido, CA: den Dulk Christian Foundation, 1990)

Journals, magazines, etc.

Bunyan, John and Powell, Martin. *The Pilgrim's Progress* (New York: Marvel Comics, 1992)

Butler, George. 'The Iron Cage of Despair and "The Unpardonable Sin" in The Pilgrim's Progress', *English Language Notes*, XXV, September 1987.

Ellis, Amy. 'Office laughter helps employees enjoy their work', *Escondido Times Advocate*, 26 September 1993, pp.G2-3.

Finley, C. Stephen. 'Bunyan among the Victorians: Macaulay, Froude, Ruskin', *Journal of Literature & Theology*, Vol. 3, No. 1, March 1989, pp.77-94.

Helm, Paul. 'Bunyan and Reprobation Asserted', *The Baptist Quarterly*, XXVII, April 1979.

Mann, James. 'What is TV Doing to America?' *U.S. News & World Report*, 2 August 1982, p.28.

Mitchell, Philip and Clarke, Greg. 'Comprehending the darkness,' *The Briefing* (2 April 1997, p.9)

Pavlac, Ross. 'Bang! Zow! Christian Comic Books Join Fight for Teens', *Christianity Today*, 2 July 1993, p.48.

Stephens, Mitchell. 'The Death of Reading', *Los Angeles Times Magazine*, 22 September 1991, p.10.

Stranahan, Brainerd P. 'Bunyan and the Epistle to the Hebrews: His Source for the Idea of Pilgrimage in *The Pilgrim's Progress*', *Studies in Philology*, 79 (1982), pp.279-96.

Tipple, Ezra S. 'Pilgrim's Progress a book for Preachers', *Methodist Review*. July 1908.

Trevelyan, G. M. 'Bunyan's England', *The Review of the Churches*. July 1928, p.319.

Wakefield, Gordon. Review of *The Persecutory Imagination: English Puritanism and the Literature of Despair*, by John Stachniewski. *Journal of Theological Studies*, October 1992, pp.749-53.

Index

Dr Barry E. Horner is pastor of Christian Fellowship Church in North Brunswick in the USA and has spent many years studying the life, ministry and literature of John Bunyan. As the host of a series of popular teaching seminars on *The Pilgrim's Progress,* and the author of a revision of the text of the allegory, he has been instrumental in bringing Bunyan's classic alive for a new generation of readers across the English-speaking world.

Further details about Dr Horner's work and publications can be found on his web site:

www.bunyanministries.org